SOVIET-AMERICAN CONFRONTATION

SOVIET-AMERICAN CONFRONTATION

Postwar Reconstruction and the Origins of the Cold War

THOMAS G. PATERSON

The Johns Hopkins University Press
Baltimore and London

Copyright © 1973 by The Johns Hopkins University Press
All rights reserved. No part of this book may be reproduced or transmitted in any form
or by any means, electronic or mechanical, including photocopying, recording, xerog-
raphy, or any information storage and retrieval system, without permission in writing
from the publisher.
Manufactured in the United States of America

The Johns Hopkins University Press, Baltimore, Maryland 21218
The Johns Hopkins University Press Ltd., London

Library of Congress Catalog Card Number 73-8120
ISBN 0-8018-1454-5

Library of Congress Cataloging in Publication data will be found on the last printed page
of this book.

FOR MY FAMILY

CONTENTS

PREFACE

Americans were determined in 1945 to avoid the crises of the past. As they prepared to shape the postwar world, they remembered the aftermath of World War I, when the United States refused to assume the international authority that its power had earned. They recalled the futile attempts in the 1920s and 1930s to avert an arms race, depression, economic nationalism, and a new and more terrible world conflagration. Their leaders resolved that the nation's stance would be more assertive and constructive: "depression and war" would be replaced by "peace and prosperity." Dean Acheson noted in early 1945 that the "great difference in our second attempt to establish a peaceful world is the wide recognition that peace is possible only if countries work together and prosper together. That is why the economic aspects are no less important than the political aspects of the peace."[1]

The purpose of this book is to study the serious problem of reconstruction in the early Cold War, when the United States was the "giant of the economic world," as President Harry S. Truman so aptly put it.[2] Although economic foreign policy often lodged itself at the center or near the center of the Soviet-American confrontation, other policy ingredients were woven into the diplomatic cloth—distorted images, fears, and irrationality, personalities and styles, the reading of historical lessons, traditional political ideals, bureaucratic lethargy, domestic politics and public opinion, and atomic-military power. To pull out one thread and bestow upon it singular importance is to sacrifice complexity for simplicity. This book is not, then, an economic interpretation of the origins of the Cold War. Rather, the diplomacy of reconstruction is considered in detail and assigned a conspicuous role in producing friction between the former Allies, but with the awareness that other diplomatic variables were also active.

This interlocked set of factors is well illustrated by the postwar ideology of "peace and prosperity," discussed in the Introduction. Simply expressed, the notion was that peace, political stability, and the containment of

[1] *Department of State Bulletin,* XXII (Apr. 22, 1945), 738.
[2] *Public Papers of the President of the United States, Harry S. Truman, 1947* (Washington, D.C., 1963), p. 168.

Communism depended upon a healthy international economy, free-flowing world trade, American exports and investments, and general American prosperity. Washington did not expend billions of dollars in loans, foreign aid, and trade only to realize narrow economic gains: an interdependent and prosperous international economy free from depression was being built up in order to achieve an open, democratic, and pacific world free from revolutionary Communism, totalitarianism, fervent nationalism, and war. Americans hoped that the 1940s would not be a reenactment of the pattern of depression and war so evident in the 1930s. They were aware that their economic power would serve as a decisive agent of preferred change.

Following the Introduction, which sorts out the various components of the "peace and prosperity" ideology and briefly traces the chronology of postwar reconstruction policies, the book is divided into two parts emphasizing the issues which bear most directly on Soviet-American relations and the origins of the Cold War. In Part I, five issues central to the diplomatic confrontation in the Soviet sphere of influence—largely centered in eastern Europe—are studied. Washington officials believed that they possessed the weapons to challenge the Soviet Union in that area but found them inadequate when measured against the Soviet presence. In Part II, focused on confrontation in the American sphere, five chapters survey the considerable power and diplomatic success of the United States in international organizations, in the Near East, in the Middle East, in western Europe, and in western Germany. The concluding chapter summarizes the importance of United States reconstruction policies to the origins of the Cold War and ventures to answer a number of questions about the well springs of American diplomatic behavior.

Access to the historical sources for the postwar period is limited by government security classifications, personal privilege, and the fact that the events are so recent. Soviet sources are shamefully restricted and manipulated. Even so, as the documentation found in this book demonstrates, there is ample data available on which to base solid, although not definitive, studies of the early Cold War. Revisions are forever in order, as the conscientious and cautious scholar will admit. But caution befits his critics as well. It is incumbent upon them to reply temperately and factually, without the unproductive labeling too often characteristic of historiographical debate on the Cold War. Otherwise, our collective effort to reconstruct the past may falter after a fitful display of rhetorical fireworks.

My dependence upon others for ideas, sources, and advice has been extensive and rewarding. Richard M. Abrams of the University of California (Berkeley), Barton J. Bernstein of Stanford University, and Armin Rappaport of the University of California (La Jolla) have read major portions of this book in its various stages, and their suggestions have retrieved me from various ruts. My friend and colleague Garry Clifford of the University of Connecticut has served as an excellent, if unpersuaded, critic. The authors cited in the footnotes provided stimulation as well as information. For their thoughtful assistance and courtesies, I also thank Les K. Adler, Thomas C. Blaisdell, Philip D. Brooks, W. Randolph Burgess, Mrs. Howard Carvin, Mark Chadwin, Alexander P. Clark, Harry Clark, Clark Clifford, Ronald Coons, Ivan Dee, Robert Ferrell, John Gaddis, Lloyd Gardner, Shirley Gilmore, Robert Griffith, Vivian Hanna, W. Averell Harriman, Paul Hoffman, A. William Hoglund, Mrs. Eric Johnston, Helen Kasper, Richard Kirkendall, Walter LaFeber, Philip D. Lagerquist, Ronald Landa, David Maselin, James McKelvey, Jack Muraskin, Edwin A. Pauley, Janet Payne, Claude Pepper, George Phillies, Paul R. Porter, Buford Rowland, Robert F. Smith, Russell C. Smith, Thomas G. Smith, Isabel Weigold, William A. Williams, Joan Wilson, and O. G. Wilson. For the index, I thank Sondra Stave.

Capable archivists are essential to creative and fruitful research. The efficient and pleasant staff of the Harry S. Truman Library was exceptional and imaginative in helping me. Diligent staffs assisted me through the massive holdings of the Library of Congress Manuscript Division and the National Archives in Washington, D.C. I thank the libraries of the University of Connecticut, the University of California (Berkeley), Harvard University, Princeton University, Cornell University, Dartmouth College, Columbia University, Syracuse University, Clemson University, Yale University, the University of Vermont, Duke University, and the University of Kentucky. Also helpful were the staffs of the United Nations Library (New York City), the Franklin D. Roosevelt Library, the Federal Records Center (Alexandria, Virginia, and Suitland, Maryland), the Chamber of Commerce of the United States Library (Washington, D.C.), the Bank of American Archives (San Francisco), and the New York City Municipal Archives and Records Center.

Generous grants from the Harry S. Truman Library Institute, the University of California (Berkeley), the American Philosophical Society, the Rabinowitz Foundation, and the University of Connecticut allowed me to reach personal papers and collections from California to New Hampshire.

The *Journal of American History, The Historian,* and Quadrangle Books have kindly permitted me to use in revised form material which first appeared as articles in their publications.

The last words must be given to Betsy, Tom, Becki, and Stephen, who closely watched the growth of this book.

SOVIET-AMERICAN CONFRONTATION

CHAPTER 1

INTRODUCTION: THE QUEST FOR PEACE AND PROSPERITY

United States diplomats who witnessed the outbreak of World War II and its ultimate costs naturally looked to the interwar years for explanations. Persuasive historical analyses sounded the common theme that economic catastrophe and extreme nationalism corroded world peace. Americans studied their own "mistakes"—their rejection of the League of Nations, high tariffs, and restrained involvement in international crises—all of which tugged at the national conscience after 1939. Woodrow Wilson's unfulfilled pleas for a stable world order of self-determination and nondiscriminatory trade were taken up anew. Cordell Hull, Franklin D. Roosevelt's secretary of state for over a decade, articulated a relationship between economics and war and the lessons of the past more effectively than most Americans. In his autobiography, published in 1948, he recalls that as early as World War I he had become convinced that "unhampered trade dovetailed with peace; high tariffs, trade barriers, and unfair economic competition, with war." The "economic dissatisfaction that breeds war" had to be eliminated.[1] With the opening of World War II, after years of depression, repressive politics, and inconclusive diplomacy, these ideas took on new importance. Leaders pledged to eradicate economic deprivation and war through their reconstruction policies.

A legion of wartime State Department and interdepartmental committees had contemplated the contours of the economically hobbled postwar world. To guide them was a set of principles developed over a period of two centuries. Foremost was the principle of nondiscrimination or equal opportunity in foreign trade, investment, and navigation. In the late nineteenth century this principle became enshrined in the words "open door." "Private enterprise," as opposed to government ownership or state-conducted foreign commerce, was another popular tenet. In the twentieth century, United States leaders increasingly subscribed to the principle of "multilateralism," or cooperation among several nations to encourage free-flowing world trade, and to the "most-favored-nation"

---

[1] Cordell Hull, *Memoirs*, 2 vols. (New York, 1948), I, 81. See also Dean Acheson's sharing of such views in Gaddis Smith, *Dean Acheson* (New York, 1972), p. 14.

principle, whereby signatories agree to extend to each other any commercial favors either grants to a third state. Cherishing these principles, although it sometimes contradicted them in practice, the United States tremendously expanded its foreign commerce and became the world's greatest trader.[2]

In the 1930s Hull created institutions to realize these doctrines. The Reciprocal Trade Agreements program and the Export-Import Bank were devoted to overcoming barriers to world trade. When the wartime committees met, they looked to these institutions and to the ideas of the past. They decided to tackle economic programs first because the principles were already established and widely accepted, because of their recent experience in the depression years, and because great areas of the world lay in ruins. They expected to encounter the least domestic opposition to economic foreign policy: many citizens did not understand the technicalities and were content to leave such policymaking to government experts. The task of the postwar planners, then, was not the creation of doctrines and agencies but their elaboration.[3]

The hope that world war would never erupt again if the United States insisted upon an open political and economic world was often offered as a counter to the somber battle reports. During the war this hope joined with national self-interest in efforts to free world trade from the shackles of the 1930s. The Atlantic Charter of 1941 was an early document illustrating the belief that economic issues and peace were linked. Roosevelt and Winston Churchill forswore territorial aggrandizement and championed self-determination and disarmament, but achievement of these goals alone would not ensure a peaceful world. Economic collaboration to improve living standards, freedom of the seas, and the right of all nations to "access, on equal terms, to the trade and to the raw materials of the world which are needed for their economic prosperity" were the other stated purposes of the Charter.[4] In numerous wartime agreements and official statements, Washington emphatically urged its principles of multilateral nondiscriminatory foreign trade and investment as the guide for the postwar world.[5]

Just before his death Roosevelt informed Congress that "we cannot

---

[2] For American principles before the 1940s, see Felix Gilbert, *To the Farewell Address: Ideas of Early American Foreign Policy* (Princeton, N.J., 1961); Walter LaFeber, ed., *John Quincy Adams and American Continental Empire* (Chicago, 1965); Walter LaFeber, *The New Empire: An Interpretation of American Expansion* (Ithaca, N.Y., 1963); Carl P. Parrini, *Heir to Empire: United States Economic Diplomacy, 1916-1923* (Pittsburgh, Pa., 1969); N. Gordon Levin, Jr., *Woodrow Wilson and World Politics: America's Response to War and Revolution* (New York, 1968); Herbert Feis, *The Diplomacy of the Dollar* (Baltimore, 1950); Joseph Brandes, *Herbert Hoover and Economic Diplomacy* (Pittsburgh, Pa., 1962); Lloyd C. Gardner, *Economic Aspects of New Deal Diplomacy* (Madison, Wis., 1964).

[3] For the wartime planning and committees see Harley Notter, *Postwar Foreign Policy Preparation, 1939-1945* (Washington, D.C., 1949), especially pp. 23-24, 133-45, 560-62; Richard N. Gardner, *Sterling-Dollar Diplomacy*, rev. ed. (New York, 1969), pp. 1-23.

[4] *Department of State Bulletin*, V (Aug. 16, 1941), 125-26 (hereafter cited as *DSB*).

[5] See, for example, the Anglo-American Mutual Aid Agreement (1942) and Hull's

succeed in building a peaceful world unless we build an economically healthy world."[6] His successor, Harry S. Truman, although lacking practical experience in diplomacy, was an enthusiastic New Deal Democrat committed to Roosevelt's programs and the traditional principles of the open door. A self-proclaimed student of history, the often brash president drew the same lessons from the past as did Cordell Hull. The day after Roosevelt's burial, Truman nervously addressed a session of Congress, asserting that national security in the future would not lie behind "geographical barriers." Rather, mutual cooperation through the machinery of the United Nations and enlarged international trade would produce a lasting peace. The United States, he proclaimed, "may well lead the world to peace and prosperity."[7]

When Truman, like Roosevelt, expressed the postwar ideology of "peace and prosperity," those simple words meant more than their catchy phraseology would suggest. This ideology drew upon the past and enjoyed wide acceptance among most segments of the political spectrum, from the liberal magazine *New Republic* to the conservative National Association of Manufacturers.[8] It constituted a rejection of the shortcomings of the 1930s and a belief that the United States possessed the wherewithal and commitment to vanquish economic and political disorder. With the tenets of "peace and prosperity" ever on their minds, Americans emerged from World War II only to enter a new international confrontation. Desperate to explain why cooperation crumbled so quickly, many called upon history and became convinced that the 1940s were potentially a replay of the 1930s, with Soviet Russia replacing Nazi Germany as the unwelcome challenger to an open world.[9] This assumption made all the more urgent the fulfillment of the goals of "peace and prosperity."

THE INTERDEPENDENT WORLD ECONOMY

As American leaders defined it, the peace and prosperity ideology had several interlocking components which directed foreign policy toward extensive

---

"Bases of Our Program for International Economic Cooperation" presented to the Moscow Conference in 1943, in Notter, *Postwar Foreign Policy Preparation,* pp. 463-64, 560-62.

[6] Samuel Rosenman, ed., *The Public Papers and Addresses of Franklin D. Roosevelt* (New York, 1950), XIII, 595 (Mar. 26, 1945). See also the statement of Secretary of State Edward R. Stettinius, Jr.: "Economic warfare, depression, hunger, poverty and despair—these are the conditions that undermine democracy and block its development, that breed tyrants and aggressors, and that turn nations one against the other." *DSB,* XII (Apr. 8, 1945), 594.

[7] *DSB,* XII (Apr. 22, 1945), 721-23.

[8] For a more extensive study of the ideology and its popular acceptance see Thomas G. Paterson, "The Quest for Peace and Prosperity: International Trade, Communism, and the Marshall Plan," in Barton J. Bernstein, ed., *Politics and Policies of the Truman Administration* (Chicago, 1970), pp. 78-112.

[9] Les K. Adler and Thomas G. Paterson, "Red Fascism: The Merger of Nazi Germany and Soviet Russia in the American Image of Totalitarianism, 1930's-1950's," *American Historical Review,* LXXV (April, 1970), 1046-64.

foreign aid, international monetary stabilization, and vigorous foreign trade—in short, an exertion of United States economic power. The first premise read that international peace depended upon economic wellbeing. One presidential committee studying the European economic crisis minced no words: "Without economic assistance Europe is lost to us and World War III becomes inevitable." Secretary of State George C. Marshall stated frankly in 1947 that the United States had "to assist in the return of normal economic health in the world, without which there can be no political stability and no assured peace."[10]

What was most troubling was the widespread devastation and suffering in Europe. "Hungry people are not reasonable people," concluded a State Department official in 1946. "Their thoughts are concerned with their own misery and particularly with the tortured cries of their hungry children. They are easy victims of mass hysteria."[11] Peace, by this definition, meant stability, and as W. Averell Harriman put it, "Political stability can only be attained through improving economic conditions."[12] "Revolution" or political disorder was often translated as "Communism," and this challenge to peace was defined as a totalitarian political force which "uses poverty to advance itself."[13] Prosperity would thus help curb totalitarianism, Communism, and war.

Another premise was that world prosperity, and hence peace, could only be fostered by healthy world trade. President Truman explained that a "large volume of soundly based international trade" was essential "to achieve prosperity for the United States, build a durable structure of world economy and attain our goal of world peace and security." On another occasion he told a Baylor University audience that "in fact the three—peace, freedom, and world trade—are inseparable."[14] Shortly after World War II, competitive economic blocs like the British sterling area and the Soviet network in eastern Europe reminded Americans of the 1930s. "Nations which act as enemies in the marketplace," William L. Clayton of the State Department said, "cannot long be friends at the council table."[15] In his famous Navy Day speech of

[10] Subcommittee on Economic and Financial Analysis, President's Committee on Foreign Aid Records, "The Effects of the Marshall Plan on Our Foreign Trade," [n.d.], Harry S. Truman Library; Marshall, in *DSB*, XVI (June 15, 1947), 1160.

[11] James A. Stilwell in *DSB*, XIV (May 19, 1946), 831.

[12] U.S., Congress, Senate, Committee on Foreign Relations, *European Recovery Program* (Hearings), 80th Cong., 2d sess. (Jan. 23, 1948), p. 908 (hereafter cited as *ERP*).

[13] James H. McGraw, publisher, in *Business Week*, May 24, 1947, p. 80.

[14] *Public Papers of the Presidents: Harry S. Truman, 1946* (Washington, D.C., 1962), p. 354 (July 23, 1946); *ibid., 1947* (Washington, D.C., 1963), p. 167 (Mar. 6, 1947) (hereafter cited as *Public Papers, Truman*). See also U.S., Congress, House of Representatives, Special Committee on Post-War Economic Policy and Planning, *Post-War Foreign Economic Policy of the United States*, 6th Report, 79th Cong., 1st sess. (May 8, 1945), p. 9.

[15] *DSB*, XII (May 27, 1945), 979. See also Paul G. Hoffman, "The Survival of Free Enterprise," *Harvard Business Review*, XXV (Autumn, 1946), 24.

1945, the president emphasized the importance of military preparedness to a durable peace and wove into his discussion such principles as freedom of the seas and inland waterways, "access on equal terms to the trade and raw materials of the world," and "full economic collaboration."[16] The Department of State *Proposals for Expansion of World Trade and Employment* (November, 1945), the accords for the International Trade Organization, the General Agreement on Tariffs and Trade (GATT), the World Bank, and the International Monetary Fund, and difficult negotiations with Britain and Russia all recorded the vigorous American counterattack against restrictions on the "open door."[17]

United States officials were quite well aware that the world economy was interdependent, and that the United States held an essential place in it. But what was especially worrisome was the potential impact of a global depression on the United States, and, conversely, depression in the United States on the world. Henry A. Wallace, although at odds with Truman on tactical questions, shared the prevailing ideology and noted: "Full employment in the United States means prosperity all over the world."[18] His successor as secretary of commerce, W. Averell Harriman, described the United States as the "financial and economic pivot of the world," articulating the popular view that "economic stagnation in the United States would drag the rest of the world down with us."[19] Secretary of State James F. Byrnes also warned in 1946 that "depressions move easily across our boundaries," and Secretary of the Interior Julius Krug popularized the idea by quipping that "depressions are as catching as the common cold."[20] In short, depressions were contagious and struck at the foundations of world peace.

Another integral part of the ideology was the assumption that a healthy and growing United States commerce was the key to world trade, United States and international prosperity, and peace. Should United States trade

---

[16] *Public Papers, Truman, 1945* (Washington, D.C., 1961), p. 434 (Oct. 27, 1945). Truman also wrote: "Sound and healthy trade, conducted on equitable and non-discriminatory principles, is a keystone in the structure of world peace and security." Harry S. Truman to Eugene P. Thomas (president, National Foreign Trade Council), Oct. 17, 1946, PPF 2097, Harry S. Truman Papers, Truman Library.

[17] U.S., Department of State, *Proposals for Expansion of World Trade and Employment* (Washington, D.C., 1950), and William Diebold, Jr., *The End of the I.T.O.* (Princeton, N.J., 1952). For GATT, see n. 59 below.

[18] *Nation's Business*, XXXIII (August, 1945), 50. See also Ronald Radosh and Leonard P. Liggio, "Henry A. Wallace and the Open Door," in Thomas G. Paterson, ed., *Cold War Critics: Alternatives to American Foreign Policy in the Truman Years* (Chicago, 1971), pp. 76-113.

[19] *Journal of Commerce*, Feb. 24, 1947.

[20] *DSB*, XIII (Aug. 26, 1945), 279; Senate, *ERP* (Jan. 18, 1948), p. 354. See also George Soule, "Will We Cooperate with Britain?" *New Republic*, CXII (Apr. 2, 1945), 442; Alvin H. Hansen, *America's Role in the World Economy* (New York, 1945), pp. 8, 23-24; Treasury Secretary Fred Vinson, in U.S., Congress, Senate, Committee on Banking and Currency, *Anglo-American Financial Agreement* (Hearings), 79th Cong., 2d sess. (Mar. 5, 1946), p. 3; Alben Barkley speech, Sept. 23, 1946, Alben Barkley Papers, University of Kentucky Library.

collapse, the shaky world economy would topple, leaving revolution, totalitarianism, and war in command. The Council of Economic Advisers was gloomy over a possible reduction in exports in 1947: "The industrial paralysis which could be expected to result in some other countries would have repercussions of major proportion upon our economy and upon world stability."[21] Indeed, postwar American foreign trade stood as a significant and in some cases crucial element in the recovery of war-torn nations simply because the United States was the largest supplier of goods to world markets. By 1947 United States exports accounted for one-third of total world exports. In the 1930s United States exports were valued at $2 to $3 billion a year, but after World War II climbed to $10 billion in 1945 and 1946 and to $14 billion in 1947.[22]

Another premise was that foreign trade ensured the economic health of the United States. "Any serious failure to maintain this [trade] flow," concluded an assistant secretary of state, "would put millions of American businessmen, farmers, and workers out of business."[23] Private and public leaders massed impressive statistics to support their contention that foreign trade represented an important segment of the economy. In 1947 almost half of the wheat production went abroad, and world food shortages after the war absorbed surpluses of citrus fruits, eggs, rice, cotton, and tobacco; 13 percent of total farm income in 1947 derived from agricultural exports. Although exports represented only about 7 percent of gross national product and about 10 percent of the production of movable goods, certain pivotal industries, such as automobiles, trucks, cola, machine tools, railroad locomotives, steel products, and farm machinery relied heavily on foreign trade for their wellbeing. In 1947, for example, exports of the Monsanto Chemical Company accounted for one-eighth of total sales, and General Motors exported about 10 percent of its sales in the postwar period. Nearly 20 percent of the employees of steel companies owed their jobs to steel exports.[24]

---

[21] *DSB*, XVII (Nov. 16, 1947), 933.

[22] U.S., Department of Commerce, *Foreign Trade of the United States, 1936-49* (Washington, D.C., 1951), p. viii; *ibid.*, *Historical Statistics of the United States* (Washington, D.C., 1960), p. 537. Also United States direct investments abroad, amounting to $12 billion in 1950, provided precious capital and revenue-producing export goods for war-devastated European nations. U.S., Department of Commerce, *Foreign Investments of the United States* (Washington, D.C., 1953), p. 2.

[23] Willard L. Thorp, in U.S., Department of State, *Problems of United States Foreign Economic Policy* (Washington, D.C., 1947), p. 3.

[24] Commerce, *Historical Statistics of the United States*, p. 542; U.S., Department of Commerce, *Statistical Abstract, 1948* (Washington, D.C., 1948), pp. 654, 662; Council of Economic Advisers, *The Impact of the Foreign Aid Program upon the Domestic Economy* (Washington, D.C., 1947), pp. 111-12; U.S., Department of Interior, *Natural Resources and Foreign Aid* (Washington, D.C., 1947), pp. 12-14, 70; Commerce, *Foreign Trade, 1936-49*, pp. 55-56; Monsanto Chemical Company, *Annual Report, 1947*, p. 14; General Motors Corporation, *Annual Report, 1948*, p. 13; Marvin Hoffenburg, "Employment Resulting from U.S. Exports," *Monthly Labor Review*, LXV (December, 1947), 675-78. According to the Bureau of Labor Statistics, in the first half of 1947, 2,364,000 of 41,963,000 nonagricultural workers were directly or indirectly employed

Although these figures seemed small at first glance, Treasury Secretary John Snyder reminded the president that the "importance of U.S. exports to the American economy is evidenced by the fact that they exceed in volume such important single elements of the national product as expenditures on producers' durable equipment, consumers' expenditures on durable goods, the net change in business inventories, the total expenditures by State and local governments or even private construction."[25] A writer for the *Harvard Business Review* observed in 1945 that "theoretically the United States can achieve full employment without any exports whatsoever," but agreed with the influential Committee for Economic Development that a "great readjustment, much inefficient production, and a lower standard of living" would be the consequences.[26] Eric Johnston, president of the United States Chamber of Commerce from 1942 to 1946, was even more pessimistic when he argued that a curtailment of foreign trade "would mean vast population shifts, and . . . new ways of subsistence would have to be found for entire geographic regions."[27]

It was convincingly argued, too, that exports paid for imports required by industry and the military. After the war it became fashionable to speak of the United States as a "have-not" nation because of the wartime drain on its resources. The director of the Bureau of Mines reported the United States "self-sufficient" in only eleven of the most critical industrial minerals. Worried leaders itemized domestic deficiencies in zinc, tin, mercury, manganese, lead, cobalt, vanadium, tungsten, chromite, industrial diamonds, nickel, bauxite, petroleum, and copper: the total amounted to more than fifty materials.[28] President Truman linked economic and military necessities when he emphasized the need for raw materials: "Without foreign trade . . . it would be difficult, if not impossible, for us to develop atomic energy."[29]

---

because of the export trade. Henry Wallace wrongly counted on foreign trade to contribute four million to five million jobs at the close of the war. See Hoffenburg, "Employment Resulting from U.S. Exports," and Henry A. Wallace to J. C. Coyle, Apr. 9, 1945, Office of Secretary, GC 95112, Box 797, Department of Commerce Records, National Archives.

[25] John Snyder to the president, "Comments on Draft of the Economic Report of the President," [n.d.], OF 396, Truman Papers.

[26] Theodore A. Sumberg, "The Government's Role in Export Trade," *Harvard Business Review*, XXIII (Winter, 1945), 167; Committee for Economic Development, *International Trade, Foreign Investment, and Domestic Employment Including the Bretton Woods Proposals* (New York, 1945), p. 10.

[27] B. C. Forbes, ed., *America's Fifty Foremost Business Leaders* (New York, 1948), p. 226. See also Harold Moulton, draft, "Economic Consideration," Oct. 10, 1947, Subcommittee on Economic and Financial Analysis, President's Committee on Foreign Aid Records, Truman Library, which noted that the United States could probably survive a collapse of trade with Europe, "but it would take at least a generation to effect the necessary readjustments—readjustments which would inevitably be accomplished by acute distress in important sectors of the economy and a long period of economic and financial instability."

[28] Senate, *ERP* (Jan. 13, 1948), p. 369.

[29] *DSB*, XXI (Sept. 12, 1949), 401.

Some forty materials from fifty-seven different countries went into the production of steel, and Harold Ickes warned in early 1946 that the nation's supplies of manganese ore, vital in steel production, would be exhausted in two years. *Steel* magazine, two years later, was alarmed to find the prediction off by only six months: "The handwriting on the wall is clear. We should get busy pronto."[30] The materials question was a salient component of the ideology, further demonstrating an awareness of the interdependence of the international economy and the need for foreign trade to ensure United States prosperity and security.

THE SWELLING OF POWER

Not only were United States leaders aware of the realities of an interdependent world, they also recognized their own comparative strength. And they intended to use it. The country possessed an enviable set of credentials. National power derived from popular support at home, which consistently applauded the exercise of that collective power. The United States unquestionably emerged from World War II as the foremost international power. One scholar has concluded that it held the "prime weapon of *destruc*tion—the atomic bomb—and the prime weapon of *recon*struction—such wealth as no nation hitherto had possessed."[31]

The United States military establishment ranked supreme in the early Cold War period. Its air force was the largest and most capable; its navy was first with twelve hundred warships and fifty thousand supporting and landing craft; its troops occupied territory and bases across the globe, including Japan, Germany, Austria, and new outposts in the Pacific. Public pressure for demobilization forced the Truman administration to reduce military forces faster than it wished to (from 12 million in 1945 to 1.5 million in 1947), but defense needs and security were not impaired because other nations were heavily devastated and the Soviet Union also demobilized (from 12 million to 3 to 4 million). Then, too, the military expenditures for fiscal years 1947 and 1948 represented one-third of the total United States budget as compared to its miniscule defense budget and might in the 1930s. The United States after 1945 was a military giant, and few denied it. While the U.S.S.R. held power confined largely to one region, eastern Europe, the United States had become a global power.[32]

[30] *Steel,* CXVIII (Feb. 4, 1946), 97, CXXII (Mar. 29, 1948), 38.

[31] Jeanette P. Nichols, "Dollar Strength as a Liability in United States Diplomacy," *Proceedings of the American Philosophical Society,* III (Feb. 17, 1967), 47. Also see the discussion of United States "capabilities" in William Reitzel, Morton A. Kaplan, and Constance C. Coblenz, *United States Foreign Policy, 1945-1955* (Washington, D.C., 1956), pp. 47-56.

[32] The United States also modernized its military establishment by unifying its services in the National Security Act (1947) under a new secretary of defense. Reitzel, Kaplan, and Coblenz, *United States Foreign Policy,* pp. 48-50, 55; Joyce Kolko and

Most officials recognized before 1947 that Russia was, as George F. Kennan put it, the "weaker force." In early 1946 Secretary of the Navy James Forrestal received a memorandum on Soviet capabilities from one of his aides:

The Red Fleet is incapable of any important offensive or amphibious operations. . . . a strategic air force is practically non-existent either in materiel or concept. . . . economically, the Soviet Union is exhausted. The people are undernourished, industry and transport are in an advanced state of deterioration, enormous areas have been devastated, thirty percent of the population has been dislocated. . . . Maintenance of large occupation forces in Europe is dictated to a certain extent by the necessity of "farming out" millions of men for whom living accommodations and food cannot be spared in the USSR during the current winter. This also aids the popular opinion that the USSR is a tremendous military power, thereby influencing political decisions to a degree out of proportion to the USSR's actual present offensive potential. . . . The USSR is not expected to take any action during the next five years which might develop into hostilities with Anglo-Americans.[33]

The nation's military superiority and its effects on diplomacy were spelled out by President Truman in October, 1945, when he asserted that through its military strength the United States would "enforce the peace of the world." "We have learned," he said, "the bitter lesson that the weakness of this great Republic invites men of ill-will to shake the very foundations of civilization all over the world."[34] When asked by Senator Claude Pepper where the American fleet would sail, Forrestal replied, "whereever there is a sea."[35] The dramatic dispatch of warships to the Mediterranean in 1946 and 1947 was only one example of this global perception.

The awesome atomic bomb had a potential rather than real place in the military arsenal. After Hiroshima and Nagasaki, many officials hoped that

---

Gabriel Kolko, *The Limits of Power: The World and United States Foreign Policy 1945-1954* (New York, 1972), pp. 91-110; Warner R. Schilling, "The Politics of Defense: Fiscal 1950," in Schilling, Paul Y. Hammond, and Glenn H. Snyder, *Strategy, Politics, and Defense Budgets* (New York, 1962), pp. 29-30. For Soviet demobilization, see Adam B. Ulam, *Expansion and Coexistence: The History of Soviet Foreign Policy, 1917-67* (New York, 1968), pp. 403-4, and Thomas W. Wolfe, *Soviet Power and Europe, 1945-1970* (Baltimore, 1970), pp. 9-11. For Soviet awareness of United States military power, consult Marshall D. Shulman, *Stalin's Foreign Policy Reappraised* (Cambridge, Mass., 1963), pp. 20-21, 285.

[33] Thomas B. Inglis to Forrestal, Jan. 21, 1946, Box 24, James Forrestal Papers, Princeton University Library; Kennan, in U.S., Department of State, *Foreign Relations of the United States, 1946* (Washington, D.C., 1969), VI, 707 (hereafter cited as *Foreign Relations* with year, volume, and page number). The foreign service chief of the *New York Times*, C. L. Sulzberger, recorded a conversation of May 7, 1946, with Walter Bedell Smith, ambassador to the Soviet Union: "He is convinced there will be no war with Russia. The Russians are too weak. They have no air force. It will take them much more than twenty years to build a good fleet, no matter how hard they try." C. L. Sulzberger, *A Long Row of Candles: Memoirs and Diaries, 1934-1954* (New York, 1969), p. 313.

[34] *Public Papers, Truman, 1945*, p. 436 (Oct. 27, 1945).

[35] Telephone conversation, Senator Claude Pepper and James Forrestal, Mar. 24, 1947, Box 91, Forrestal Papers.

the ghastly demonstration of this weapon's destructive power, combined with the United States monopoly of it, would constitute enough of a threat to force some diplomatic concessions. Its presence was always implicit at the conference table, even though United States negotiators never overtly threatened its use. Secretary of War Henry L. Stimson recorded in his diary that Secretary of State James F. Byrnes "wished to have the implied threat of the bomb" at the London Foreign Ministers meeting (September, 1945). Indeed, Byrnes "looks to having the presence of the bomb in his pocket" at the conference.[36] Both Britain and Russia were immediately alarmed by this unilateral handling of the bomb, and the Soviets ordered their scientists to speed up their atomic development project.[37] Not until they exploded their atomic bomb in 1949 did the United States lose its monopoly. But that monopoly never meant much as a diplomatic device. In essence, it created fear and anxiety and loomed in the background as a symbol of United States technological genius and destructive ability to which other nations would aspire.

Closely linked to this military prominence was international political power. In control of Japan, Italy, and parts of Korea and Germany after the war, the United States could greatly shape their internal history. In Japan General Douglas MacArthur excluded the Soviets from joint participation, wrote a new constitution, established a representative government, and built a base at Okinawa. Thus Japan was securely placed within the United States sphere of influence for years.[38] United States interference in the internal affairs of Latin America remained a part of western hemispheric relations after the war. Through the Act of Chapultepec (1945) and the Rio Pact (1947), and continued aid to military governments, political strength and "friends" were acquired.[39]

In the United Nations Organization, which was constructed by the great powers as an instrument to reflect their control of world affairs, the United States frequently won its way through bloc voting. In essence, it possessed a "hidden veto" because a majority of the members were "friends" of or dependent upon Washington. Almost twenty Latin American governments repeatedly voted with Washington on important questions. Using its majority, Washington could avoid the veto which an outnumbered Moscow employed

[36] Quoted by Barton J. Bernstein, from Stimson diary in "American Foreign Policy and the Origins of the Cold War," in Bernstein, *Politics and Policies of the Truman Administration,* p. 36. See also Thomas G. Paterson, "Potsdam, the Atomic Bomb, and the Cold War: A Discussion with James F. Byrnes," *Pacific Historical Review,* XLI (May, 1972), 225-30.

[37] A. J. R. Groom, "U.S.-Allied Relations and the Atomic Bomb in the Second World War," *World Politics,* XV (October, 1962), 123-37; G. K. Zhukov, *The Memoirs of Marshal Zhukov* (New York, ca. 1969; 1st Eng. ed., 1971), pp. 674-75.

[38] Herbert Feis, *Contest over Japan* (New York, 1967); John W. Dower, "Occupied Japan and the American Lake, 1945-1950," in Edward Friedman and Mark Selden, eds., *America's Asia: Dissenting Essays on Asian-American Relations* (New York, 1971).

[39] David Green, "The Cold War Comes to Latin America," in Bernstein, ed., *Politics and Policies of the Truman Administration,* pp. 149-95.

time and time again. When the Soviets did veto a Security Council action, the United States could often circumvent it by utilizing alternative machinery such as the General Assembly. Also effective were threats of a "financial veto" because the United States paid a sizeable share of the organization's operating budget. The Soviets, however unenviable their own practices, sharply criticized this decisive United States hold on the United Nations.[40]

Joined to this military and political pre-eminence was the overwhelming economic power of the United States. Its businesses owned or controlled 59 percent of the world's total known oil reserves by 1947; its automobile production then was eight times that of France, England, and Germany combined, and four years later it turned out seven million cars, compared to Russia's 65,000. It was the largest producer and consumer of coal and steel in the world and at mid-century held one-third of the world's merchant fleet (gross tonnage). General Motors president Charles Wilson bragged in 1948 that with only 6 percent of the world's area and 7 percent of its population, the United States had 46 percent of the world's electric power, 48 percent of its radios, 54 percent of its telephones, and 92 percent of its modern bathtubs. The economic power of American bathtubs may have been lost on foreigners, but that of its capital and durable goods manufacturing was not. Countries in dire need of economic rehabilitation could not ignore the fact that in 1948 the United States produced about 41 percent of the goods and services in the world and was the source of almost half its total industrial output.[41] Secretary Forrestal tied this economic power to other elements of

[40] John G. Stoessinger has pointed out that "nearly 80 per cent of the Soviet Union vetoes [105 in the period 1946-1969] have been rendered less effective in one way or another and 24 per cent have been circumvented by action of the United Nations itself." Edward Rowe demonstrates that in the first twenty-one General Assembly sessions (1945-1966) the United States (except in five sessions) had at least a two-thirds majority on its side on Cold War issues. John G. Stoessinger, *The United Nations and the Superpowers: United States-Soviet Interaction at the United Nations,* 2d ed. (New York, 1970), p. 10; Edward T. Rowe, "The United States, the United Nations, and the Cold War," *International Organization,* XXV (Winter, 1971), 59-78. See also Frederick H. Gareau, *The Cold War, 1947 to 1967* (Denver, Colo., 1969); Gabriel Kolko, *The Politics of War* (New York, 1968), pp. 467-79. For Soviet complaints that the United Nations was an instrument of United States diplomacy, see W. Gottleib, "A Self-Portrait of Soviet Foreign Policy," *Soviet Studies,* III (October, 1951), 201-3; Robert R. McNeal, "Roosevelt through Stalin's Spectacles," *International Journal,* XVIII (Spring, 1963), 202-4.

[41] One wartime committee summarized United States economic power early: "Because of its relatively great economic strength, the favorable balance-of-payments position, and the importance of its market to the economic well-being of the rest of the world, the influence of the United States on world commercial policies far surpasses that of any other nation." "Summary of the Interim Report of the Special Committee on Relaxation of Trade Barriers," Dec. 8, 1943, in Notter, *Postwar Foreign Policy Preparation,* p. 622. Ernest Bevin concluded in June, 1947, that the United States was "in the position today where Britain was at the end of the Napoleonic Wars. When those wars ended Britain held about 30 per cent of the world's wealth. The U.S. today holds about 50 percent." *Foreign Relations, 1947,* III, 255. Figures are from *DSB,* XVI (Mar. 23, 1947), 554-55 (oil); Mira Wilkins and Frank E. Hill, *American Business Abroad: Ford on Six Continents* (Detroit, Mich., 1964), p. 357, and Harry A. Bullis, *A*

national strength: "As long as we can out-produce the world, can control the sea and can strike with the atomic bomb, we can assume certain risks otherwise unacceptable in an effort to restore world trade, to restore the balance of power—military power—and to eliminate some of the conditions which breed war."[42]

American leaders used words like "giant," "center," and "pivot" to describe their country's economic position. Leo Crowley, head of the Foreign Economic Administration, noted in early 1945 that the president "is now in a better bargaining position in dealing with our Allies than he is likely to be either before or after the end of the war," because other nations are "heavily dependent" upon the United States for both war and postwar materiel.[43] Even earlier, in 1944, Harriman wrote that "economic assistance is one of the most effective weapons" with which to influence events in eastern Europe.[44] As this book will demonstrate, government officials understood their nation's exclusive power and without much reluctance attempted to exploit their advantage.

Other governments, especially in European countries desperately in need of reconstruction aid, recognized this power. Soviet officials constantly remarked on United States economic strength while at the same time predicting, on the basis of rigid and distorting dogma, that the capitalist nations were heading for depression. Philip Mosely has confirmed that "when the Soviet leaders look at America, they think primarily of its great economic power."[45] Foreign Minister V. M. Molotov dipped into the *World Almanac* in 1946 to point out how World War II had strengthened the United States economy, and asked what "equal opportunity" in foreign trade and investment would really mean when the United States had no peers.[46] Then,

Businessman Views a Changing World (Minneapolis, Minn., 1952), p. 21 (autos); U.S., Department of Commerce, *Statistical Abstract, 1953* (Washington, D.C., 1953), p. 954 (merchant fleet); Wilson, in Forbes, *America's Fifty Foremost Business Leaders*, p. 447; David M. Potter, "The American Economic System," in Lyman Bryson, ed., *An Outline of Man's Knowledge of the Modern World* (New York, 1960), p. 456.

[42] Walter Millis, ed., *The Forrestal Diaries* (New York, 1951), pp. 350-51 (Dec. 8, 1947).

[43] Leo Crowley, "Memorandum Relative to Present Bargaining Power of the President," Jan. 20, 1945, Folder 52, James F. Byrnes Papers, Clemson University Library.

[44] *Foreign Relations, 1944* (Washington, D.C., 1966), IV, 951 (Mar. 13, 1944). Harriman later wrote the secretary of state: "When it comes to matters of greater importance, we should make it plain that their failure to conform to our concepts will affect our willingness to cooperate with them, for example, in material assistance for reconstruction." He went on to explain that on matters of "vital" importance, the United States should tell the Soviets "that we are prepared to take the consequences if they adhere to their position. In such cases, I am satisfied that in the last analysis Stalin will back down." *Ibid.*, p. 997 (Sept. 20, 1944).

[45] Philip E. Mosely, "Soviet-American Relations since the War," *The Annals of the American Academy of Political and Social Science*, CCLXIII (May, 1949), 202.

[46] And Andrei Zhdanov said, "Of all the capitalist powers, only one—the United States—emerged from the war not only unweakened, but even considerably stronger economically and militarily." Andrei Zhdanov, *The International Situation* (Moscow, 1947), pp. 11-12. V. M. Molotov, "The Danube and Economic Problems," in *Problems*

too, American economic power and the willingness to employ it for diplomatic leverage reinforced in the Soviet mind the Communist teaching that capitalist countries are acquisitive and aggressive and that imperialism results from their drive to expand economically to evade depressions at home.[47]

The record is replete with examples of American diplomatic forcefulness sustained by a self-conscious awareness of power. The Truman administration was not helpless, defensive, drifting, or ignorant in its Cold War diplomacy. The most famous example of its position is the White House confrontation between Truman and Molotov in April, 1945, when the president, less than two weeks in office, vigorously chided the shocked Russian diplomat and warned that no reconstruction aid would be forthcoming unless the Soviets accepted the American interpretation of the Yalta accords. Truman in fact told his advisers just before this meeting that "if the Russians did not wish to join us [in establishing the United Nations] they could go to hell."[48] Shortly after the incident, Truman informed Joseph Davies, former ambassador to Russia, "I gave it to him straight 'one-two to the jaw.' I let him have it straight."[49]

This language amounted to more than mere rhetoric or an exuberant style; the tough words were backed by a growing confidence in United States power. Less than a month after the Potsdam Conference Secretary Byrnes drew a lesson: "the only way to negotiate with the Russians is to hit them hard, and then negotiate."[50] The president, declaring the United States the "greatest naval power on earth" and meaning it, insisted in the fall of 1945 that "we shall not give our approval to any compromise with evil."[51] And in September, 1946, when Byrnes was having a difficult time with the stubborn Russians over peace treaties with the German satellites, Truman cabled him in Paris: "Do everything you can to continue but in the final analysis do whatever you think is right and tell them [the Russians] to go to hell if you have to."[52] Although its leaders had a sense of their powerful rank in world

---

of Foreign Policy: Speeches and Statements, April 1945-November 1948 (Moscow, 1949), pp. 209-14.

[47] Frederick C. Barghoorn, "The Soviet Critique of American Foreign Policy," Columbia Journal of International Affairs, V (Winter, 1951), 5-14; Adam Ulam, "Soviet Ideology and Soviet Foreign Policy," World Politics, XI (January, 1959), 153-72; Gottlieb, "A Self-Portrait of Soviet Foreign Policy," pp. 185-205 (esp. 203-4).

[48] Foreign Relations, 1945 (Washington, D.C., 1967), V, 253. See Truman's account in Harry S. Truman, Memoirs, 2 vols. (New York, 1955-56), I, 82.

[49] Quoted in John L. Gaddis, The United States and the Origins of the Cold War, 1941-1947 (New York, 1972), p. 205.

[50] See Paterson, "Potsdam, the Atomic Bomb, and the Cold War," p. 228.

[51] Public Papers, Truman, 1945, pp. 432, 433 (Oct. 27, 1945).

[52] Truman to Byrnes, Sept. 24, 1946, Folder 52, Byrnes Papers. See also Truman, Memoirs, I, 552, and the statements of Secretary of War Robert Patterson, General Dwight D. Eisenhower, and General John P. Deane in late 1946 on the importance of economic power as a diplomatic weapon, in Bruce Kuklick, American Policy and the Division of Germany: The Clash with Russia over Reparations (Ithaca, N.Y., 1972), pp. 224-25.

affairs and were not reluctant to flex their muscles, both rhetorically and actually, as succeeding chapters will show, the influence of the United States ultimately never reached as far as its power, and many of its hopes for the postwar period went unfulfilled.

CONTRADICTIONS AND ANXIETIES

United States power, of course, was not absolute, and both internal and external restraints at times inhibited its exercise. Congress always had to be persuaded to spend more for foreign aid and to abide by the administration's trade principles. Persuasion takes patience, and the Truman administration could not always move at the pace it desired. Congress was especially sticky on the reduction of tariffs and trade privileges, and thus a contradiction between America's conduct and doctrine was created. The machinery of the World Bank, the International Monetary Fund, the United Nations, and the Export-Import Bank sometimes moved with annoying slowness. The Russians and British engaged in conspicuous discriminatory practices, and each country maintained or began to forge empires which served as barriers to United States influence. The emergence of the Soviet Union as a contending world power, backed by an ideology which struck directly at the "American way," seemed particularly alarming. Recurrent crises in Europe and the Far East aroused uncertainties about United States security, and Latin America seemed less and less compliant as a sphere of influence. Then, too, anxieties about a postwar depression undercut the national optimism. A world in ruins seemed an increasingly unlikely place to realize equal economic opportunity, multilateralism, and political freedom. At a time when the United States was an economic behemoth, wealthy and expanding, and much of Europe remained a "rubble heap," as Winston Churchill put it, many countries turned in self-defense to economic methods anathema to Washington—import controls, nationalization, trade preferences, bilateral treaties, and subsidies.

The United States itself established trade restrictions. The president failed to control congressmen eager to give tariff protection to the products of their districts. Further, it was believed that the Soviet Union must be confronted with all weapons possible, including the interruption of world trade through export controls. The State Department also was forced to fight skirmishes at home. The Department of Agriculture, especially in 1945-1946, advocated international commodity agreements to set minimum and maximum prices and regarded "free trade with fear."[53] Domestic price supports, the subsidizing of agricultural exports by the Commodity Credit Corporation and by the Economic Cooperation Administration, and tariffs and quotas on agricultural imports—all violated the announced Truman trade

[53] Allen J. Matusow, *Farm Policies and Politics in the Truman Years* (Cambridge, Mass., 1967), p. 91. See also *Fortune*, XXXII (August, 1945), 115.

program, as did subsidies to shipping interests and sugar producers, government purchases of rubber, barter deals with India for manganese, and "buy America" provisions in the Stockpiling Program. In the Middle East, American oil companies, with Washington's backing, entered into cartel arrangements with British firms. Some companies were involved in cartels in matches, screws, and electrical equipment, among others, and some merely continued their prewar cartel activity.[54] Winthrop G. Brown of the State Department had to admit that "we have had in this country a certain amount of State trading. . . ."[55]

The United States also built up preferential trade relations with Cuba and the Philippines, prompting Russian and British criticism. *Pravda* wrote that "economic relations between the Philippines and the USA have been re-established on the old notorious basis of 'free trade' of economic preference for the USA, and discrimination in regard to other countries,"[56] and the *Economist* (London) chided Americans for a double standard:

In spite of their loudly proclaimed devotion to free enterprise and competition, they regard competitive imports as an evil to be guarded against by prohibitive import duties, embargoes, and quotas. Many of them object to the continued presence of European possessions in the Western Hemisphere, but see no incompatability in American requisition of bases on the far sides of the Pacific and Atlantic Oceans—nor in telling the Russians what they should do in Poland and the Balkans, and the British what they should do in Palestine, India, and Siam.[57]

Under Secretary of State Will Clayton, who bore the task of bringing goals and practice into some kind of alignment, admitted that "if we want to be honest with ourselves, we will find that many of the sins that we freely criticize other countries for practicing have their counterpart in the United States."[58] He felt handicapped in trade negotiations (such as those for the

---

[54] For violations of the Truman trade program, see C. Addison Hickman, *Our Farm Program and Foreign Trade* (New York, 1949); Alex F. McCalla, "Protectionism in International Agricultural Trade, 1850-1968," *Agricultural History*, XLIII (July, 1969), 329-43; Raymond F. Mikesell, *United States Economic Policy and International Relations* (New York, 1952), p. 303; Raymond F. Mikesell and Hollis B. Chenery, *Arabian Oil: America's Stake in the Middle East* (Chapel Hill, N.C., 1949), pp. 9, 120; Senate, *Anglo-American Financial Agreement*, pp. 124 (Mar. 6, 1946), and 445-46, 456 (Mar. 19, 1946); George W. Stocking and Myron W. Watkins, *Cartels in Action* (New York, 1946); Gabriel Kolko, "American Business and Germany, 1930-1941," *Western Political Quarterly*, XV (September, 1962), 713-28.

[55] U.S., Congress, Senate, Committee on Foreign Relations, *Proposed Treaty of Friendship, Commerce and Navigation between the United States and the Italian Republic* (Hearings), 80th Cong., 2d sess. (Apr. 30, 1948), p. 10.

[56] *Soviet Press Translations*, I (November, 1946). Also see Hans Heymann, *We Can Do Business with Russia* (Chicago, 1945), p. 153.

[57] Quoted in *Iron Age*, CLVIII (Aug. 8, 1946), p. 146.

[58] Gardner, *Sterling-Dollar Diplomacy*, p. 378. See also David A. Baldwin, *Economic Development and American Foreign Policy, 1943-62* (Chicago, 1966), p. 99; Lamar Fleming to John C. Whites, May 14, 1945, Will Clayton Papers, Truman Library.

ambitious General Agreement on Tariffs and Trade of 1947) because of those sins and because the British refused to yield much on their imperial preferences, citing as reasons their own economic crisis and insufficient United States concessions.[59]

Some leading businessmen and government officials came to realize that the economically disrupted postwar world was hardly conducive to multi-lateralism, and the government itself moved farther and farther away from this policy. By 1950 the Department of State noted that the United States conducted the "great mass of our business through bilateral relations with more than 70 governments. These involve questions of trade and travel, private investment and governmental assistance, and countless matters of daily business which affect us all."[60] But Washington officials did not think their advocacy of the open door and their contradictory actions placed them in a hypocritical position. They argued that tariff reductions and a more liberal trade practice would simply take time—that critics should not expect the United States to change its habits overnight. Commodity agreements and subsidies for domestic interests, argued Clayton, were temporary measures during the adjustment to peace.[61] Bilateralism, state trading, import and export controls, and cartels, whether practiced by the United States or other nations, were, presumably, accepted only as temporary evils. Once the world regained its economic health, the administration argued, such trade impediments could be permanently eliminated.

If trade barriers weakened United States economic power, anxieties about the country's postwar economic health also eroded confidence in that power. Both during and after the war, Americans and foreigners expected an economic collapse in the United States. When the French Institute of Public Opinion asked why Washington had proposed a European reconstruction program in 1947, over half the French respondents said the plan was designed to ensure foreign markets for United States goods to avert depression.[62] Although Soviet propagandists and theorists, with the notable exception of Eugene Varga, also predicted an immediate economic crisis, that prediction did not originate in France or Moscow.[63]

[59] For GATT, see *Journal of Commerce*, Mar. 15, 1947; Matusow, *Farm Policies*, pp. 95-97; Sumner Welles, "Pressure Groups and Foreign Policy," *Atlantic Monthly*, CLXXX (November, 1947), 63-67; Gardner, *Sterling-Dollar Diplomacy*, pp. 349-61.
[60] *DSB*, XXII (Apr. 3, 1950), 531.
[61] Senate, *Anglo-American Financial Agreement* (Mar. 6, 1946), p. 124. See also House, *Post-War Economic Policy*, 6th Report, p. 41.
[62] Poll of September, 1947, in Harry B. Price, *The Marshall Plan and Its Meaning* (Ithaca, N.Y., 1955), p. 85.
[63] *New Times* (Moscow), July 1, 1945, pp. 15-19; *Foreign Relations, 1945*, V, 851-66; Margaret Carlyle, ed., *Documents on International Affairs, 1947-1948* (London, 1952), pp. 116-21 (Stalin interview with Harold Stassen); Ulam, *Expansion and Coexistence*, p. 410; Eugene Varga, "The Approach of an Economic Crisis in the Capitalist World," *Political Affairs*, XXVI (March, 1947), 264-68; Frederick C. Barghoorn, "The Varga Discussion and Its Significance," *American Slavic and East European Review*, III (October, 1948), 214-36; Shulman, *Stalin's Foreign Policy Reappraised*, pp. 32-35.

Within the United States fears of economic slump fed on the unhappy experiences of the 1930s. Some believed that the shaky prewar economy might re-establish itself. As the Committee for Economic Development noted: "Memories of depression and mass unemployment in the last decade are still vivid—thrown into strong relief by the recent experience of wartime full employment."[64] Through 1945 and 1946 observers differed on the business outlook, with those predicting a downturn having the edge. Amidst the uncertainty, Secretary of the Treasury John Snyder attempted to alleviate the gloom by declaring it "bad psychology to be continually talking about 'depression' and 'recession' when we have all the elements for a continued prosperous period."[65]

In early June, 1947, the *Journal of Commerce* reported that an "international economic crisis is being freely predicted today. . . . In this country, an approaching collapse is ascribed to the exhaustion of purchasing power abroad."[66] President Truman fought against this pessimistic mood: "Despite many gloomy predictions, there is no convincing evidence that a recession is imminent."[67] But by the middle of 1947 forecasts of recession were on the increase. This may be partly explained by the economic distress in Europe, partly by the administration's own warnings that continued European depression would have unfortunate domestic and international economic and political consequences unless programs such as the Truman Doctrine and the Marshall Plan were approved.[68] There was growing concern, too, that inflation and the alarming trend of rising prices would precipitate economic disaster.

Decisionmakers were aware that their references to depression fortified Soviet theory and rhetoric. Secretary Forrestal recorded that several passages in a draft of the president's message to Congress in early 1948 about the "low standard of living in this country on the part of millions of families and the foreboding of a coming depression" would serve as "excellent propaganda for the Kremlin."[69] During the 1948 presidential campaign John Foster Dulles

[64] Committee for Economic Development, *Toward More Production, More Jobs, and More Freedom* (New York, 1945), p. 7.

[65] *Journal of Commerce*, Oct. 31, 1946. Also see Everett E. Hagen and Nora Kirkpatrick, "Forecasting Gross National Product and Employment during the Transition Period," *Studies in Income and Wealth*, X (1947), 94-109; Michael Sapir, "Review of Economic Forecasts for the Transition Period," *ibid.*, XI (1949), 273-351; W. S. Woytinsky, "What Was Wrong in Forecasts of Postwar Depression?" *Journal of Political Economy*, LV (April, 1947), 142-51.

[66] *Journal of Commerce*, June 3, 1947.

[67] *Public Papers, Truman, 1947*, p. 279 (June 16, 1947).

[68] United States exports to Europe in 1947 showed the effects of economic distress and reduced buying power there. From a peak of $565,180,000 in May, 1947, they dropped to $470,952,000 in July, to $404,312,000 in November, and to $400,892,000 in January, 1948. In 1947 the United States exported goods worth $14 billion. In 1948 the figure dropped about $3 billion, and in 1949 it declined another $0.5 billion. *Survey of Current Business*, XXVIII (April, 1948), 5-21; Commerce, *Foreign Trade, 1936-49*, p. 42.

[69] Millis, *Forrestal Diaries*, p. 356 (Jan. 6, 1948).

informed Thomas Dewey that "Soviet foreign policy is encouraged and stiffened by predictions in high quarters in the United States that [a] Republican victory will bring serious internal depression to our country."[70]

The various aid programs, especially the large-scale Interim Aid project and Marshall Plan of 1947-1948, reduced fears about the economy and kept sales abroad from sagging disastrously. Nevertheless, a recession hit in the third quarter of 1948 and lasted until the second quarter of 1950. Exports continued to decline, and about 26 percent of the total drop in output during the period was due to the slackening of that trade. But foreign aid unquestionably blunted some of the sharper edges of the recession by placing $6.45 billion in the hands of Europeans and other foreigners buying in United States markets in 1948 and 1949.[71]

In 1947, before the recession began, many observers believed that inflation at home, rather than reduced buying abroad, would cause economic decline. Inflationary tendencies were at work, and Europe's purchase of goods scarce in the United States did contribute to them.[72] As the *Journal of Commerce* put it, the country had a choice "between higher prices or lower exports."[73] Neither inflation nor foreign aid to bolster exports was welcome, but government officials and some labor and business leaders thought that at least prices could be controlled through anti-inflationary policies.[74] In June Truman stated the problem in historical perspective: "To say that we should abandon our efforts directed toward enduring world peace and freedom because these efforts create economic problems is like saying that we should have abandoned our war effort because it created economic problems."[75] Foreign aid and foreign trade—the exertion and extension of economic

[70] John Foster Dulles to Thomas Dewey, Sept. 24, 1948, John Foster Dulles Papers, Princeton University Library.

[71] According to M. I. Ghozlan: "The increase in government expenditures on national defense and international affairs took place . . . at a critical stage in the development of the recession, namely the latter half of 1948 and the first half of 1949, and was therefore of considerable value in supporting the weakening economy during that period." M. E. Ghozlan, "The Recession of 1948-1949 in the United States" (Ph.D. dissertation, Yale University, 1954), p. 459 (see also pp. 494-95); Ilse Mintz, *American Exports during Business Cycles* (New York, 1961), p. 12; Congressional Quarterly Service, *Evolution of Foreign Aid, 1945-1965* (Washington, D.C., 1966), p. 25.

[72] Between August, 1945, and August, 1948, the cost of living rose 35 percent and wholesale prices 61 percent. In 1947 an international wheat shortage, the result of a poor European crop and bad weather in the United States, caused wheat prices to skyrocket. There were also shortages in coal, steel, some industrial equipment, and nitrogen fertilizers. Lester V. Chandler, *Inflation in the United States, 1940-1948* (New York, 1951), pp. 216, 229-30; Interior, *Natural Resources,* pp. 7-10; *Journal of Commerce,* Sept. 2, 1947.

[73] *Journal of Commerce,* Sept. 19, 1947.

[74] See, for example, Philip Murray (CIO) in Senate, *ERP* (Feb. 3, 1948), p. 1300; Americans for Democratic Action, press release, Oct. 2, 1947, Clark Clifford Papers, Truman Library; Committee for the Marshall Plan, Executive Committee minutes, Jan. 16, 1948, Box 105, Winthrop Aldrich Papers, Baker Library, Harvard University.

[75] "Statement by the President," press release, June 5, 1947, Box 15, Clifford Papers.

power—were simply too important to both United States and world prosperity, to the effort to contain Communism and the Soviet Union (and hence to world peace), to be allowed to fade. Prominent officials accepted the conclusion of the influential National Advisory Council on International Monetary and Financial Problems that "any temporary sacrifice" demanded from the economy by foreign aid "will be small compared to the long-range advantages to the United States of a peaceful, active, and growing world economy."[76]

The words "long-range" are important to the peace and prosperity theme. The Truman administration did not argue that foreign aid was essential to head off an imminent recession. Rather, it stressed the long-range economic and political importance of such assistance. When discussing inflation and exports, government and business leaders emphasized the temporary and controllable nature of inflation and the long-run and worldwide significance of exports to peace and prosperity. Washington looked anxiously beyond the present to the future. Could the United States remain at peace in a world vulnerable to Communism because of economic dislocation? Could it be secure and prosperous in an economically weak world that turned increasingly to systems which challenged both its ideals and foreign trade? Could it afford to lose its lucrative European markets and its foreign sources of strategic materials? Could it withstand both the economic and political consequences of global economic chaos? The significant question was not whether a decline in foreign trade would bring an immediate depression at home but whether the interdependent world economy, linked by United States exports and economic power, would become viable and prosperous enough to stave off unstable and revolutionary politics—in short, Communism. These were troubling questions; all the economic power the nation possessed would be rendered diplomatically useless if they were answered in the negative.

RECONSTRUCTION DIPLOMACY IN THE EARLY COLD WAR

Despite these contradictions, anxieties, and unsettling questions, government leaders expressed a remarkable confidence that they could forge an open world. Indeed, they were often overoptimistic, either ignoring the restraints on United States power or consigning them a temporary function. Foreign policy constituted more than simply "ensure peace" or "stop Communism" or "avert capitalist depression" or "expand markets and raw materials sources." These objectives were intimately related, as the ideology of peace and prosperity explained so well. Consistent with these goals was the

[76] United States National Advisory Council on International Monetary and Financial Problems, *Statement of the Foreign Loan Policy of the United States Government*, 79th Cong., 2d sess. (Mar. 1, 1946), H. Doc. 489, p. 5.

intention to become the most powerful voice in international affairs and thereby to mold the postwar world in the image of the United States. Economic power enjoyed high rank as an instrument for that self-conscious thrust.

To argue thus is not to say that reconstruction diplomacy followed a neat master plan. United States principles were consistently articulated and goals doggedly pursued, but there were moments of introspection and gradual modification, times of haphazard application and inadequate coordination. The trend in the early Cold War years was toward a cohesive program of trade, aid, and loans, finally realized in the Truman Doctrine, Marshall Plan, and the rehabilitation of Germany. The North Atlantic Treaty Organization (NATO) and National Security Council Paper No. 68 (NSC 68) represented a similar coalescence in the military program. Implicit in this trend was the use of a "tough method" with the Russians, as Truman put it.[77]

Diplomacy in this period can best be described as moving in "spurts"—that is, relatively short periods in which leaders, after interim months of trial and error, summarized, re-evaluated, and clarified their thinking and took more affirmative action. Because these brief periods of intense thought and decision occurred within a long-term trend toward coordination, and because there was little deviation from revered principles, the "spurts" cannot be labeled dramatic turning points. They were induced by self-assessment, by the fruition of months of gradual activity, or by the pressure of events at home and abroad. The announcement of the Truman Doctrine in March, 1947, for example, actually derived from all three factors. Several "spurts" can be recognized: (1) late 1943 to mid-1944; (2) April-August, 1945; (3) February-June, 1946; (4) September-October, 1946; (5) February-June, 1947; (6) early 1948. They should not be taken as rigid boundary marks but rather as times in which thought and decision coalesced.

Late 1943 to Mid-1944

Americans began thinking about the contours of the postwar world early in the war, and toward the end of the conflagration they took steps to fulfill both wartime and postwar aims. In November, 1943, the United States joined other Allies in creating the United Nations Relief and Rehabilitation Administration (UNRRA), the result of more than a year of study. The new relief institution was designed to feed, clothe, shelter, and dispense medicine to millions of helpless people in Europe and the Far East. Because the United States provided about three-quarters of UNRRA funds, it looked upon UNRRA as an agency which would meet its goals of relieving human discontent and economic chaos, and creating political stability. The agency's

[77] Truman statement of April, 1945, quoted in Gaddis, *United States and the Origins of the Cold War,* p. 205.

establishment thus reflected a combination of sincere humanitarianism and national interest.[78]

At about the same time, United States diplomats opened the question of a postwar loan to the Soviet Union, and in February, 1944, reconstruction-conscious Soviet leaders demonstrated their keen interest by asking for $1 billion. A twofold motivation lay behind the overture. As Ambassador Harriman indicated, sizeable postwar Soviet-American trade financed by a loan might help ease his country's adjustment to a peacetime economy, and a loan could have value in forthcoming diplomatic negotiations with Russia. The question of a loan became a major topic in discussions on how best to counter Soviet influence in eastern Europe. Harriman noted in March that postwar economic assistance was "one of the most effective weapons at our disposal" to influence events in Europe and the Balkans.

In June, 1944, the president of the Chamber of Commerce, Eric Johnston, made his celebrated trip to Russia and was granted a rare and serious interview with Stalin in which postwar trade prospects were excitedly discussed. In Iran, with Washington's encouragement through appeals to the open door, United States oil companies filed concession requests and directly challenged the predominant Anglo-Iranian Company. An international scramble for oil seemed in the offing, with far-reaching consequences. Also significant was the opening in July of the Bretton Woods Conference of forty-four nations in the New Hampshire mountains. After months of planning, and following the lead of the United States and Britain, it established the International Bank for Reconstruction and Development (World Bank) and the International Monetary Fund. Governed by the principles of multilateralism and the free flow of trade and currencies (and by United States power), these new institutions were assigned the duties of ensuring postwar economic stability and hence peace.

By the middle of the year, then, the United States had, in essence, articulated its reconstruction goals, created three major institutions to fulfill those goals, begun to discuss postwar trade and aid with the Russians, and moved into competition for Middle Eastern oil. Events from then to about April, 1945, marked a gestation period in which policymakers at the Quebec, Dumbarton Oaks, and Yalta conferences grappled inconclusively with the problems of how to disperse power within a new international organization (the United Nations), how to avert Soviet dominance in eastern Europe (particularly Poland), and how to treat postwar Germany. In the German case, the Allies could not agree on the amount of reparations to be paid, and the United States awkwardly embraced an imprecise program named the Morgenthau Plan after the secretary of the treasury. In January the Russians revived the dormant question of a postwar loan and audaciously asked for $6 billion. Surprised Washington officials pondered the request. The

[78] For the most part, footnotes for the remainder of this chapter will be omitted because the topics are discussed and documented thoroughly in forthcoming chapters.

State Department also watched warily as a bloody civil war in Greece threatened peace in the Near East.

April–August 1945

A number of ideas jelled in this next period, as the United States, sensing the war's end and its own postwar economic power, attempted to fashion a United States-oriented world order and to challenge with a "tough method" those nations resisting its aims. In April, 1945, Harriman and the new president, Truman, hardened on the loan to Russia and decided to hold it as a weapon to force Soviet concessions. Molotov felt the brunt of this stiffening position in his tussle with Truman on April 23, and Senator Arthur M. Vandenberg at the United Nations Conference in San Francisco was elated that "F.D.R.'s appeasement of Russia is over."[79] At that conference, the United States, using the votes of the Latin American states, firmly orchestrated the refusal to seat the provisional (pro-Soviet) government of Poland and the decision to seat Argentina, detested by the Soviets for what seemed to be its tolerance of Nazi Germany.

Washington abruptly terminated Lend-Lease in early May, causing the Soviets to charge that economic pressure was being used against them. Although the termination order was modified to allow some shipments to Russia, it was intended as a warning to the Russians not to expect American generosity without diplomatic concessions. Concurrently, a program for the economic control of Germany was issued (JCS/1067), reflecting Morgenthau's ideas for a corrective peace. Truman signed it without enthusiasm. The military governor of the American zone, General Lucius Clay, evinced immediate distaste for the plan and began a retreat from it. The Allied Reparations Commission began to function in June, and immediately the American and Soviet commissioners disagreed on the amount of reparations and on German ability to pay. By the summer of 1945, it appeared that most United States leaders were leaning to a "constructive" rather than a "corrective" peace.

In June and July, 1945, Congress, usually by large votes, passed important legislation. The Trade Agreements Act, authorizing the administration to reduce tariffs in return for reductions by other nations, was extended for three years. The president asked for and received $3.5 billion to expand the Export-Import Bank, soon to become the major agency for dispensing reconstruction loans. That same month the Senate approved United States membership in the United Nations, the Food and Agriculture Organization, and the World Bank and Fund. After joining these institutions, the United States scuttled UNRRA the following month. Congressmen who favored direct control of relief dollars for diplomatic benefit joined Truman

---

[79] Arthur H. Vandenberg, Jr., ed., *The Private Papers of Senator Vandenberg* (Boston, 1952), p. 176.

administration officials who found with chagrin that UNRRA could not be used as an American diplomatic weapon in eastern Europe. Over the protests of a number of war-damaged nations, Washington set a termination date of December, 1946, for the relief agency.

The Potsdam Conference of July 17-August 2, 1945, figured prominently in reconstruction diplomacy. Not only did Truman and Byrnes bargain assertively and impatiently and come away convinced that the Russians were bent on obstructing a viable peace, but several decisions of particular note were taken. Britain, Russia, and the United States created the Council of Foreign Ministers, wherein they would struggle for at least two years to write peace treaties for Germany's satellites and coordinate the Allied zones in Germany. The conferees also decided at Potsdam to disarm, demilitarize, and denazify the Germans, as well as to follow a set of economic principles. German industry would be dismantled to the point where it could not serve military purposes. The Allies decided also that Germany would be treated as a "single economic unit." Finally, each power would draw reparations from its own zone.

The Potsdam agreements on Germany later provided some of the most divisive issues in the Soviet-American confrontation; at the same time they represented a vigorous but unsuccessful attempt by President Truman to get Britain and Russia to accept the principle of freedom of navigation on international waterways like the Danube. Truman was most insistent on this issue and summarized Washington's position well, but Stalin, who considered the river within the Soviet sphere, much as the Suez Canal was within the British, asked for delay on the question. Truman, furious that one of his pet principles had been ignored, returned from Potsdam all the more committed to acting tough with the Russians, especially by denying them any part in the postwar control of Japan or any knowledge of the atomic bomb. He would, however, attempt to pry concessions from them on eastern Europe by continuing to hold out the hope of a large loan. An invitation to submit a new loan application was tendered to the Russians on August 9, one week after Potsdam and the day on which the last atomic bomb fell on Nagasaki. V-J Day came at last on August 15, and World War II was over.

From August, 1945, to early 1946—an interim period—attention was drawn to crises in Iran and Greece, where Communist-led rebels threatened to tear the two governments from their close relationship with Britain and the United States. Crudely exercised Soviet influence in eastern Europe also aroused concern in Washington. Monthly protest notes were combined with refusals to grant loans to eastern European countries. United States negotiators were frustrated in their attempts at the London (September-October) and Moscow (December) conferences to obtain meaningful changes in that region. The only good news in this interim period came in December, when, after months of tiring negotiations, Britain and the United States signed a financial agreement whereby Washington extended a $3.5 billion loan in return for a British promise to reduce its restrictive trading practices in the future. Meanwhile, the question of credits for Russia remained uncertain. Over all, the interim period was one of unsettled issues and mounting tension. Shortly after the Moscow Conference, however, Truman ordered his advisers to launch a more vigorous diplomacy. A new spurt began in February, 1946.

February–June, 1946

Crises, opportunities, and ideas merged in February. Defeated for a long time in its attempts to influence affairs in eastern Europe and looking to the first meeting of the World Bank in March, the United States thought it a propitious moment to reopen the loan question. On February 21, after months of silence on the matter, the State Department informed the Soviet Union that it would begin negotiations on a postwar loan, but that the agenda must include events in eastern Europe, Soviet membership in the World Bank, and a variety of open door topics like free navigation of rivers. Also, the Iranian crisis was heating up: the Iranians were urging a Security Council investigation of Soviet interference.

The re-opening of the loan question coincided with three major independent statements about the course of postwar relations. On February 22 Chargé George F. Kennan sent an impressive eight-thousand-word telegram to the State Department from Moscow. Discussing the "basic features" of Soviet ideology and behavior, Kennan's alarming document found the Soviet leaders uncompromising, warlike, aggressive, neurotic, subversive, and intent upon destroying "our traditional way of life." Furthermore, Russia would only pay "lip service" to international economic cooperation. He ended on a note of caution and guarded optimism when he added that the "Soviets are still by far the weaker force."[80] The telegram was just what a number of officials were looking for—an authoritative, persuasive, and simple essay which explained with clarity just how intransigent and threatening Russia was. Secretary Forrestal soon had Kennan recalled from Moscow and installed as a lecturer at the National War College. The telegram was read widely in Washington, and most officials ignored Kennan's cautionary words and focused instead on his hard-hitting analysis of Soviet behavior.[81]

Secretary Byrnes and bipartisan leader Vandenberg were coming to similar conclusions independently. They had always followed a tough policy toward Russia, but now they were more open about it. In a speech of February 28 Byrnes spoke bleakly of the suspicion and distrust between the great powers. Standing under the umbrella of the United Nations, and with the Iranian crisis in mind, he declared that the United States would "act to prevent aggression," and emphasized the importance of military strength toward that

---

[80] *Foreign Relations, 1946*, VI, 696-709.
[81] For Kennan's impact on the Truman administration's thinking, see Thomas G. Paterson, ed., *Containment and the Cold War: American Foreign Policy since 1945* (Reading, Mass., 1973).

goal. He denounced "coercion," "subterfuges such as political infiltration," and "penetrations of power." The day before on the Senate floor Vandenberg had asked, "What is Russia up to now?" His answer was not lucid, but he implied that the Soviets were embarked on a path of global expansion.[82]

In March the United States backed Iran in the Security Council, refused a Soviet request to delay the proceedings, and witnessed a Soviet walkout. By April the Iranian crisis, to all intents, ended when the Soviets agreed to pull back from Azerbaijan in exchange for an oil concession. On March 5 Churchill delivered his famous "iron curtain" speech, with Truman conspicuously in attendance on the speaker's platform. Although United States officials disapproved of Churchill's call for an Anglo-American alliance, they were friendlier to his denunciation of Soviet intrusions in eastern Europe. Shortly after the address, between March 8 and 18, the first meetings of the World Bank and Fund took place in Savannah, Georgia. The United States so dominated the gathering that even the British protested—but cautiously, because the British loan agreement was still before Congress (it passed in May) and they were desperate for aid. There was little doubt that the Bretton Woods institutions would serve Washington's purposes. In Greece, elections which the rebels boycotted produced a sizeable vote for the conservatives. American leaders were generally pleased with the results because now they could back a Greek regime elected under "democratic" procedures, yet the civil war flared up again, and more American warships and loans went to Greece in the spring of 1946. In Germany the Allies finally agreed on a level of industry plan and could now proceed with economic rehabilitation. General Clay, in a bold step, stopped all reparations shipments to Russia from the American zone in Germany in an attempt to force Russia to accept German "economic unity."

The United States also kept up its pressure on eastern Europe. Poland was granted credits after its government promised to practice multilateralism; a month later the offer was withdrawn because Poland did not seem to be moving fast enough. Trying to achieve the principle of free navigation on the Danube, officials in the American zone in Austria seized several hundred river vessels belonging to Yugoslavia and Czechoslovakia. Byrnes's refusal in June to accept a Soviet concession for "preliminary" talks on eastern Europe in conjunction with loan negotiations killed prospects for a loan and was one more sign of the stiffening attitude toward Russia and the determination to use economic pressure in the Cold War.

During the summer of 1946, in the Bretton Woods agencies, the Near East, the Middle East, Germany, and eastern Europe, the United States seemed more confident and affirmative in its use of economic power.

[82] For a discussion of the mood in early 1946, see ch. 9, "Getting Tough with Russia: The Reorientation of American Policy, 1946," in Gaddis, *United States and the Origins of the Cold War;* Byrnes, in *DSB,* XIV (Mar. 10, 1946), 355-58; Vandenberg, in *Congressional Record,* XCII, 79th Cong., 2d sess. (Feb. 27, 1946), 1692-95.

Moreover, Washington presented the Baruch Plan on the international control of atomic weapons, offering to give up its monopoly only after other nations had taken a series of steps which denied them authority over fissionable materials and development work. United States officials thought it a generous offer, but the Russians considered it too risky because until the last step was taken the United States alone would hold the bomb. Economic power and atomic power would continue as United States weapons. Truman summarized the point on April 6, 1946, in his Army Day speech: the "United States today is a strong nation; there is none stronger." It would tolerate no aggression and would continue to work against the 1930s economic nationalism which had "poisoned international relations." Somewhat surprisingly, in view of the occasion, the president reiterated United States trade principles and pledged that his country's economic power would help Europe recover. From spring to fall, the nation began to follow through on many of these decisions.

September–October, 1946

United States diplomacy further jelled in September and October. Byrnes established a State Department policy of refusing aid to countries friendly to Russia. As for Germany, in a much-publicized speech in Stuttgart on September 6 he once again explained the importance of German economic unity and stated that the United States would proceed with as much unification as it could obtain—by which he meant merger of the American and British zones. Neither the Soviets nor the French were interested in such unity, so this policy frankly recognized that Germany was going to be divided for a long time. He also recommended lifting some of the restrictions on German industry. At about the same time, the Truman administration announced it would henceforth maintain a permanent fleet in the Mediterranean and conveyed to the Soviet Union its strong support of Turkey in the latter's refusal to share control of the Dardanelles. After a thorough "re-evaluation" of policy toward Greece, Truman decided that it was vital to United States security and would be a recipient of aid. In Iran, with strong American encouragement, the government ousted opposition party members (Tudeh, mostly Communist) from the cabinet and began to lean heavily on Ambassador George V. Allen for advice. The Near and Middle East were being drawn closer to American influence.

In September the sole critic within the cabinet of the "get tough with Russia" approach and an advocate of aid to Russia was forced out of the government after he spoke at a Madison Square Garden political rally. " 'Getting tough' never brought anything real and lasting—whether for schoolyard bullies or businessmen or world powers," Henry A. Wallace concluded. "The tougher we get, the tougher the Russians will get."[83]

---

[83] *Vital Speeches,* XII (Oct. 1, 1946), 738-41.

Wallace was talking to minds that had been made up. Indeed, his removal prompted Truman and Byrnes to reassert their foreign policy. In September Truman asked presidential assistant Clark Clifford to prepare a report on Soviet-American relations, and Clifford consulted several top officials before handing the president a long memorandum reaffirming a forceful foreign policy backed by military and economic power.[84]

From October to February reconstruction diplomacy endured one of those interim periods. Diplomats were testing their recent decisions and wondering whether to increase commitments. Greece continued to attract a great deal of attention. Although aid flowed to the Greek regime and warships offshore symbolized United States hostility toward the advancing rebels, such actions no longer seemed adequate. The ambassador's cables to Washington became more frantic, and the administration, uncertain, sent a study mission to Greece. Britain appeared incapable of aiding the Greeks further. The Soviet-Turkish squabble persisted, and Washington continued its ineffective protests about the blatant Soviet presence in most of eastern Europe. Frustrated in its attempt to impose the principle of free navigation and recognizing the folly of seizing the Danubian vessels, Washington reluctantly ordered them released. Frustrating to the Truman administration, too, was the Republican victory in the November congressional elections. It raised questions about how well the administration had explained its foreign policy and whether it should apply even more pressure to the Russians, whom the United States blamed for most of the world's troubles.

February–June, 1947

The Truman Doctrine, so dramatically announced by the president on March 12, 1947, represented a new spurt and further coalescence of thought. The Greek civil war taxed British resources severely and aggravated Britain's own economic crisis in the winter of 1946-1947. Although United States leaders believed the rebels to be extensions of Moscow who were trying to create another Soviet satellite, not until the British announced on February 21 that they would leave Greece by the end of the next month did Washington undertake a full-scale aid program. For the next few days Truman met with advisers and congressmen, and his speechwriters began to piece together a major address.

The president went before a special joint session of Congress on March 12 and delivered an alarmist speech. It was actually not much different from many previous administration speeches except that this time Truman summarized in grand but simple fashion what United States diplomacy would henceforth be: "I believe that it must be the policy of the United States to support free peoples who are resisting attempted subjugation by armed minorities or by outside pressures." He asked Congress for $400 million to

[84] Memorandum in Arthur Krock, *Memoirs* (New York, 1968), pp. 422-82.

assist the economic stability and military establishments of Greece and Turkey. The world, he said, was divided into "two ways of life," the American and the Communist, and nations would have to choose between them. The Truman or containment "doctrine" became the most persistent guide to United States diplomacy in the Cold War. It was a hanger with many hooks on which an array of global policies could be accommodated.

The Moscow Foreign Ministers Conference, which opened on March 10 and dragged on into April, proved to be a further catalyst to such thought and behavior. Secretary of State George C. Marshall returned home convinced that the Russians would not agree to any economic cooperation for Germany and that they were eager to see western Europe collapse so that the Communists could take power. Concurrently, the Economic Commission for Europe was organized, and some American officials thought it a possible vehicle for reconstruction, but the general trend in Washington was toward a major United States directed plan. Truman, Dean Acheson, Clayton, and Marshall began to shape their ideas as the discouraging economic and political reports from abroad continued to be registered in Washington. They decided to raise the German level of industry because German production, especially steel and coal, was so vital to production throughout western Europe. They imposed export controls on United States goods in order to channel crucial items to western Europe and to isolate Russia and eastern Europe. Marshall created a Policy Planning Staff in the State Department in late April and instructed its new director, George Kennan, to recommend a recovery program for Europe. On May 8 Acheson revealed some of the new thinking in a key speech to cotton growers in the deep south. Europe was collapsing economically, he warned, and the United States, in the interest of peace and prosperity, had to launch a massive aid program. Economic instability threatened political order.

Within the State Department a number of memoranda were routed to the Planning Staff. On May 23 that committee submitted a report to Marshall calling for a major recovery program initiated by the Europeans. Next came intense discussion, with Clayton stirring State Department officials with vivid descriptions of the crisis in western Europe. On May 29 Marshall confirmed a speaking engagement for the Harvard University commencement and instructed his assistant, Charles E. Bohlen, to draft his speech. In late May Congress approved Truman's February 21 request for $350 million in relief earmarked especially for Greece, Austria, China, and Italy. There was little fanfare on June 5; Marshall actually discouraged drama and headlines. But he wanted it understood that the Europeans would have to draw up a new program and submit it to Washington. The speech itself, delivered awkwardly to a bored audience, was a summary of thinking within the administration. Marshall said simply that the United States would help any European nation recover through a joint reconstruction program. His speech represented the new opinion that piecemeal loans were inadequate to meet the crisis. The Marshall Plan would become America's most applauded Cold War program.

Early 1948

From June, 1947, until the spring of 1948, the details of previous decisions were filled in. Negotiations with western European nations produced agreement, through the new Committee of European Economic Co-operation, on a multi-billion-dollar program. The Economic Commission for Europe, which had Russia as a member, was bypassed, and Russia and its neighbors boycotted the Marshall Plan. To counter this economic offensive, in the summer of 1947 Russia signed a number of restrictive trade treaties with eastern European nations, tying them together in the Molotov Plan. The old Comintern was revived in October as the Cominform. The Anglo-American allies lifted many restrictions on German heavy industry, and the dismantling of factories slowed down. In the fall of 1947, the president appointed a committee to conserve food at home so that more could be shipped to western Europe, and Congress authorized interim aid amounting to $597 million to meet reconstruction needs until the Marshall Plan could be launched.

In early February a Communist coup d'état in Czechoslovakia confirmed fear that the Soviets were an expansionist threat. Many Italians predicted that the Communists would score electoral victories unless the United States took action. Russia also seemed uncompromising to the United States delegates to the Danubian Conference in February. It was the one postwar conference where the Russians controlled a majority of the votes, and they ran the meeting without deference to American sensibilities: the decision was that the Soviets would control the river. Moved by events such as these, as well as by predictions from the military that war with Russia was not an impossibility, Congress passed the Marshall Plan, and Truman signed it on April 3. The amount was large—about $5 billion for the first year. At the same time, western Germany was being revived and its currency reformed, and full-scale export controls imposed in March stopped most United States exports to the Soviet sphere.

By the spring of 1948 the United States had a coordinated reconstruction program and funds to implement it. It still could not achieve an open world, yet its economic power had been enlisted to salvage what it could from the wreckage of the war by assisting those nations who became part of a United States-dominated sphere of influence. The failure to create a world of peace and prosperity derived from the Soviet-American confrontation, which, in turn, as later chapters will suggest, sprang in considerable measure from the determination of the United States to use its massive power to reconstruct the world its way. By the spring of 1948 the antagonists were in control of their restrictive spheres of influence, and, indeed, the world seemed to be following the scenario Americans had wanted so much to avoid.

PART I
Confrontation in the
Soviet Sphere

CHAPTER 2

DIPLOMATIC WEAPON: THE ABORTIVE
LOAN TO RUSSIA

Reconstruction was a postwar priority for most European nations, and the American articulation of the peace and prosperity theme held out some hope that the United States would employ its great economic power to revive all of Europe. Yet Washington presumed that nations requesting aid would make important concessions to help bring about certain postwar goals; that is, that recipient countries would accept its principles in international relations. To a government reluctant to offer concessions on such terms, economic pressure was applied. If such pressure failed to achieve cooperation, Washington declared the government obstructionist and a threat to peace and prosperity and isolated it from the benefits of United States trade, investment, and aid. Such was the pattern in economic relations between the United States and Russia and eastern Europe, and the issue of the loan to Russia brought it into focus.

Ambassador to Moscow W. Averell Harriman cabled the Department of State in January, 1945, that the Soviet Union placed "high importance on a large postwar credit as a basis for the development of 'Soviet-American relations.' From his [V. M. Molotov's] statement I sensed an implication that the development of our friendly relations would depend upon a generous credit."[1] Reconstruction was for Russia a matter of "prime importance,"[2] and Soviet leaders hoped that the United States would help finance it. In the period 1943-1945, a loan to Russia might have served as peacemaker, but by

[1] *Foreign Relations, Conference at Malta and Yalta, 1945* (Washington, D.C., 1955), 313 (Jan. 6, 1945). See also Albert Z. Carr, *Truman, Stalin, and Peace* (Garden City, N.Y., 1950), p. 13. I wish to thank Mr. Harriman for kindly granting me permission to examine those parts of his private papers dealing with economic relations with the Soviet Union. This chapter is a much revised and updated version of my article, "The Abortive American Loan to Russia and the Origins of the Cold War, 1943-1946," *Journal of American History*, LVI (June, 1969), 70-92.

[2] Memorandum by Oscar Cox, May 16, 1945, Box 99, Oscar Cox Papers, Franklin D. Roosevelt Library. Many observers believed that Russia placed reconstruction at the top or near the top of its priorities. Charles de Gaulle visited Russia in late 1944 and noted that "authorities applied the watchword *reconstruction* in the most spectacular manner." Charles de Gaulle, *The War Memoirs of Charles de Gaulle: Salvation, 1944-1946*, trans. Richard Howard (New York, 1960), p. 67.

mid-1946, both nations had become increasingly uncompromising on major
issues, and the usefulness of a loan to the United States, to Russia, and to
amicable relations had been called into serious doubt. "Whether such a loan,"
Secretary of State Edward R. Stettinius, Jr., later wrote, "would have made
the Soviet Union a more reasonable and co-operative nation in the postwar
world will be one of the great 'if' questions of history."[3] Some historians
have simply dismissed the loan question as unimportant.[4] The unavailability
of thorough Soviet historical sources certainly makes any conclusive answer
to Stettinius' surmise impossible. However, a considerable amount of evidence suggests that the United States' refusal to aid Russia's postwar
reconstruction through a loan similar to that granted Britain in early 1946[5]
may have contributed to a continuation of a low standard of living for the
Russian people, with detrimental international effects; to a harsher Russian
policy toward Germany and eastern Europe; and to unsettled and inimical
Soviet-American relations.

World War II had been cruel to the Russians. Coupled with the deaths of
millions was the devastation of Minsk, Stalingrad, 1,710 towns, and 70,000
villages. Over 30,000 industrial plants and 40,000 miles of railroad line had
been destroyed. In 1945 Soviet agricultural output was about half the 1940
level. One Department of State study reported that $16 billion in fixed
capital, or one-quarter of the prewar level, had been lost, and the chief of the
United Nations Relief and Rehabilitation Administration (UNRRA) mission
in Byelorussia recorded that that republic alone had suffered 800,000 dead
and 1,215,000 dwellings and 4,000 bridges razed.[6] To help repair the massive
war damage, the Soviet government looked eagerly to the United States.

THE BEGINNING

Shortly after his arrival in Moscow in October, 1943, Harriman asked to meet
with A. I. Mikoyan, Soviet commissar for foreign trade, to discuss aid for
Russia's postwar reconstruction. Harriman found the Russians "intensely
interested." He told Mikoyan that healthy postwar trade between the two

[3] Edward R. Stettinius, Jr., *Roosevelt and the Russians: The Yalta Conference*
(Garden City, N.Y., 1949), p. 121.

[4] Arthur M. Schlesinger, Jr., "Origins of the Cold War," *Foreign Affairs*, XLVI
(October, 1967), 45; Herbert Feis, *From Trust to Terror: The Onset of the Cold War,
1945-1950* (New York, 1970), pp. 71-75.

[5] See Chapter 8 below for the British loan.

[6] *New York Times*, Feb. 9, 1946 (statistics presented at the Nuremberg trials); Harry
Schwartz, *Russia's Postwar Economy* (Syracuse, N.Y., 1947), p. 12; *Foreign Relations,
Yalta*, p. 322; statement by Richard Scandrett, [n.d. (1946)], Box 58,000, UNRRA
Records, United Nations Library, New York City. See also Marshall MacDuffie, chief of
UNRRA mission to the Ukraine, "First Monthly Report," Apr. 2, 1946, Box 59,000,
ibid.; Henry L. Stimson diary, XLIX (Nov. 10, 1944), Henry L. Stimson Papers, Yale
University Library; Peter Grimm, "Russia Seen from Within: An Account of a Relief
Mission Visit," *International Conciliation*, no. 429 (March, 1947), 119-42.

countries financed by credits "would be in the self-interest of the United States to be able to afford full employment during the period of transition from war-time to peace-time economy."[7] At the Moscow Conference of October-November, the United States delegation recommended preliminary discussions on aid for Russia's postwar rehabilitation.[8] Donald M. Nelson, War Production Board chairman, visiting with Premier Joseph Stalin in Moscow about the same time, told him that the United States had a "great surplus capacity for producing the goods that you need. We can find a way to do business together."[9] Harriman, aware of Russian priorities, informed the secretary of state in November, 1943, that "this question of reconstruction is considered by the Soviet Government as, next to the war, the most important political as well as economic problem that confronts them."[10] The ambassador began to see diplomatic advantages in this Russian problem.

After the Teheran Conference of late 1943 Harriman and Molotov discussed the aid question, at Molotov's initiative. Harriman suggested that the Soviets tell the United States "the specific type and quantity of equipment which were most urgently needed and over what period." He broached the possibility of a credit from Washington and recorded that Molotov showed the "keenest interest."[11] But there was no definite loan policy, and Harriman cabled home for instructions. Meanwhile he formulated his own position more carefully. In early 1944 he called for a small loan at first, with firm control and approval of specific projects by Washington. He reiterated that Soviet orders for United States products would ease "dislocations to our employment problems" and noted again that Russia "places the utmost importance" on economic cooperation with the United States. But he also advised Washington that aid to Russia "is a factor which should be integrated into the fabric of our overall relations rather than dealt with independently in its purely commercial and economic aspects." For Harriman, then, a loan to Russia served two purposes: to expand United States

[7] W. Averell Harriman, "Certain Factors Underlying Our Relations with the Soviet Union," Nov. 14, 1945, W. Averell Harriman Papers (in his possession); *Foreign Relations, 1943* (Washington, D.C., 1963), III, 781-86; see also p. 588.

[8] *Foreign Relations, 1943*, I, 739.

[9] Donald M. Nelson, *Arsenal of Democracy: The Story of American War Production* (New York, 1946), pp. 423-24; *Foreign Relations, 1943*, III, 710-16, 788.

[10] *Foreign Relations, 1943*, III, 788-89. Secretary of State Cordell Hull was not keen about a postwar loan to Russia but thought that the state-trading Russians might adjust their trade practices to fit into the United States multilateral trade program if a loan depended upon it. Herbert Feis, *Churchill, Roosevelt, Stalin: The War They Waged and the Peace They Sought* (Princeton, N.J., 1957), p. 642. A State Department report at about the same time was also cool about aid to Russia; it argued that Russia had few goods to sell to the United States and that Soviet-American trade would remain small. *Foreign Relations, 1943*, III, 722-23.

[11] Postwar aid was not discussed with the Soviets at Teheran, although Roosevelt, Harry Hopkins, and Harriman talked about it privately within the United States delegation. Robert E. Sherwood, *Roosevelt and Hopkins: An Intimate History* (New York, 1948), p. 777; William A. Williams, *American-Russian Relations, 1781-1947* (New York, 1952), p. 274; Harriman, in *Foreign Relations, 1944*, IV, 1033 (Jan. 7, 1944).

trade and thereby avert a postwar depression and to influence "overall relations" with Russia.[12]

In January, 1944, Mikoyan asked Harriman how large a postwar loan the Soviet Union could expect. Harriman, lacking specific instructions, could not answer. On February 1 Mikoyan himself suggested a figure of $1 billion to run for twenty-five years at 0.5 percent interest. Harriman demurred; he found the amount too large, the repayment schedule too liberal, and the interest rate too low.[13] The State Department still had no defined policy on a loan to Russia and instructed Harriman to limit himself to "generalities" because Washington was worried about the legal limitations on loans to Russia imposed by the provisions of the Johnson Act.[14]

Harriman was annoyed with this lethargy because he saw the diplomatic leverage—"competitive advantage"—in a loan. Furthermore, "the Soviets place great importance on knowing now our general attitude toward their reconstruction problems and if we push aside the consideration of their whole program doubts may be aroused as to our serious intents." He urged further that a loan might encourage the Russians to cooperate "with us on international problems *in accordance with our standards. . . .*" In March, 1944, Harriman was more precise: "I am impressed with the consideration that economic assistance is *one of the most effective weapons* at our disposal to influence European political events in the direction we desire and to avoid the development of a sphere of influence of the Soviet Union over Eastern Europe and the Balkans."[15] Harriman's earlier interest in a loan as a roadblock to depression had now almost entirely given way to its use as a diplomatic weapon, but others seemed more concerned about the economy at home than about developing new diplomatic weaponry.

Some businessmen studied the loan question in 1944. When Eric Johnston visited Stalin in June to discuss postwar trade, he anticipated significant commercial contacts and knew that a loan would be "the nub of our trade" with the Soviets. This articulate businessman assured Stalin that he would promote a postwar loan for Russia when he returned to the United States. Harriman welcomed Johnston's trip, although he insisted that Johnston

---

[12] *Foreign Relations, 1944*, IV, 1034-35. Hopkins apparently opposed Harriman's recommendation for itemization of projects because of the traditional Soviet reluctance, as in the case of Lend-Lease, to divulge information, Feis, *Churchill, Roosevelt, Stalin*, p. 643.

[13] The figures, Mikoyan said, were based on Russia's reconstruction plans. *Foreign Relations, 1944*, IV, 1041-42.

[14] *Ibid.*, p. 1043 (Feb. 4, 1944). The Johnson Act of 1934 forbade private loans to foreign governments which were in default of financial obligations to the United States. Since the Export-Import Bank, which alone had authority to extend credits for developmental purposes and the export of capital goods, guaranteed private loans or made payments directly to United States producers rather than to the credit recipients, the Johnson Act was applicable to Russia, which had long refused to repay the indebtedness incurred by the Kerensky government.

[15] *Ibid.*, pp. 1049-50 (Feb. 9, 1944), p. 1055 (Feb. 14), p. 951 (Mar. 13) (italics added). Harriman toyed with the idea of utilizing Lend-Lease machinery for postwar aid.

consult with him first and talk about trade with the Russians only in general terms.[16]

In Washington, some Treasury Department officials, at the request of Secretary Henry Morgenthau, prepared a report which matched Johnston's enthusiasm for trade and credits. Harry D. White's memorandum argued that a loan to Russia was both feasible and desirable because the United States could replenish its depleted stock of raw materials from Russian sources. He named manganese, tungsten, graphite, zinc, chrome, and mercury, among others, and stressed that the United States was inescapably dependent on foreign sources. Russia could exchange these raw materials for a loan of $5 billion. White was optimistic about expanded Soviet-American trade after the war, and he repeated what Nelson and Harriman had said earlier—that Russia "could make an important contribution to the maintenance of full employment during our transition to a peace economy." He concluded in the peace and prosperity idiom, that a loan "would provide a sound basis for continued collaboration between the two governments in the postwar period."[17] Morgenthau endorsed White's study and later urged the president to extend an even larger loan.

A FORMAL REQUEST AND A SCHISM

On January 3, 1945, Molotov handed Harriman the first formal request for a postwar loan. At the same time, Churchill, Stalin, and Roosevelt were settling the place and date for a Big Three meeting (Yalta), and it seemed likely that the loan question would become one of the elements in the diplomatic bargaining. Harriman was extremely annoyed by the detailed Soviet aide-mémoire and chastised Molotov for his "strange procedure" in presenting the "curiously worded document." The Soviet request was indeed bold:

The Soviet Government accordingly wishes to state the following: Having in mind the repeated statements of American public figures concerning the desirability of receiving extensive large Soviet orders for the postwar and transition period, the Soviet Government considers it possible to place orders on the basis of long-term credits to the amount of 6 billion dollars. Such orders would be for manufactured goods (oil pipes, rails, railroad cars, locomotives and other products) and industrial equipment. The credit would

[16] *Nation's Business, XXXII* (October, 1944), 21-22; *New York Times*, July 22, 1944; *Foreign Relations, 1944*, IV, 956, 972.

[17] Memorandum, Harry D. White to Henry Morgenthau, Mar. 7, 1944, part II:23, Harry D. White Papers, Princeton University Library; reprinted in U.S., Congress, Senate, Committee on Interior and Insular Affairs, *Accessibility of Strategic and Critical Materials to the United States in Time of War and Our Expanding Economy*, 83rd Cong., 2d sess. (1955), S. Rep. 1627, pp. 370-72. White recommended that the loan run for thirty years at a 2.1 percent interest rate. Harriman warned against "exaggerated optimism" about postwar Soviet-American trade. *Foreign Relations, 1944*, IV, 958 (Apr. 1, 1944).

also cover orders for locomotives, railroad cars, rails and trucks and industrial equipment placed under Lend-Lease but not delivered to the Soviet Union before the end of the war. The credits should run for 30 years, amortization to begin on the last day of the 9th year and to end on the last day of the 30th year. Amortization should take place in the following annual payments reckoned from end of 9th year: First 4 years 2½% of principal; second 4 years 3½%; third 4 years 4½%; fourth four years 5½%; last 6 years 6%. Soviet Government will be entitled to pay up principal prematurely either in full or in part. If the two Governments decide that because of unusual and unfavorable economic conditions payment of current installments at any time might not be to mutual interest, payment may be postponed for an agreed period. Annual interest to be fixed at 2½ [2¼%].

The United States Government should grant to Soviet Union a discount of 20% off the Government contracts with firms, of [on] all orders placed before end of war and falling under this credit. Prices for orders placed after the end of the war should be left to agreement between the American firms in question and Soviet representatives.

Harriman implored Washington to "disregard the unconventional character of the document and the unreasonableness of its terms and chalk it up to ignorance of normal business procedures and the strange ideas of the Russians on how to get the best trade." He chided the Russians for starting "negotiations on the basis of 'twice as much for half the price.' . . ." Any loan, he argued, should be dependent upon Russian behavior in overall international relations. "I feel strongly," he added, "that the sooner the Soviet Union can develop a decent life for its people the more tolerant they will become." But such a concern was secondary, and he again demanded complete United States control of the funds "in order that the political advantages may be retained and that we may be satisfied that the equipment purchased is for purposes that meet our general approval."[18]

Harriman's reaction was curious. The United States had certainly been approached before by foreign governments with detailed requests for aid; in fact, later, it was to insist that the Marshall Plan recipients draw up just such proposals. And it is diplomatic practice to ask for more than one expects to get. Harriman should not have been surprised that Russia was aware of the "repeated statements of American public figures concerning the desirability of receiving extensive large Soviet orders," for Nelson, Johnston, and he himself had mentioned this consideration. What perhaps disturbed him most was the boldness, thoroughness, and independent attitude expressed in the

---

[18] *Foreign Relations, 1945* (Washington, D.C., 1967), V, 942-43 (Jan. 4, 1945), 945-46 (Jan. 6); Harriman, "Certain Factors." At the same time the Russians indicated willingness to sign the Fourth Protocol for Lend-Lease. The loan question probably did not receive much attention during 1944 in large part because debate over the Fourth Protocol (especially the interest rate for goods which might be shipped after the war) languished. The Fourth Protocol was finally signed on April 17, 1945, but did not mention interest rates. See Martin F. Herz, *Beginnings of the Cold War* (Bloomington, Ind., 1966), pp. 160-62; *Foreign Relations, Yalta*, p. 320; *ibid., 1945*, V, 957.

Russian request, for Russia had taken the initiative with the first detailed proposal, and Harriman seemed fearful that the United States had lost some diplomatic leverage.

Assistant Secretary of State Will Clayton agreed with Harriman in late January that caution was in order, perhaps because of the forthcoming Yalta Conference: "From a tactical point of view, it would seem harmful to us to offer such a large credit at this time and thus lose what appears to be the only concrete bargaining lever for use in connection with the many other political and economic problems which will arise between our two countries."[19] A State Department memorandum, sharing the sentiments of Harriman and Clayton, concluded that "the U.S.S.R. will be in a position to take a highly independent position in negotiations regarding foreign credits." The report also held that Russia could recover without such aid, that trade with Russia would remain minimal, and that Russia might not even repay.[20] But few officials were willing to kill a loan altogether because it was still possible that Russia might make concessions: join the United Nations, participate in the Bretton Woods institutions, establish a "proper role" for the United States in Rumania, Bulgaria, Hungary, Germany, Poland, Czechoslovakia, and the Balkan nations, and establish a "proper basis in Iran."[21]

In early January Secretary Morgenthau had dissented vigorously from the State Department's policy of deliberate hesitancy. He opposed the use of economic power as a political weapon, advised Roosevelt to present the Russians with a "concrete plan" for reconstruction aid, and recommended a $10 billion loan at 2 percent interest to be amortized over a period of thirty-five years. Repeating White's warnings about raw materials shortages, Morgenthau also reminded the president that "this credit to Russia would be a major step in your program to provide 60 million jobs in the post-war period."[22] But at a meeting with Secretary of State Stettinius and Roosevelt on January 10, Morgenthau encountered the active opposition of the State Department. Roosevelt agreed with the State Department that the loan question should not be raised at the Yalta Conference. As he told the disappointed Morgenthau, "I think it's very important that we hold back and

[19] Foreign Relations, 1945, V, 966 (Jan. 20, 1945).

[20] Ibid., pp. 939-40 (Jan. 4, 1945). The report appears to have been based on an OSS study which is summarized in Samuel Lubell to Bernard Baruch, [n.d.], Bernard Baruch Papers, Princeton University Library. Despite this suggestion that Russia might not repay, many observers were aware of Russia's good credit reputation, aside from the Kerensky debts, which the Soviets never recognized. See New York Times, Jan. 26, 1945; E. C. Ropes, "Credits to Soviet Agencies in the United States," American Review on the Soviet Union, VI (May, 1945), 10-15; Nation's Business, XXXII (October, 1944), 22; Alexander Gerschenkron, Economic Relations with the U.S.S.R. (New York, 1945), p. 19; Jan F. Triska and Robert M. Slusser, The Theory, Law, and Policy of Soviet Treaties (Stanford, Calif., 1962), p. 286.

[21] Foreign Relations, 1945, V, 960 (Jan. 17, 1945).

[22] Henry Morgenthau to the president, Jan. 1, 1945, part II:23, White Papers; Morgenthau to the president, Jan. 10, 1945, ibid.; Foreign Relations, Yalta, pp. 309-10, 315.

don't give them any promises of finance until we get what we want."[23] The idea seemed to be that continued Soviet hope for a loan would bring more diplomatic advantages than the actual granting of it. Morgenthau, who believed that this position was too demanding and that the president was letting a valuable chance for cooperation slip by, complained that "both the President and Stettinius were wrong and that if they wanted to get the Russians to do something they should. . . . do it nice. . . . Don't drive such a hard bargain that when you come through it does not taste good."[24]

Shortly thereafter the State Department's reluctance to discuss the loan question publicly was revealed. James Reston of the *New York Times* called Morgenthau on January 24 to tell him that he planned to write a story on a $6 billion loan for Russia. Morgenthau, concerned about Reston's source of information, quickly notified the State Department that he himself had not divulged any information regarding the diplomatic maneuverings on the loan. Under Secretary Joseph C. Grew talked with Reston by telephone and requested that he "go slow" on the subject. The Reston article appeared in the *Times* two days later, and its largely accurate contents demonstrated that Reston had a knowledgeable friend in high office. Reston concluded his article by stating that the administration did not find the time "propitious" for discussing the loan.[25]

Apparently it was not propitious to discuss the loan with the Russians at the Yalta Conference (February 4-11) either, for there was virtual silence on the subject.[26] Yalta was characterized by compromise, and the United States achieved some diplomatic success as far as the issues of Poland, Germany, and the United Nations were concerned. The loan question was implicit at the conference, at least in the minds of the diplomats, for the Soviet request had been filed only a month earlier and United States officials had deliberately decided not to discuss it directly. Roosevelt apparently continued to believe that there was more diplomatic value in keeping the Soviets uncertain and hopeful than in offering aid at that time.[27]

[23] John M. Blum, *From the Morgenthau Diaries: Years of War, 1941-1945* (Boston, 1967), III, 305.

[24] *Ibid.* James F. Byrnes also dissented from the Morgenthau position. James F. Byrnes, *All in One Lifetime* (New York, 1958), p. 310.

[25] Memorandum of conversation, Jan. 24, 1945, VI, Conversations, Joseph C. Grew Papers, Harvard University Library.

[26] Molotov did mention once that the Russians hoped to receive reparations in kind from Germany and long-term credits from the United States. Stettinius replied that the United States was willing to discuss credits at any time in either Moscow or Washington. *Foreign Relations, Yalta*, p. 610. For the conference, consult Diane Shaver Clemens, *Yalta* (New York, 1970).

[27] Leo Crowley, head of the Foreign Economic Administration, recalled a conversation with President Roosevelt on March 30, 1945: "I also told him that it would be a great mistake to give any consideration to a loan of that size until we knew something about what the peace objectives of Russia were going to be. He concurred very definitely in my views, telling me he had yet to obtain any concession from Marshal Stalin. . . ." Leo T. Crowley to Harold Faber, Oct. 4, 1955, Folder 922, Byrnes Papers.

In a message to the State Department on April 11, 1945, one day before Roosevelt's death, Harriman was pessimistic about any postwar economic cooperation with Russia. Although the Russians were "keen" to obtain the $6 billion credit, he believed that "it certainly should be borne in mind that our basic interests might better be served by increasing our trade with other parts of the world rather than giving preference to the Soviet Union as a source of supply." The United States should undertake a domestic conservation program and end its dependence upon Soviet imports of manganese ore by seeking supplies in Brazil, Africa, and India.[28] Should a loan agreement ever occur, Harriman wanted strict United States control over the funds because "it is not possible to bank goodwill in Moscow. . . ." But he cautioned that "it would be inadvisable to give the Soviets the idea that we were cooling off on our desire to help . . ."; the loan still retained value as diplomatic "leverage" on the issues growing out of eastern Europe, Turkey, and China.[29] Ten days later Harriman was in Washington, where he again told State Department officials that it would be quite satisfactory for loan negotiations to "drag along" because delay afforded the "greatest element in our leverage."[30] Oscar Cox, deputy administrator of the Foreign Economic Administration, was disturbed by a conversation with Harriman at San Francisco five days later: "He seems to be trending towards an anti-Soviet position."[31]

Truman, required suddenly to handle the difficult and growing foreign policy problems facing the nation, relied heavily upon subordinates, and Harriman was prepared and eager to advise him. In the transition from one administration to another, Harriman's views on the loan, already widely held, were reaffirmed. On April 23, 1945, Truman and Harriman, among others, met with Molotov in Washington to discuss the question of Poland's government. The exchange was acrimonious, and the blunt and impatient president addressed Molotov as though he were speaking to a rebellious Missouri ward politician. He warned that Russia's international behavior would affect United States decisions on postwar aid because "legislative appropriation was required for any economic measures in the foreign field and . . . he could not hope to get these measures through Congress unless there was public support for them."[32] At the United Nations Conference in San Francisco following the Molotov-Truman confrontation, Senator Arthur H. Vandenberg, architect of the bipartisan foreign policy and a delegate to the conference, recorded in his diary: "Stettinius added that he explained to

[28] As late as 1947, the United States was buying one-third of its manganese ore, one-half of its chromium, and more than one-half of its platinum from the U.S.S.R. See Chapter 3 below for Soviet-American trade.
[29] *Foreign Relations, 1945*, V, 995-96 (Apr. 11, 1945). See also Millis, *Forrestal Diaries*, p. 39.
[30] *Foreign Relations, 1945*, V, 845 (Apr. 21, 1945).
[31] Diary, Apr. 26, 1945, Cox Papers.
[32] *Foreign Relations, 1945*, V, 256-57. See also Truman, *Memoirs*, I, 74-82.

Molotov that future Russian aid from America depends entirely upon the temper and the mood and the conscience of the American people—and that Frisco is his last chance to *prove* that he deserves this aid. This is the best news in months." To this Vandenberg added his famous bit of hyperbole: "F. D. R.'s appeasement of Russia is over."[33]

Truman's scruples about public opinion and congressional impediments, expressed many times by administration figures, raise a number of questions. Neither the Roosevelt and Truman administrations nor the professional diplomats in the State Department ever prepared the public or Congress for a loan to Russia in the 1943-1946 period. In fact, public discussion was discouraged, as we have seen, and certainly there was no attempt to demonstrate to the Soviet Union that the United States considered the issue an important one for immediate negotiation. The State Department was slow to recommend that the restrictive Johnson Act be repealed and that Export-Import Bank funds be expanded. In 1944 the secretary of state received such recommendations from the interdepartmental Committee on Foreign Economic Policy, and in his budget message to Congress in January, 1945, Roosevelt repeated the suggestion,[34] but it was not until July, 1945, that Truman specifically asked Congress to increase the lending power of the Export-Import Bank from $700 million to $3.5 billion, with the idea that $1 billion of these funds could be set aside for Russia should a loan agreement be worked out. The administration did *not* have to apologize to Congress for suggesting that funds might go to Russia, a full-scale public congressional debate never occurred, and Truman got the increase he requested as well as removal of the Johnson Act obstruction.[35] Over a year and a half after Mikoyan and Harriman first discussed postwar aid, the impediments to a loan were finally removed.

It was not so much public opinion or Congress in 1945 which served as a restraint on loan policy—for the president had persuasive powers which often shaped or created the "public" opinion the administration wanted to hear—but rather Roosevelt, Truman, and Harriman themselves, among others, who deliberately stalled negotiations as a form of diplomatic pressure on the Soviets. The calculated delay was hardly conducive to amicable relations, and,

33 Vandenberg, *Private Papers*, p. 176.

34 American Bankers Association Subcommittee, "Notes on Conference on International Monetary Proposals," Oct. 22-25, 1944, Box 18, Winthrop Aldrich Papers, Baker Library, Harvard University; Rosenman, *Public Papers and Addresses of Roosevelt*, XIII, 478 (Jan. 3, 1945); *Foreign Relations, 1945*, V, 949.

35 Part of the hearings were in "executive session," and hence there is no record. U.S., Congress, Senate, Committee on Banking and Currency, *Export-Import Bank of 1945* (Hearings), 79th Cong., 1st sess. (July 17-18, 1945). Even Senator Robert Taft, who opposed the British loan later, remarked: "I would say that $1,000,000,000 is a fair amount to be used in the next year to finance trade with Russia." *New York Times*, July 18, 1945. The act passed the House on July 13 by a vote of 102-6. The Senate passed it by voice on July 20. Later, the Johnson Act was, in effect, repealed because all nations which were members of the International Monetary Fund, an institution Russia thought of joining but never did, were exempted. See Chapter 7 below.

as Oscar Cox noted, "the Soviet Union unquestionably doubts whether we really mean business on this subject."[36]

CUTTING BACK LEND-LEASE TO RUSSIA

Harriman also saw diplomatic value in the generous Lend-Lease aid to Russia. Early in 1945, for example, he suggested that Washington tell Moscow that petroleum products shipped under Lend-Lease would be curtailed unless the Russians halted their penetration of the Rumanian oil industry.[37] He helped formulate the decision of May 11, 1945, only three days after V-E Day, to reduce drastically Lend-Lease aid to Russia, which was not yet at war with Japan. The Russians were surprised and angered by the abrupt decision; Stalin complained to Harry Hopkins on May 27 that "the manner in which it had been done had been unfortunate and even brutal. . . . If the refusal to continue Lend-Lease was designed as pressure on the Russians in order to soften them up then it was a fundamental mistake." Hopkins assured the Soviet leader that the United States did not intend to use Lend-Lease as a "pressure weapon" because the United States was "a strong power and does not go in for those methods."[38] Yet the Lend-Lease suspension was handled in such a way as to antagonize Russia, and the Soviets considered it a hostile act.[39]

Scholars differ in their interpretations of the decision. Some argue that it did indeed constitute economic pressure aimed directly at the Soviets.[40] Others believe that the Truman administration was simply and clumsily fulfilling the law as written by Congress (and watched over by congressmen) that at the end of the war Lend-Lease should terminate.[41] There is evidence to support both interpretations because the Truman administration proceeded with the dual intention of pressuring the Russians and satisfying congressional opinion. Yet for the history of Soviet-American relations, the

[36] Oscar Cox to Leo Crowley, May 28, 1945, Box 65, Cox Papers. See also Cox's complaint that "we have done nothing effective about it since they first raised the question." Memorandum by Oscar Cox, May 16, 1945, Box 99, *ibid.* Cox did, however, suggest that it would be easier to get legislation once Russia joined the war against Japan.

[37] *Foreign Relations, 1945,* V, 649-50. For evidence that other officials discussed the possibility of terminating Lend-Lease to Russia as diplomatic pressure, see Hull, *Memoirs,* II, 1448; George C. Herring, Jr., "Lend-Lease to Russia and the Origins of the Cold War, 1944-1945," *Journal of American History,* LVI (June, 1969), 97, 105; *New York Times,* Jan. 7, 1945. For the issue of Rumanian oil, see Chapter 5 below.

[38] Paraphrase from *Foreign Relations: Conference of Berlin (Potsdam),* 2 vols. (Washington, D.C., 1960), I, 33, 35.

[39] For a recent Soviet assessment which sees the curtailment and the loan as interrelated, see Victor Issraeljan, *The Anti-Hitler Coalition* (Moscow, 1971), pp. 391-94.

[40] See, for example, Gar Alperovitz, *Atomic Diplomacy* (New York, 1965), pp. 35-39; Kolko, *Politics of War,* p. 500; Bernstein, "American Foreign Policy and the Origins of the Cold War," pp. 27-28.

[41] Compare, for example, Herring, "Lend-Lease to Russia"; Feis, *From Trust to Terror,* p. 228; Gaddis, *United States and Origins of the Cold War,* pp. 217-20.

more important consideration was the coercion of Russia: the cutback order must be viewed in the context of the administration's thinking about economic power as diplomatic leverage. Although Harriman and others knew full well that Moscow would read a sharp reduction in Lend-Lease as economic pressure, they made no effort to soften the sudden blow, and, in fact, the administration braced itself for the Soviet cries of protest which it expected.

On May 9 Secretary Stettinius, in the midst of tense negotiations with the Soviets at the San Francisco Conference, conferred with Harriman on Soviet-American relations. He agreed with Harriman, who was to return to Washington to counsel the president, that "we should *begin curtailing at once* our Lend-Lease shipments to Russia and scrutinize carefully requests for shipments after July 1st with a view to our own interests and policies." Stettinius went on: "generally in our attitude toward the Russians with respect to Lend-Lease and similar matters we should *be firm while avoiding any implication of a threat or any indication of political bargaining.*"[42] The Lend-Lease issue was intertwined with Washington's thinking on overall relations with the Soviets.[43] The evidence suggests that officials expected, not unhappily, that the Soviets would be irritated and that the curtailment would influence general Soviet-American relations, but that the reduction should be done in such as way as to shield the United States from a charge of crude "political bargaining." Moscow got the message, but because lower-echelon officials fulfilled the decision of May 11 with such zeal that they even turned back ships already at sea, the administration's application of economic pressure was quite conspicuous and naked.

Harriman and officials from a number of agencies involved in aid to Russia prepared the memorandum of May 11 for the president calling for the substantial reduction of Lend-Lease, except for goods which would assist Soviet operations in the Far East. The president concurred.[44] Both Acting Secretary of State Joseph Grew and the head of the Foreign Economic Administration, Leo Crowley, anticipated the Russian response. Crowley "wanted to be sure that the President thoroughly understands the situation and that he will back us up and will keep everyone else out of it. He [Crowley] stated that we would be having difficulty with the Russians and he did not want them to be running all over town looking for help."[45] Although

[42] *Foreign Relations, 1945*, V, 998 (italics added). Stettinius did not mention any congressional requirements compelling such a curtailment.

[43] George Herring shows from research in the Stettinius Papers that both Harriman and Stettinius saw the interlinking of Lend-Lease with other problems, but he gives a literal reading to the words that the United States should avoid "any indication of political bargaining." This writer, on the other hand, from the evidence presented below, believes that these diplomats meant no blatant or crude threat. The fact that they were so upset with the Soviet Protocol Committee's handling of the curtailment order would confirm this interpretation. Herring, "Lend-Lease to Russia," p. 105.

[44] *Foreign Relations, 1945*, V, 998-1000.

[45] Memorandum of conversation, May 11, 1945, III, Conversations, Grew Papers.

Truman wrote in his memoirs that the abrupt termination was a mistake made by Grew and Crowley and that he had not read the cessation order, the evidence from the Crowley-Grew conversation indicates that he did know its implications. Furthermore, Secretary of War Henry L. Stimson recorded in his diary for May 11, the day of the president's memorandum, that he and the State Department believed that because the war was over Lend-Lease to the U.S.S.R. should cease and Russia should apply for continued aid and justify her needs like other nations. Stimson noted that Truman agreed with this view and that he "was trying to pull in the extravagance. . . ."[46]

There is evidence from events of the next day that government officials fully expected the order to stir up a Soviet "hornets' nest," as Truman later put it.[47] On May 12 Grew informed the Soviet chargé d'affaires that deliveries of supplies under Lend-Lease to Russia "will be adjusted immediately to take into account the end of organized hostilities in Europe."[48] That same day, Grew was active on the telephone. Harriman told him that "we would be getting a 'good slashback' from the Russians but that we would have to face it." Harriman added, as he again linked the curtailment to other issues, that "the Russians were going on in a high-minded way about colonies being given their freedom when they were at the same time subjugating Poland and [Harriman] said we should take this seriously." The Soviet chargé d'affaires telephoned and complained to Grew that he had heard that even the loading of material on ships had been ordered discontinued. The Soviet Protocol Committee, which carried out the order, that morning had in fact stopped all loading and also recalled ships already at sea, so that any goods intended for the European theater could be halted. When the Soviet chargé asked about this, Grew apparently was not aware of the action and replied that the rumor was incorrect.[49]

Many diplomats like Harriman disapproved of the Soviet Protocol Committee's strict interpretation of the cancellation directive, when it became known, and Truman quickly ordered continued loading and sailing, but with careful screening so that only goods headed for the Far East were released.[50] His reduction order stood, however. Officials rapidly went to work to explain publicly what had happened. Crowley prepared a statement: "In view of the end of hostilities in Europe a careful reexamination is being made of

---

Crowley recounts his role in the *Milwaukee Journal,* Aug. 18 and 19, 1969. He writes that F. D. R. also wanted Lend-Lease aid to Russia shut off after the war in part as economic pressure—to get concessions from Stalin.

[46] Diary, May 11, 1945, LI, Stimson Papers.

[47] Truman, *Memoirs,* I, 228.

[48] *Foreign Relations, 1945,* V, 1001.

[49] Memoranda of conversation, May 12, 1945, VII, Conversations, Grew Papers.

[50] For a discussion of reduced Lend-Lease shipments to Russia between V-E and V-J days, see Robert W. Coakley and Richard M. Leighton, *Global Logistics and Strategy, 1943-1945,* United States Army in World War II (Washington, D.C., 1968), pp. 694-99; Herring, "Lend-Lease to Russia," pp. 109-10; Herbert Feis, *Between War and Peace: The Potsdam Conference* (Princeton, N.J., 1960), pp. 329-33.

lend-lease programs with a view to allocating materials to theaters where they are most needed." Grew liked these innocuous words because they "did not bring the Russians in directly. . . ." He added that "this whole thing is full of dynamite."[51] Crowley and Grew issued similar statements in the next few days, and Truman repeated them in his own words at his May 23 press conference.[52]

On May 14, Stimson joined the issues of the atomic bomb and economic power (Lend-Lease) in his diary: "I called it a royal straight flush and we mustn't be a fool about the way to play it. They can't get along without our help and industries and we have coming into action a weapon which will be unique."[53] In short, Stalin probably got the message Washington wanted him to receive when he complained of economic coercion. A more gradual cutback may not have changed Russian positions on most diplomatic questions, but it served as a demonstration of American firmness. There was no attempt to cushion the blow, except Hopkins' belated conversation with Stalin.

It is not clear that the Lend-Lease Act required the Truman administration to cut back aid to the Soviet Union. There is some evidence to suggest that aid under the law could have continued so long as the president deemed it necessary to national defense.[54] There were, for example, further war-related functions in the European theater—the military occupation of Europe—which involved the Russians. There was some public hostility toward continued Lend-Lease aid, but as pointed out above, the Truman administration never sought to alter that sentiment or to explain that aid after V-E Day was important. Washington was without question justified (by law) in curtailing Lend-Lease, but the interpretation it gave to the law derived from the assumption that economic power as a diplomatic weapon would make the Russians more pliable; a different assumption could have produced a different interpretation. The reduction in Lend-Lease aid occurred at the same time that the administration was stalling on the loan question; the issues in both cases were the same—postwar reconstruction—and Stalin probably made the connection.

ANOTHER REQUEST AND MORE DELAY

President Truman himself endorsed the basic premise that economic power was a valuable weapon in the growing confrontation with the Soviet Union.

[51] Memorandum of conversation, May 12, 1945, VII, Conversations, Grew Papers.

[52] New York Times, May 13 and 15, 1945; Public Papers, Truman, 1945, p. 68. Truman helped prepare Crowley's statement of May 13. Oscar Cox Diary, May 14, 1945, Cox Papers.

[53] Diary, May 14, 1945, LI, Stimson Papers.

[54] See Walter N. Thayer to Oscar Cox, Aug. 14, 1945, Box 75, Cox Papers; Dean Acheson, Present at the Creation: My Years in the State Department (New York, 1969), p. 122; Alperovitz, Atomic Diplomacy, pp. 38-39.

In early June, he met with Colonel Bernard Bernstein, who reported to Secretary Morgenthau that the president "didn't seem at all pessimistic about his relations with the Russians because he felt we held all the cards and that the Russians had to come to us." The "cards" were a loan and technical assistance, according to Truman. The president commented further on the destruction in Russia and the threat of starvation in some areas. "That was why he felt he had the cards in American hands," Colonel Bernstein informed Morgenthau, "and he made very clear that he proposed to play them as American cards."[55]

A month later the administration seemed prepared to discuss credits to the U.S.S.R. at the Potsdam Conference.[56] Just before Truman left for the meeting, the head of the Office of War Mobilization and Reconversion, Fred Vinson, advised him that "a sound and adequate program of credits for foreign reconstruction would directly and immediately benefit the United States in both its domestic economy and its foreign policy." He suggested that the United States could loosen Soviet control of eastern Europe through the extension of a loan, "our ace in the hole."[57] Yet the subject did not come up at Potsdam, even though Truman later contended that he had gone there planning to offer help for Russian reconstruction. He said that all Stalin wanted to talk about was the ending of Lend-Lease.[58] The Potsdam records do not reveal that Stalin pushed the Lend-Lease issue, but why neither the United States nor Russia introduced the subject of a loan remains a puzzle.

On August 9, 1945, only three days after an atomic blast leveled Hiroshima, Harriman informed the Russians that the Export-Import Bank was willing to consider (in Washington) Soviet proposals for postwar aid. On August 28 the Russians presented the Bank with a request for $1 billion, the figure Mikoyan first used in February of the previous year, but this time at 2.375 percent interest. The drop from $6 billion was necessitated by the Bank's lending power limitation of $3.5 billion. Although the Bank's interest rate of 3 percent was inflexible, the National Advisory Council on International Monetary and Financial Problems, set up in July to coordinate foreign loan policy, approved a loan to Russia "in principle," and in

[55] U.S., Congress, Senate, Judiciary Committee, 90th Cong., 1st sess., *Morgenthau Diary (Germany)*, 2 vols. (Washington, D.C., 1967), II, 1555.

[56] *Foreign Relations, Berlin*, I, 181.

[57] Vinson to Truman, July 14, 1945, Central Files, Office of War Mobilization and Reconversion Records, National Archives (courtesy of Barton J. Bernstein).

[58] *New York Times*, Feb. 14, 1950. When Truman was at Potsdam, Donald Nelson urged him to foster Soviet-American trade relations and recounted for him his attempts to establish a business delegation to handle economic relations between the two nations: "I could find no way to get the proposal out of the State Department pigeonhole." Nelson to Truman, "Stimulating World Economic Revival," filed July 31, 1945, OF 396, Truman Papers. At about the same time Herbert Feis dismissed the notion that a loan would affect the Soviet position in Poland. He argued that a loan should be offered only if the political air cleared—on the unsupportable assumption that an American loan would not reduce postwar tensions. Herbert Feis, "Political Aspects of Foreign Loans," *Foreign Affairs*, XXIII (July, 1945), 609-19.

September Truman agreed that Export-Import Bank negotiations "should go forward," but apparently to be contingent upon State Department approval.[59]

When a group of congressmen, members of the House Special Committee on Post-War Economic Policy and Planning, met with Stalin in Moscow in September, the Russian leader remarked that the United States had not initiated discussions on the Soviet request, but he was optimistic that "there are possibilities for the trade between the United States and Russia to increase."[60] He told Senator Claude Pepper of Florida, who met with him on a separate occasion, that it would be "suicide" for Russia to use any loan funds for military purposes.[61] There was some apprehension in the United States that Russia might utilize its aid for armaments;[62] Stalin's response was to sketch a bleak picture of Russia's reconstruction tasks and to point out specific serious deficiencies in heavy equipment, railroad cars, and grain. "Our internal market is bottomless," he said, "and we can swallow God knows how much." George F. Kennan, then stationed in the embassy in Moscow, commented, "it is possible that his emphasis on Russian reconstruction problems was meant to impress the Congressmen favorably with a view to credits; but in general I think that he was sincere in the things he said."[63] The crucial question was whether Stalin would shift his foreign policy in return for a loan. Some of the visiting congressmen believed that the United States should use the loan to "influence Russian policy more to our own standards and our liking," but Harriman seemed increasingly skeptical that such pressure could now produce favorable diplomatic results.[64] Byrnes seemed to share Harriman's view: in November, 1945, he wrote that the

[59] *Foreign Relations, 1945*, V, 1037; *ibid., 1946*, I (Washington, D.C., 1972), 1403, 1408, 1418. The British interest rate for their loan was 2 percent, for which Congress appropriated special funds (see Chapter 8 below). The question of a loan to Russia lay dormant from late August until October while the Soviet Union and the United States haggled over an agreement on "pipeline" (ordered but not delivered) Lend-Lease goods, which was reached on October 15. It covered the Soviet purchase of approximately $400 million of Lend-Lease supplies on order, with an interest rate of 2.375 percent on the unpaid balance, the first payment to be made in 1954. This agreement received almost no press coverage and was not printed in U.S., Department of State, *United States Treaties and Other International Agreements*, until 1956; see VII, pt. 3, ser. 3662, pp. 2819-27.

[60] It is curious that Stalin mentioned $6 billion rather than the smaller request. "Conversation between Stalin and Members of the House Special Committee on Post-War Economic Policy and Planning," Sept. 14, 1945, Box 47, Claude Pepper Papers, Federal Records Center, Suitland, Maryland.

[61] "Conversation with Stalin," Sept. 14, 1945, Box 46, *ibid.*

[62] See, for example, *Foreign Relations, 1945*, V, 878 (Byrnes), and n. 66 below.

[63] George F. Kennan, "Excerpts from a Draft Letter Written at Some Time during the First Months of 1945," *Slavic Review*, XXVII (September, 1968), 482. The letter was undated, and Kennan has mistakenly placed it in early 1945.

[64] Pepper favored a loan. Claude Pepper, "Travelogue," [n.d.], Box 49, Pepper Papers.

Department of State "has been pursuing policy of not encouraging active discussions and at present matter is dormant."[65]

In November the House Special Committee on Post-War Economic Policy and Planning issued a report on economic reconstruction in Europe which acknowledged that the Soviet economy was in massive disarray because of the German scorched-earth policy. Economic cooperation with Russia should be effected, but certain points had to be clarified before a "sound relationship" could develop. First, Russia must assure the United States that its aid would not finance a military buildup. Second, the Russians must make a "full and frank disclosure" of their production statistics. The next three demands centered on the Soviet presence in eastern Europe: Russia must withdraw its occupation forces, disclose its trade treaties with that area, and ensure that relief supplies were distributed on nonpolitical grounds. The remaining points reflected the "open door": protection of American property in eastern Europe; "free entry" of American planes flying ordinary Russian air routes; protection of American copyrights in Russia; and the granting of visas in "adequate quantities."[66]

Shortly after this report was issued, Harriman assessed the status of the loan question. United States economic policy toward Russia, he said, had "so far added to our misunderstanding and increased the Soviets [sic] recent tendency to take unilateral action." Moreover, our loan policy "has no doubt caused them to tighten their belts as regards improvement of the living conditions of their people and may have contributed to their avaricious policies in the countries occupied or liberated by the Red Army." He added that Russia worked under long-range plans and by this time had probably formulated its program without United States credits.[67] Hence, any aid rendered would be over and above such a plan. He called for a review of Soviet-American economic relations, apparently with the idea of denying Russia any further UNRRA assistance, from which he believed the United States realized little diplomatic benefit. Harriman's assessment indicated that the use of economic power for diplomatic concessions had thus far failed. Russia had not been swayed.

[65] *Foreign Relations, 1945*, V, 1048. See also *New York Times*, Oct. 24, 1945, and *Journal of Commerce*, Oct. 25, 1945. At his October 24 press conference, Byrnes was either reluctant to discuss the loan question or was not yet well informed about it (he spent much of September at the London conference) because he repeatedly said he did not know much about it and that it was the "business" of Crowley's office. The latter statement was curious since the loan question was discussed by the National Advisory Council, where sat Will Clayton of the State Department. Transcript, press conference, Oct. 24, 1945, Folder 554, Byrnes Papers.

[66] U.S., Congress, House, Special Committee on Post-War Economic Policy and Planning, 8th Rept., *Economic Reconstruction in Europe*, 79th Cong., 1st sess. (1945), pp. 10-11, 31-33.

[67] "Certain Factors," Nov. 14, 1945, Harriman Papers. See also *Foreign Relations, 1945*, V, 935-36 ("Report Prepared by Mr. Thomas P. Whitney").

One Moscow correspondent noted at about the same time that observers there thought that American leaders "are most interested in using that country's favorable economic position to promote United States political aims" and that Moscow publications repeatedly criticized "dollar diplomacy" and "atom diplomacy."[68] By the end of 1945, the United States had not initiated aid negotiations with Russia; the contrast with the successful conclusion of the British loan negotiations on December 6 was stark. President Truman did not clarify the loan question—for Americans or Russians—at his press conference of December 7:

Q. Mr. President, have you any plans for starting negotiations with Soviet Russia for a loan? They have asked for $6 billion, I believe.
The President. If they have, it has never been officially given to me. They never asked me for a $6 billion loan, since I have been President.[69]

Truman may have evaded the question in part because the State Department had not briefed him carefully. He failed to mention why no negotiations had started, and he failed to set the record straight about the new figure of $1 billion. Just six days earlier the State Department had decided to withhold a loan "until we have received concrete and tangible assurance and supporting evidence that [Soviet] economic policies are in general accord with our announced international economic policies."[70]

The State Department continued to stall negotiations in early 1946 with the declared intention of placing "the initiative for any further discussions upon the Soviets."[71] This was a curious procedure, since the request for aid rested in Washington awaiting response. But Washington wanted Russian membership in the newly organized World Bank and International Monetary Fund in the hope of changing restrictive Soviet trade habits and also sought an open door in eastern Europe. The State Department waited, hoping that Soviet reconstruction needs would require Russia to come to the United States to make concessions. Moscow waited, believing that the United States needed to finance exports to Russia to head off a depression.[72] Meanwhile, a conference of the economic counselors and advisers to United States missions in Europe met in Paris from January 28 to February 2, 1946, and decided that the United States should insist on full reciprocity in any forthcoming loan negotiations—that is, should withhold aid unless Russia accepted the principle of multilateralism and opened the door in eastern Europe.[73] Shortly thereafter Clayton informed the National Advisory Council that the State Department would soon open loan negotiations with the Russians.[74]

[68] *New York Times*, Dec. 6, 1945.
[69] *Public Papers, Truman, 1945*, p. 527.
[70] *Foreign Relations, 1946*, I, 1138 (Dec. 1, 1945).
[71] Memorandum by Emilio G. Collado, Feb. 4, 1946, *ibid.*, VI, 825. See also pp. 822-24.
[72] *Ibid.*, p. 824, and *ibid.*, I, 1388n. See also Feis, *From Trust to Terror*, p. 73.
[73] Harriman to author, Nov. 20, 1967; *DSB*, XIV (Mar. 3, 1946), 327-29.
[74] *Foreign Relations, 1946*, I, 1421.

THE QUESTION IS OPENED

On February 21, 1946, State Department officials handed the Russian chargé
a note drafted by Harriman. It explained that the $1 billion credit was "one
among a number of oustanding economic questions" between Russia and the
United States. The note suggested negotiations in Washington on the loan and
several other issues, including a general settlement of Lend-Lease (Soviet
purchase of Lend-Lease items in Russia); claims of American nationals against
Russia; copyright protection; free navigation of rivers, civil aviation; and a
treaty of friendship, commerce, and navigation. The negotiations should
consider policies designed to assist "the peoples liberated from the domination of Nazi Germany and the peoples of the former Axis satellite states of
Europe to solve by democratic means their pressing economic problems"—in
short, the status of eastern Europe. The note further suggested that the Soviet
Union send "observers" to the first meeting of the World Bank and
International Monetary Fund scheduled for March 8.[75] The Truman administration had decided to resurrect the loan question, although some advisers
like Kennan were pessimistic that important concessions could be secured,
since Russia would pay only "lip service" to international economic cooperation.[76] The published State Department documents do not show clearly why
at that moment Washington reversed its policy, although the immediacy of
the first Bank and Fund meeting and the fact that delaying tactics had not
worked probably explain the shift.

Early in March, unnamed officials in the State Department informed a
New York Times correspondent, who reported the story on the front page,
that the State Department's laxity of the previous months was due to
administrative confusion: the Soviet loan request had been "lost" since
August, misplaced during the transfer of the papers of the Foreign Economic
Administration (overseer of the Export-Import Bank during and shortly after
the war) to the State Department.[77] What is the scholar to make of this
bizarre report, which until recently went unchallenged? Arthur M.
Schlesinger, Jr., accepts the story of administrative clumsiness, although he
admits that the explanation "only strengthened Soviet suspicions of American purposes."[78] George F. Kennan, on the other hand, comments that
"there've been a lot of statements that we lost the paper and so forth—it was

[75] *Ibid.*, VI, 828-29.
[76] *Ibid.*, p. 703 (Feb. 22, 1946). On February 28, shortly after opening the loan
question, Byrnes delivered a vigorous and widely reported speech which indicated that
the loan issue was being raised at a time of deep Soviet-American hostility. He said that
the United States "cannot allow aggression to be accomplished by coercion or pressure
or by subterfuges such as political infiltration." *DSB*, XIV (Mar. 10, 1946), 357. Then,
too, the loan was resurrected about the time when Churchill was bemoaning the "iron
curtain" in eastern Europe—a phrase which Stalin deeply resented. *New York Times*,
Mar. 14, 1946.
[77] *New York Times*, Mar. 2 and 3, 1946.
[78] Schlesinger, "Origins of Cold War," p. 44.

not lost. It was always there in the files."[79] Indeed, the evidence is convincing that neither the loan request nor the topic of the loan was lost. The State Department may have feigned administrative confusion in order to explain its long silence concerning the request.

The Soviet reply of March 15 arrived about a week after a Russian observer attended the initial conference of the World Bank and Fund at Savannah, Georgia, as the United States had requested. The Soviets also agreed to discuss a long-term credit, Lend-Lease, and a treaty of friendship, commerce, and navigation, but none of the other items.[80] On that same day, Henry A. Wallace, secretary of commerce and an advocate of a loan to Russia, urged the president to make "a new approach along economic and trade lines." Critical of the current handling of economic relations with Russia, he asked the president to appoint a "new group" to undertake negotiations. And he summarized the importance of postwar aid; "We know that much of the recent Soviet behavior which has caused us concern has been the result of their dire economic needs and their disturbed sense of security. The events of the past few months have thrown the Soviets back to their pre-1939 fears of 'capitalist encirclement' and to their erroneous belief that the western world, including the USA, is invariably and unanimously hostile."[81] Truman later wrote: "I ignored this letter of Wallace's."[82] In essence, Wallace was answered by Kennan, in a telegram to the secretary of state on March 20: "I think there can be no more dangerous tendency in American public opinion than one which places on our Government the obligation to accomplish the impossible by gestures of good will and conciliation toward a political entity constitutionally incapable of being conciliated."[83]

The reply to the Soviets, dispatched on April 18, applauded them for agreeing to discuss some questions and for sending an observer to Savannah. But Byrnes insisted in his letter that a credit of $1 billion should be tied closely to "the creation of an international economic environment permitting a large volume of trade and expanding mutually beneficial economic relations among nations." The letter went on to state—without mentioning specifically the Soviet economic penetration of eastern Europe—that "certain of the questions which might stand in the way of sound development of these relations should be freely discussed. . . ." Byrnes also noted that the discussions would be facilitated by full Soviet membership in the World Bank and Fund.[84] One news correspondent commented, "the conditions laid down by

[79] Transcript, "Cold War Seminar," Institute for Advanced Study, Princeton, N.J., Feb. 15, 1968, p. 40.

[80] *Foreign Relations, 1946*, VI, 829-30. See also *Wall Street Journal*, Mar. 4, 1946; *Journal of Commerce*, Mar. 21, 1946.

[81] Henry Wallace to the president, Mar. 15, 1946, Office of Secretary, GC 90034, Commerce Records.

[82] Truman, *Memoirs*, I, 556.

[83] *Foreign Relations, 1946*, VI, 723.

[84] *Ibid.*, pp. 834-37. For vigorous U.S. protests against Soviet trade treaties with eastern European nations, see Chapter 5 below.

the United States are still regarded as so rugged from the Soviet point of view that there was little expectation among informed officials that the Russians would accept them."[85]

The Russians, as is discussed more fully in a later chapter, were not eager to adopt United States trade principles and to reject the state-trading practices that its economic and social system required and that had been in use since the early years of the Soviet government. They were also wary about joining the World Bank and Fund, both dominated by American dollars, economic principles, voting power, and leadership. They believed they could derive little economic benefit from membership and would have to reverse a long-time policy and divulge details about the Russian economy to the Bank.[86] Nor were they willing to accept an economic open door in eastern Europe, for they looked upon the whole principle as a disguise for United States expansion into the area.

In mid-May, 1946, the Soviet chargé in Washington, Nikolay V. Kovikov, told Acting Secretary of State Dean Acheson with some alarm of his fear that the Export-Import Bank was no longer keeping aside $1 billion for the possible loan to Russia.[87] His fear was correct, and his discovery posed a dilemma for the Truman administration because domestic politics and concern about political stability in France influenced the status of the loan at that point. The State Department had decided in April that the Bank should no longer reserve $1 billion for Russia, because the Soviet-American "conversations" were not proving fruitful and because France was about to hold elections which could be influenced favorably, from Washington's point of view, if further French economic instability could be forestalled. The National Advisory Council concurred, and in May France was granted $650 million.[88]

The administration knew that it was politically dangerous to go to Congress in mid-1946 for more money for the Export-Import Bank to cover a Russian loan or for a special appropriation for Russia. The issues of Iran, eastern Europe, and Germany were bitter ones, and Truman was reluctant to place another controversial issue in the political arena on the eve of the congressional elections.[89] In short, the State Department was in the position of having offered to negotiate with the Russians for money it did not have and probably could not get.

85 John H. Crider, New York Times, Apr. 21, 1946.

86 See Chapter 7 below. Some appreciation of the Russian difficulties in accepting U. S. trade principles can be found in Herbert Feis, "The Conflict over Trade Ideologies," Foreign Affairs, XXV (January, 1947), 217-28.

87 Foreign Relations, 1946, VI, 838-39. The uncommitted portion of the Export-Import Bank's total lending power as of June 30, 1946, was $820 million. Export-Import Bank of Washington, Second Semiannual Report to Congress, January-June, 1946 (Washington, D.C., 1946), p. 31.

88 Foreign Relations, 1946, I, 1430-32.

89 New York Times, Apr. 11, 1946; John C. Campbell, The United States in World Affairs, 1945-1947 (New York, 1947), p. 375; Foreign Relations, 1946, VI, 842-43; ibid., I, 1430-35.

To the State Department's dismay, the Soviets made a concession when they formally communicated with Washington again on May 17. They had earlier agreed to negotiate Lend-Lease, a treaty, and a loan. Now, however, they were "prepared to exchange in a preliminary fashion opinions" on the questions of claims, copyright protection, and eastern Europe. The note did not refer to the World Bank or Fund but did concur with the previous American suggestion that civil aviation and river navigation be discussed in separate negotiations.[90] The Department seemed bewildered; one officer noted that the Export-Import Bank did not have enough money to meet the request and that an open debate in Congress over more funds "might well worsen our relations with the U.S.S.R." He saw two alternatives: first, "to take advantage that the Soviet reply of May 17th gives to break off gracefully loan negotiations with the Soviet Union"; second, to postpone any request to Congress until "we have a clearer picture of the likelihood of successful negotiations with the U.S.S.R."[91]

Washington's actions came closest to the first alternative. On June 13 Byrnes informed the Soviets that the United States appreciated the Soviet willingness to "widen the scope of the negotiations. . . ." but stated that Washington was "unable to agree to a merely preliminary exchange of opinions on some of the questions. . . ." Finally, he insisted that Soviet participation in the World Bank and Fund would facilitate the negotiations.[92] In short, complete Soviet agreement with the United States agenda for negotiations was required, and the Soviet concession was virtually ignored. The loan issue appeared dead.

To salvage something, the State Department decided in September, 1946, to split the issues of Lend-Lease and a loan in the hope that at least a settlement of Lend-Lease could be effected.[93] In October, Harriman told the National Press Club that the loan was no longer a "current issue."[94] Indeed, the general question of assistance to Russian reconstruction was seldom mentioned again until June, 1947, when Secretary Marshall offered dollars to a European recovery program. Russia did not participate in the Marshall Plan, and that finally resolved the issue of postwar aid to Russia.

The history of the abortive Russian loan posits some provocative questions. Would the Soviet Union have sought such heavy reparations from former Axis countries in eastern Europe had a loan been granted? Harriman suggested that the Russians would not have been so "avaricious." He also stated that the Russians might not have followed a "unilateral" course in eastern Europe had a loan been granted. Morgenthau argued, according to his biographer, John Blum, that a postwar credit to Russia would "soften the

[90] Foreign Relations, 1946, VI, 842.
[91] George F. Luthringer, Office of Financial and Development Policy, in ibid., pp. 842-43 (May 23, 1946).
[92] Ibid., pp. 844-46.
[93] Ibid., pp. 853-66.
[94] "Address," Oct. 15, 1946, Harriman Papers.

Soviet mood on all outstanding political questions."[95] And in June, 1945, Grenville Clark asked President Truman: "Now that Russia has regained self-confidence and military strength, is it surprising that without firm promises of aid from the United States . . . she should seek other methods of self-protection?"[96]

As for Germany, one scholar writes that a loan might have taken "the acrimony out of the Russian attitude on reparations."[97] Albert Z. Carr, an associate of Donald Nelson, believed it "altogether probable that these two matters, an American credit and German reparations, were closely linked in Soviet political thinking, for our attitude toward both questions profoundly affected the rate of Russia's postwar recovery."[98] Indeed, as early as 1944, the ambassador to Great Britain, John G. Winant, linked the two issues and, according to one of his former staff members, argued that "the Russian need for material aid in repairing the vast destruction in the Soviet Union was bound to make the Soviet government particularly eager to receive reparations deliveries from Germany on a large scale."[99] United States leaders did not doubt that there was a direct connection between Russia's reparation demands and her reconstruction needs. Edwin Pauley, American reparations ambassador, wrote in 1947, "it can be assumed . . . that Russia's intransigent position on unification and reparations is due to a desire to obtain the maximum amount of industrial and consumer goods from Germany, to meet internal political prestige needs and to help rebuild the Soviet industrial machine."[100] Reporter Edgar Snow noted in the same year that "Ivan" was asking: "Did America offer Russia a serious alternative to reparations?"[101]

Harriman commented that the absence of reconstruction aid probably caused the Russians "to tighten their belts as regards improvement of the living conditions. . . ."[102] Others have noted that the demands of reconstruction and the absence of aid required heavy sacrifices from the Russian people, in part because consumer goods held a secondary priority.[103] Gunnar

95 Blum, *From Morgenthau Diaries*, III, 306.

96 Grenville Clark to Truman, June 2, 1945, quoted in Gardner, *Economic Aspects*, p. 318.

97 J. P. Nettl, *The Eastern Zone and Soviet Policy in Germany, 1945-50* (London, 1951), p. 40.

98 Carr, *Truman, Stalin, and Peace*, p. 41.

99 Philip E. Mosely, *The Kremlin and World Politics: Studies in Soviet Policy and Action* (New York, 1960), p. 176.

100 Edwin Pauley, "Paper on German Reparations, Revised, November 17, 1947," Edwin Pauley Papers (in his possession). See also *Foreign Relations, 1944*, IV, 968; *Foreign Relations, Yalta*, p. 610; Gardner, *Economic Aspects*, p. 314; William McNeill, *America, Britain and Russia: Their Cooperation and Conflict, 1941-1946* (London, 1953), pp. 443-44.

101 Edgar Snow, *Stalin Must Have Peace* (New York, 1947), p. 91.

102 See n. 67 above.

103 Schwartz, *Russia's Postwar Economy*, pp. 108-10. Schwartz believes, however, that United States aid would not have significantly upgraded the Soviet economy because by late 1947 Russia had achieved considerable recovery from the war's devastation. See also Frederick Schuman, *The Cold War: Retrospect and Prospect*, 2d ed. (Baton Rouge, La., 1967).

Myrdal, head of the Economic Commission for Europe, is correct, however, in pointing out that a loan's "possible direct influence on economic reconstruction and development in the Soviet Union should not be exaggerated, but as an element in building up a spirit of friendly cooperation and giving a momentum to trade it would have been of great importance."[104] Finally, what effect did the failure to grant Russia a loan have on the United States goal of multilateralism? We can suggest, as did Vera Micheles Dean in 1947, that Russia was forced to meet its needs through bilateral barter agreements—anathema to multilateralism.[105]

At the close of the war, Stalin told Harriman: "I will not tolerate a new *cordon sanitaire.*"[106] The hesitancy to grant a loan and the use of aid as a diplomatic weapon while Washington was granting Great Britain a handsome loan at an interest rate of less than 2 percent, Chiang Kai-shek was denying Soviet requests for joint companies in Manchuria, a Russian oil concession in Iran was refused, General Lucius Clay had halted German reparations shipments from the American zone of Germany to Russia, and France and Italy were receiving considerable aid—all fed Soviet fears that the United States was creating an international bloc and replaying the events which took place after World War I.[107] As Wallace put it in a letter to Truman in July, 1946, "From the Russian point of view, also, the granting of a loan to Britain and the lack of tangible results on their request to borrow for rehabilitation purposes may be regarded as another evidence of strengthening of an anti-Soviet bloc."[108]

The proposed American loan to Russia was never given the opportunity to demonstrate whether it could serve as a peace potion for easing increasingly bitter Soviet-American relations. The Truman administration—over the objections of Morgenthau, Nelson, White, and Wallace, among others—decided to employ the loan as a diplomatic weapon before negotiations began rather than as a diplomatic tool at the conference table. Few nations or individuals are eager to enter negotiations when the attitude of the other party is simply "our way or not at all." The diplomatic use of economic power by any nation possessing it is to be expected and may be helpful in achieving fruitful and mutually beneficial negotiations. But if that power thwarts negotiations or is employed to buttress demands which alone are held to be the sine qua non for peaceful settlement, the result is schism and conflict.

[104] Gunnar Myrdal, *An International Economy: Problems and Prospects* (New York, 1956), p. 138.
[105] Vera Micheles Dean, "Russia's Foreign Economic Policy," *Foreign Policy Reports*, XXII (Feb. 1, 1947), 279.
[106] Averell Harriman, *Peace with Russia?* (New York, 1959), p. 12.
[107] See, for example, Joseph Stalin's response to Winston Churchill's "iron curtain" speech in *New York Times*, Mar. 14, 1946.
[108] Wallace to Truman, July 23, 1946, reprinted in "The Path to Peace with Russia," *New Republic*, CXV (Sept. 30, 1946), 404.

CHAPTER 3

COLD WAR CASUALTY: TRADE WITH RUSSIA

United States trade with the Soviet Union after the war was largely dependent upon foreign aid. When the loan failed to materialize and United States-financed UNRRA assistance declined in 1946, the expectations that postwar Soviet-American trade would prosper collapsed. The peace and prosperity theme provided most of the reason for such expectations in the late war years, but the growing antagonism between the former allies convinced many Americans that exports to Russia should be controlled in order to reduce shipments of potential military items, to hinder Soviet reconstruction, to punish the wayward ally, and to divert goods to western Europe. After much preparation, Washington initiated a formal system of controls in early 1948, and the Soviet Union retaliated in late 1948. By the time of the Korean War, Soviet-American trade had become negligible. It had never been extensive, but it became both a cause and a casualty of the postwar Soviet-American confrontation.

EARLY EXPECTATIONS

During World War II and for a short time thereafter, many businessmen and government officials spoke optimistically of postwar trade with Russia. One of the most active and informed advocates of new trade departures, as noted earlier, was the president of the United States Chamber of Commerce, Eric Johnston. In mid-1944 he undertook a five-thousand-mile trip through the Soviet Union, visiting factories, interviewing workers as well as Premier Stalin, accumulating statistics on Soviet needs, and carrying with him a team of reporters who were stunned by the favorable and generally unrestricted Soviet treatment he was accorded. Johnston was impressed; he predicted that Russia would turn to the United States for heavy machinery to rebuild and to raise its standard of living. The United States, in turn, would welcome shipments of ores, gold, oil, and timber. Indeed, Russia might become the United States' "most eager customer when the war ends."[1] He played down ideological differences and assumed that capitalists and Communists could trade without serious impediments. Speaking informally to Mikoyan, he said jokingly, "I like your manganese. . . . It does not know it is Socialist. It would just as soon go into a furnace in Pittsburgh as in Stalingrad. . . . And you like our machine tools. They do not know that they are capitalistic."[2]

Others shared Johnston's optimism. Ernest C. Ropes, a Russian trade expert in the Department of Commerce, repeatedly made the point that trade with the Soviet Union would and should expand in the postwar years in the interests both of peace and of a healthy economy. He predicted that Russia would purchase large quantities of automobiles, refrigerators, machine tools, and other heavy equipment, and expected that companies like Ford Motor would sign new technical assistance contracts.[3] Jack Warner of Warner Brothers was interested in expanding the film trade in Russia; Chase National Bank began negotiating for the purchase of gold; General Electric, International Telephone and Telegraph, and Du Pont all took Soviet orders near the close of the war; and the Radio Corporation of America and Westinghouse were other prominent corporations stirred by the trade potential.[4] Opinion polls indicated that trade would increase significantly, and Henry Wallace, Donald Nelson, and Harry White tried to maintain such positive public sentiment.[5] The officials of the City of Baltimore and of Bethlehem Steel,

[1] Quoted in *Nation's Business*, XXXII (October, 1944), 21-22. For accounts of Johnston's Russian excursion and his views, see *Foreign Relations, 1944*, IV, 972, 973-74, 979; Harrison E. Salisbury, "Russia Beckons Big Business," *Collier's*, CXIV (Sept. 2, 1944), 11ff.; Eric Johnston, "My Talk with Joseph Stalin," *Readers Digest*, XLIII (October, 1944), 1-11.

[2] Speech, luncheon given by A. I. Mikoyan (Moscow), June 3, 1944, Eric Johnston Papers, Spokane, Washington.

[3] See Ropes's works and ideas in "The Shape of United States-Soviet Trade, Past and Present," *Slavonic and East European Review*, XXII (August, 1944), 1-15; "Credits to Soviet Agencies in the United States," *American Review on the Soviet Union*, VI (May, 1945), 10-15; *Doing Business with Russia* (Washington, D.C., 1945); "Opportunities for Russian-American Trade Expansion," *Dun's Review*, LV (May, 1947), 11, 58; "American-Soviet Trade: 1917-1947," *Soviet Russia Today*, XVI (November, 1947), 14ff.; *New York Times*, Feb. 16, 1945, July 31 and Sept. 24, 1946.

[4] Memorandum of conversation (Warner), VII (June 15, 1945), Conversations, Grew Papers; J. C. R. to W. W. Aldrich (Chase National), May 16, 1945, Box 110, Aldrich Papers; *Nation's Business*, XXXIII (March, 1945), 46; *Foreign Relations, 1944*, IV, 1079; Paterson, "Economic Cold War," p. 211n.

[5] Business executives polled by *Fortune* placed Russia second to South America and just ahead of Asia as the area in which they expected to increase foreign business, and over 90 percent thought it was to the long-term advantage of the United States to promote trade with Russia. In an American Institute of Public Opinion poll (March, 1945) most respondents picked trade as what the United States had most to gain from the Soviet Union after the war. *Fortune*, XXXII (September, 1945), 238; Hadley Cantril, *Public Opinion, 1935-1946* (Princeton, N.J., 1951), p. 962; Henry A. Wallace and Andrew J. Steiger, *Soviet Asia Mission* (New York, 1946); Nelson, *Arsenal of Democracy*; memorandum, Harry White to Henry Morgenthau, Mar. 7, 1944, part II: 23, White Papers.

which was based there, hoped to enjoy considerable profits from improved trade with Russia; manufacturers of transportation equipment and machine tools envisioned large Soviet markets; and many businessmen looked forward to an influx of Russian manganese ores and other vital raw materials.[6] One outstanding example of business interest in the Soviet market was the 1945 edition of the *Catalogue of American Engineering and Industry,* published in Russian by the Soviet Union for its purchasing agents. Seven hundred United States companies spent $250,000 to advertise in the volume, which was prepared with the help of the United States-based AMTORG Trading Corporation, the official buying and selling agency for the Soviet Commissariat for Foreign Trade.[7]

A number of leaders argued that Soviet-American trade would smooth diplomatic relations and help stave off a postwar economic slump. James McGraw of McGraw-Hill agreed with Henry Wallace that expanded trade might "prevent the world splitting into two hostile ideological camps."[8] Former ambassador to Russia Admiral William H. Standley echoed the popular idea that Russian purchases of surplus production would cushion the postwar depression, and Professor Selig Perlman stated emphatically that "Russia is the very market we need for our industries exposed to the greatest economic hazard."[9] Perlman added that trade would serve a diplomatic purpose: "We have no sword big enough to brandish over Russia, but we can deeply influence her foreign policy, her plan for Western Europe, and for certain portions of Asia, by the inducement of assisting her in her economic restoration and expansion. Our economic necessity might thus become the foundation of our diplomatic opportunity."[10] One of Donald Nelson's aides reported after a conference with the Soviet premier, "Stalin made no secret of his feeling that trade with the United States would provide a basis for political co-operation with the West."[11]

The Soviets have always been admirers of United States products, technical skill, engineers, and businessmen, and Stalin wanted to continue the

---

[6] *Baltimore Sun,* July 29, 1944; *Hartford Times,* July 14, 1944; *Fortune,* XXXI (January, 1945), 155ff.; Hans Heymann, *We Can Do Business with Russia* (Chicago, 1945), p. 123; William Mandel, "Russia—Our Biggest Postwar Market?," *Advertising and Selling,* XXXVII (May, 1944), 29; *Nation's Business,* XXXIII (March, 1945), 46; *Iron Age,* CLVI (Aug. 9, 1945), 99; *Steel,* CXVII (July 30, 1945), 54; *New York Times,* Mar. 18 and Aug. 27, 1945; Valery J. Tereshtenko, "American Soviet Trade," *Soviet Russia Today,* XV (February, 1945), 8ff.; Perkins, "Can Our Foreign Customers Pay," pp. 49, 51.

[7] *Fortune,* XXXI (January, 1945), 156; Ladislas Farago, "AMTORG: Its Business Is Business with Russia," *United Nations World,* I (July, 1947), 29-31.

[8] *Fortune,* XXXI (January, 1945), 156; *New York Times,* May 5, 1945 (Wallace).

[9] *New York Times,* Feb. 21, 1945 (Standley); Harriman and Nelson, in Chapter 2 above; Selig Perlman, "Some Reflections on Russia and the Future of Russian-American Relations," in Thomas C. T. McCormick, ed., *Problems of the Postwar World* (New York, 1945), pp. 340-41.

[10] Perlman, "Some Reflections," pp. 340-41.

[11] Carr, *Truman, Stalin, and Peace,* p. 24.

flow of goods begun under the Lend-Lease program.[12] He was frank in setting forth his country's desire for machinery made in the United States because, though expensive, its quality was superior.[13] This attitude was reflected in the exceptionally cordial reception given to businessmen like Johnston, who quipped: "I think sometimes that they have a great deal more admiration for American businessmen than we have in our own country."[14] Diplomats and journalists enjoyed less freedom and respect in Russia, prompting the associate editor of *Time* to say that "businessmen in Russia can get things done that other foreigners cannot."[15] And an AMTORG representative commented in 1947, "believe it or not, American big business is our only remaining friend in the United States."[16]

But this enthusiasm, which certainly reflected the general wartime mood toward Russia,[17] was challenged by a few doubters, most of whom cited the historical record. The editor of *American Exporter*, for example, stressed the small part Russia had played in world trade before the war.[18] Indeed, prewar trade statistics did not invite optimism for the postwar period. From 1925 to 1937, both Russian imports and exports accounted for only 1.5 percent of total international trade. American exports to Russia before the war seldom rose above 2 percent for all American exports, and imports from Russia hovered around 1 percent of total American imports. Lend-Lease shipments to the Soviet Union in the war period altered this pattern significantly, and it was this commercial interchange—especially in machinery—which Stalin and some large corporations hoped to perpetuate.[19]

Some government officials were not altogether as convinced as Ernest

[12] See Lewis S. Feuer, "American Travelers to the Soviet Union, 1917-32: The Formation of a Component of New Deal Ideology," *American Quarterly*, XIV (Summer, 1962), 119-49; Peter Filene, *Americans and the Soviet Experiment, 1917-1933* (Cambridge, Mass., 1967); *New York Times*, Nov. 1, 1967.

[13] See Chapter 2 above and *Foreign Relations, 1943*, III, 713.

[14] In Heymann, *We Can Do Business*, pp. vii-viii.

[15] Sam Welles, "Report on Russia," June 19, 1947, doc. 60, General File, President's Committee on Foreign Aid Records.

[16] Quoted in Farago, "AMTORG," p. 31..

[17] For favorable wartime attitudes toward Russia, see Paul Willen, "Who 'Collaborated' with Russia?," *Antioch Review*, XIV (September, 1954), 259-83.

[18] *New York Times*, July 6, 1945. See also the strong position of Edmund A. Walsh, president of Georgetown University, that trade with "dictatorial" Communists was politically dangerous. *Ibid.*, Apr. 4, 1945.

[19] Percentage and value of American exports to Russia:

1935: 1.1 percent ($24.4 million)	1938: 2.3 percent ($69.7 million)
1936: 1.4 percent ($33.4 million)	1939: 1.8 percent ($56.6 million)
1937: 1.3 percent ($42.9 million)	1940: 2.2 percent ($86.9 million)

Percentage and value of American imports from Russia:

1935: 0.9 percent ($17.7 million)	1938: 1.2 percent ($23.5 million)
1936: 0.9 percent ($21.4 million)	1939: 1.1 percent ($25.0 million)
1937: 0.9 percent ($27.2 million)	1940: 0.8 percent ($20.8 million)

In 1942, Russia took 17.6 percent of U.S. exports; in 1943, 23.1 percent; in 1944, 24.3 percent. Alexander Baykov, *Soviet Foreign Trade* (Princeton, N.J., 1946), pp. 89, 95; Gerschenkron, *Economic Relations with the U.S.S.R.*, p. 20.

Ropes that the postwar trade picture with Russia would improve. As early as 1942, a high-ranking Lend-Lease official predicted that Russia would place large postwar orders in central Europe and Italy, rather than in the United States, in order to tie those economies to the Soviet Union. It was faulty, he concluded, to expect the Soviet marketplace to help the United States avert "post war problems."[20] In 1943, members of the Interdepartmental Committee on Commercial Relations with the Soviet Union played down potential trade, arguing that Russia had few goods Americans needed.[21] When the United States contemplated expanding its consulates in the Soviet Union in 1945, the case was made not that they would enlarge trade but that they would serve as diplomatic "observation" posts.[22] Harriman, always alive to the diplomatic advantages of trade, urged caution and expressed the uncertainty of many diplomats: "On the one hand we should allay the *exaggerated optimism* as to the possible volume of post war trade with the USSR . . . , without, on the other hand, minimizing its importance. . . ."[23]

Other businessmen and officials hesitated because of commercial and financial problems growing out of the Bolshevik Revolution. An aide to Thomas W. Lamont, board chairman of J. P. Morgan and Company, told Lamont in 1944 that bankers would never forget the repudiation of the World War I debt and the expropriation of American property in Russia.[24] The National City Bank, Guaranty Trust Company, New York Life Insurance Company, and International Harvester were among the firms which lost their holdings after the Revolution. Some managed to recover a fraction of their assets, but the overall experience was souring.[25] Then, too, some observers were irritated that, as George F. Kennan put it, "there is absolutely no protection of either property interest of patentees or of US national interest in this connection."[26] Some worried that United States patents would not be respected and that machinery shipped to Russia might be duplicated, reproduced, and even exported to compete with the original product.[27] The Singer Manufacturing Company, for one, saw its property (valued by the company at about $100 million) confiscated without compensation after 1917. To Singer's further dismay, the Russians were soon manufacturing Singer sewing machines to compete with the "genuine" article.[28] The

20 John N. Hazard to Charles Bunn, Apr. 27, 1942, *Foreign Relations, 1942*, III, 758-59.

21 Memorandum, Elbridge Durbrow, *ibid., 1943*, III, 722-23.

22 *Ibid., 1945*, II, 1166.

23 *Ibid., 1944*, IV, 958 (italics added).

24 Memorandum to T. W. L., May 29, 1944, Box 128, Thomas W. Lamont Papers, Baker Library, Harvard University.

25 Donald G. Bishop, *The Roosevelt-Litvinov Agreements: The American View* (Syracuse, N.Y., 1965), pp. 142-44.

26 *Foreign Relations, 1945*, V, 850.

27 Joseph Grew to Edward S. Mason, May 15, 1945, CXXIII, Grew Papers; *Foreign Relations, 1943*, III, 795-97.

28 Heymann, *We Can Do Business*, p. 195.

Caterpillar Tractor Company took Singer's experience as a lesson during the war and refused to disclose to the Russians specific information regarding the manufacture of their tractors because there was no guarantee that the Soviets would not begin producing similar vehicles after the war.[29]

The growing diplomatic crises of 1945 in eastern Europe, the continued Soviet-American verbal clashes, the absence of a loan to Russia, which Johnston considered the "nub of our trade," and the lack of Soviet participation in multilateral nondiscriminatory trade schemes all dampened trade hopes.[30] Harriman and Kennan were especially wary because they saw few advantages for the United States in a strictly commercial agreement and did not trust Russia to fulfill the provisions of a treaty. They insisted that a state which conducts its foreign trade through a monopoly does not have the flexibility to fulfill the United States goals of multilateral trade.[31] Acheson responded that Russia, as a member of an international trade association, would be obliged "to purchase foreign goods up to a minimum value in return for tariff and other trade barrier reductions on part of other countries," but the skeptics in the American embassy in Moscow were not convinced,[32] nor was there much enthusiasm for a treaty of "friendship, commerce, and navigation" which the U.S.S.R. Committee of the State Department drafted and sent on to Kennan for comment. Kennan thought that negotiating such a treaty was "quite useless" because few benefits would accrue to the United States from it.[33]

Some observers noted that the failure to establish political and commercial accords introduced a substantial element of risk into Soviet-American trade. The president of Dresser Industries warned that Washington, to achieve its diplomatic objectives, might make a hasty decision to cut back trade with Russia. He recommended that the government guarantee commercial transactions with the Soviet Union to eliminate the "immediate pocket book hazard which would wrong American manufacturers exporting goods," should the government unexpectedly impose a ban.[34] It is not surprising, then, that one business journal found trade experts in 1945 "quizzical" about postwar trade prospects.[35]

---

[29] *Foreign Relations, 1943*, III, 797.

[30] Johnston, in *Nation's Business*, XXXII (October, 1944), 22.

[31] *Foreign Relations, 1945*, II, 1337-39, 1348-49, 1350-52, 1355-58; *ibid., 1946*, VI, 728-31.

[32] *Ibid., 1945*, II, 1348-49.

[33] *Ibid., 1946*, VI, 728-31. See also *ibid., 1945*, V, 912-13; George F. Kennan, *Memoirs, 1925-1950* (Boston, 1967), pp. 268-69.

[34] H. N. Mallon, "Relations between United States Manufacturers and Foreign Governments," October, 1945, Office of Secretary, GC 93126, Box 748, Commerce Records.

[35] *Nation's Business*, XXXIII (May, 1945), 19.

BEGINNING TO LOOK ELSEWHERE: 1946

The years 1946 and 1947 were ones of uncertainty. Some companies were still trading with Russia, and a few optimists continued to de-emphasize ideological factors. Johnston was still arguing in 1946 that the world had "enough room for capitalism and communism," a writer in the magazine of the United States Chamber of Commerce concluded that state trading and private trading were "not necessarily contradictory,"[36] and the case of the Warner and Swasey Company showed how easily ideological differences could be subordinated—the president of the company was a member of the pro-trade American-Russian Chamber of Commerce at the very time when the company was financing anti-Soviet, anti-Communist advertisements in major business magazines.[37] Charles Prince, formerly with the United States Chamber of Commerce, called for a new commercial treaty to protect foreign-owned private property and patents in Russia, to exchange information, to arrange for granting of credits, and to outlaw dumping and discrimination, but the proposal received little attention.[38]

Corporate giants like International Telephone and Telegraph, Radio Corporation of America, and General Electric continued to enlist and fill Soviet orders in 1946, and by the end of the year about fifty United States firms held technical assistance contracts with the Soviet Union.[39] Ropes and Lewis L. Lorwin of the Commerce Department returned from an official visit to Russia, undertaken at the request of Secretary Wallace, to predict that it would buy $2 billion worth of United States products if the necessary credits were extended.[40] Shortly after his ouster from the Truman cabinet, Wallace publicly recommended that the president send a special trade mission to Moscow to take advantage of what seemed an optimistic mood among American businessmen, and that he seek agreements to export United States machinery and import timber, metallic ores, furs, paper and pulp, and vegetable drugs.[41]

One organization particularly interested in promoting trade with Russia

---

[36] Johnston, in Senate, *Anglo-American Financial Agreement* (Mar. 19, 1946), p. 464; L. G. Dillon, in *Nation's Business*, XXXIV (July, 1946), 59.

[37] See postwar issues of *Business Week* for Warner and Swasey advertisements.

[38] Prince proposal in *Congressional Record*, 79th Cong., 2d sess., XCII (June 21, 1946), A3666-69.

[39] Stella K. Margold, *Let's Do Business with Russia: Why We Should and How We Can* (New York, 1948), pp. 101-2; *Journal of Commerce*, Dec. 18, 1946.

[40] *New York Times*, June 20, July 7 and 31, Sept. 20 and 24, 1946.

[41] Wallace, "Path to Peace with Russia," p. 405. See also Donald R. Crone and Eugene Bouianovsky, "U.S. Advertising in Soviet Publications," *Foreign Commerce Weekly*, XXIV (Aug. 17, 1946), 27ff. In September Donald Nelson made public a letter he had sent to Stalin renewing his recommendation that a "commission of American businessmen" enter trade talks in Russia. "Do you not still believe that this plan would bring our countries closer together?" *New York Times*, Sept. 1, 1946.

was the American-Russian Chamber of Commerce. Representatives from Chase National Bank, General Electric, Radio Corporation of America, Armco International, International Business Machines, Fruehauf Trailer, and the Thomas A. Edison Company joined executives from some middle-sized companies in this organization. Incorporated in 1916 and reorganized in 1926, its mainstay was Reeve Schley, a vice-president of Chase National Bank and during the war a special assistant to the administrator of Lend-Lease. In addition to the anticipated profits, trade would smooth diplomatic ripples, according to Schley: "Trade can be carried on without the embarrassments of differences of religious thought, social ideals or internal economic problems. To be sure, knowledge and understanding through trade, is a slow process, but the reconciliation of the two systems will inevitably be a slow process."[42]

But trade impediments, shortages in the United States, and diplomatic schism destroyed some of this optimism. Distillation Products Industries, a division of Eastman Kodak, and the Ross Gear and Tool Company turned down Soviet orders; steel companies diverted more and more steel from Russia to meet domestic demands; and the Soviet Union was excluded from third-quarter 1946 tinplate allocations.[43] Some companies not trading with Russia complained about those that did: the General Shale Products Corporation protested to Washington in mid-1946 that it could not acquire dryer cars because Chase Foundry and Manufacturing was shipping all available cars to Russia. General Shale criticized this "favoritism toward a foreign power."[44] Governor Earl Warren of California charged that the A. O. Smith Company of Milwaukee was giving perference to a Russian order for gas pipeline over an El Paso company which had contracted to construct a natural gas pipeline from Texas to California.[45] With the Cold War tensions developing, manufacturers became more cautious; some asked the Atomic Energy Commission about the propriety of shipping certain goods to Russia; the industrial magazine *Steel* advocated holding up "questionable shipments until the recipient nations clarify their positions to our satisfaction."[46] A poll in the fall of 1946 recorded that 65 percent of those questioned believed that the United States should stop shipments of food, equipment, and other supplies to Russia.[47]

[42] Reeve Schley to John Foster Dulles, Sept. 14, 1946, Category II, Dulles Papers. For earlier Schley views and activities, see Filene, *Americans and Soviet Experiment*, pp. 114-15; *The Chase*, March-April, 1942, p. 411; and obituary in *New York Times*, June 27, 1960.

[43] R. W. Albright to Bernard Baruch, Mar. 14, 1950, part XI:1, Baruch Papers (on Distillation Products); *Steel*, CXVIII (Jan. 7, 1946); *Iron Age*, CLVIII (July 4, 1946), 105.

[44] William L. Sells to Congressman Carroll Reece, Aug. 10, 1946, UNRRA folder, John W. Snyder Papers, Truman Library.

[45] *Iron Age*, CLVIII (Oct. 31, 1946), 96; *Journal of Commerce*, Oct. 19, 1946.

[46] Bernard Baruch to David Lilienthal, Dec. 19, 1946, part XI:1, Baruch Papers; *Steel*, CXIX (Sept. 2, 1946), 61.

[47] Cantril, *Public Opinion, 1935-1946*, p. 740 (A.I.P.O. poll of Sept. 11, 1946).

One journal noted that businessmen, troubled by the diplomatic squabbles, "are forgetting their dream of a great Russian market."[48]

Some congressmen encouraged this negative attitude. In March, 1946, a group of representatives led by John Taber of New York, John M. Vorys of Ohio, Francis Case of South Dakota, Clare E. Hoffman of Michigan, and Everett Dirksen of Illinois unsuccessfully introduced legislation to stop shipments of Lend-Lease goods yet undelivered but scheduled for Russia under the agreement of October 15, 1945. At the turn of the year, Congress did suspend such cargoes.[49] The House Special Committee on Post-War Economic Policy and Planning joined the sentiment against trade with Russia in late 1946 by strongly urging that restrictions be imposed on Soviet commercial agents in the United States and that United States patents and "industrial secrets" be protected through careful screening.[50]

Both Kennan and the new ambassador to Moscow, Walter Bedell Smith, continued to be pessimistic about Soviet adherence to a trade agreement, and Smith advised using trade as a weapon in diplomatic bargaining with the Soviets.[51] Secretary Forrestal was much impressed with a study prepared by a member of his staff which argued that Russia would eventually be an economic power challenging the United States, and concluded with an analogy that was to become popular: "It would seem just as short-sighted for us to strengthen Russia in any way as it was for us to strengthen Japan by continuing to sell her oil and scrap iron at a time when her policies were actively opposed to our own."[52] Soon after succeeding Wallace as secretary of commerce, Harriman recommended that the State Department withhold from Russia captured German technological information: "Perhaps this scientific enrichment to them [Russians] of knowledge developed by the United States might be of some value to you in subsequent negotiations."[53]

---

[48] *Nation's Business,* XXXIV (October, 1946), 25.

[49] Actually, shipment continued until March 26, 1947, for those articles title to which had passed to the U.S.S.R. before December 31, 1946. H. Bradford Westerfield, *Foreign Policy and Party Politics: Pearl Harbor to Korea* (New Haven, Conn., 1955), p. 209; *New York Times,* Nov. 15, 1947; U.S., Department of Commerce, Office of International Trade, "United States Trade with the U.S.S.R. in 1947," *International Reference Service,* V (April, 1948).

[50] House, *Economic Reconstruction in Europe: Progress Report,* pp. 36-37.

[51] *Foreign Relations, 1946,* VI, 703, 745-46.

[52] Edward F. Willet, "Dialectical Materialism and Russian Objectives," Jan. 14, 1946, Box 17, Forrestal Papers. Throughout 1946 there were annoyed rumblings against the U.S.S.R. as a trade competitor in Europe. A Soviet trade treaty with Sweden brought a State Department protest and spirited Swedish and Russian replies that the United States was meddling in their sovereign affairs. Other American and British fears grew out of Soviet trade with Switzerland, Denmark, and Norway, and, as will be discussed in Chapter 5 below, Soviet penetration of eastern European economies. *New York Times,* July 26 and 28, Aug. 8, 11, and 30, Sept. 1 and 3, Oct. 6, Nov. 30, and Dec. 12, 1946.

[53] Harriman to James F. Byrnes, Nov. 15, 1946, Harriman Papers. For an intriging account of the Soviet-American contest to "exploit" German rocket scientists and technical knowledge and Washington's success in that competition, see Clarence G. Lasby, *Project Paperclip: German Scientists and the Cold War* (New York, 1971).

He also ordered the Office of Technical Services to cease filling Russian orders for copies of technical and scientific publications.[54] Finally, despite Soviet requests, none of the 2,300 surplus ships sold abroad went to the Soviet Union.[55]

Trade with Russia declined sharply from 1945 to 1946. In 1945, the United States exported $1.838 billion in goods to Russia, largely under the Lend-Lease and relief programs; in 1946 such exports had dropped to $358 million, of which only $53 million represented cash purchases. Imports from Russia increased, from $54 million in 1945 to $101 million in 1946, but this slight growth was hardly enough to overcome the overall trade decline or to realize Stalin's prediction in December of 1946 that "the expansion of world trade would benefit in many respects the development of good relations between our two countries."[56]

ECONOMIC PRESSURE AND DIPLOMACY: 1947

Advocates of a cutback in trade with Russia became more vocal in early 1947. One congressman remonstrated against pig iron shipments to the Soviet Union, and the chairman of the House Merchant Marine Committee, Alvin F. Weichel, introduced a bill to prohibit exports until Russia made a "satisfactory settlement" for the ninety-five American merchant ships it received during the war.[57] Shortly after the president's hard-hitting speech on the Truman Doctrine, Senator Ralph Flanders of Vermont introduced a joint resolution to embargo trade until Russia accepted Washington's interpretations of the Yalta and Potsdam agreements. He called for economic pressure against the Soviet Union: "Our present means of bargaining are economic. They are the persuasive arguments which we bring to the council table in requiring of Russia that she keep her agreements and become a willing and cooperative member of the United Nations. Whenever and wherever there is an economic need of Russia's which we can fill, it must be contingent on her continuing wholehearted cooperation."[58] Congressman Norris Poulson of California compared the loading of gasoline on twelve Russian tankers in Los Angeles to U.S. shipments to Japan before Pearl

54 See the story in *Steel*, CXXII (Feb. 2, 1948), 78.

55 In August, 1945, for example, the U.S. Maritime Commission approved sale of seventy-five "Liberty" ships to France, fifty to Italy, forty-two to the Netherlands, and fourteen to Norway. *Journal of Commerce*, Aug. 5, 1946; *New York Times*, Nov. 15, 1947.

56 Figures in U.S., Congress, Senate, *Interim Aid for Europe* (Washington, D.C., 1947), pp. 184-85; *J. V. Stalin on Post-War International Relations* (London, 1947), p. 19.

57 *Congressional Record*, 80th Cong., 1st sess., XCIII (Feb. 3, 1947), 747; *New York Times*, Mar. 5, Nov. 18, and Dec. 13, 1947.

58 "Interview with Senator Ralph Flanders over WNAC, Boston," Mar. 15, 1947, Box 133, Flanders Papers; *New York Times*, Mar. 15, 1947.

Harbor, and Bernard Baruch joined the demand for tighter controls on exports of machinery and vehicles to the Soviet Union.[59] The Special House Committee on Post-War Economic Policy and Planning issued a strongly worded report early in 1947 which stated that controls should be placed on the export of capital goods as "bargaining pressure" and to impede Russian "industrial development that can only be deleterious to the interests of a secure and peaceful world...."[60] President Truman himself stimulated restrictionist thought in early 1947 with his flamboyant anti-Soviet rhetoric and his request that Congress give him power to determine, through licensing control, those countries which could receive United States exports of arms and munitions: "In the interests of world peace articles supplying a foreign establishment cannot be left free from Government supervision so far as exports are concerned."[61]

Major companies trading with Russia began to react to this keenly negative sentiment. Dresser Industries asked for a clarification of government policy. It indicated that its trade in oil equipment with the Soviet Union was profitable, but stated that "if accepting further business from those people is inimical to the over-all interest of the United States, then we do not want any part of such business."[62] Some companies receiving orders for goods which could conceivably go into the production of atomic energy stalled until guidelines could be established.[63] General Electric, troubled by a Russian order for heavy electrical equipment valued at $11 million, asked the State Department for advice. Under Secretary Robert Lovett replied that the department "would not be unhappy if General Electric could find adequate commercial reasons for refusing this business." General Electric then stiffened its terms, only to find that Russia still wanted to consummate the deal. At this point, Lovett recommended that the order be accepted to avoid an "open break" with Russia on export policy.[64] John Abbink, president of McGraw-Hill International and prominent member of the influential National Foreign Trade Council, was less cautious and urged an embargo on machinery to a "potential enemy"; he added, "the lesson of Japanese treachery has not been forgotten."[65] The Chamber of Commerce contended that the shipment of

[59] *Congressional Record,* 80th Cong., 1st sess., XCIII (June 17, 1947), A2928; draft speech, July 21, 1947, Memoranda-Misc. 1947 folder, Baruch Papers. See also Congressman Alvin F. Weichel to W. C. Foster, July 8, 1947, Office of Secretary, GC 93126, Box 748, Commerce Records.

[60] House, *Economic Reconstruction in Europe: Progress Report,* p. 25.

[61] *Public Papers: Truman, 1947,* p. 206 (Apr. 15, 1947, message).

[62] H. N. Mallon to Harriman, Sept. 22, 1947, Office of Secretary, GC 93126, Box 748, Commerce Records. Apparently the company did not complete all of its contracts with Russia. Margold, *Let's Do Business,* p. 98.

[63] Ferdinand Eberstadt to Lewis L. Strauss (Atomic Energy Commission), Oct. 27, 1947, Harriman Papers.

[64] Robert A. Lovett to C. Tyler Wood, Oct. 14, 1947, *ibid.*

[65] National Foreign Trade Council, *Report of 34th National Convention,* p. 457.

steel products should be discontinued because "we do not want to contribute to the rearmament of Russia. . . ."[66]

The Second DeControl Act of 1947, recommended by the president only one week after his dramatic announcement of the Truman Doctrine and passed in July, gave the executive branch the authority to control exports. It was designed to help the government curtail the export of goods in short supply at home. It also allowed control of the distribution of goods abroad, in order to curb trade with Russia as well as to direct needed items to the European Recovery Program.[67] Another restriction was the requirement that would-be recipients of United States products file detailed reports stating their probable consumption, actual imports, current production, and reserve stock position of each product desired. Russia was reluctant to divulge economic statistics and indeed had laws on the books forbidding such revelations.[68] In fact, the information requirement trimmed back oil shipments considerably because Russian officials refused to submit the requested data. Secretary of State Marshall ruled against "special treatment" for Moscow. In response to a senator's query about oil shipments to Russia after mid-1947, Acting Secretary of Commerce William C. Foster admitted both "political and economic considerations" behind export control policy.[69]

Basic steel products were added to the control list in early summer, 1947, and since the U.S.S.R. again refused to supply the requested information, steel exports were curbed. Locomotives and freight cars were treated similarly.[70] In December the Department of Commerce informed Russian trade officials that AMTORG's orders for railway dump cars had been rejected because of domestic shortages but that the United States hoped soon "to set up a modest quota for freight cars which we can license in accord with our policy of endeavoring to take care of certain of the more essential requirements of *friendly* foreign countries."[71] However, freight cars were shipped to Poland in "the belief that it would result in increased shipments of Polish coal to the countries of western and northern Europe."[72] The export

[66] Minutes, Board of Directors meeting, Nov. 22, 1947, Chamber of Commerce Library, Washington, D.C. See also *New York Times*, sec. 3, Nov. 9, 1947, for Russian difficulty in finding businessmen eager to sell equipment to them, and *ibid.*, Dec. 2, 1947, for congressional requests that the Commerce Department reveal the names of companies doing business with Russia so that a "blacklist" could be initiated.

[67] U.S., Department of Commerce, *First Quarterly Report under Second Decontrol Act of 1947* (Washington, D.C., 1947).

[68] Margold, *Let's Do Business*, pp. 138-39.

[69] Marshall to Harriman, Aug. 5, 1947, Harriman Papers; William Foster to Senator Scott Lucas, July 7, 1947, Office of Secretary, GC 93126, Box 748, Commerce Records. Also David Bruce to Congressman Mike Mansfield, Nov. 25, 1947, *ibid*; Bruce to AMTORG Trading Corp., Aug. 27, 1947, *ibid.*

[70] Thomas C. Blaisdell to Senator Leverett Saltonstall, Apr. 27, 1948, Box 750, *ibid.*; Harriman to Neil Morgan, Dec. 22, 1947, Harriman Papers.

[71] David Bruce to AMTORG, Dec. 22, 1947, Office of Secretary, GC 93126, Box 749, Commerce Records (italics added).

[72] W. A. Harriman to Senator Forrest C. Donnell, Dec. 18, 1947, *ibid.*

of synthetic rubber products to Russia was also restricted.[73] At year's end about 20 percent of all exportable products had become subject to controls, with particular restrictions on exports to Russia and Spain.[74]

By the end of 1947, the United States was making determined efforts to cultivate manganese shipments from countries other than Russia. India was a prime target; experts were dispatched, found the railway system a shambles, and encouraged increased United States exports of steel to that troubled country. United States Steel and Bethlehem Steel were also searching for manganese deposits in Brazil. A participant at a meeting of the President's Materials Policy Commission later concluded that the "seriousness of the manganese supply started a concerted effort to examine all possible sources for manganese" and that United States aid in the form of transportation equipment assisted that effort.[75]

Public criticism of Soviet-American trade became louder as the Truman administration began to publicize its Marshall Plan and Interim Aid program in late 1947. The Department of Commerce files bulged with letters of protest, and 70 percent of the respondents in one poll stated that the United States should halt all shipments of oil, machinery, and industrial products to Russia.[76] One irate person made the absurd charge that the Caterpillar Tractor Company was shipping to the Soviet Union caterpillar bodies "with gunmounts on them" which would some day be converted into tanks.[77] In November, Congressman John Davis Lodge of Connecticut asked whether the "time has come to use the economic pistol, so to speak, in connection with Russia and her satellites with regard to export control licenses"; Joseph Bryson, a representative from South Carolina, compared shipments of "war materials" to Russia with those to Japan before 1941.[78] Analogies with World War II became very popular during the Cold War. Both Congressman

[73] William C. Foster to Jerome Lewine, Dec. 8, 1947, Box 749, *ibid.*

[74] U.S., Congress, Senate, Committee on Foreign Relations, *European Recovery Program: Basic Documents and Background Information,* 80th Cong., 1st sess. (Washington, D.C., 1947), pp. 181-82. Under the new export policy established in March of 1948, restrictions on trade with Spain were apparently relaxed. Some leaders began in 1947 to call for the inclusion of Spain in Washington's plan for a united Europe. In March of 1950 Franco secured a $62.5 million loan from the United States, although Truman found Spain ideologically intolerable. In 1951, Truman recognized Franco Spain and sent an ambassador, and in 1953 Spain granted the United States military bases. Between 1945 and 1963, Spain received $865 million in nonmilitary aid and $521 million in military aid from the United States. See LaFeber, *America, Russia, and Cold War,* p. 126; Congressional Quarterly Service, *Evolution of Foreign Aid,* p. 7.

[75] Minutes, President's Materials Policy Commission, Mar. 29, 1951, Box 5, President's Materials Policy Commission Records, Truman Library (statement by John Croston).

[76] See the Gallup poll in *Iron Age,* CLX (Dec. 25, 1947), 119.

[77] David H. Harts to Congressman Leslie C. Arends, Oct. 13, 1947, Office of Secretary, GC 93126, Box 748, Commerce Records. The company replied that it had not shipped anything to Russia since early 1946 (an UNRRA shipment). Caterpillar Tractor to Department of Commerce, Box 749, *ibid.*

[78] U.S., Congress, House, *Emergency Foreign Aid* (Nov. 13, 1947), p. 121; *Congressional Record,* 80th Cong., 1st sess., XCIII (Nov. 20, 1947), 10678.

Taber and Harold Stassen, for example, charged Truman with "appeasement" for allowing continued exports to Russia.[79] New York Congressman Robert Ross supported a resolution to stop exports of machinery to Russia and declared: "Unless we use every weapon at our command to win this cold war, we are likely to find some of these materials coming back to us in the form of sharpnel in the event we have a hot war."[80] On December 9 Congress blocked shipment of $20 million worth of equipment (saw mills, diesel engines, steel, and pipe) purchased by Russia from the War Assets Administration.[81] In late 1947, Harriman stated the administration position: "I do not believe in making loans or grants to the USSR and her satellites, nor do I believe in sending them supplies that will be of direct military assistance."[82]

There were still a few voices spelling out the advantages of trade with Russia. Ropes continued to write and speak, and Henry Wallace continued to argue that importing Russian raw materials would help the American economy.[83] The executive director of the Institute of Foreign Trade, J. Anthony Marcus, predicted that the Russian market would consume at least $10 to $15 billion of United States products in the next ten years. How would the Soviets pay? One-third, he said, would come in commodities, such as timber resources; another third in gold, platinum, and other precious metals, the mining of which would be easily increased through improved technology; and the remaining third would be financed by a long-term credit. He advocated the influx of American technical know-how to the Soviet Union and inspection trips by Russian officials to the United States. Improved trade would not only enhance the American economy, he believed, but would also reduce Russian fears and ignorance of the United States.[84]

For a short time the Soviet Union itself nurtured the hope that the United States would find trade irresistible. Its press wrote, as had some United States businessmen earlier, that capitalism and socialsm could collaborate in economic matters and that Russia was eager for an expansion of Soviet-American trade relations.[85] The magazine of the Communist Party, *Bolshevik*, repeated the common argument that the United States was heading for a postwar depression which only the extension of loans abroad and increased foreign trade could avert. Russia, it stated, would be willing to participate in the

[79] *New York Times,* Nov. 24 and 26, 1947. For a discussion of analogies with World War II and the reappearance of phrases like "appeasement" and "Munich," see Adler and Paterson, "Red Fascism."

[80] *Congressional Record,* 80th Cong., 1st sess., XCIII (Dec. 18, 1947), 11635. For other congressional opinion, see *ibid.,* Nov. 24 and 25, Dec. 2, 4, 8, 10 and 11, pp. 10767, 10853, 10879, 10997, 11068, 11183, A4343, A4349, A4350, A4460, A4689, A4672.

[81] Margold, *Let's Do Business,* p. 137; *New York Times,* Dec. 10, 1947.

[82] Draft, Harriman to Neil Morgan, Dec. 15, 1947, Office of Secretary, GC 93126, Box 749, Commerce Records.

[83] Ropes, in n. 3 above; Wallace, in *New York Times,* June 17, 1947.

[84] *Ibid.,* Feb. 5, Mar. 15, and July 30, 1947.

[85] *Ibid.,* May 14, 1947.

growth of that trade.[86] Later in 1947, however, irritation over United States commercial restrictions became evident. Moscow blamed Washington for the failure of Anglo-Russian trade negotiations, insisting that "dollar diplomacy" had dictated British foreign policy.[87] In the fall of 1947, AMTORG applied counter-pressure: it announced that henceforth all contracts would contain a provision that unless Washington had granted export licenses by the scheduled time of shipment, AMTORG reserved the right to cancel the contract. This new procedure alarmed manufacturers who produced items to unique Russian specifications. At this point, many leaders contended that *all* United States exports should be placed under licensing control to end the existing government practice of placing items under control without adequate notice.[88]

Trade statistics for 1947 demonstrated the adverse effect of export controls, official and public opinion, Soviet irritation, and the reluctance of companies to continue taking and servicing Soviet orders. Exports to Russia amounted to $149,069,000, down by $209,000,000 from 1946. Imports from Russia totaled $77,102,000, as compared with the 1946 figure of $100,486,000. The Soviet Union accounted for only 1 percent of total United States exports in 1947.[89]

EXPORT CONTROLS, THE COLLAPSE OF TRADE, AND THE COLD WAR

The Department of Commerce announced in mid-January, 1948, that as of March 15 all United States exports to Europe would be subject to export controls and that licenses would be required. Up to that point, export controls had existed mostly for foodstuffs, fuels, and metals.[90] "Even though a commodity is not in short supply," the Department explained, "export control according to end use and destination remains an exceedingly effective method of implementing United States foreign policy."[91] The new licensing process was designed to channel goods to the Marshall Plan countries, to reduce trade with Communist nations, and to halt the flow of any potential military products to the Soviet Union.

Harriman was pleased that businessmen would now have lucid directives from the government on questions of Soviet trade and dismissed the objection of some critics that the control system violated the liberal trade

[86] *Ibid.*, May 25, 1947.
[87] *Ibid.*, Aug. 16, 1947.
[88] *Ibid.*, Sept. 11 and Nov. 2, 1947.
[89] Commerce, *Foreign Trade of the United States, 1936-49*, pp. 42, 46.
[90] U.S., Department of Commerce, *Second Quarterly Report under the Second Decontrol Act of 1947* (Washington, D.C., 1948), pp. 12-13.
[91] U.S., Department of Commerce, *Thirty-Sixth Annual Report of the Secretary of Commerce* (Washington, D.C., 1948), p. 178.

principles established by the Truman administration, stating that such principles were no longer applicable at a time when such a large part of the rest of the world traded on a controlled basis.[92] But the State Department, which had the unhappy task of trying to reconcile liberal trade pronouncements with restrictionst practices, tried to limit the controls to military items and was "more liberal" than either the Commerce or Defense departments in allowing shipments to Communist nations.[93] The State Department's "liberalism" annoyed the new secretary of commerce, Charles Sawyer, and he later frankly charged that the State Department tended to "favor the interests of other countries; the Defense Department usually supported the Commerce Department in an effort to promote and protect the interests of the United States."[94] In fact, it was the Department of Commerce Office of International Trade which was given authority to approve or deny export license applications, and all exports to eastern Europe and the Soviet Union had to be cleared by military agencies.[95]

The export controls reduced trade quite effectively. Total exports to Russia in 1948 amounted to only $28,000,000. In 1949, the figure was $6,617,000. Exports in the fourth quarter of 1949 amounted to only $200,000, compared to the quarterly average of $88,000,000 in 1946 and $37,000,000 in 1947. Only $700,000 in American goods were shipped to Russia in 1950, and by 1953 the figure was negligible.[96] Some companies no longer sought trade with Russia, but those who did found that between March, 1948, and March, 1950, the Truman administration denied applications for shipments to Russia amounting to $38,000,000, and approved only $13,900,000.[97] Both Westinghouse and General Electric, for example, were denied the opportunity to ship equipment to the Soviet Union, because "this material would not be in the national interest. . . ."[98]

These trade figures raise an important question: why the United States did not place a total embargo on trade with Russia, and thus exert maximum economic pressure. Under Secretary of Commerce William C. Foster articulated the Truman administration's answer in 1947 when he admitted that the United States was partially dependent upon certain Russian imports.[99] He explained that one-third of all manganese ore (vital to steel production),

92 Harriman to Robert Lowe (National Foreign Trade Council), Feb. 20, 1948, Harriman Papers; Millis, *Forrestal Diaries,* p. 359 (Jan. 16, 1948, cabinet meeting).

93 Willard Thorp, former assistant secretary of state, to author, May 22, 1967.

94 Charles Sawyer, *Concerns of a Conservative Democrat* (Carbondale, Ill., 1968), pp. 184-85.

95 John R. Steelman to Max Sorenson, Apr. 3, 1948, OF 275A, Truman Papers.

96 Commerce, *Foreign Trade of the United States, 1936-49,* p. 42; Nicolas Spulber, *The Economics of Communist Eastern Europe* (New York, 1957), p. 464; U.S., Department of Commerce, *Export Control and Allocation Powers,* 11th Quarterly Report (Washington, D.C., 1950), p. 2.

97 Commerce, *Export Control and Allocation Powers,* p. 24.

98 Loring K. Macy to J. C. Moffatt, Oct. 13, 1949, Office of Secretary, GC 93126, Box 753, Commerce Records; T. C. Blaisdell to W. R. Herod, Oct. 7, 1949, *ibid.*

99 Foster to John F. Schwieters, Dec. 29, 1947, Box 749, *ibid.*

one-half of all chromium ore, and more than half of all platinum imported in 1947 came from the Soviet Union.[100] Congressman George Sadowski of Michigan added nickel to the list and stated: "Now if Joe Stalin wanted to be mean to us he would say: 'Let us cut off trade with the United States and not give them any more ore.' We would be in a fine fix."[101] Indeed, in March, 1948, the United States had only a six-month supply of manganese ore in stock.[102] The Truman administration's stockpiling program emphasized manganese and chrome, but the U.S. Steel Corporation thought the program would fall short, and *Iron Age* also asked the disturbing question: "The United States hasn't been too cooperative with Russia. We shut off machine tool and other strategic material shipments. So far she hasn't retaliated. But she could and the big question is, when?"[103]

In December, 1948, in the midst of the Berlin blockade, the Soviet Union finally responded; curbs on valuable shipments of raw materials to the United States were announced. The Russians believed that this pressure, especially the reduction in manganese exports, would threaten the United States economy and loosen restrictions on exports of machinery to Russia (although the announced explanation was that the manganese was needed domestically).[104] Whereas $2.7 million in manganese and chrome had been imported from Russia in December of 1948, the figure for January slumped to $1.2 million. In March imports amounted to only $600,000, and in all of 1950 the United States acquired only 3 percent of its manganese from Russia. By April, 1950, Russian manganese imports had dropped from first to fifth place, and by 1954 no Russian ore was shipped to the United States.[105] In July of 1949 one government official explained that increased cargoes of manganese from India, South Africa, Cuba, Brazil, Mexico, and the Gold Coast "have altered the general situation to a degree where we no longer need to depend on the Russians."[106]

[100] *Iron Age,* CLX (Dec. 11, 1947), 118. For appreciation of the possible retaliatory effects (reduction of Russian manganese and chromium exports) of an American embargo, see *New York Times,* Nov. 28, 1947 (James Reston), Dec. 5 (Robert A. Lovett), Dec. 7 (Foster), Dec. 11 (Hanson W. Baldwin), Dec. 22 (Senator Millard E. Tydings of Maryland), Mar. 24, 1948 (George Bell of Office of International Trade), Mar. 26 and 27 (Harriman).

[101] *Congressional Record,* 80th Cong., 1st sess., XCIII (Dec. 4, 1947), 11056.

[102] *Steel,* CXXII (Mar. 29, 1948), 38.

[103] *Iron Age,* CLXII (Dec. 16, 1948), 133. For Soviet irritation with export controls, see *DSB,* XVIII (May 23, 1948), 682. For American concern about manganese sources and supplies, see *Steel,* CXXIII (Oct. 11, 1948), 75; CXXII (Mar. 29, 1948), 38; CXXII (Apr. 5, 1948), 152; Julius Krug and Thomas J. Hargraves, telephone conversation, Munitions Board, Apr. 28, 1948, Box 49, Krug Papers.

[104] L. M. Herman, "Russian Manganese and the American Market," *American Slavic and East European Review,* X (1951), 272-81; *Business Week,* Jan. 15, 1949, p. 21; *Steel,* CXXIV (Jan. 31, 1949), 32.

[105] *Steel,* CXXIV (Apr. 4, 1949), 65; CXXIV (May 23, 1949), 67; CXXVI (Apr. 24, 1950), 53; Senate, *Accessibility of Strategic and Critical Materials,* p. 14; Herman, "Russian Manganese," p. 272.

[106] The Phillipines replaced Russia as the largest supplier of chrome to the United States. Quotation from *Steel,* CXXV (July 4, 1949), 42.

In the early years of the Cold War, both Russia and the United States attempted to use trade as a diplomatic weapon. Russia used trade to bind the eastern European states more closely to it and to punish enemies (Yugoslavia in 1948 and the United States in 1949). The United States applied economic pressure to eastern Europe and Russia in both loan and trade questions. Washington's sanctions did not work: the Soviet Union recovered economically, in part by exploiting its eastern European neighbors and in part by de-emphasizing consumer goods at home. Compelled to take its foreign business elsewhere, it tightened its control over the economies of eastern Europe, also cut off from United States loans and trade. As Gunnar Myrdal has noted, the export controls "greatly helped Stalin, and his cadre of politicians throughout the bloc to consolidate his empire."[107] They encouraged Russia to be more self-sufficient, and helped Russian economic planners, who knew exactly what to expect in the way of trade with the United States. Finally, Russian military preparedness and strength were not seriously handicapped by these restrictions.[108] Washington could not have predicted all of these failures, locked as it was in a vigorous struggle with Moscow for international influence and determined to use every means, including trade, to win. Yet the severence of trade both reflected and excerbated the embittered confrontation.

[107] Gunnar Myrdal, *Challenge to Affluence* (New York, ca. 1962), p. 114. See also Vladimir Katkoff, *Soviet Economy, 1940-1965* (Baltimore, 1961), p. 435; Spulber, *Economics of Communist Eastern Europe*, p. 453.

[108] U.S., Commission on Foreign Economic Policy, *Staff Papers* (Washington, D.C., 1954), p. 448; Myrdal, *Challenge*, pp. 114-15.

CHAPTER 4

THE DILEMMA OF POWER:
UNITED STATES RELIEF POLICY AND UNRRA

The postwar international relief program, like East-West trade, was both agent and victim of the Soviet-American confrontation. The millions of hungry, bewildered, and displaced people—Communist and non-Communist—left behind by World War II looked to the United States for relief. Their governments were hesitant to believe, however, that the United States, despite its reputation for humanitarianism, would enthusiastically endorse and finance a massive postwar relief program without demanding returns on its expenditure. The immediate returns were not difficult for United States leaders to perceive because they viewed the question through the lens of the peace and prosperity notion. "We cannot ignore great masses of starving people," an eminent publisher told the House Foreign Affairs Committee, "without our desired peace being threatened."[1] A State Department officer declared that the United States would undertake a relief program to establish "a more stable world order."[2] Not only would stability result from such a venture, but also, as the peace and prosperity theme indicated, the economy would benefit. Recipients of relief expenditures would buy American products, thereby boosting the postwar economy, easing reconversion, and sustaining jobs.[3] As one critical journalist put it, in asking for compassion for Europe's suffering: "If humanity and moral obligation will not move us, let us remember that devastated countries make poor markets, that poverty is contagious in the modern economy, and that pestilence too can spread."[4]

The significant question for a postwar relief program was whether it would be United States-directed and dominated or administered through an international organization. Further, the question of who would control the distribution of food and medicine was crucial. In 1943, when the United

[1] Eugene Meyer (*Washington Post*), in U.S., Congress, House, Committee on Foreign Affairs, *Further Participation in Work of UNRRA* (Hearings), 79th Cong., 1st sess. (Nov. 19, 1945), p. 118.
[2] Francis B. Sayre, in *DSB*, IX (Oct. 23, 1943), 275.
[3] See, for example, *ibid.*, p. 276; "UNRRA—Or Nothing," *New Republic*, CXIII (Oct. 22, 1945), 517-18; "Dead Customers Cannot Help World Recovery," *Christian Century*, LXII (Sept. 26, 1945), 1085.
[4] I. F. Stone, "If They Ask for Bread," *Nation*, CLX (Apr. 7, 1945), 379.

States helped organize the United Nations Relief and Rehabilitation Administration, it publicly applauded this program run by an international
organization with no political, racial, or national tests for potential recipients.
But as Washington became increasingly aware of its economic power and of
the value of food as a diplomatic tool and as tensions between Russia and the
United States in Europe increased, it abandoned UNRRA and adopted a
unilateral program of political relief. The nationalism of all countries
receiving UNRRA goods, the suspicions and encumbrances of the Congress,
the unstable conditions in recipient countries, and the Truman administration's conviction that favorable results could best be ensured through direct
control of relief combined to undermine and destroy UNRRA. As happened
repeatedly in these years, diplomatic lines were rigidly drawn and alternative
solutions were rejected. Dean Acheson expressed this attitude clearly when he
told a Senate committee in 1947 that the United States "took a very strong
position that the future relief, our future relief, should be granted in
accordance with our judgment and supervised with American personnel."[5]

The idea for an international relief program for areas liberated from
Hitler's grasp was not original with any one person or nation. The governments
of Great Britain, the United States, and Russia individually prepared plans for
an international organization in 1942 and, with China, entered into several
discussions before emerging with a draft proposal in 1943. Forty-four nations
signed the result—the UNRRA Agreement—on November 9, 1943, at the
White House. The agency and its members pledged themselves to "plan,
coordinate, administer or arrange for the administration of measures for the
relief of victims of war in any area under the control of any of the United
Nations through the provision of food, fuel, clothing, shelter and other basic
necessities, medical and other essential services."[6]

The Department of State insisted during the various stages of negotiations
that the head of the new program be an American. The United States also
joined Britain, Russia, and China in concentrating authority in a Central
Committee of the four nations (later enlarged), which had wide powers when
the general Council was not in session. All members had one vote in the
Council, and decisions were made by a simple majority vote, although United
States economic power wielded an influence on most votes. As expected,
Herbert H. Lehman, governor of New York from 1932 to 1942, was named
UNRRA director-general. Lehman held this post until March, 1946, when he
was succeeded by a more conspicuous New Yorker, Fiorello La Guardia,
three-term mayor of New York City.

UNRRA was slow in getting underway because of dislocations in transportation, civil wars (as in Greece and China), procurement and distribution

[5] Senate, *Assistance to Greece and Turkey* (Mar. 24, 1947), p. 37.
[6] Quoted in George Woodbridge et al., *The History of the United Nations Relief and
Rehabilitation Administration*, 3 vols. (New York, 1950), I, 4. For the formation of
UNRRA see *ibid.*, I, 3-32; Milton O. Gustafson, "Congress and Foreign Aid: UNRRA,
The First Phase, 1943-1947" (Ph.D. dissertation, University of Nebraska, 1966), ch. 1.

snarls, and difficulties in recruiting personnel, but before its demise in mid-1947 it had dispensed nine million tons of food, built hundreds of hospitals, administered medicine to prevent threatened epidemics of diphtheria, typhoid, cholera, tuberculosis, and venereal disease, revived transportation systems and industries, and cared for over one million displaced persons. Expenditures amounted to about $4 billion ($3 billion in commodities), and the United States provided about $2.7 billion, or roughly three-quarters of the total.[7] The agency alleviated considerable individual suffering and rehabilitated crippled regions of Europe and the Far East.[8]

China was the largest recipient of UNRRA supplies ($518 million) and, with Italy ($418 million), Greece ($347 million), and Austria ($135 million), absorbed about half of UNRRA assistance. Yet it was the rest of the money which received the most attention from the media, the Congress, and the White House because it went to people living in eastern Europe. Western European governments had decided to negotiate directly with supplying nations like the United States, to use their own foreign exchange, and to avoid international machinery like UNRRA. UNRRA programs in Poland ($478 million), Yugoslavia ($416 million), Czechoslovakia ($261 million), and the Soviet republics of the Ukraine ($188 million) and Byelorussia ($61 million) came under close scrutiny.[9] Comments like Francis Sayre's in 1943 that the "future of American interests and of humanity" were at stake in UNRRA yielded, soon after the war ended, to widespread charges that the taxpayers' money was being used to shore up Communist regimes via UNRRA, and that the United States was helpless to prevent this unless it killed UNRRA altogether.[10]

THE UNPOPULARITY OF UNRRA IN THE UNITED STATES

Popular suspicion of UNRRA arose soon after its founding. Many congressmen were annoyed because they had not been included in the initial

[7] Contributions were voluntary and based on 1 percent of the member nation's national income. Congress authorized the first assessment of $1.350 billion on March 28, 1944, and a second assessment of the same amount on December 18, 1945. There were five appropriations, some reluctantly and belatedly granted after vigorous debate: June 30, 1944 ($800 million); December 14, 1945 ($550 million); December 28, 1945 ($750 million); May 27, 1946 ($135 million); and July 23, 1946 ($465 million). Woodbridge, *UNRRA*, I, 113.

[8] *Ibid.*, I, 234, 409, 433, 434-42; II, 518; III, 500. See also Wilbur A. Sawyer, "Achievements of UNRRA as an International Health Organization," *American Journal of Public Health*, XXXVII (January, 1947), 41-58; Virginia Rishel, "War on Postwar Pestilence," *Hygeia*, XXV (September, 1947), 680-81.

[9] For complete statistics, including those for small UNRRA programs in Albania, the Dodecanese Islands, Ethiopia, Finland, Korea, the Philippines, and San Marino, see Woodbridge, *UNRRA*, III, 428.

[10] Francis Sayre to Senator Charles McNary, Nov. 3, 1943, Box 12, Francis Sayre Papers, Library of Congress.

negotiations and because membership in UNRRA came by Roosevelt's executive order rather than by treaty. Among them was Senator Arthur H. Vandenberg, always alert to any attempt by the State Department to bypass Congress. When Secretary of State Cordell Hull replied unconvincingly to his protest about improper procedure, Vandenberg, according to Acheson, was moved to "rotund hyperbole" and a "hot flame" of indignation. Congressional complaints about prerogative stung the State Department, and Acheson later wrote, "I can only plead that it no more occurred to me that Congress would feel left out of organizing a relief organization than in not being included in a Washington Community Chest drive."[11]

There were other reasons for "unsettled" congressional relations with UNRRA, however.[12] Some congressmen believed that since UNRRA received so much United States assistance it should hire their constituents. Congressman Sol Bloom of New York became less enthusiastic about UNRRA as the agency rejected the people he sent to be hired. Senator Lister Hill of Alabama recommended many of his constituents, most of whom UNRRA found unqualified. To accommodate Hill's dissatisfaction and deflect attacks, UNRRA took the extraordinary step of setting up special candidate interviews in Birmingham.[13] One of the more dramatic and ridiculous complaints against UNRRA came in 1944 from Congressman Fred A. Hartley of New Jersey, who waved a woman's dress around during a House speech and charged that UNRRA intended to transport six million expensive seersucker dresses to Europe as relief. Why not plain cloth, he asked. The reply from the Foreign Economic Administration was that the dresses numbered 850,000; they were surplus and factory rejects; the material was not seersucker but a substitute; they had been ordered by the FEA for the War Department to be used as relief in military zones; and recipients would pay for the clothing—UNRRA was not even involved.[14] Government agencies and UNRRA were forced to devote valuable time and expense to reply to such misinformed attacks and hearsay. Often the agency became a convenient target for frustrated special-interest groups. For example, in October, 1944, the Polish-American Congress, a strongly anti-Soviet organization, berated UNRRA's work in Poland and called for Polish relief "under the American flag and under American supervision, which, in the present circumstances, can alone prevent American gifts becoming instruments of expansionist political pressure."[15]

Increased antagonism beset UNRRA in 1945. The Red Cross continued to ask Congress for special funds and did not coordinate its activities well with UNRRA, raising some question as to why the Red Cross could not do the

[11] Acheson, *Present at the Creation*, pp. 71-72.
[12] Gustafson, "Congress and Foreign Aid," p. 142.
[13] *Ibid.*, pp. 148-49, 162-63.
[14] *Ibid.*, p. 142.
[15] Quoted in Arthur Bliss Lane, *I Saw Poland Betrayed* (Indianapolis, Ind., 1948), pp. 59-60.

whole job.[16] Henry L. Stimson was alarmed that UNRRA trucks might be used by Tito's forces in Yugoslavia and that some Russians had received UNRRA appointments in the Balkans.[17] *Life* magazine called for the "junking" of UNRRA because it was not feeding western Europe, and *Fortune* added that UNRRA "leaves even the paupers unimpressed."[18] Diplomats in the field were also nurturing doubts about UNRRA. From Moscow, Harriman arued that UNRRA aid to White Russia and the Ukraine should be delayed until Russia "cooperated in reestablishing normal interchange of goods in Europe . . . ," and said he feared that "UNRRA aid may well tend to permit the Soviet authorities to maintain a larger army than they otherwise would by assisting to fill the gap which the Russian people appear to be demanding for a more comfortable existence"—in short, UNRRA might relieve "the discontent of the Russian people over their not obtaining more consumer goods."[19] Ambassador Laurence A. Steinhardt complained from Prague that the Czechs were unaware that most UNRRA goods came from the United States; in fact, they believed that Russia had donated them. Furthermore, "by having put UNRRA deliveries in the hands of the local committees, UNRRA . . . gave the Communists a potent political weapon."[20] There were difficult relations between UNRRA and Poland in 1945 because the UNRRA mission there was headed by a Russian, and UNRRA dealt with the Lublin Poles rather than with the exiled group in London.[21] Diplomats in Greece and Yugoslavia also reported that political partisans were abusing UNRRA aid. Ambassador Lincoln MacVeagh reported that Britain controlled UNRRA in Greece as "frank spheres-of-influence politics, in the same manner as recent British action in influencing the making and breaking of Greek Governments."[22] Unconfirmed rumors from Belgrade in mid-1945 suggested that the Communist Party was manipulating food and medical supplies for political advantage.[23]

The preponderance of such negative reports in Washington in 1945 cooled official enthusiasm for UNRRA. Ambassador to Belgium Charles Sawyer recalled that he told President Truman in July, 1945, that the United States had to stop "playing Santa Claus to Europe," and that the president agreed that UNRRA was a wasted effort.[24] Oscar Cox of the FEA noted on May 29

[16] Gustafson, "Congress and Foreign Aid," pp. 157-58.

[17] *Ibid.*, p. 159.

[18] "The Trouble with UNRRA Is So Basic That We Had Best Wind It Up and Start Over," *Life*, XIX (Nov. 5, 1945), 48; "Europe: From Freedom to Want," *Fortune*, XXXI (May, 1945), 261.

[19] *Foreign Relations, 1945*, II, 1023 (Aug. 29, 1945).

[20] Quotation from Steinhardt to Francis Williamson, Oct. 20, 1945, Box 83, Steinhardt Papers; also James F. Byrnes to Peter Alexejev, chief of mission, Czechoslovakia, Oct. 15, 1945, Box 60,000, UNRRA Records, United Nations Library, New York City; *Foreign Relations, 1945*, II, 1028-29.

[21] *Foreign Relations, 1945*, II, 958, 966, 968, 973, 975-78, 998.

[22] *Ibid.*, p. 227 (June 18, 1945).

[23] *Ibid.*, pp. 999-1000.

[24] Sawyer, *Concerns*, p. 156.

of the same year that Truman was leaning toward a United States relief effort and away from UNRRA.[25] Congressional criticisms mounted through 1945: UNRRA cost too much and showed little results; it backed Communist regimes; it was not supervised by Americans; it was overstaffed, overpaid, inefficient, and too slow; and it drained items in short supply from the United States.[26] Congressman Alvin E. O'Konski of Wisconsin commented that he was "more concerned about freedom than ... about food," and, demonstrating a short memory for World War II, asked where the call for UNRRA assistance came from: "Does it come from the people who have given their all for freedom? Not at all. This call for more clothing, more food, and more medicine comes from the chiselers and the gangsters and the racketeers that have forced a government against the will of those people."[27] The irrepressible Congressman Walter Judd of Minnesota picked up a rumor that in China UNRRA was deliberately bypassing missionaries in hiring personnel and publicly chastised the organization before he could be assured that no such discrimination existed.[28]

Congressional visits to UNRRA missions abroad did little to dissipate these hostile impressions. About a hundred representatives traveled to Europe in the summer of 1945 to see the destruction wrought by the war. Their contacts with UNRRA, as one historian has written, constituted a "superficial inspection."[29] Predisposed to criticize an international organization which lay outside direct United States control, they came home with undocumented charges and little factual knowledge of UNRRA's work. Indeed, one Russian in the international organization was enough to frighten the congressman away. A group from the House Foreign Affairs Committee returned from a short excursion to the Warsaw mission and asked for the resignation of Mikhail Menshikov, the chief of the mission and a Russian, because, they charged, he was distributing supplies in such a way as to back the provisional Communist government.[30] When Menshikov was replaced by Charles M. Drury, a Canadian military officer, Ambassador Arthur Bliss Lane accused Drury of "Communist tendencies" and suggested a security check because, like Menshikov, "the substantiating evidence of the foregoing is that he has permitted UNRRA supplies to be used advantageously for the support of persons politically friendly to the present Polish Provisional Government."[31]

25 Oscar Cox Diary, May 29, 1945, Cox Papers.

26 See, for example, U.S., Congress, House, Committee on Appropriations, *United Nations Relief and Rehabilitation Administration, 1946* (Hearings), 79th Cong., 1st sess. (October, 1945), pp. 36-37, 94, 194-97; *New York Times*, Oct. 3, 1945; House, *Further Participation*, pp. 57, 210-11; Gustafson, "Congress and Foreign Aid," pp. 186-231.

27 Quoted in "The Reactionaries Fight Relief," *New Republic*, CXIII (Nov. 12, 1945), 620.

28 Gustafson, "Congress and Foreign Aid," p. 160.

29 *Ibid.*, p. 163.

30 *Ibid.*, p. 166. Lehman charged that Menshikov, who became deputy director-general, sent information to the Russian embassy. Allan Nevins, *Herbert H. Lehman and His Era* (New York, 1963), pp. 277-78.

31 Lane to Frederick B. Lyons, Sept. 16, 1946, Arthur Bliss Lane Papers, Yale University Library.

The confusion and the difficulty of confirming or squashing such rumors is demonstrated by Lane's later praise for Drury's UNRRA work in Poland.[32]

Another delegation, headed by Representative Victor E. Wickersham of Oklahoma, arrived on short notice in Prague in the evening of August 25, 1945. Members of the UNRRA mission in Czechoslovakia were appalled at the desultory manner in which the group gathered information. On the evening of August 28, three of the congressmen met with UNRRA officials in a hastily called meeting which lasted less than an hour, much of which was devoted to demands by Wickersham that the United States, as the largest contributor to the agency, should exercise more control. UNRRA officials reported that "most of the questions asked showed a fundamental lack of knowledge as to UNRRA, its basic principles, its constitution, its policies, and even its membership."[33] The delegation left the next morning, and the UNRRA staff was pessimistic and chagrined after this brief encounter with their congressional critics: "We attempted to correct misapprehensions but succeeded only to a limited extent. If Committee's subsequent opposition to UNRRA is based on such casual lopsided and opinionated attitude as evidenced here, without inviting factual information from Mission experts, its findings cannot be of much value to Congress."[34] Indeed, there was no reason for optimism. Congressman Everett Dirksen of Illinois reflected widespread public opinion when he announced on his return from Europe in July of 1945 that "UNRRA has developed an odor and the time is at hand to carefully audit its personnel, its accounts and its activities."[35] Despite such hostility, however, Congress appropriated large contributions to UNRRA in December, 1945.

Such attacks became more vociferous and damaging in 1946, yet were repeatedly based on misinformation. Charges and rumors circulated that UNRRA was a haven for Soviet spies and inept administrators, that relief supplies to Communist countries allowed Russia to divert funds to other purposes, perhaps military, and that Washington should emphasize European reconstruction rather than relief.[36] *Life* suggested in late 1946 that UNRRA officials in Poland represented "a grim travesty of the charitable impulse," and the chairman of the Federal Reserve Board, Marriner Eccles, stated flatly

[32] Lane, *I Saw Poland Betrayed*, p. 214.

[33] Mission officers Glassey, Shute, and Hitchcock to P. I. Alexejev, Aug. 29, 1945, Box 60,009, UNRRA Records.

[34] Prague mission to UNRRA London, Sept. 6, 1945, *ibid.* See also Gustafson, "Congress and Foreign Aid," pp. 167-68, for a critical congressional visit to the mission in Greece.

[35] *New York Times*, July 1, 1945.

[36] See, for example, "Our Assistance to Soviet Bloc: Billion for Relief and Loans," *U.S. News*, XXI (Sept. 6, 1946), 15-16; *New York Times*, Aug. 14 and 22, Nov. 17, 1946; *Journal of Commerce*, July 26, 1946; *Chicago Daily Tribune*, May 8, 1946 (Congressman Bartel J. Jonkman of Michigan); *Fortune*, XXXIII (May, 1946), 95; *Nation's Business*, XXXIV (June, 1946), 98; "Get a Horse: UNRRA's End Still Leaves Americans Faced with the Big Job of World Rehabilitation," *Life*, XXI (Dec. 30, 1946), 18; John B. Martin, "Middletown Revisited: Snapshots of Muncie at Peace," *Harper's*, CXCIII (August, 1946), 111; Nevins, *Lehman*, pp. 276, 278, 432n.

that "we ought to stop sending food to countries in the Soviet zone."[37] On the other side of the political spectrum, a *Nation* writer charged that a "small, reactionary clique of would-be rulers" around Chiang Kai-shek were using UNRRA for their political benefit and that Washington was ignoring their corruption and continuing to support Chiang.[38]

Two hot issues detrimental to UNRRA were aid to Yugoslavia and Dirksen's "free press" amendment. In mid-April, 1946, Secretary of War Robert P. Patterson informed Secretary Byrnes that the War Department suspected UNRRA trucks and trailers of having an "actual or potential military value in Yugoslavia." He also noted that UNRRA delivery of C-47 aircraft would result "in our assisting the Yugoslav armed forces, at least to the extent of releasing to them resources that would otherwise be required to support their national economy." Concerned that Tito might employ UNRRA supplies against American troops stationed in the disputed territory of Venezia Giulia (Trieste), Patterson recommended that the State Department find ways to halt the shipment of potential military items to Yugoslavia.[39] In the next few weeks Yugoslav-United States relations deteriorated: Tito severely curtailed the United States' use of Yugoslav air routes and air fields, and Byrnes considered withdrawing representation at the ambassadorial rank. Trieste, claimed by both Italy and Yugoslavia, continued as a disruptive issue; United States and British troops were poised for a possible military clash there. General Draja Mihailovich's trial and execution for treason and the forcing down by Yugoslav aircraft of a United States plane which had violated Yugoslav air rights further aggravated matters.[40] In August Yugoslavia shot down two United States planes which had strayed into its territory, apparently because of bad weather. The loss of lives resulting from this incident prompted vigorous protests.[41] Byrnes instructed the State Department on August 28 "to do everything that we properly can to stop shipments of supplies of any sort by UNRRA for Yugoslavia. I think you realize the implications of an organization to which the United States contributes 73% continuing to supply a government guilty of such outrageous and unfriendly conduct as Yugoslavia."[42]

Herbert Hoover and an irritated public mounted a campaign against UNRRA's Yugoslav operation. The International Longshoremen's Association (AFL) refused for three weeks to handle UNRRA goods to Tito, and the E. I. Du Pont Company announced it would not supply goods to UNRRA destined

---

[37] "Poland Abuses UNRRA," *Life*, XXI (Dec. 16, 1946), 19; Eccles, in *San Francisco Chronicle*, Dec. 4, 1946.

[38] Ilona Ralf Sues, "The UNRRA Scandal in China," *Nation*, CLXIII (July 20, 1946), 70-71.

[39] *Foreign Relations, 1946*, VI, 887-88 (Apr. 17, 1946).

[40] *Ibid.*, pp. 893-925.

[41] *Ibid.*, pp. 925-29.

[42] *Ibid.*, p. 930.

for Yugoslavia.[43] But the State Department was bewildered and cautious: it did not want to intrude blatantly in the affairs of the agency and was reluctant to take the drastic step of imposing economic sanctions against Yugoslavia. Both Patterson and Forrestal, however, insisted that Washington protest to UNRRA and suspend the United States share of UNRRA aid to Yugoslavia. Byrnes agreed but, noting that Belgrade had met American demands and that there was no way to curb UNRRA shipments to Yugoslavia "without having our good faith questioned," he reluctantly ruled out any interruption of the organization's activities there.[44]

Earlier congressional and diplomatic complaints that Tito was corrupting UNRRA by using its donations for political purposes were hardly quieted by Director-General La Guardia's report in October, 1946, that an investigating commission headed by Sir Humphrey Gale, a British general and former assistant to General Eisenhower, had found no violations of UNRRA in Yugoslavia.[45] Indeed, Will Clayton warned La Guardia in a telephone conversation that the report should be looked at suspiciously because it "constitutes a substantial whitewash of the Yugoslavian Government and its cooperation with UNRRA."[46] These incidents further poisoned UNRRA's standing in the United States and contributed to the decision to abandon it.

The "free press" amendment was another troublesome issue, and here too the State Department felt it necessary to avoid overt manipulation. Again it attempted to maintain a semblance of support for an international organization and to withstand congressional attacks until the time when the Truman administration could extricate itself from UNRRA and adopt a program of unilateral aid. As Byrnes told the State Department, nothing should be done which might call into question the "good faith" of the United States in its relations with an international body, but the "free press" issue made it almost impossible for the State Department to weather the critical storm.

In late 1945, Congressman Clarence Brown of Ohio and Congressman Dirksen offered an amendment to the UNRRA appropriation act which would halt relief shipments to nations which denied American newsmen the opportunity to report freely on UNRRA activities. The amendment grew out of the belief that reporters were unduly restricted in travel, were unable to report that the United States was the source of most UNRRA supplies, and

---

[43] *Ibid.*, p. 932; Lowell W. Rooks, acting director-general, to Fiorello La Guardia, Aug. 28, 1946, Box 2739, La Guardia Papers, Municipal Archives and Records Center, New York City; *New York Times*, Sept. 10, 1946; Gustafson, "Congress and Foreign Aid," pp. 269-72. See also Eric L. Pridonoff, "How UNRRA Bolstered Tito," *American Mercury*, LXIV (January, 1947), 13-19. Pridonoff was a former economic officer at the United States embassy in Belgrade.

[44] *Foreign Relations, 1946*, VI, 932-33, 946-47, 950-51.

[45] In October congressmen were upset that steel rails had been diverted from China to Yugoslavia by UNRRA. Gustafson, "Congress and Foreign Aid," pp. 258, 269-76; *Foreign Relations, 1946*, VI, 945.

[46] *Foreign Relations, 1946*, VI, 967.

that recipient nations were deliberately withholding information on the key United States role or misrepresenting UNRRA aid as national in origin. The Brown-Dirksen amendment passed, but was striken by the Senate.[47]

When the last UNRRA appropriation bill came before Congress in mid-1946 Dirksen tried again. He particularly wanted shipments to the Ukraine and Byelorussia to be stopped, ostensibly because the press had been denied access there. Actually, he wanted to punish the Russians for their international transgressions; he hoped to use relief as a diplomatic weapon to say "that we expect Russia to cooperate."[48] Congressional leaders Christian Herter of Massachusetts, Karl E. Mundt of South Dakota, and Clare Boothe Luce of Connecticut, among many others, supported the resurrection of the Brown-Dirksen amendment. It passed Congress by 228 to 85 votes, with only one Republican vote recorded in opposition. The Senate modified the amendment by providing that the State Department was to determine whether reports on UNRRA had been censored and that Washington could halt relief only if a "reasonable number" of press representatives from the United States had been refused the opportunity to report freely on UNRRA activities.[49]

The passage of this amendment by both houses, even in its watered-down form, seemed a defeat for the Truman administration, which opposed it. The administration position was determined not only by its distaste for meddling openly in an international organization but also by evidence refuting Dirksen's charges: both Acheson and Clayton denied that reporters were restricted in the Soviet republics and said that individual recipients were aware that UNRRA goods largely originated in the United States. While admitting censorship in the Soviet Union, Clayton informed Senator Kenneth McKeller of Tennessee that no evidence existed that Russia had restricted information on the distribution of UNRRA supplies.[50] But Byrnes, although he opposed the amendment as an ultimatum which would probably have the opposite effect from what was intended, weakened his department's position when he wrote that he favored the "intrinsic merit of the suggestion" for greater press freedom.[51]

What the Truman administration could not ignore was the extensive

---

[47] The amendment grew out of several similar amendments. Dirksen's original amendment, for example, stated that the president would decide whether "satisfactory arrangements" for the press had been made before relief could start again. Brown's original was much tougher: no relief to countries with any kind of censorship or barriers to the American press. Gustafson, "Congress and Foreign Aid," pp. 207-10; Woodbridge, *UNRRA*, I, 116-17.

[48] Quoted in Gustafson, "Congress and Foreign Aid," p. 253.

[49] *Ibid.*, pp. 252-59.

[50] Clayton to McKeller, July 4, 1946, XXB, Richard Scandrett Papers, Cornell University Library; Gustafson, "Congress and Foreign Aid," pp. 252, 253; *New York Times*, July 4, 1946.

[51] Byrnes to Congressman Cavendish W. Cannon, *Foreign Relations, 1945*, II, 1035 (Oct. 31, 1945).

evidence that reporters, especially in the Ukraine and Byelorussia, did have unprecedented freedom of movement and reporting and that recipients recognized the source of UNRRA aid. Richard Scandrett, the chief of mission in Byelorussia and formerly a successful New York lawyer, informed UNRRA headquarters in July, 1946, that "irrespective of any censorship regulation I am completely convinced that UNRRA operations in Byelorussia are unrestricted and that intention of government is that such operations be reported as fully as foreign correspondents desire." Brooks Atkinson and Drew Middleton of the *New York Times* had been allowed substantial freedom in inspecting what they wished, including collective farms. It was true, of course, he continued, that reports had to be filtered through the Soviet censorship apparatus, but very few correspondents found their stories altered.[52] Truman said he was satisfied that there were no serious limits on reporting UNRRA activities in Poland and Czechoslovakia.[53] Even John Fischer, a former journalist and disaffected UNRRA official, admitted in his generally critical *Why They Behave Like Russians* (1946), "the Soviet government had agreed that we should have complete freedom to travel throughout the Ukraine, talk to people through our own interpreter, and observe without obstruction what happened to UNRRA goods. This agreement was kept to the letter."[54]

Lehman pointed out that the problem was not that recipients failed to appreciate the United States contribution but rather that they considered UNRRA an American agency because its goods carried the label "made in the U.S.A." In Poland UNRRA was called "UNRRA Amerikanski," and even Pope Pius made the same mistake.[55] Fischer believed that the "United States got more than its fair share of credit for UNRRA supplies," and in late 1945 the Prague mission countered rumors and criticisms like those of Ambassador Steinhardt that many Czechs considered UNRRA relief a Russian gift: "Mission has evidence through press cuttings, film releases as well as personal experience of individual members investigating distribution, that public is aware of origin of supplies and rather has tendency to consider UNRRA American organization. Mission finds average Czechoslovak citizen relatively well informed, readily recognizing American makes and UNRRA markings on supplies. On contrary, it is often necessary to explain that certain supplies

[52] Scandrett to La Guardia, July 5, 1946, XXB, Scandrett Papers; "Summary," 1946, XXA, *ibid.*; memorandum, July 4, 1946, *ibid.*

[53] Gustafson, "Congress and Foreign Aid," pp. 249-50.

[54] John Fischer, *Why They Behave Like Russians* (New York, 1946), pp. 24-25. *The Washington Post* commented on November 3, 1945, that "every country maintains some barriers to obtaining news. Newspapermen were excluded, for example, from the executive session of the House Appropriations Committee which acted on the UNRRA request for funds."

[55] House, *UNRRA, 1946* (Oct. 11, 1945), pp. 72-73; UNRRA mission in Poland to L. G. Holliday (British embassy, Warsaw), 1946, UNRRA Records.

also come from U.K., Canada, New Zealand, India, etc."[56] As the official UNRRA historian later put it, "the major contributing country, therefore, had little cause for concern that its generosity was not well known."[57] Yet these refutations had little effect upon a Congress determined to reap political benefits from its appropriations or upon the Truman administration, which had never been enthusiastic about international relief and had decided in 1945 that UNRRA should be terminated the following year.

THE TERMINATION OF UNRRA

From the beginning, both the Roosevelt and Truman administrations perceived UNRRA as a temporary relief program. The Roosevelt administration in 1943 envisioned only a three-year project, and Congress set June 30, 1946, as the termination date for the first authorization (later extended to June 30, 1947, to complete usage of second authorization funds).[58] Byrnes recommended that funds be cut off in 1946 in a July 30, 1945, letter to Truman, and Clayton told the House Foreign Affairs Committee in late 1945, "I would hate very much to see UNRRA develop into a general international relief organization. . . ."[59] Congress and Truman were really not in conflict; they were traveling the same route, but Truman was more aware of the potential embarrassment from an abrupt severance of ties with UNRRA and more desirous of waiting out its brief lifespan. The historian, therefore, must view with suspicion Acheson's words to the same House Foreign Affairs Committee a short time after Clayton made his statement: "UNRRA is not just another agency which we can alter or discard to suit some temporary convenience for it has become one of the foundation blocks of our whole effort to secure a functioning international organization."[60] Congressional attacks did not force the administration to withdraw from UNRRA; they simply reinforced administration thinking. Never did the State Department undertake a significant public information program to counter misconceptions about UNRRA and to argue for a long-term international relief project.[61]

56 Fischer, *Why They Behave*, p. 54; Prague mission to Washington headquarters, Sept. 29, 1945, quoted in Sutherland Denlinger, "A Narrative of Public Information in Prague," [n.d.], Box 756, UNRRA Records. See also *Foreign Relations, 1945*, II, 1037, 1056; Marshall MacDuffie, chief of mission, Ukraine, to UNRRA (Washington), Apr. 30, 1946, Box 59,000, UNRRA Records. MacDuffie resigned in protest against the Dirksen amendment.

57 Woodbridge, *UNRRA*, I, 299. See also *New York Times*, May 21, 1947.

58 Gustafson, "Congress and Foreign Aid," p. 66; House, *Further Participation* (Nov. 14, 1945), pp. 4, 7.

59 Byrnes to Truman, July 30, 1945, OF 423, Truman Papers; House, *Further Participation* (Nov. 14, 1945), p. 38.

60 House, *Further Participation* (Nov. 20, 1945), p. 159.

61 There is evidence that State Department liaison officers with congressional committees were cool toward UNRRA. Gustafson, "Congress and Foreign Aid," pp. 167-68.

At the third UNRRA Council meeting in London in August, 1945, the United States secured a termination date of December 31, 1946, for UNRRA in Europe.[62] Truman and Byrnes did not go to the fourth Council in Atlantic City in March, 1946; the State Department instead appointed Congressman Sol Bloom, chairman of the House Foreign Affairs Committee, to head the United States delegation. In his opening address, Bloom momentarily set aside his prepared text to urge the Council to extend UNRRA beyond 1946: "You cannot stop now.... Something must be done."[63] The Truman administration was embarrassed but unmoved. The other dramatic event at Atlantic City was Lehman's resignation and La Guardia's appointment as director-general. Lehman stated publicly that he was resigning because of ill health but in private said that he was disgusted with Truman's movement toward unilateral relief and his failure to initiate domestic controls to ensure adequate grain shipments abroad. Apparently Truman's appointment of a confirmed advocate of relief for diplomatic purposes, Herbert Hoover, to lead an independent Emergency Famine Committee earlier in the year had been a crushing blow to Lehman.[64]

The fifth Council in August, 1946, in Geneva spelled the end for UNRRA. Clayton confirmed that the United States intended to terminate the organization.[65] When the British delegate seconded the decision, UNRRA was doomed. Richard Scandrett, the Byelorussian chief of mission, reported after the meeting, "I had little opportunity to affect the Council decisions, most of which had been planned in advance, and were largely determined by Will Clayton...."[66] The opposition of the Greek, Polish, Czech, Soviet, and Chinese delegates was ignored. As the donor of about three-fourths of UNRRA's funds, Washington could dictate terms.[67] At the sixth Council in Washington in December La Guardia resigned, saying, "we have demonstrated to the world that forty-eight nations can work in harmony, that forty-eight nations, bent on doing good, can carry on a great mission. Let not that be lost to history."[68] The delegate from Byelorussia, as did many others, despite their unhappiness with UNRRA's demise, expressed his "deep appreciation to the governments of contributing countries, especially the United States, United Kingdom, Canada, Brazil, Australia, and others...."[69] UNRRA completed most of its work by the close of 1946 and officially ceased operations on June 30, 1947.

One of the reasons given by the State Department for the withdrawal of support from UNRRA was unconvincing: Clayton and Acheson argued that

[62] Woodbridge, *UNRRA*, I, 41-47.
[63] Quoted in Gustafson, "Congress and Foreign Aid," p. 241.
[64] *Ibid.*, pp. 240-41; "Lehman Resigns in Disgust," *New Republic*, CXIV (Mar. 25, 1946), 398; Nevins, *Lehman*, pp. 296-99.
[65] Woodbridge, *UNRRA*, I, 47.
[66] "Summary," XXA, Scandrett Papers.
[67] UNRRA, *Journal: Fifth Session of the Council*, V (Aug. 9, 1946), 35-42.
[68] Quoted in Woodbridge, *UNRRA*, I, 50.
[69] *Ibid.*

the crisis in food was largely over and that only a few countries needed further help. Those who did require aid, Clayton added, could probably find a way of financing their own food imports.[70] But Acheson, in his recently published memoirs, now admits that many people at the time regretted UNRRA's death because relief needs were still apparent: "Indeed the Food and Agriculture Organization (FAO) was predicting food shortages of famine proportions."[71] The diplomatic adviser to UNRRA agreed: "every reliable report makes it clear that there are going to be millions of hungry men, women, and children in Europe in 1947. The United Nations Food and Agriculture Organization gives the grim warning that the world faces a grain shortage in 1947 of about 8,000,000 tons."[72] FAO reported in July that the relief problem had not improved over the last year, and UNRRA estimated that Poland needed $200 million in food imports for 1947 just to maintain the minimum individual daily subsistence level of 1,800 calories.[73] Finally, the State Department's own estimates belied Clayton's public statements. A secret report listed the relief deficits of Austria, Greece, Hungary, Italy, Poland, Trieste, and China, all UNRRA recipients, at $596 million for 1947.[74] In short, there was still a serious need for a major relief program.

The more important reason for terminating UNRRA was expressed in testimony to congressional committees. As Acheson told the Senate Foreign Relations Committee in early 1947, "if you have an international organization which controls the allocation of funds, we have only one voice out of many voices and many votes...."[75] He later wrote that UNRRA was inefficient, that supplies "went to the wrong places and were used for the wrong purposes" (to hostile eastern Europe), and that "internationally administered relief had been a failure."[76] Clayton stated before the House Foreign Affairs Committee that relief "could be handled more efficiently and

[70] *DSB*, XV (Aug. 1, 1946), 249; *Journal of Commerce*, Dec. 9, 1946; Frederick J. Dobney, ed., *Selected Papers of Will Clayton* (Baltimore, 1971), pp. 173-74 (Aug. 15, 1946).

[71] Acheson, *Present at the Creation*, p. 201. For criticisms of Clayton, see "After UNRRA What?" *Nation*, CLXIII (Aug. 10, 1946), 144-45.

[72] Memorandum, Francis Sayre, [n.d.], Box 12, Sayre Papers.

[73] United Nations, Food and Agriculture Organization, *Second Annual Report of Director-General* (Washington, D.C., 1947), p. iii; "Poland's Minimim Requirements for 1947 from UNRRA or Successor Organization," UNRRA Council V, doc. 13, July 24, 1946, Box 6, UNRRA Records. For other reports emphasizing the continued threat of hunger, see memorandum of press conference, Sept. 5, 1946, Scandrett Papers; UNRRA press release, June 30, 1947, Box 59,001, UNRRA Records; "Twelfth Monthly Report," Ukraine Mission, Mar. 1, 1947, Box 59,000, *ibid.*; Interior, *Natural Resources and Foreign Aid*, p. 6.

[74] "Foreign Relief Needs in 1947," State Department, Apr. 14, 1947, Box 178, Tom Connally Papers, Library of Congress. A FAO estimate of $583 million was not far from that of the State Department. John C. Campbell, *The United States in World Affairs, 1945-1947* (New York, 1947), p. 464.

[75] Senate, *Assistance to Greece and Turkey* (Mar. 24, 1947), p. 37.

[76] Acheson, *Present at the Creation*, p. 201.

expeditiously without the cumbersome mechanism of an international relief agency."[77]

The abandonment of UNRRA was consistent with the United States treatment of other postwar international organizations like the United Nations, the World Bank and International Monetary Fund, and the Economic Commission for Europe, as we shall note. Unless they could be controlled by the United States they were sidestepped in favor of unilateral programs. American foreign policy, stimulated by visions of postwar power, gravitated toward foreign aid programs which, as Acheson put it, were "in accordance with our judgement and supervised with American personnel."[78]

THE DEFENSE OF UNRRA

There were, of course, defenders of UNRRA, people inside and outside the organization who did admit that UNRRA was troubled, that the "acids of national interest are eating away at the substance of international cooperation,"[79] that fair distribution was difficult in China and Greece because of civil war there, that UNRRA's accounting procedures were often haphazard because of attempts to minimize paperwork in the interest of speedy delivery, that Communists ate UNRRA food, that the free movement of newsmen was sometimes inhibited by censorship laws and harrassment, that UNRRA did house a number of inefficient employees, and that UNRRA relief on occasion was used for political purposes.[80] But, as one columnist wrote, "no relief job could deal adequately with a world in ruins, and no critic has a basis for judgement who has not seen the conditions UNRRA had to face."[81] Despite political impediments, civil wars, the disruption of transportation, late

[77] House, *Relief Assistance to Countries Devastated by War* (Feb. 25, 1947), p. 2.
[78] See n. 5 above.
[79] Samuel D. Marble, "What Has Happened to UNRRA," *Christian Century*, LXII (Feb. 21, 1945), 238.
[80] Woodbridge, *UNRRA*, II, 388-91; Nevins, *Lehman*, p. 277; B. I. Jacot (UNRRA) to chief of mission, Prague, Jan. 25, 1946, Box 60,009, UNRRA Records; Campbell, *United States in World Affairs, 1945-1947*, p. 333; Gustafson, "Congress and Foreign Aid," p. 176.
[81] Anne O'Hare McCormick, *New York Times*, Aug. 5, 1946. For opinion largely favorable to UNRRA and its continuation, see Rishel, "War on Postwar Pestilence"; Sawyer, "Achievements of UNRRA"; Daniel Lang, "The Hens Aboard the *Pepperell*," *New Yorker*, XXII (Apr. 27, 1946), 53-59; Lowell W. Rooks, "UNRRA's Record in Yugoslavia," *American Mercury*, LXIV (May, 1947), 635-39; Donald S. Howard, "After UNRRA—What?" *Survey Graphic*, XXXVI (April, 1947), 236ff.; "La Guardia's Hungry World," *New Republic*, CXIV (Apr. 1, 1946), 428-29; Edgar M. Wahlberg, "We Give a Lift to Greece," *Christian Century*, LXIII (Jan. 16, 1946), 77-79. In mid-1946 the CIO and American Jewish Congress, among others, asked for another year of life for UNRRA. Gustafson, "Congress and Foreign Aid," p. 261. See also *Journal of Commerce*, Dec. 5, 1946, for other groups opposing "food as a weapon of foreign policy."

contributions from members, especially the United States, the huge numbers of hungry and displaced people, and the short time available to build a viable program, UNRRA worked well. At its demise it had gone far in improving its staff, correcting abuses (impounding aid to China, for example, because Chiang diverted it from Communist areas), creating a tighter organization, and streamlining accounting methods. Some congressmen who returned from visits to UNRRA missions applauded the agency's work and appreciated the problems it had to confront. Christian Herter reported in October, 1945, that UNRRA had improved in efficiency and described its successful and extensive relief operations throughout Europe. He added that a significant part of the responsibility for a number of incompetent UNRRA personnel must rest with the State Department because of its unwillingness to release qualified individuals to the organization.[82] Few governments fearful of postwar crisis were eager to send their best men to UNRRA, yet it had built up a competent staff by the end of 1946.[83]

Its defenders also denied the charges that UNRRA in eastern Europe was manipulated by Communists for political advantage. The record is mixed, of course; clear discrimination in the distribution of goods existed at one time or another in every recipient country, Communist or not. But the evidence is convincing that the distribution—given the magnitude of the assignment—was remarkably and predominantly fair and that criticisms were often derived from rumors and secondhand information. Many of the reports which flowed to Washington from embassies abroad were inconclusive and admitted that, as Ambassador to Yugoslavia Richard C. Patterson put it, "valid evidence is scant and substantiation difficult."[84] The diplomatic correspondence is scattered with "perhaps," "it may be possible," "no estimate available," and "information . . . inadequate."[85] As noted, the Truman administration found after investigation that the charges about newsmen were largely unfounded. UNRRA officials devoted an inordinate amount of time to amassing evidence that UNRRA was not a simple tool of Communists in eastern Europe.[86]

Discriminatory distribution of relief was often confused with the obstructions imposed by chaotic transportation systems immobilized by the war. The question was not really "discrimination," but "distribution." As the UNRRA mission in Yugoslavia explained the distinction:

[82] *Congressional Record*, 79th Cong., 1st sess., XCI (Oct. 10, 1945), 9545-47. See also report of congressional visit to Italy in Gustafson, "Congress and Foreign Aid," pp. 167-68.

[83] Nevins, *Lehman*, pp. 280, 290.

[84] *Foreign Relations, 1945*, II, 1056 (Dec. 26, 1945).

[85] *Ibid.*, pp. 987, 989, 999-1000.

[86] See Paul F. White, chief of mission, Ukraine, "Sixth Monthly Report," Sept. 1, 1946, Box 59,000, UNRRA Records; C. M. Drury, chief of mission, Poland, to *Life* editors, Jan. 20, 1947, Box 75,024, *ibid.*; M. E. Hays, acting chief of mission, Poland, to Molly Flynn, UNRRA (Washington), Feb. 15, 1947, *ibid.*; *New York Times*, Sept. 1, 1945; Nevins, *Lehman*, pp. 265-66.

Observation of distribution in all states receiving UNRRA supplies has been continuous. Because of transport difficulties it has not been physically possible to distribute supplies equitably to all areas of need. . . . *In all areas observers give no evidence of discrimination though because of autonomy of local government units in distributing supplies methods vary somewhat between different localities.* . . . In many ports supplies so small as to permit only small distribution to small percentage of population classified as being in greatest need. *No evidence of any discrimination and any discrimination in so classifying.*[87]

It is unquestionable that UNRRA aid relieved individual hardship and collective discontent in some of the eastern European countries and indirectly shored up governments there. La Guardia stated the issue bluntly: "Let's get down to the business of feeding communists. UNRRA food is eaten by communists. It just so happens that there are many more communists than others in some countries we supply. UNRRA's purpose is to feed hungry people. . . . UNRRA doesn't ask the politics or religion of the people it feeds."[88] Even Ambassador Arthur Bliss Lane saw no alternative in late 1945: "For reasons of humanity we cannot allow Poland to starve during the coming winter. . . ."[89] La Guardia asked a rhetorical but important question: "Does the Government of the United States intend to adopt a policy which will make innocent men and women suffer because of the political situation which makes their Government unacceptable to the United States?"[90] In arguing against the "free press" amendment, the *Youngstown* (Ohio) *Vindicator* noted "it is much as if the Community Chest in Youngstown should refuse aid to a starving mother and her children, because it did not like her landlord."[91]

FOOD AND CONFUSION IN THE UNITED STATES

Friends of UNRRA also recounted the chaotic and selfish story of the problems of supply and demand, consumption, conservation and rationing, and procurement of food in the United States—all of which, combined with the often late American payments to UNRRA, helped impede its operations

[87] Quoted in Carl B. Spaeth to Clair Wilcox, *Foreign Relations, 1945*, II, 1020 (Aug. 10, 1945).

[88] UNRRA press release (Washington), June 28, 1946, Box 59,002, UNRRA Records.

[89] Lane to Christian Herter, Sept. 26, 1945, Lane Papers.

[90] Quoted in David Horowitz, *The Free World Colossus* (New York, 1965), p. 70. At the United Nations General Assembly in the fall of 1946, La Guardia chastised the United States for wanting to give aid only to those countries "chosen, picked and acceptable to our government." Quoted in Campbell, *United States in World Affairs, 1945-1947*, p. 335.

[91] Nov. 2, 1945. Quoted from "The Press Fights Back," Box 82, Cox Papers. See also *Washington Post*, Oct. 23, 1945.

and strained its relations with the United States. Allen Matusow has
chronicled well the confused and shortsighted domestic program, inadequate
conservation plans, unsuccessful voluntary efforts and public appeals, and
partial success in exporting food and supplies to hungry areas.[92] The Truman
administration relaxed rationing and price controls and diverted about 270
million bushels of wheat to livestock rather than to the destitue abroad.
Secretary of Agriculture Clinton P. Anderson and Congress focused primary
attention on potential overproduction and surplus in the United States rather
than on world famine. Consumers and farmers at home came first; "America
cannot feed the world."[93] Truman refused to initiate a rationing program,
but by juggling prices and restricting the use of grain in alcohol, he did
increase grain shipments significantly in 1946. However, UNRRA pointed out
early in the year that its supply of bread grains was 40 percent off
requirements and that it was 41 percent short of food supplies during
March.[94] Americans were eating more and better than before the war, and
perhaps, as one commentator remarked, "America itself is too well fed to
understand the depth of human suffering in other countries."[95] La Guardia,
who once protested that "ticker-tape ain't spaghetti," stated the problem
sharply: "We have also been greedy, greedy with our stomachs and greedy for
our pocketbooks."[96] But Lehman's and La Guardia's appeals for more
effective United States cooperation with UNRRA were largely futile, and the
agency "remained a neglected if petulant stepchild."[97]

Although Washington would not order rationing, it did promote voluntary
"eat less" campaigns at home to deflect criticism and to achieve some food
conservation. In February of 1946, as noted above, Truman called on the
dean of post-World War I relief programs, Herbert Hoover, to chair an
Emergency Famine Committee consisting of twelve prominent citizens,
including Henry Luce, George Gallup, and Chester Davis. Truman did not
even consult Lehman, and the UNRRA director-general resigned, in part
because the new committee would simply duplicate much of UNRRA's work.
Actually the committee was essentially an advertising agency, set up to issue
assurances that the federal government was concerned and that something
was being done. The committee tried to sell a voluntary rationing program to

[92] Matusow, *Farm Policies*, chs. 1 and 2.

[93] Anderson, quoted in *ibid.*, p. 10.

[94] *Ibid.*, p. 7-17, 28-29; Campbell, *United States in World Affairs, 1945-1947*, pp.
325-28; *New York Times*, Mar. 17, 1946; UNRRA press release, Apr. 15, 1946, Box
62,008, UNRRA Records.

[95] "UNRRA," McNaughton Report, Nov. 16, 1945, Box 8, McNaughton Papers.

[96] Quoted in Matusow, *Farm Policies*, p. 29; speech, Apr. 19, 1946, Box 2738,
La Guardia Papers.

[97] Matusow, *Farm Policies*, p. 7. As one example of the problem, the United States
failed to supply vital hospital textiles. Woodbridge, *UNRRA*, I, 436, 441. For other
complaints see "The World Needs Our Help," *New Republic*, CXIII (Dec. 10, 1945),
779-81; I. F. Stone, "Fumbling with Famine," *Nation*, CLXII (Mar. 23, 1946), 335-36.

the public; it prepared a list of thirty-nine ways to save on critical foods and ambitiously asked the public to cut down on its food intake by 50 percent.[98] Truman implored Americans not to "ignore the cry of hungry children," and the Advertising Council, which during the war had assisted the government in selling bonds and patriotism, joined the Famine Committee in publicizing the food crisis.[99] The Lipton Company sponsored a promotional scheme against hunger and found the public goodwill it created beneficial to the corporation, and the fashionable Waldorf-Astoria hotel joined the "eat less" campaign by informing its patrons that the management would serve white bread only on request and would offer only one roll and one piece of toast unless the guest asked for more.[100] But Hoover's return to relief questions was unsuccessful: "After six weeks of well-publicized preaching, it admitted that its voluntary program was inadequate and that its meager savings had been offset by increasing feeding of wheat to livestock."[101]

After launching the Famine Committee, Hoover toured three continents as Truman's food ambassador. He was optimistic when he returned, challenging UNRRA's statements about the crisis and reporting to the president that world food requirements had been exaggerated because of faulty calculations. Hoover's statistics were questioned, and according to his critics at home, the effect of his trip was to reduce the public awareness of the seriousness of the problem and to assuage the nation's conscience. His open hostility to UNRRA—he wanted to shut it down by September, 1946—and his desire to use food to achieve foreign policy goals further obstructed postwar relief efforts and strained relations with UNRRA.[102] A Communist daily newspaper in Yugoslavia was much harsher than were his critics at home: "If Hoover is interested in free elections there is sufficiently wide scope for him in the U.S.A. where he can use his authority to see that negroes also acquire the right freely to express their will at elections. . . . UNRRA is not his endowment."[103]

In September, 1947, still bothered by world food shortages and domestic criticism, Truman appointed a Citizens' Food Committee. Chaired by the dynamic thirty-eight-year-old head of Lever Brothers, Charles Luckman, and made up of members of various interest groups, the Committee committed itself to "all-out methods" to help the public win "this war against starvation as they have won all wars."[104] With a grant of $250,000 from the federal government, the committee hired David Noyes, a Los Angeles advertising

[98] Matusow, *Farm Policies*, pp. 27-28; Nevins, *Lehman*, p. 297.

[99] Truman, *Memoirs*, I, 473.

[100] Advertising Council, *Annual Report, 1946*; UNRRA press release, Mar. 21, 1946, Box 60,008, UNRRA Records.

[101] Matusow, *Farm Policies*, p. 29.

[102] *Ibid.*, pp. 33-34; Kolko, *Politics of War*, p. 498.

[103] *Borba*, quoted in *East Europe*, III (Sept. 18, 1946), 12.

[104] Luckman, in *New York Times*, Sept. 26, 1947.

man, to promote a "save food" and "waste less" campaign. Catchy peace and prosperity slogans such as "Save Wheat, Save Meat, Save the Peace" and "Waste Makes Want—Want Makes War" were part of the public relations appeals.[105]

Behind the slogans lay the profound fear that continued hunger abroad would undermine United States foreign policy. As a leading member of the Citizens' Food Committee frankly admitted at the first meeting in October: "I think a year ago we could have said humanitarianism, saving people from starvation. We did talk about democracy, too. But today there is a battle on and our national security is involved, and everything else is subordinate to that."[106] Only two months later the Luckman committee retired to an advisory capacity, claiming that it had succeeded in obtaining "pledges" for savings of 100 million bushels of wheat. Many of the promises went unfulfilled, and voluntary conservation failed, but a jump in grain prices made it less profitable to use grain for fattening livestock, and by early 1948 domestic wheat supplies were much larger than expected. Combined with new foreign aid programs, increased exports from Argentina, and a bumper crop in Australia, the threat of famine in Europe in 1948 was largely eliminated.[107]

UNRRA AND THE COLD WAR

When Washington helped organize UNRRA, it tried to structure it so that United States influence would be potent—with an American as director-general and a Central Committee, for example. Its large financial contribution added to its power, and Congressman John M. Vorys of Ohio, a strong backer of UNRRA in the House in 1944, further argued that Washington would dominate UNRRA because of the sizable Latin American membership under its control.[108] Additional influence derived from the Anglo-American Combined Food Board, through which UNRRA requests for allocations had to be funneled.[109] Acheson said frankly in 1944 that "U.N.R.R.A. has to come to us to ask for goods and for money."[110] Congressmen often treated it like an

---

105 U.S., Department of State, *Third Report to Congress on the United States Foreign Relief Program* (Washington, D.C., 1948), p. 10; Theodore A. Wilson and Richard D. McKinzie, "The Food Crusade of 1947," *Prologue*, III (Winter, 1971), 136-52; *New York Times*, Sept. 26, 1947; John Gray, *Business without Boundary: The Story of General Mills* (Minneapolis, Minn., 1954), pp. 276-77.

106 "Proceedings of the Citizens' Food Committee," Oct. 1, 1947, UNRRA Files, Lehman Papers.

107 *New York Times*, Nov. 21 and Dec. 4, 1947; Matusow, *Farm Policies*, pp. 160-61, 165-66.

108 Gustafson, "Congress and Foreign Aid," p. 106.

109 *Ibid.*, p. 88; I. F. Stone, "UNRRA's Battle," *Nation*, CLXII (Mar. 30, 1946), 361-62.

110 U.S., Congress, House, Committee on Appropriations, *Foreign Economic Administration Appropriation Bill for 1945* (Hearings), 78th Cong., 2d sess. (May 10, 1944), pp. 272-73.

American institution and called upon UNRRA officials as if they were employees of the Department of Commerce. Lehman had to say constantly, "I must be in a position to tell Congress. . . ."[111]

Without question, United States influence in UNRRA was conspicuous, and major policy decisions had to have its approval. It was the United States which pushed for UNRRA aid to Italy even though it was a former enemy and supposedly ineligible for assistance under the plan. Italy became the second largest recipient of UNRRA aid ($418 million).[112] In 1945 the Soviet Union asked UNRRA to help relieve the Ukraine and White Russia, and requested $700 million. The figure was high, and to meet it UNRRA would have had to appeal for more funds from the United States. But Byrnes and Harriman were adamant: the need was not that great; the Soviets had foreign exchange resources to purchase food imports; they could expect dollars in loans from the World Bank and the Export-Import Bank. Byrnes's suggestion that a loan to Russia would satisfy Soviet relief needs was in stark contrast with the fact that "the Soviets have stated informally to UNRRA that they have made this request because Lend-Lease and credit negotiations have 'failed.' "[113] The United States could not stop aid to the Ukraine and White Russia entirely without grossly violating the terms of UNRRA. Washington agreed to $250 million, and "Clayton hated to give them that."[114] Both John G. Winant, ambassador to Britain, and Acheson argued for extension of this aid. Both noted that there was no legal way to kill the Soviet request, that Russia was being treated differently from other UNRRA members, and that Russia's wartime and postwar devastation was greater and its standard of living lower than other European countries. They added that it would be "disastrous" to deny relief to Russia at the same time that the United States was attempting to include the ex-enemies Austria and Italy in UNRRA's programs.[115] There were other examples of United States influence in UNRRA at the policy level, but the question of the final distribution of goods produced and purchased with American dollars in the "field"—of lack of control—still plagued Washington.[116]

---

[111] John Perry, "Why UNRRA Has Failed," *Harper's*, CXCII (January, 1946), 84; Lehman to McFeller, Sept. 12, 1945, UNRRA Files, Lehman Papers.

[112] Gustafson, "Congress and Foreign Aid," pp. 154-55.

[113] Ambassador John G. Winant to secretary of state, *Foreign Relations, 1945*, II, 1004 (Aug. 6, 1945). See also *ibid.*, pp. 1010-11, 1021, 1022, 1026-27.

[114] Transcript, Emilio G. Collado, Nov. 6, 1958, Marshall Plan Project, Ellen Clayton Garwood Papers, Truman Library.

[115] Winant, in *Foreign Relations, 1945*, II, 1024-25 (Sept. 4, 1945); Acheson to Harriman, *ibid.*, pp. 1025-27 (Sept. 8, 1945).

[116] The United States, for example, attempted to influence the appointment of UNRRA employees in the Ukraine. Cable 2616, London to Washington, Jan. 3, 1946, Box 59,000, UNRRA Records. The United States persuaded the UNRRA Council to pass a resolution asking member nations (that is, Russia) with occupying forces in UNRRA-receiving countries to refrain from using land and indigenous resources and from impeding the equitable distribution of imported and indigenous goods. Woodbridge, *UNRRA*, I, 44; *New York Times*, Mar. 27, 1946.

A corollary of this dilemma existed in the case of UNRRA's personnel. An American was director-general, and 983 of 1,136 headquarters employees were of United States nationality in late summer, 1945. Only 1,108 United States nationals, of a total of 6,816, were employed outside headquarters, although in White Russia 17 of 18 UNRRA officials were American, as were 10 of 11 in the Ukraine.[117] These figures, the fact that English was the official language of UNRRA, and the obvious United States influence in the Washington headquarters led smaller nations and Russia to think that UNRRA was dominated by the United States.[118] This notion would have been further reinforced had it been widely known that in 1945 the chief of the Office of Strategic Services (OSS) tried to enlist the help of UNRRA in American spy operations abroad. William Donovan offered Lehman a number of men to fill UNRRA positions to serve as OSS information-gatherers, but Lehman turned down the suggestion.[119] However, although there were many Americans in prominent positions in UNRRA, they were employed by an international organization and for the most part refused to knuckle under to United States pressure. Failing to control UNRRA employees and the final distribution of UNRRA supplies, the Truman administration ended the problem by ending UNRRA.

After the death of UNRRA, American leaders recalled their embittered relations with the organization in order to buttress their contention that henceforth the United States itself should dispense relief on a unilateral basis. Vandenberg spoke of "vicious dissatisfactions" with UNRRA, and Clayton insisted that the Marshall Plan be a closely supervised United States venture because UNRRA had been "extravagant."[120] Secretary Forrestal, upon surveying the relief record in late 1947, asked: "We missed the boat on UNRRA. Is there any way of catching it on our relief work this Winter?"[121] The post-UNRRA relief authorization bill of May, 1947 ($350 million) provided for aid to Austria, Greece, Italy, China, Trieste, and two eastern European nations, Poland and Hungary. Relief missions were to be "com-

---

[117] House, *UNRRA, 1946,* p. 32; MacDuffie to La Guardia, June 29, 1946, XXB, Scandrett Papers; "Summary," XXA, *ibid.*

[118] In late 1945 there were only fourteen Russians outside headquarters and five within. By September, 1946, the maximum of forty-nine Russians in UNRRA was reached. House, *UNRRA, 1946,* p. 32; Woodbridge, *UNRRA,* I, 244-46; Perry, "Why UNRRA," pp. 83-84. Polish leaders complained to Ambassador Lane in early 1946 that the United States forced UNRRA to cut grain shipments to Poland for "political" reasons. Lane to secretary of state, *Foreign Relations, 1946,* VI (Feb. 26, 1946), 401-2.

[119] Nevins, *Lehman,* p. 277.

[120] *Congressional Record,* 80th Cong., 1st sess., XCIII (Apr. 8, 1947), 3197; "Clayton Reminiscences," Oral History, Columbia University Library, pp. 196-97.

[121] Forrestal to Robert Lovett, Oct. 25, 1947, Box 126, Forrestal Papers. See also complaints about UNRRA help to Polish Communists in Stanton Griffis, ambassador to Poland, to Harriman, Aug. 12, 1947, Harriman Papers; Parker Buhrman, embassy in Warsaw, to Congressman Charles Eaton, Oct. 3, 1947, Tray 18831, Committee on Foreign Affairs, House Records.

prised solely of American citizens who shall have been investigated by the Federal Bureau of Investigation." Each recipient nation had to allow American newsmen and government officials unrestricted travel, and "full and continuous publicity will be given within such country as to purchase, source, character, scope, amounts and progress of the United States relief programs. . . ."[122] When Clayton was asked whether Poland and Hungary could accept such provisions, he replied: "I think the conditions that we lay down, while fair and proper, would be so tough that probably some of these countries might not accept."[123] The legislation gave the Truman administration the flexibility to set the amounts each nation would receive. When Congress finally appropriated the relief money, the figure had dropped to $332 million, and there was an understanding that Poland and Hungary were excluded.[124]

The United States looked for diplomatic profits from the new expenditure in terms of order, stability, prosperity, and anti-Communism. In Italy, for example, shipments of coal and wheat were ostentatiously welcomed by the United States ambassador. Local officials crowded around, praised the United States, and advertised its presence with fanfare. The Italians were soon to hold major national elections, and the pragmatic and physical merits of adherence to United States foreign policy goals were made clear to millions of Italians. Rations carried the words: "The supplies you are receiving came from the United States."[125]

La Guardia launched a series of attacks on the administration's adoption of political relief. He blasted the "reversion to power politics, the use of food relief as a weapon of foreign policy—an approach to world problems utterly opposed to the concept of the United Nations and wholesome international collaboration."[126] In late 1946 he proposed an alternative, a United Nations Emergency Food Fund to help finance food purchases by Yugoslavia, Austria, Greece, Hungary, Italy, and Poland. Nations able to do so would

---

[122] Senate, *ERP: Basic Documents*, p. 171.

[123] House, *Relief Assistance to Countries Devastated by War* (Feb. 25, 1947), p. 2.

[124] Cleona Lewis, *The United States and Foreign Investment Problems* (New York, 1948), p. 198.

[125] Senate, *ERP*, p. 795; Clinton P. Anderson, *Outsider in the Senate: Senator Clinton Anderson's Memoirs* (New York, 1970), pp. 70-71. One of the prominent examples of this use of political relief was Yugoslavia's break with Russia. A famine struck Yugoslavia in 1950, and the United States extended $50 million to that country. An assistant secretary of state explained the Truman administration's thinking: "Although the purely humanitarian aspects of our aid are important, they are not the major consideration; in the light of present world conditions, they are a minor consideration." Noting the schism between Tito and Stalin, he argued that the "granting of this aid at this time has great political and strategic advantages to the U.S." George Perkins, "Statement . . . on Aid to Yugoslavia," Dec. 4, 1950, Tray 2820, Foreign Relations Committee, Senate Records.

[126] La Guardia petition, Nov. 13, 1946, UNRRA Files, Lehman Papers. See also Senate, *Assistance to Greece and Turkey* (Mar. 26, 1947), p. 131; Ira A. Hirschmann, *The Ember Still Burns* (New York, 1949).

contribute to the Fund, but none would be allowed to give more than 49 percent of its anticipated $400 million. A small staff drawn from the United Nations Secretariat would administer the program. Despite the support of Denmark, Peru, Norway, and most of the potential recipients named and the willingness of Brazil, France, Austria, Venezuela, and the Netherlands to accept a compromise between the unilateral United States scheme and the Food Fund, the idea died, largely because of Washington's opposition.[127]

The Food Fund, UNRRA, and international cooperation in general were catalysts and casualties of Soviet-American friction and the political complications of the postwar world. And yet UNRRA, with all of its shortcomings, was a postwar institution in which Communists and non-Communists together attempted to provide the basic requirements for survival. UNRRA saw compromise and compassion. Soviet officials cooperated, and mission officers in the Ukraine often expressed their satisfaction with the cooperation they had experienced.[128] As Howard K. Smith commented: "It is a highly important key to the Cold War that with UNRRA—that is, aid with no strings tied, internationally administered—American observers were for the first time allowed free run inside Soviet Russia."[129] With the death of UNRRA, a large corps of experienced international civil servants was lost. It appears that former UNRRA employees were discriminated against or rejected for employment in later United States-controled programs like aid to Greece and Turkey under the Truman Doctrine.[130]

The tragedy of UNRRA was that the United States was bent on using its economic power to shape its desired postwar world. The Soviet Union and other Communist nations could only look with suspicion upon American relations with UNRRA. They remembered the period after World War I and political relief. *Pravda* interpreted the Dirksen amendment as an attempt to "intimidate" the Soviet Union, and the overt American success in restricting UNRRA aid to the two Soviet republics further rankled Russia.[131] Although the Food and Agriculture Organization, the International Refugee Organization, and the World Health Organization carried on some UNRRA functions, their funds and activities were small in scale. The Soviet Union never joined the first two and dropped out of the last in 1949. The troubled relations with UNRRA had a conspicuous impact on all U.S. foreign aid programs after 1946, especially the Truman Doctrine and the Marshall Plan. Washington henceforth limited assistance to non-Communists and supervised that assistance outside the United Nations machinery.

127 Woodbridge, *UNRRA*, I, 425; Senate, *Assistance to Greece and Turkey* (Mar. 26, 1947), pp. 120-31 (La Guardia); "Proposed Food Fund Debated: Many Viewpoints on Measures To Continue UNRRA Work," *United Nations Weekly Bulletin*, I (Nov. 25, 1946), 36-38.
128 See, for example, Marshall MacDuffie, "Second Monthly Report," May 1, 1946, Box 59,000, UNRRA Records; Paul F. White, "Ukranian Mission History," [n.d.], Box 755, *ibid.*
129 Howard K. Smith, *The State of Europe* (New York, 1949), p. 94.
130 Perry, "Why UNRRA," p. 86; Gustafson, "Congress and Foreign Aid," p. 281.
131 Gustafson, "Congress and Foreign Aid," p. 256.

CHAPTER 5

THREATS AND FEARS: THE OPEN DOOR IN
EASTERN EUROPE

The UNRRA controversy pointed up a fact that Washington disliked but
ultimately could not alter—Soviet and Communist influence in eastern
Europe. American leaders believed that the conspicuous Soviet presence in
the area threatened their avowed goals of peace, political democracy,
prosperity, open trade, and security, and that the fate of eastern Europe
directly affected the national interest. The Soviet presence there was often a
repressive one, but even when it was not, Americans felt somehow responsible
for rolling it back, though, as Walter Lippmann noted, eastern Europe's status
did not threaten United States security, and Washington had few diplomatic
tools to work with in that area.[1] An active, noisy, and offensive foreign
policy vis-à-vis the Soviet sphere was followed. Non-recognition, atomic
diplomacy, and the manipulation of loans and trade, however, not only failed
to change the arrangement of power but tended to exacerbate Soviet fears
and led to a further tightening of the Soviet grip.[2]

This intense postwar interest in the Soviet sphere of influence derived in
part from questions of trade, investment, nationalization, loans, navigation on
the Danube, reparations, and relief. Washington feared a closing of the
economic door. But this concern for economic issues arose from more than
the drive toward and protection of business profits. The Truman administration sought the economic open door for much the same reasons it sought free
elections: both were traditional American ideals, and their fulfillment in
eastern Europe would reduce Soviet influence and augment that of the
United States in the postwar international competition called the Cold War.
Washington and Moscow recognized that economic relationships were part of
general foreign relations, and that economic ties meant influence upon other

---

[1] Walter Lippmann, "A Year of Peacemaking," *Atlantic Monthly*, CLXXVIII
(December, 1946), 35-40; Walter Lippmann, *The Cold War* (New York, 1947);
Barton J. Bernstein, "Walter Lippmann and the Early Cold War," in Paterson, *Cold War
Critics*, pp. 18-53.
[2] For the abortive loan to Russia and its relationship to eastern Europe see Chapter 2
above; for the recognition issue see Lloyd C. Gardner, *Architects of Illusion: Men and
Ideas in American Foreign Policy, 1941-1949* (Chicago, 1970), ch. 4; for atomic
diplomacy, see Alperovitz, *Atomic Diplomacy*, and Bernstein, "American Foreign Policy
and the Origins of the Cold War," pp. 32-36.

nations (but, of course, in varying degrees). Washington tried to orient the world toward the United States, but it is difficult to call its policy toward eastern Europe sinister and aggressive. Yet it was a direct challenge to Russia. Americans believed they were responding defensively to Soviet machinations, failing to recognize that Moscow, Prague, Warsaw, and Belgrade perceived United States foreign policy as offensive and meddlesome. In the long run Washington's assertive policy was detrimental to the independence of the eastern European nations, for it made Russia keep a closer watch over its neighbors.

Finding that it was difficult to shape events in eastern Europe, the United States decided to isolate that region by early defining it as a sealed bloc and cutting it off from loans and trade. Secretary Byrnes stated the issue simply in September, 1946: "We must help our friends in every way and refrain from assisting those who either through helplessness or for other reasons are opposing the principles for which we stand."[3] This chapter will discuss the fears for the open door in eastern Europe which helped shape Byrnes's thinking.

FEARS, INVESTMENTS, AND TRADE

The chief of the State Department's Division of Eastern European Affairs complained in May, 1945, that Soviet trade agreements threatened to "create an almost airtight economic blackout in the entire area east of the Stettin-Trieste line."[4] "Economic blackout," "engulfment," "economic colony," "penetration," "closed economic orbit," and "exclusive influence" became frequent descriptions of Soviet economic relations with neighboring countries.[5] Harriman insisted that Russia "cease special economic monopolies," and the United States minister in Hungary speculated in early 1946 that Russia "bids fair to advance steadily in this area and elsewhere in Europe much as Nazi Germany advanced through the late thirties." Hungary, he predicted, would soon "become an economic colony of USSR from which western trade will be excluded and in which western investments will be totally lost."[6] In late 1946 a congressional committee endorsed the Truman administration's protests and deplored in vigorous language "economic enslavement" and "political terrorism" in eastern Europe.[7] Secretary Byrnes summarized these fears publicly at the 1946 Paris Peace Conference, when he declared that the United States opposed treaties "which tend to restrict and divert trade or distort international economic relations to the prejudice of the

---

[3] *Foreign Relations, 1946,* VII, 223.

[4] Elbridge Durbrow, in *ibid., 1945,* V, 853.

[5] *Ibid.,* pp. 934-35; *ibid., 1946,* VI, 14, 258-60, 267, 293, 377, 821; *ibid.,* IV, 818; memorandum by F. M. A., Jan. 5, 1944, Box 12, Lubin Papers.

[6] Harriman, in *Foreign Relations, 1945,* V, 1351 (Dec. 15, 1945); H. F. Arthur Schoenfield, in *ibid., 1946,* VI, 260 (Feb. 15, 1946).

[7] House, *Economic Reconstruction in Europe, Progress Report,* p. 28.

great majority of the United Nations and of world peace and prosperity."[8]

American assets in eastern Europe do not explain this alarm, for they amounted to about $560 million, or about 12 percent of all such assets in Europe and Britain and only 4 percent of all American investments in the world. Only $278,600,000 of that figure represented investments in American-controlled enterprises (as distinct from securities and individual property holdings[9]). International Telephone and Telegraph, Standard Oil of New Jersey, Socony-Vacuum Oil, Anaconda Copper, International Business Machines, Universal Pictures, Colgate-Palmolive-Peet, Royal Typewriter, Ingersoll Rand, Ford Motor, and Corn Products Refining were some of the corporations active in eastern Europe.

Poland and Czechoslovakia accounted for the largest investment. American-controlled business in Poland represented investments of $108,800,000; the corresponding figure for Czechoslovakia was $67,100,000. At least fifty United States companies held property in Poland, with Anaconda Copper prominent; Socony-Vacuum owned about 12 percent of Poland's oil refineries at the close of the war. International Telephone and Telegraph was active in Czechoslovakia, and Socony-Vacuum controlled about 14 percent of Czech petroleum refining, valued by the company at $15,000,000. Standard Oil of New Jersey and Socony-Vacuum controlled 34 percent of all Hungarian oil refineries, with Standard valuing its property at $20,000,000; Standard's subsidiary, MAORT, was responsible for almost one-third of all oil produced in Europe; Ford Motor had an assembly plant, and International Telephone and Telegraph, Eastman-Kodak, and International General Electric held Hungarian properties also. Total American assets in Hungary stood at $62,300,000, of which $21,700,000 were listed as interests in American-controlled enterprises. Standard Oil of New Jersey and Socony-Vacuum conducted 10 percent of Rumanian oil refining; Standard Oil's holdings were valued at $33,000,000. Total American assets in Rumania amounted to $66,100,000 ($52,400,000 in controlled firms), including a Ford assembly plant. Corresponding figures were $50,300,000 ($22,000,000) for Yugoslavia; $11,800,000 ($6,600,000) for Bulgaria; and $1,300,000 (negligible) for Albania.[10]

[8] DSB, XV (Aug. 25, 1946), 354. For other complaints about the limitations on trade and investment in eastern Europe, see House, Economic Reconstruction in Europe, 8th Rept., pp. 31-33; Fortune, XXXII (July, 1945), 110; Journal of Commerce, Aug. 24 and Oct. 29, 1945, Feb. 20 and Sept. 20, 1946; Thomas B. Inglis, "Russian Economic Penetration of Satellite Area," Dec. 28, 1945, Box 100, Forrestal Papers; George Kennan to secretary of state, Jan. 4, 1946, Harriman Papers; Nation's Business, XXXIII (January, 1945), 25-26; Herbert Feis, "Political Aspects of Foreign Loans," pp. 609-19; Business Week, Nov. 10, 1945, p. 111, Jan. 26, 1946, p. 107; NFTC, Report of 33rd National Convention (Nov. 11, 1946), p. 52; Senate, Interim Aid (Nov. 14, 1947), pp. 239, 247 (John F. Dulles); Senate, Anglo-American Financial Agreement (Mar. 6, 1946), p. 177.
[9] U.S., Department of Treasury, Census of American-Owned Assets in Foreign Countries (Washington, D.C., 1947), p. 68.
[10] Ibid.; Arthur Bliss Lane to Donald Russell, Jan. 15, 1947, Lane Papers; "Report

United States trade with eastern Europe was never substantial. The prewar average (1936-1938) for exports to that region represented only 2.1 percent ($62,297,000) of total United States exports, and although the immediate postwar figures are greater, they consist largely of UNRRA shipments. From July to December, 1945, exports to eastern Europe amounted to $206,840,000, but UNRRA accounted for $201,560,000 of the total. In 1946, the eastern European nations took $431,152,000 in American exports and in 1947, $222,254,000. Again UNRRA was important; it accounted for $380,403,000 and $86,296,000 of the total in these years. The impact of trade controls and UNRRA's demise is evident in the export figures for 1948 and 1949: $103,260,000 and $72,264,000. Most of these exports consisted of cotton, machinery, and vehicles, although the last two categories, as in the case of Russia, dropped markedly with the introduction of controls. By 1952 trade with eastern Europe was negligible.[11]

SOVIET PENETRATION OF EASTERN EUROPEAN ECONOMIES

What alarmed Washington more than the possible reduction in trade and investments was the Soviet Union's assertion of influence in eastern European economies through bilateral treaties, reparations collections, and joint-stock companies. Whereas the United States interpreted these arrangements as signs of Russia's generally aggressive behavior, Russia saw them as defensive measures to protect Soviet security and its rightful fruits of victory over the Axis, and as necessary for reconstruction and industrialization.[12] As noted, the United States tried unsuccessfully to reduce these arrangements, which struck at multilateralism and the open door, through its loan policy toward Russia.

One of the first squabbles occurred in Rumania, and a State Department officer depicted the controversy as a test of postwar Soviet-American commercial relations.[13] In late 1944, eager for reparations, the Soviets carted

---

of the Group on American Petroleum Interests in Foreign Countries," I (Oct. 15, 1945), Box 19, Special Committee Investigating Petroleum Resources, Senate Records; *Journal of Commerce,* Mar. 8, 1946, June 10 and 11, 1947; "Compensation for Socony-Vacuum Oil Company," 1947, Box 55, Steinhardt Papers; European Gas and Electric Company of the Standard Oil Company, *Standard Oil Company (New Jersey) and Oil Production in Hungary by MAORT* (New York, 1949); Wilkins and Hill, *American Business Abroad,* pp. 348-49; *Foreign Relations, 1946,* VI, 284; *Business Week,* Mar. 11, 1950, p. 142.

[11] Imports from eastern Europe after the war averaged only 2 percent of total imports to the United States. Commerce, *Foreign Trade of the United States, 1936-49;* Commerce, *Export Control and Allocation Powers,* 5th Quarterly Report, p. 42; *ibid.,* 8th Quarterly Report, p. 20; *ibid.,* 12th Quarterly Report, p. 23; Erik Thorbecke, *The Tendency towards Regionalization in International Trade, 1928-1956* (The Hague, 1960), p. 35.

[12] "The Russian Sphere in Europe: Economic Planning in Eastern Europe," *The World Today,* III (October, 1947), 432-45.

[13] John A. Loftus, in *DSB,* XIII (Aug. 5, 1945), 173.

off oil equipment from Rumania, some of which a Standard Oil of New Jersey subsidiary claimed as its property. Washington protested, but the issue of ownership was confused. Russia insisted that the oil equipment was in fact German-owned because the company had served wartime Axis oil needs and had acquired machinery from Germany during the war. Under the armistice agreements, German property in the ex-enemy states was to go toward Soviet reparations. On this interpretation of ownership, Russia signed an agreement with Rumania in early 1945 which gave the Soviets all existing oil products as German assets.[14] Harriman denounced Russian "sharp practices," and he and Grew contemplated curtailment of Lend-Lease oil shipments to the Soviet Union as a response.[15] But Russia did not grab the entire Rumanian oil industry, as Grew had mistakenly predicted, and Washington was temporarily sanguine that a settlement of the ownership issue was possible.[16] The Potsdam Conference in mid-1945 established a joint Soviet-American investigating committee, and Byrnes stated the United States position strongly: "Equitable settlement requires either return of equipment taken in equal condition or replacement with material of equal quality. Compensation for material not replaced and for other damages sustained should be paid in dollars."[17] The meetings eventually broke down, and the oil commission was disbanded in July, 1947.[18] Washington had lost this contest, which it considered a test of the open door.

A somewhat similar crisis arose in Hungary, where Standard Oil's subsidiary (MAORT) clashed with the Soviets. In this case, the Soviets seized control of production and removed little equipment. Pro-German Hungarians had managed MAORT during the war, and the German war machine had used MAORT oil. For this reason, the Russians prohibited representatives of the company from visiting MAORT's property in late 1945, and in early 1946 Soviet officials announced that they would take over the production of Hungarian oil. MAORT officials complained vigorously, and Secretary Byrnes chided the Russians for their unilateral action and for wasting oil resources. Byrnes instructed Harriman to protest that "MAORT is suffering heavy and irreparable losses of both gas and oil because of Soviet disregard for sound oil field practices in insisting that the Company maintain an excessive production rate." He insisted on Soviet withdrawal from the Hungarian oil industry.[19]

---

[14] G. I., "Rumanian Oil: Nationalization and Foreign Interests," *The World Today*, V (January, 1949), 9; *Foreign Relations, Berlin*, I, 420-23; *ibid., 1945*, V, 661.

[15] Draft note, Harriman to secretary of state, Jan. 8, 1945, Harriman Papers; *Foreign Relations, Berlin*, I, 425-26; *ibid., 1945*, V, 649-50.

[16] *Foreign Relations, 1945*, V, 647-49; *ibid., Berlin*, I, 395, 420-21.

[17] *Ibid., 1945*, V, 658.

[18] *Ibid.*, pp. 662-66; *ibid., 1946*, VI, 625. Washington also wanted Rumanian oil to flow to western Europe for postwar recovery. *Ibid., Berlin*, I, 943, 945-46, 947; II, 606, 1379-81.

[19] European Gas and Electric, *Standard Oil Company*, p. 7; *New York Times*, Apr. 4, 1946; *Foreign Relations, 1946*, VI, 284, 328.

Company representatives in Hungary lobbied with United States diplomats and, in November, 1946, called the Soviet intrusion "an affront to American diplomacy...."[20] In February, 1947, at about the same time as the signing of the Hungarian peace treaty which provided for equality of economic opportunity, Soviet officials withdrew from MAORT properties, and, as the company put it, "MAORT returned to almost normal operations."[21] But this success was soon set back by the issue of nationalization, as we shall note.

The Department of State was disturbed also by the rash of joint-stock companies and bilateral agreements in eastern Europe. Trade treaties with Bulgaria in March, with Rumania in May, and with Hungary in August, 1945, gave Russia new influence in their economies. Using former German assets as their share, the Russians organized companies in Rumania in oil, navigation, civil aviation, banking, and others on a fifty-fifty basis. Under the Hungarian treaty, eight joint companies were established; before 1949 they were important only in civil aviation and bauxite mining. They employed only 1.1 percent of all workers in Hungarian manufacturing by 1948; another forty all-Russian companies accounted for only 2.6 percent of manufacturing workers.[22] One State Department report at the Potsdam Conference indicated, with some hyperbole, that "this kind of exclusive penetration is at variance with the general commercial policy of this Government, which looks toward the expansion of trade and investment on a multilateral, non-discriminatory basis."[23] Russia, applying its own version of the open door, replied in August, 1945, that the treaties did not discriminate against other nations.[24]

By mid-1946 Russia had signed barter agreements with Bulgaria, Rumania, Hungary, Poland, and Czechoslovakia. Poland was compelled, by an agreement of August, 1945, to deliver 6.5 million metric tons of coal per year to Russia until the end of the occupation in Germany. Although Russia later relieved Poland of this burden, Washington was particularly upset because it wanted Polish coal for the recovery of western Europe. The agreement with Rumania also required that nation to ship a large part of its exports, including oil, to Russia.[25] These barter agreements were anathema to the goals of unrestricted trade and United States influence in eastern Europe.

---

[20] European Gas and Electric, *Standard Oil Company,* p. 43.

[21] *Ibid.,* p. 9.

[22] Spulber, *Economics of Communist Eastern Europe,* pp. 189, 191; Andrew Gyorgy, *Governments of Danubian Europe* (New York, 1949), p. 55; Ygael Gluckstein, *Stalin's Satellites in Europe* (Boston, 1952), pp. 30-32, 58-62; Elizabeth Wiskemann, "Hungary," in R. R. Betts, ed., *Central and South East Europe, 1945-1948* (London, 1950), p. 109. For a complete list of Soviet trade treaties, see Triska and Slusser, *A Calendar of Soviet Treaties.*

[23] *Foreign Relations, Berlin,* I, 422.

[24] *Ibid., 1945,* V, 656-57.

[25] *New York Times,* May 7, 1946; *Journal of Commerce,* Sept. 16, 1946; Dewar, *Soviet Trade;* S. Z. Tomczak, *Soviet Economic Experiments in Poland* (Newtown, England, 1946); Stella K. Margold, "Economic Life in Russia's Orbit: I," *Harvard Business Review,* XXVIII (September, 1950), 66; *Foreign Relations, 1945,* V, 544-45.

Related to these commercial arrangements was Russian eagerness for reparations. The armistice agreements, which the United States signed, provided that Hungary, Rumania, and Bulgaria ship capital equipment or current output to Russia. As noted, American oil property became ensnarled in the question. Washington admitted that the armistice agreements were vague but would not concede that the property it claimed, even though controlled and expanded by the Germans during the war, was subject to reparations.[26] It further protested that the June, 1945, Soviet-Hungarian reparations agreement placed too heavy a burden on the Hungarian economy and impeded reconstruction. The Russians replied that the United States itself was retarding recovery by holding Hungarian property in the American zone of Germany.[27] Some precision emerged from the peace treaties of 1947 with Hungary and Rumania, which Washington signed. Each nation was required to pay $300 million in reparations, with $200 million from each country going to Russia.[28]

Russia consistently sought economic advantages in eastern Europe, and with the exception of Yugoslavia, succeeded in gaining them.[29] Washington's protests failed to reverse Russian economic arrangements in eastern Europe but did effectively challenge similar ones in Iran and China in 1946.[30] The constant insistence on the open door derived not only from traditional ideology but also from the realization that the open door was one of the few available ways to challenge Soviet influence in eastern Europe. The policy failed because of predominant Soviet power and the paucity of American economic interests in the area and because the open door philosophy clashed with the indigenous movement toward socialism exemplified by nationalization.

NATIONALIZATION

The eastern European countries did not nationalize key sectors of their economies in unison. Non-Communist Czechoslovakia first announced a postwar nationalization program on October 24, 1945; 80 percent of that

[26] *Foreign Relations, Berlin*, I, 421-32; "Report" cited in n. 10 above.

[27] *Foreign Relations, Berlin*, I, 369; *ibid., 1946*, VI, 265-66, 286, 326; Gluckstein, *Stalin's Satellites*, p. 60; Campbell, *United States in World Affairs, 1945-1947*, pp. 157-58.

[28] Bulgaria was exempt. See Senate, *Treaties of Peace*. Russia reaped propaganda benefit in 1948 by reducing the Hungarian and Rumanian reparations debts by half.

[29] Yugoslavia rejected Soviet requests for joint companies in oil and banking in 1946. Two Russian-Yugoslav transport companies, organized in 1947, disbanded in 1948. Gluckstein, *Stalin's Satellites*, p. 32; Vladimir Dedijer, *Tito* (New York, 1953), pp. 326-27; Vladimir Dedijer, *The Battle Stalin Lost: Memoirs of Yugoslavia, 1948-1953* (New York, 1971), pp. 73-77, 90.

[30] For Iran, see Chapter 9 below. For China, see U.S., Department of State, *United States Relations with China* (Washington, D.C., 1949), pp. 118-24, 596-98; Tang Tsou, *America's Failure in China, 1941-50* (Chicago, 1963), pp. 335-38.

country's industry was scheduled for government ownership. After more nationalization in 1948, only 5 percent of industrial production and 17 percent of the physical plant remained in private hands. Poland followed in January, 1946, but its program was an extension of prewar nationalization. As of 1938, for example, all Polish production of alcohol, tobacco, aircraft, automobiles, telegraph services, and potassium salts was government-owned, and coal, natural gas, chemicals, smelting, and marine transportation were partially nationalized. Although there was no postwar nationalization law in Yugoslavia until December, 1946, there too some nationalization had occurred earlier. In January, 1946, Hungary nationalized its coal mines and in November five heavy industries, but until the nationalization act of early 1948, one-quarter of heavy industry and four-fifths of the rest of industry were privately operated. Until December, 1947, only 6 percent of Bulgarian industry was owned by the government. Nationalization in Rumania was planned in 1947, but a full-scale act was not passed until June, 1948. By 1950 about 90 percent of total Rumanian industrial production was nationalized.[31]

The official United States position held that nationalization was the right of any sovereign nation but that prompt and adequate compensation was due foreign-owned companies, and most nations did promise compensation. In practice, however, Washington was irritated by nationalization, attempted to slow it down or thwart it, and insisted on such rapid payments from these war-devastated and financially unstable nations that eastern European leaders believed the United States to be hostile and intrusive. In Poland, Ambassador Arthur Bliss Lane frequently protested that the Poles did not give "definite assurances to American interests as to compensation . . ."; Ambassador to Czechoslovakia Laurence A. Steinhardt opposed nationalization of the Czech oil industry altogether and tried to convince Czech officials that their action was futile.[32] Both men appealed to Washington to withhold postwar loans until the two nations met compensation demands. Washington flatly refused to recognize the Rumanian nationalization law of 1948. The United States insisted that the legislation violated the 1947 peace treaty because it nationalized American property but exempted Soviet-owned enterprises, and hence violated the most-favored-nation clause of the treaty (Article 31-c). The State Department also rejected the Rumanian program because it did not provide for "prompt, adequate, and effective compensation" and because it

---

[31] Samuel L. Sharp, *Nationalization of Key Industries in Eastern Europe* (Washington, D.C., 1946), pp. 3-5; Richard F. Starr, *The Communist Regimes in Eastern Europe: An Introduction* (Stanford, Calif., 1967), p. 85; Dewar, *Soviet Trade*, pp. 35-36; Gluckstein, *Stalin's Satellites*, pp. 39-42; Ghita Ionescu, *Communism in Rumania, 1944-1962* (London, 1964), 161-65.

[32] The United States proposed the establishment of a mixed commission to handle nationalization cases in Poland. Lane to Selden Chapin, Apr. 29, 1946, Lane Papers; Steinhardt to Harold F. Sheets (Socony-Vacuum), Aug. 27, 1945, Box 83, Steinhardt Papers; *Foreign Relations, 1946*, VI, 378, 380, 386-87.

was "discriminatory." The companies affected were Standard Oil and Socony-Vacuum.[33]

In Hungary MAORT resisted nationalization. After 1947 the Communists attempted to control the company's hiring practices, pricing, and management. The government appointed a "controller" for MAORT in May, 1948, apparently after MAORT rejected its attempt to buy the company. Arrests of leading MAORT officials, both Hungarian and foreign, and forced "confessions" of sabotage further inflamed the controversy.[34] The State Department commented that the Hungarian charges of sabotage and the abuse of the men "are characteristic of the methods employed by police states, where the rights and dignity of the individual are, in practice, ignored."[35] In September, 1948, the Hungarian government officially nationalized MAORT, or, as the company put it, "seized [it] from its legal owners."[36] Washington called the action "wholly arbitrary and unwarrantable."[37]

In late 1945 the attaché of the United States embassy in Moscow reported, with the endorsement of Ambassador Harriman, that in eastern Europe "programs of nationalization and government control of industry and transport are being inspired and supported by Moscow."[38] The popular, if not the official, assumption in the United States was that the Soviet Union was forcing nationalization schemes upon governments as part of its economic exploitation of the region. The evidence suggests, however, that eastern European nationalization was indigenous, that it was a logical extension of similar prewar activities, that it was designed to hasten industrialization, and that Russia followed a mixed policy. One close student of the subject has written: "The trend toward nationalization of industrial and financial undertakings was a general phenomenon in Europe after World War I. . . . Consequently the present transition to state ownership of entire industries is actually less drastic and not as shocking as it would be in a country with a highly-developed and functioning capitalist system."[39] Ambassador Steinhardt admitted that such postwar programs followed a trend; he wrote that nationalization "is a normal development in Europe by

[33] In 1946, Brigadier General Cortlandt Van R. Schuyler, U.S. Representative to the Allied Control Commission for Rumania, appealed for fewer government controls and more "private enterprise" in Rumania. The State Department instructed Schuyler to avoid criticizing Rumanian "intervention in private business." *Foreign Relations, 1946,* VI, 591, 610; *DSB,* XIX (Sept. 26, 1948), 408.

[34] *Journal of Commerce,* Mar. 8, 1946, and June 10, 1947; *DSB,* XIX (Dec. 12, 1948), 736-38; European Gas and Electric, *Standard Oil Company,* pp. 10-27, 44-55.

[35] Quoted in European Gas and Electric, *Standard Oil Company,* p. 14.

[36] *Ibid.,* p. v.

[37] Earlier in 1946, Washington held that Hungary had no right to nationalize while under an armistice agreement. *Foreign Relations, 1946,* VI, 285; European Gas and Electric, *Standard Oil Company,* p. vi; *DSB,* XIX (Dec. 12, 1948), 736-38.

[38] Thomas P. Whitney, in *Foreign Relations, 1945,* V, 935.

[39] Sharp, *Nationalization,* pp. 3, 5.

reason of the impoverished soil, absence of important natural resources, lack of capital to invest, and that long before the war much new enterprise in Europe was financed by governments so that nationalization began in this manner even before the war and is less of an ideology than a necessity."[40]

Almost all postwar political parties supported nationalization.[41] Czech leader Jan Masaryk emphasized the lack of private capital and the need to industrialize and told the United Nations General Assembly in 1947 that nationalization had become "the irretrievable program of Europe today."[42] The British were nationalizing in their zone of Germany in 1945-1946. Czech President Eduard Beneš told United States officials that he saw state socialism and nationalization as possible bulwarks against Communism in his country.[43] Eastern European leaders also complained that prompt and adequate compensation to owners of nationalized companies was unrealistic, given the war's devastation, the shortage of dollars, and the costs of recovery. As the non-Communist Czech minister of foreign trade stated: "In order to assure that these operations [compensation] shall be financially bearable for Czechoslovakia, they must be preceded by a favorable development of our trade balance, so that our financial balance may be able to stand the transfer of considerable sums."[44] A Polish official pointed out that compensation was a slow process because it "burdens the whole state and delays its reconstruction."[45] Then too, the Soviet Union actually opposed nationalization in some countries because it might delay shipments of eagerly sought goods from eastern Europe. The Rumanian Communist Party, in fact, played down nationalization in 1946.[46] However, despite the complexity of the issue, nationalization appeared to be part of an aggressive Soviet pattern, as did the controversy over the control of the Danube River.

THE OPEN DOOR AND THE DANUBE CONTROVERSY

"For ten years I spent my time in the Vatch prison on the banks of the Danube," recalled a Hungarian Communist Party leader in 1946. "From the window of my cell I could observe all the ships which plied the river. I must record the fact that in the whole ten years I did not detect one American ship among them, and therefore do not understand why Americans manifest such tremendous interest in Danubian navigation."[47] Prewar United States trade

---

[40] Steinhardt to William Diamond, May 27, 1947, Box 84, Steinhardt Papers.

[41] Kolko, *Politics of War*, pp. 392, 411.

[42] *United Nations Weekly Bulletin*, III (Sept. 30, 1947), 429.

[43] *Foreign Relations, 1945*, V, 555.

[44] Quoted in William Diamond, *Czechoslovakia between East and West* (London, 1947), pp. 132-33.

[45] Quoted in Sharp, *Nationalization*, p. 46.

[46] Ghita Ionescu, *The Break-Up of the Soviet Empire in Eastern Europe* (London, 1965), 26-27; Ionescu, *Communism in Rumania*, p. 161.

[47] Matthias Rakoczi, quoted by Eugene Varga, *Pravda*, Nov. 2, 1946, in *Soviet Press Translations*, III (Jan. 15, 1947), 8.

on and interest in the Danube was in fact negligible—in stark contrast with Washington's vigorous concern for the river after World War II.[48] A Yugoslav delegate to the Paris Peace Conference of 1946 depicted the controversy between Russia and America over the scenic Danube as "a struggle for spheres of influence,"[49] but Senator Arthur Vandenberg, a delegate to the meeting, put it differently. Although the United States had no commercial interest in the Danube, "it had an emphatic interest in international peace and security and in avoiding trade barriers which invited discrimination and friction."[50]

The United States, under the principle of free navigation of international waterways in the postwar world, called in 1945 for an interim international Danube authority to establish regulations on that important eighteen-hundred-mile river, which originates in the Black Forest and winds its way through several countries to the Black Sea. Members of this commission were to include the United States, Britain, France, and the riparian states (including Russia), with United States participation derived from and justified by its occupation of Austria, a riparian state.[51] For Washington, however, the Danubian issue was larger than the principle of free navigation or narrow economic interests. A river free of trading impediments and open to all nations would stimulate commerce, tie the Danube into an interdependent, Western-oriented world economy, and contribute to European reconstruction and hence to peace. Western participation in the control of the river could also serve as a means of observing and perhaps checking Soviet influence in eastern Europe. As the Department of State concluded in early 1946: "US should use this policy as to Danube River, in so far as possible, to promote principles of freedom of commerce and navigation in East-Central Europe and to support political independence of peoples of this region."[52]

Russia countered the call for an international commission with the argument that only riparian states should govern the river and that for the duration of the postwar occupation military authorities should assume its control. The Danube issue touched directly the Soviet sphere of influence, prestige, and military security. Moscow looked askance at any commission which granted conspicuous representation to a hostile West seeking to reduce Soviet influence in Europe. It looked upon the Danube as the United States looked upon the Panama Canal and Britain the Suez Canal—as an imperial lifeline. Its desire to have the major voice in authority over the river was

[48]For prewar history see Stephen Gorove, *Law and Politics on the Danube: An Interdisciplinary Study* (The Hague, 1964).

[49] *Foreign Relations, 1946,* III (Washington, D.C., 1970), 759 (Oct. 10, 1946).

[50] *Ibid.,* p. 598 (Sept. 30, 1946).

[51] *Ibid., Berlin,* I, 329-31; *ibid., 1945,* II, 1366, 1384-85. The riparian states were Germany, Austria, Czechoslovakia, Hungary, Rumania, Yugoslavia, Bulgaria, Russia, and the Ukraine.

[52] *Ibid., 1946,* V, 229 (Feb. 26, 1946). See also *ibid., 1945,* II, 1373-82 (Oct. 22, 1945); John C. Campbell, "Diplomacy on the Danube," *Foreign Affairs,* XXVII (January, 1949), 315-27. Dean Acheson wrote on March 28, 1946, that the free navigation principle applied to the Danube was a "method of supporting political independence of peoples of this region." *Foreign Relations, 1946,* V, 233.

intensified by memories of 1921, when it was excluded from the international control commission while the non-riparian states Britain, France, and Italy were granted membership.[53] Joseph Davies, a former ambassador to Russia, indicated another factor: "The Danube Basin with its 'Iron Gate' has been for centuries recognized as a vital strategic military highway of Europe. In case of war between Russia and the West, it is of primary military importance."[54] The Soviets could only see the commission as an intrusion into their sphere of influence under the guise of the supposedly neutral open door principle. As one writer asked in *Pravda*, why did not the United States apply the principle of freedom of navigation "generally to those international waterways in which all maritime countries are interested, namely, to the Suez, Panama and Kiel Canals?"[55]

For President Truman, freedom of navigation on inland waterways was a principle of considerable importance, for he was convinced that world history demonstrated that the major wars of the past two centuries had erupted in the lands watered by the Rhine and Danube. Internationalization of these two rivers would limit the chances of war ever breaking out again. He also appealed for a network of canals to link European waterways, to bring together "the breadbasket with the industrial centers through a free flow of trade."[56] He was apparently endorsing and perpetuating Franklin D. Roosevelt's idea of a Tennessee Valley Authority for central Europe.[57]

Truman carried these ideas to the Potsdam Conference of July, 1945, where he hoped to persuade Stalin to accept them. According to Robert D. Murphy, United States political adviser for Germany, "Truman's favorite project at that time was the internationalization of inland waterways. . . ."[58] The president proposed that an international control commission for the Danube be established and that the principle of free navigation be accepted. He also argued that waterways like the Black Sea Straits and the Danube should be free of fortifications, but he did not mention the fortified Suez and Panama canals. When Winston Churchill endorsed Truman's general propositions and made it clear that he excluded the Suez from them, Foreign Minister V. M. Molotov pressed him: "If it was such a good rule why not

[53] *Foreign Relations, 1945,* II, 1376-77, 1381; *ibid., Berlin,* I, 326-28; Charlotte B. Rasmussen, "Freedom of the Danube," *Current History,* XII (January, 1947), 27-31.
[54] Diary, July 30, 1945, Box 19, Joseph Davies Papers, Library of Congress.
[55] Eugene Varga. See n. 47 above.
[56] Truman, *Memoirs,* I, 236. The Hungarian prime minister visited the United States in 1946 and commented shortly thereafter that Truman seemed to be "especially interested in the Danube. . . ." Ferenc Nagy, *The Struggle behind the Iron Curtain* (New York, 1948), p. 228. Also see Truman's Navy Day address of October 27, 1945. *Public Papers, Truman, 1945,* pp. 431-38.
[57] Jonathan Daniels, *The Man of Independence* (Philadelphia, 1950), p. 284; Doris S. Whitnack and David Handler, "Danubian Transportation Problems in Relation to Development of the Basin," *DSB,* XIV (June 30, 1946), 1108-10; George Kiss, "TVA on the Danube?" *Geographical Review,* XXXVII (April, 1947), 274-302; Gardner, *Architects of Illusion,* pp. 73-74.
[58] Robert D. Murphy, *Diplomat among Warriors* (Garden City, N.Y., 1964), p. 277.

apply it to the Suez."[59] Churchill was evasive, and it appears that neither he nor Truman would grant "any equivalent concessions" to the Russians.[60] Stalin asked for postponement of the question of internationalization, stating that the Russian delegation had not come to Potsdam prepared to discuss the issue. It was evident that neither the United States nor Britain would entertain his recommendation that Turkey and Russia determine the control of the Black Sea Straits, especially since they were governed by a convention from which Russia was excluded which allowed Turkey to shut off navigation during a threat of war. He finally accepted Truman's suggestion that the question of waterways be referred to the London Foreign Ministers Conference.[61] Nevertheless, Truman was angered by Stalin's apparent rebuff of his pet project. He concluded in his *Memoirs* a few years later that Stalin's lack of enthusiasm for internationalization of waterways "showed how his mind worked and what he was after. . . . The Russians were planning world conquest."[62] It was a grand conclusion drawn from an inconclusive discussion of a question—the Danube—about which most Americans were ignorant and which seemed minor indeed compared to the dramatic crises in Poland, Germany, and the United Nations.

No agreement was reached at the foreign ministers' meetings in late 1945. When the United States opened the Russian loan question in early 1946, the issue reappeared. At that time the United States attempted to pressure eastern Europe and Russia into a settlement on its terms through the use of about eight hundred Danubian vessels. This fleet, constituting about one-third of all barges on the Danube, belonged to Bulgaria, Yugoslavia, Hungary, and Czechoslovakia. The Germans confiscated them during the war, and at the close of the war General Mark W. Clark moved many of them into the waters of the American zones in Austria and Germany. "It seemed to me," he wrote, "that they would be a kind of ace up our sleeve in bargaining with the Russians, since the barges would be essential when river traffic was resumed."[63] Washington let it be known quietly that they would not be released to their legal owners until the principle of free navigation was

[59] *Foreign Relations, Berlin,* II, 365.

[60] Gardner, *Architects of Illusion,* p. 82.

[61] For the record of the Potsdam Conference on the free navigation problem, see *Foreign Relations, Berlin,* II, 303-4, 366, 397-98, 527, 577-78, 654-58, 1427-28; *The Tehran, Yalta, and Potsdam Conferences: Documents* (Moscow, 1969), pp. 232-34, 251-52, 259, 292, 305-7, 340. See also Murphy, *Diplomat,* pp. 277-78; James F. Byrnes, *Speaking Frankly* (New York, 1947), p. 129. Truman wrote in his *Memoirs* (I, 377) that he included the Panama and Suez canals in his proposal, but the Potsdam records indicate that he did not.

[62] Truman, *Memoirs,* I, 412. Murphy has written: "The earnestness of the President's speech was evident. . . . Everybody could see that the President was intensely interested in this matter, more than many of us believed justified at that moment, and Byrnes did his best to get some action on it." Murphy, *Diplomat,* pp. 277-78.

[63] Mark W. Clark, *Calculated Risk* (New York, 1950), p. 464. See also Clark's *From the Danube to the Yalu* (New York, 1954), pp. 7-8.

accepted for the Danube. A State Department official explained to Ambassador Steinhardt: "We cannot continue to hold the Czech barges indefinitely and in time will have to give them back, but, along with the others, they constitute *the only bargaining weapon* which the United States has in establishing the principle of free navigation."[64]

This rather blunt procedure, which violated the very principle the United States wanted endorsed, prompted Yugoslavia and Czechoslovakia to request the Economic and Social Council of the United Nations to direct the United States to return the craft. On September 21, 1946, the Danubian fleet issue was placed on the agenda, and debate was initiated by Yugoslavia a week later. The Yugoslav delegate said that the immobilization of the fleet was disrupting his country's transportation system by overtaxing railroads, impeding the shipment of UNRRA goods, and delaying valuable cargoes of coal and building materials. He further stated that Washington had informed Belgrade in April that the fleet was tied to the principle of free navigation. Czechoslovakia supported the Yugoslav protests, lamenting the detrimental effect of the action on economic reconstruction, and Russia lined up behind its neighbors.[65]

The United States delegate to the Council, Ambassador John G. Winant, was uncomfortable because he himself believed the United States was perpetrating an injustice. Reluctantly he submitted a proposal that a conference of riparian states and of nations occupying Germany and Austria be convened to settle the question, and he again linked the restitution of the craft to the principle of free navigation. He also introduced another explanation for the Washington's intransigence: the vessels were being held "as an offset to American property which has been seized or nationalized and for which no compensation arrangements have yet been made."[66] The Yugoslav delegate's cry of "the Danube for the Danubians" was in vain: the Council rejected the Yugoslav appeal that the United States be instructed to release the barges and passed the proposal for a Danubian conference.[67] Winant, in protest to the Department of State for its obstinacy on the question, resigned his position that year.[68]

At the Paris Peace Conference in the fall of 1946, the issue of free navigation and the confiscated fleet aroused vigorous debate. The United

[64] Francis Williamson to Steinhardt, July 1, 1946, Box 51, Steinhardt Papers. Robert D. Murphy put it strongly on May 2, 1946: "Those 800 vessels held by the U.S. forces constitute greater bargaining power than originally believed, and the most important factor in negotiations with the Soviets" on the Danubian issue. *Foreign Relations, 1946,* V, 251. See also *ibid.,* VI, 315, 339; *ibid.,* V, 262; Campbell, *United States in World Affairs, 1945-1947,* pp. 422-23.

[65] United Nations, Economic and Social Council, *Official Records,* 1st year, 3d sess. (New York, 1946), pp. 9, 38, 62-72.

[66] *Ibid.,* pp. 68, 74-76.

[67] *Ibid.,* pp. 76, 153-55; Bernard Bellush, *He Walked Alone: A Biography of John Gilbert Winant* (The Hague, 1968), pp. 224-25.

[68] Bellush, *He Walked Alone,* p. 225.

States wanted the peace treaties to provide for international control and free navigation, and the Russians wanted no mention of those principles at all.[69] Molotov piously protested that "one cannot agree with such methods of treating small states." He criticized dollar and sterling diplomacy: the Soviet Union could not "concur when a strong Power tries to exploit its temporary advantages at a time when many countries have not yet healed their war wounds." He also posed a number of penetrating questions: "Are the advocates of the principle of 'equal opportunity' willing to apply it to the Suez Canal? Are the advocates of the principle of 'equal opportunity' willing to apply it to the Panama Canal as well?"[70]

In October by a two-thirds majority the Conference voted to include a clause in the peace treaties with former German satellites endorsing the principle of freedom of navigation on the Danube and of a permanent Danube commission. It was a hollow American victory, for the most crucial issue was control, and that Russia already had. Yet it gave the United States the opportunity to resolve the embarrassing problem of the seized vessels. As one State Department official noted: "It may be that we have extracted the maximum bargaining value from our retention and we could perhaps capitalize on return of barges to a greater extent now than we can at some later date." He feared that Russia would eventually veto any free navigation and that the United States would be left with a "noble gesture and no result." If there was a chance that the Soviets might think that the United States had weakened its position, "I would favor holding the barges until Hell freezes over." But the new clauses offered a way to let go of the vessels, and Truman, at the State Department's recommendation, ordered them returned.[71] The decision essentially amounted to a realization that this "dog-in-the-manger policy was producing little except ill-will," as John C. Campbell put it.[72] The barges began moving on the Danube in November, but one State Department officer was disappointed at the Czech reaction to the release. "The Czechs might have at least given the news some prominence in the press," he complained, "if they do not want to miss chances to regain our good will."[73]

The Council of Foreign Ministers agreed in December, 1946, to arrange a meeting of the Danubian states, France, Britain, and the United States to effect an agreement on control, the conference to take place within six months after the entry into force of the peace treaties with Hungary, Rumania, and Bulgaria. The treaties became law in September, 1947, and the

---

[69] *Foreign Relations, 1946,* III, 598-600, 758.

[70] V. M. Molotov, *Problems of Foreign Policy: Speeches and Statements, April 1945-November 1948* (speech of Oct. 10, 1946) (Moscow, 1949), pp. 217, 218-19, 211. See also *DSB,* XV (Oct. 20, 1946), 711.

[71] U.S., Department of State, *Treaties of Peace with Italy, Bulgaria, Roumania, and Finland* (Washington, D.C., 1947); *Foreign Relations, 1946,* III, 604, 626, 811, 816; *ibid.,* IV, 79-80, 468-69, 496, 922, 933, 946; *ibid.,* V, 276, 279-80 (the quoted statement, by John Hickerson, deputy director of European affairs, appears on p. 276).

[72] Campbell, *United States in World Affairs, 1945-1947,* p. 423.

[73] James W. Riddleberger to Steinhardt, Dec. 2, 1946, Box 51, Steinhardt Papers.

conference was scheduled to meet in March, 1948. On February 27, 1948, the United States asked that it be postponed until the end of the year, in the hope that by then Austria would have signed a peace treaty and could participate as an equal. Austria would support the United States position, and Washington knew that the Danube conference would be the first international meeting since the war in which the Soviet Union was not in the minority and outvoted by the West. After much disagreement, Russia and the United States compromised on July 30, 1948, as a date for the meeting. Moscow rejected the American proposal that Austria be seated despite the absence of a peace treaty but did accept Austrian participation on a consultative basis.[74]

In early 1948 President Truman and Grenville Clark, a distinguished lawyer and United World Federalist, entered a private debate which demonstrated again Truman's deep commitment to his internationalization scheme. Clark, in an address to a New York City audience in February, urged, among other proposals, that international waterways between oceans and seas be placed under the control of the United Nations. He did not mention the Danube but specifically singled out the Black Sea Straits, the Panama and Suez canals, and the Straits of Gibraltar.[75] He sent a copy of the speech to Truman, who quickly responded that he had pressed unsuccessfully for internationalization of waterways at Potsdam. "I don't know what people expect from Governments represented by Molotov, Vishinsky, and Gromyko," the president said. "They have fixed ideas and those ideas were set out by Peter the Great in his will—I suggest that you read it." This "will" supposedly illustrated Russian aggressive intentions, and although Truman was clearly reciting a distorted history in this instance because scholars considered the "will" a forgery, the correspondence indicates again his firm belief that Soviet failure to endorse internationalization was an aggressive gesture.[76]

It was not long after this exchange that the Danube Conference met in Belgrade. Although the meeting lasted from July 30 to August 18, the outcome was evident on the first day. There was a Soviet majority, and Russia pressed its advantage, even to the point of excluding English as an official language. Andrei Y. Vyshinsky bossed the meeting: "I would say in general that what is acceptable in the United States draft can be found in the

[74] Fred L. Hadsel, "Freedom of Navigation on the Danube," *DSB*, XVIII (June 20, 1948), 787-93, 797.
[75] Grenville Clark, "A Settlement with Russia—Its Necessity for World Order," Feb. 7, 1948, Stimson Papers.
[76] Truman letter, Feb. 18, 1948, quoted in John Garry Clifford, "Historical Analogies, President Truman, and Peter the Great's 'Will' " (unpublished manuscript, 1970, in the author's possession), p. 5. According to the copy of the document which Clark possessed, Peter the Great wrote: "My successors will make her [Russia] a great sea destined to fertilize impoverished Europe, and if my descendents know how to direct the waters, her waves will break through all opposing banks." Copy in Stimson Papers. The author thanks Professor Clifford for calling the Clark-Truman debate to his attention and for offering helpful suggestions on the Danube controversy.

Soviet draft and what is not in the Soviet draft cannot be accepted."[77] United States Ambassador Cavendish V. Cannon's arguments that international control and free navigation would ensure world peace and prosperity aroused no enthusiasm in the solid bloc of seven riparian states. Even Yugoslavia, under heavy attack from Stalin for deviation, voted with Russia, suggesting, as in the case of Rumania, that prewar resentment against Western involvement in the Danube was still active.[78] By a vote of seven to three (France, Britain, and the United States), Russia carried its proposal for riparian control of the Danube. The request for open navigation and nondiscrimination on the river was defeated. The Soviet Union and its allies also rejected a formula whereby the new Danubian commission would report to a body of the United Nations (where United States influence would probably be dominant). Finally, with chances of success very slim indeed, the United States asserted that the international commission established in 1921 was still legal and that France and Britain therefore could not be excluded from Danubian control. Nothing could have annoyed the Russians more because of their bitterness over their exclusion from the 1921 commission. The conference ended with riparian control and no provision for free navigation. France and Britain did not even record their final abstentions; the United States cast the only negative vote. The Western participants refused to be bound by the convention, and by the end of 1948 only about two hundred miles of the river remained open to Western traffic.[79] The Soviet Union now had a major artery for its developing empire.

The United States left the conference embittered. Washington had hoped that an open Danube would facilitate commerce and hence assist the Marshall Plan. Cannon commented angrily, "I know of no previous international conference where a majority of the participants, with cynical solidarity, have refrained from proposing even minor changes in the text laid before them for discussion."[80] Nor were there many changes in the Danube's role in international politics thereafter. The Soviet Union denied certain rights to Yugoslavia in the new Danube commission (including visas to travel to the meetings); after Stalin's death, Yugoslavia was back in the fold, and multilateral programs and technical improvements were initiated; in 1960 Austria joined the commission. Meanwhile, the Western members of the defunct 1921 commission held a brief meeting in Rome in 1953 and decided not to disband.[81]

<hr>

[77] DSB, XIX (Aug. 22, 1948), 219.

[78] David T. Cattell, "The Politics of the Danube Commission under Soviet Control," American Slavic and East European Review, XIX (October, 1960), 383-84. For Cannon speeches, see DSB, XIX (Aug. 15, 1948), 197-99; ibid. (Aug. 22, 1948), 220; ibid. (Sept. 5, 1948), 291-92.

[79] Vyshinsky, in Pravda, Aug. 4, 1948, in Soviet Press Translations, III (Oct. 1, 1948), 519-24; Campbell, "Diplomacy on the Danube," pp. 322-27; Gyorgy, Governments of Danubian Europe, pp. 63-64.

[80] DSB, XIX (Sept. 5, 1948), 291.

[81] Cattell, "Politics of the Danube Commission," pp. 384-94.

The Danube became a Cold War casualty and a symbol—to Washington, of a closing door, both political and economic, in eastern Europe; to the Russians, of a Western attempt to challenge the Soviet Union. President Truman's marked attention to the question and the deep East-West schism the controversy encouraged provide a case study of Soviet-American competition for influence in Europe. It joined the concatenation of dramatic issues such as free elections in Poland, the Truman Doctrine and Greece, and the Marshall Plan, all of which, according to popular sentiment in the United States, were attempts to roll back Soviet influence in Europe. The debates over the Danube, nationalization, reparations, trade treaties, and joint-stock companies exacerbated and reflected the postwar confrontation.

WAS THE OPEN DOOR CLOSED?

Was the trade and investment door closed in the early years of the Cold War? Did the Soviets seal off eastern Europe behind an "iron curtain" before 1947? Did an impenetrable Soviet bloc exist immediately after the war? The answers must be tentative and suggestive because of thè paucity of available Soviet historical sources. Yet considerable evidence suggests that in the 1945-1946 period, the Soviet Union was uncertain, halting, and defensive in its relations with the eastern European nations and did not have a master plan for the region. Its mixed behavior in eastern Europe is evident: independence and democratic politics for Finland and Czechoslovakia (until 1948); free elections in Hungary in the fall of 1945, with the Communists polling less than 20 percent of the vote; a firm hand in Poland and Rumania; elections in Austria in 1945; and independence for Tito's Yugoslavia. Without doubt there was a Soviet sphere of influence in the immediate postwar years, but the thesis that an inexorably aggressive Russia established a close-knit bloc is open to question. Not until 1947-1948 did it tighten its grip on eastern Europe through the Cominform, the Molotov Plan, coups, and blatant political repression. The flexibility of the 1945-1946 period—evidence that a bloc did not exist—is demonstrated by a study of the open door issue in eastern Europe and the relationship between United States loan policy and independence in that region.

Professor John K. Galbraith challenged the popular attitude in 1946: "Soviet influence in eastern Europe has not resulted in the totally closed system that so often has been pictured in recent months."[82] Barbara Ward also denied that the "total state" had been imposed on that area, and, although there is no doubt that United States trade and investment met impediments, throughout the postwar years opportunities remained avail-

---

[82] John K. Galbraith, *Recovery in Europe* (Washington, D.C., 1946).

able.[83] The chronology and the nature of the nationalization programs are important, for they were indigenous and traditional, and many of them came late in the Cold War. Czechoslovakia, next to Yugoslavia the most independent eastern European state, was first with its nationalization; Rumania, one of the least independent, was last (June, 1948). It does not appear that nationalization constituted a Soviet effort to close the door, nor were the programs so extensive that all private enterprises were eliminated. Then, too, Russia seized little American-owned property; when it did confiscate property it had usually been German-owned at some time during the war. Secretary Stettinius noted in mid-1945 that "the satellite governments apparently have not attempted to discriminate against American property, nor have the Russians made a practice of demanding American-owned plants and factories under the respective reparations clauses."[84] As of June 22, 1945, he could account for only two cases of Russian seizure of American property: oil equipment in Rumania and a bulb factory in Hungary, both properties Russia considered German.

The evidence of continued trade between the United States (and western Europe) and eastern Europe further challenges the notion that the door to the East closed. Stalin told the Special Committee on Post-War Economic Policy and Planning in September, 1945, that Russia did not object to eastern European trade with other nations: "We understand that an American company [Dodge] would like to set up a plant in Rumania and that investment should be this way: 30% Russian, 30% American. We were asked if we had any objections. We have no objections." The Committee later reported that an American automobile firm was in fact offered such participation in a mixed company.[85] *Business Week* confirmed the Russian attitude in 1946, writing that despite Russian penetration of mixed companies, "doors have not yet been closed to similar participation by U.S., British, and other business interests."[86] In mid-1946 Rumania negotiated in the United States with Kaiser-Frazer and Nashville Bridge for their participation in American-Russian-Rumanian companies, and in the next year both Standard Oil of New Jersey and Westinghouse (each with a 10 percent interest) participated in the Rumanian-American Trading Corporation.[87] The

[83] Barbara Ward, "Europe Debates Nationalization," *Foreign Affairs*, XXV (October, 1946), 44-58.
[84] *Foreign Relations, Berlin*, I, 428. See also William B. Cowles, "Recovery in American Claims Abroad," *Harvard Business Review*, XXV (Autumn, 1946), 104-5; *New York Times*, Apr. 22, 1946.
[85] "Conversation between Stalin and Members of the House Special Committee on Post-War Economic Policy and Planning," Sept. 14, 1945, Box 46, Pepper Papers; House, *Economic Reconstruction in Europe*, 8th Rept., p. 43.
[86] *Business Week*, Apr. 20, 1946, p. 107.
[87] *Journal of Commerce*, Aug. 2, 1946; Alfred W. Barth to Winthrop Aldrich, May 9, 1947, File II, Box 110, Aldrich Papers. In 1947 Chase National Bank loaned Banque

Czechs continued to trade with the West, and President Beneš in early 1946 told Steinhardt that he did not expect Russia to insist on disrupting such trade.[88] Steinhardt assisted the Czechoslovak Glass Works in reaching customers in the United States, and the Czech minister of foreign trade recalled that "our trade with the Western countries still far surpassed that with Russia and the countries of the Soviet sphere, which in the most favourable circumstances could not reach more than 40 percent."[89] The Polish-American Supply Company, a combination of Polish businessmen and the government, appealed for more trade with the United States in 1947, and Bulgaria and Yugoslavia arranged barter agreements with American companies in 1946 and 1947.[90] As Vera Micheles Dean concluded in 1948: "Contrary to the impression sometimes prevalent in the United States, the Polish government, far from favoring a policy of self-sufficiency or an economic iron curtain, has fostered trade with all countries irrespective of political differences. Like Czechoslovakia, Poland has played an active part in the European Economic Commission—especially in its Coal Committee."[91]

Trade figures for eastern Europe further challenge the notion that there was a closed economic system early in the Cold War. Without question East-West trade declined, but by 1950 only one-third of eastern Europe's trade was with Russia. Non-Communist countries' exports to eastern Europe (including Russia) remained fairly constant in 1947-1949 at $1.3 billion a year. The United States during the Marshall Plan years anticipated more East-West trade; the sharp decline actually began in 1950 and lasted into the late 1950s.[92]

Although trade within the Soviet sphere of influence increased significantly after the war, a closed trade bloc did not develop, despite Russia's post-Marshall-Plan attempts to create one.[93] In late 1947, a leading international banker noted that Russia was having trouble "trying to hold" eastern Europe together economically: "In an economic sense, no Molotov

Nationale de Roumanie several million dollars. *Ibid.*, Mar. 8, 1947. See also *Foreign Relations, 1946*, VI, 641-42, 645, 669, 671.
    [88] *Foreign Relations, 1946*, VI, 178n. Also see pp. 189-90.
    [89] Czechoslovak Glass Works to Steinhardt, Jan. 6, 1947, Box 50, Steinhardt Papers; Ripka, *Czechoslovakia Enslaved*, p. 131.
    [90] *Journal of Commerce*, June 12 and Sept. 8, 1947; *East Europe*, III, no. 93 (July 31, 1946), 11; N. K., "East-West Trade," pp. 98, 99-101.
    [91] Vera M. Dean, "Economic Trends in Eastern Europe–I: Czechoslovakia and Poland," *Foreign Policy Reports*, XXIV (Apr. 1, 1948), 27.
    [92] U.S., Congress, Senate, Committee on Banking and Currency, *East-West Trade* (Hearings) (1968), pt. 2, p. 787; Raymond F. Mikesell and Jack N. Behrman, *Financing Free World Trade with the Sino-Soviet Bloc* (Princeton, N.J., 1958), p. 4.
    [93] Trade within eastern Europe, including Russia, increased from 1 percent of world trade in 1938 to 3 percent in 1948 and to 8 percent in 1953. By 1954, Soviet intrabloc trade had risen to ten times the prewar volume. Thorbecke, *Tendency*, p. 7; U.S., Commission on Foreign Economic Policy, *Staff Papers* (Washington, D.C., 1954), pp. 445-46.

bloc can be formed."[94] Clayton, Steinhardt, and Thomas Blaisdell (Commerce Department) agreed that Russia simply could not meet eastern Europe's economic needs and therefore would fail to establish a bloc economy.[95] As one student of the area wrote in 1949: "The tremendous tasks of postwar reconstruction have forced the Soviet government to compromises of all types. It had to allow Eastern Europe governments to trade with the West. . . ."[96]

President Truman's statement that Russia blocked East-West trade after Potsdam fails to reflect the complexity and checkered pattern of foreign economic relations in eastern Europe.[97] Washington exaggerated Soviet policy there, and its own export controls of early 1948 (affecting Russia too) contributed to the closing of the door. Between March, 1948, and March, 1950, the Department of Commerce rejected export applications for shipments to eastern Europe totaling $150 million, or 36 percent of the total requested. There is no account of applications never filed because of known restrictions, especially on vehicles and machinery. The United States pressured Marshall Plan countries to agree to restrictions on "strategic" goods. By 1951 these countries, organized in a Coordinating Committee (COCOM) in 1950, embargoed 90 percent of the items regarded by Washington as strategic.[98] It is clear that the United States helped close the door in eastern Europe and that fears for the open door, in both the economic and political sense, were exaggerated in the immediate postwar years.

[94] Per Jacobson, Bank for International Settlements, to Randolph Burgess, Oct. 22, 1947, Proposals folder, President's Committee on Foreign Aid Records.
[95] "Comment on Mr. Grenville Clark's Memorandum of December 1st, 1948 Regarding United World Federalists' Policy," Jan. 17, 1949, William L. Clayton Papers, Rice University Library; Steinhardt to William Diamond, May 27, 1947, Box 84, Steinhardt Papers; draft memorandum, "Export Policy toward Eastern Europe," T. C. Blaisdell, Aug. 12, 1948, Commercial Policy folder, Thomas C. Blaisdell Papers, Truman Library.
[96] Gyorgy, *Governments of Danubian Europe*, p. 57. According to Zsoldos Laszlo, in *The Economic Integration of Hungary into the Soviet Bloc: Foreign Trade Experience* (Columbia, O., 1963), p. 95, the Hungarian economy after 1950 was "imperfectly integrated with the Soviet Bloc." For similar views, see William Diebold, Jr., "East-West Trade and the Marshall Plan," *Foreign Affairs*, XXVI (July, 1948), 712-13; Dewar, *Soviet Trade*, pp. 4, 13-14, 22-23.
[97] *New York Times*, Feb. 14, 1950.
[98] Office of Secretary, GC 93126, Boxes 748, 751-53, Commerce Records; Commerce, *Export Control and Allocation Powers*, 11th Quarterly Report, p. 1; Committee on the Present Danger, "Limitations of Trade of the Free World with the Soviet Bloc as a Condition of U.S. Foreign Aid," July 18, 1951, East-West Trade folder, Theodore Tannenwald Papers, Truman Library. During the 1950s some of the Marshall Plan countries resisted the pressure from Washington and shipped goods to eastern Europe. Senator James P. Kem of Missouri retaliated with a provision in the Battle Act of 1951 that countries which shipped strategic goods to Communist-dominated nations were ineligible for United States aid. U.S., Department of State, *The Battle Act Report, 1966* (Washington, D.C., 1966); Price, *Marshall Plan*, pp. 168-70.

CHAPTER 6

THE DIPLOMACY OF THE DOLLAR: LOANS, INDEPENDENCE, AND THE SOVIET SPHERE

One of the few diplomatic tools available to American officials to pry Eastern Europe open to United States influence was economic assistance. Washington conducted a conscious and active diplomacy after the war through the granting or denying of loans to eastern European nations. When that maneuver failed to move the area out of the Soviet orbit, United States aid was cut off, and eastern Europe fell more deeply under Russian influence. Demonstrating some flexibility, Washington treated Finland and Yugoslavia as exceptions and gave them aid without "strings," thus helping to ensure their independence, but Czechoslovakia, Poland, Rumania, and Hungary were considered Soviet fiefs and members of a tight bloc. If they could not be wooed from their foreign policy alignment with Russia—and Washington soon learned that its economic diplomacy was inadequate for that task, then they had to be isolated from the benefits of American loans and trade. Aid without "strings"—given simply to preserve what was left of independence in eastern Europe and to maintain links between that area and the United States—was not tolerated. Secretary Byrnes's simple prescription of September, 1946, merits repeating: "We must help our friends in every way and refrain from assisting those who either through helplessness or for other reasons are opposing the principles for which we stand."[1]

Americans faced a dilemma. If Washington extended considerable aid with "strings" to eastern Europe, the Soviets might be aroused to halt it. If the United States refused aid altogether, eastern Europe would become more dependent on Russia. The resolution of the dilemma would have been a non-threatening, cautious economic foreign policy without "strings." Russia would tolerate reasonable—but not exploitative or binding—Western economic relations with its sphere.[2] But the Truman administration defined

[1] *Foreign Relations, 1946*, VII, 223.
[2] See the evidence in Chapter 5 above and Andrei Zhdanov's statement: "The Soviet Union has never objected to using foreign, and in particular American, credits as a means capable of expediting the process of economic rehabilitation. However, the Soviet Union has always taken the stand that the terms of credits must not be extortionate, and must not result in the economic and political subjugation of the debtor country to the creditor country." Zhdanov, *International Situation*, p. 40.

"friends" and "principles for which we stand" in narrow terms and followed a conspicuous diplomacy designed to weaken the Soviet presence.

THE TRAGEDY OF CZECHOSLOVAKIA

After World War II, Czechoslovakia clung precariously to a middle ground in the developing bipolar world, attempting to perpetuate its independence and interchanges with western Europe and the United States and at the same time to build and nurture a strategically important and sincere friendship for Russia.[3] Well before the Communist coup of February, 1948, however, American leaders defined Czechoslovakia, a democratic socialist nation, as a Soviet satellite and virtually wrote the fledgling country off as "lost." Crucial reconstruction aid was denied and the Soviet domination that Washington had prematurely imagined became stark reality.

United States foreign policy experts grappled with three troublesome questions in Czechoslovakia in 1945: removal of American and Soviet troops, the declaration by Soviet authorities that two plants claimed by the International Telephone and Telegraph Corporation (ITT) were "war trophies," and the relationship between the Czech nationalization program, loans, and United States goals in eastern Europe. Both the Americans and the Russians refused to withdraw their troops until it was certain that the withdrawal would be simultaneous; after some hesitation both nations removed their soldiers in December, 1945. That month, too, after American protests to Moscow that the ITT factories were American-owned and important to Czech reconstruction, Russia dropped it claim to one of the plants and demanded 50 percent ownership of the other.[4]

The third issue was more divisive. In early 1945 the United States was anxious about Czechoslovakia's postwar intentions concerning nationalization. Ambassador Laurence A. Steinhardt successfully persuaded the Department of State to defer any loan decision by the Export-Import Bank until the Czech nationalization program had been announced.[5] In October, the non-Communist government led by the respected Eduard Beneš nationalized

---

[3] It was not surprising that Czechoslovakia looked more to Russia than to the United States after Munich. The impression was prevalent "among many Czechoslovak leaders that Russia's pre-eminent role in Eastern Europe was not only inevitable but actually desirable in view of the assumed German enmity." Ivo Duchacek, "Czechoslovakia," in Stephen D. Kertesz, ed., *The Fate of East Central Europe* (Notre Dame, Ind., 1956), p. 197.

[4] *Foreign Relations, 1945,* IV, 420-509.

[5] Steinhardt was a lawyer in the New York firm of Guggenheimer, Untermyer, and Marshall until the early 1930s. He entered government service in 1933 as an envoy to Sweden. He then served as ambassador to Peru (1937-39), Russia (1939-41), Turkey (1942-45), Czechoslovakia (1945-48), and Canada (1948-50). He died in 1950. His papers in the Library of Congress contain important letters to and from business associates, prominent friends, and Department of State officers. *Foreign Relations, 1945,* IV, 551.

American-owned and controlled enterprises valued at $109 million. Such companies as Socony-Vacuum, ITT, Remington Rand, Corn Products Refining, and Standard Oil of New Jersey were affected; John Foster Dulles of Sullivan and Cromwell represented several other claimants.[6]

At first, Steinhardt was confident that the Czechs would compensate these businesses for nationalized property, although he recognized that their shortage of dollars would make such compensation difficult.[7] He became impatient and more demanding as the Czech government struggled with the problem. He and the State Department came more and more to see Czechoslovakia as a prime target for the diplomatic use of economic power. Loan policy under Steinhardt's and Byrnes's guidance was aimed at slowing down nationalization, securing adequate compensation for American property, and, more significant, orienting Czech foreign policy toward the United States.

Hoping to export surplus cotton, the Truman administration began negotiations with Czechoslovakia in October, 1945, for a $20 million cotton credit. This credit was granted on July, 1946, but after nationalization negotiations for a large loan (Czechoslovakia had requested $300 million in September) moved more slowly. The State Department and Steinhardt agreed the previous December that a loan of $25 to $35 million was feasible, yet in early 1946, Steinhardt was arguing for delay until Czech-Soviet trade relations clarified and because the Czechs were already receiving UNRRA shipments. Byrnes assured Steinhardt that no loan would be granted until the Czechs revealed their trade agreements with Russia, until they assured the United States of adequate compensation, and until they agreed to abstain from measures which might impede multilateral trade.[8]

In the first half of 1946 Steinhardt's attitude hardened. He insisted that "a large American loan to any foreign government in which the Communist Party is strongly represented will be availed of by them indirectly to entrench their position and extend their grip."[9] He recalled the defaulting upon World War I loans, claimed that the Czechs did not need a large reconstruction loan, mentioned again UNRRA aid, and stressed the importance of compensation.

---

[6] Treasury, *Census of American-Owned Assets,* p. 68; U.S., Congress, Senate, Special Committee to Investigate Petroleum Resources, "Report of the Group on American Petroleum Interests in Foreign Countries," I, Oct. 15, 1945, Senate Records; *Business Week,* Mar. 11, 1950; memorandum, "Compensation for Socony-Vacuum Oil Company," 1947, Box 55, Steinhardt Papers; Steinhardt to Dulles, Dec. 26, 1946, Box 83, and June 18, 1946, Box 50, *ibid.; Foreign Relations: Berlin,* I, 428.

[7] Steinhardt to Dulles, Dec. 26, 1945, Box 83, Steinhardt Papers.

[8] *Foreign Relations, 1945,* IV, 549-57; *ibid., 1946,* VI, 178-80, 182-83, 203-4. In May, 1946, the United States also extended a $2 million tobacco credit.

[9] *Ibid.,* p. 187. See also pp. 181-82, 185-88, 195, 200-203, 205-6. Steinhardt wrote to the European representative of Socony-Vacuum: "Should you hear of an Export-Import Bank reconstruction loan to Czechoslovakia, do not let this alarm you as one of the conditions of the loan will be adequate and effective compensation for American nationalized properties." Steinhardt to Harold Sheets, May 16, 1946, Box 50, Steinhardt Papers.

He also tried, but without success, to dissuade Washington from adding another $40 million to the $10 million already offered Czechoslovakia for the purchase of surplus United States property in Europe, which the Foreign Liquidation Commission was eager to sell. In July, to Steinhardt's dismay, negotiations for a $50 million reconstruction loan were proceeding well because the Czechs promised to open talks on compensation.

Steinhardt filed a stinging dissent. Mere promises of compensation, he contended, were not enough to justify a loan. The reconstruction loan was "our last trump" in securing compensation. But his reasoning went beyond the narrow compensation issue to the question of the place of Czechoslovakia in world affairs. Earlier he had cabled the State Department that "since election of May 26 [in which the Communists polled 38 percent of the popular vote] there has been an unmistakable though indefinable tendency on part of some officials of Czech government to show increasing indifference towards western powers." He noted that the Czechs were "self-satisfied" and not thirsting for United States aid and that the bargaining authority of a loan seemed significantly diminished.[10] Overemphasizing the "indifference" of some political figures, he virtually ignored the eagerness of Beneš, Hubert Ripka, and Jan Masaryk—non-Communist officials—for aid.

Steinhardt's position received dramatic and surprising support from Byrnes at the Paris Peace Conference on August 30.[11] The Czechs sent ten officials to the meeting, two of whom were Communists. At one point in the discussions, these two Communist delegates applauded a Soviet charge that the United States was trying to force its will upon weaker nations through its lending power. Infuriated, Byrnes ordered Washington to prevent the unused portion of the surplus property credit of $40 million from being utilized and to suspend the Czech application for a $50 million reconstruction loan. Henceforth the United States should aid "friends," he said, and not subsidize "the Communist control of Czechoslovakia." He would not tolerate "vilification of the United States and distortion of our motives and policies."[12] A more cautious Will Clayton believed that since the United States had already set prerequisites for the reconstruction loan, it had a "moral commitment" to proceed with the loan if the Czechs met the conditions. Nevertheless, the Export-Import Bank loan application was suspended and the surplus property credit was taken back.[13]

Byrnes's decisions, seemingly motivated by the handclapping incident at

[10] *Foreign Relations, 1946,* VI, 206n, 209.

[11] On August 29 Acheson noted that the negotiations were bogged down over the compensation issue, with already confiscated, as opposed to nationalized, property causing disagreement. *Ibid.,* pp. 215-16.

[12] *Ibid.,* pp. 216-17.

[13] *Ibid.,* pp. 220, 224, 229. One of the reasons given for the suspension of the surplus property credit was that Czechoslovakia planned to sell some of the property to Rumania. For this complicated secondary issue, see *ibid.,* pp. 220-23, 225, 227-28; James F. Byrnes, *All in One Lifetime* (New York, 1958), p. 364; *Central European Observor,* XXIII (Nov. 8, 1946), 353.

Paris, derived from the larger question of Czech friendship for Russia: "You must bear in mind . . . that up to the very end of this conference Czechoslovakia has consistently opposed the United States and voted invariably with the Slav bloc on every important issue. . . . I should wish to see much more substantial evidence of Czechoslovak independence and friendship toward the United States before resuming any form of economic assistance which some members of its delegation here profess to believe may lead to Czechoslovakia's 'economic enslavement.' "[14] The secretary had expressed such sentiments in his September 24, 1946, cable dividing the world into "friends" and opponents. As John C. Campbell has commented: "The answer to the accusation of dollar diplomacy apparently was to give the accuser a real taste of it. It was a rather unprecedented move, to which there was some opposition within the U.S. Government, on the ground that Czechoslovakia was not lost and that economic aid would strengthen ties with the west."[15]

Byrnes's decision seems curious. It was supposedly triggered and justified by the actions of only two members of a delegation of ten. It assumed that Czechoslovakia had a Communist-dominated government. In fact, after the May, 1946, elections, nine of the twenty-six top-level officials of the government were Communist, and the Communists held 114 of 300 seats in the Constituent National Assembly. The Prime Minister (Klement Gottwald) was a Communist, other critical cabinet posts such as Information and Interior were held by the same party, the Social Democrats often voted with the Communists in the majority, and Czechoslovakia did pursue a foreign policy closely attuned to that of Moscow.[16] But to label this government, with Jan Masaryk as foreign minister and Beneš as president, "Communist," as Byrnes did, was to ignore the facts. Even Steinhardt pointed out that in the elections of 1946 "the vote recorded was the expression of the will of the people in a democratic manner."[17] There was far more freedom in Czechoslovakia than anywhere else in eastern Europe.[18]

Beneš tried to explain the complex state of affairs to Steinhardt in December, 1946. He insisted that a number of the Communists in the cabinet were "good patriots" and pointed out the importance of preserving Czech independence. He asked Steinhardt to appreciate the reality of circumstances in which a small country contiguous to Russia found itself and the necessity of avoiding "reprisals" from its neighbors. Steinhardt recorded Beneš's explanation: "Under circumstances Masaryk [at Paris] has deemed it

[14] *Foreign Relations, 1946*, VI, 233.

[15] Campbell, *United States in World Affairs, 1945-1947*, p. 157.

[16] *Foreign Relations, 1946*, IV, 204-5; Josef Korbel, *The Communist Subversion of Czechoslovakia, 1938-1948: The Failure of Coexistence* (Princeton, N.J., 1959), pp. 153-55.

[17] *Foreign Relations, 1946*, VI, 199.

[18] Philip Mosely noted that as late as the fall of 1947 there was considerable political freedom. "Czechoslovakia, Poland, Yugoslavia: Observations and Reflections," *Political Science Quarterly*, LXIII (March, 1948), 4-5.

preferable to vote with Soviet Union on almost every occasion that Poland and Yugoslovakia had done so, convinced that United States was not harmed thereby whereas Czechoslovakia might benefit. *He pointed out that as result of Czechoslovakia's voting record Soviets had scrupulously refrained from interfering in Czechoslovakia's internal affairs* and that in consequence moderates were making steady progress in leading country back to democratic ways."[19] What Czechoslovakia sought to maintain was its independence; few United States leaders appreciated this effort. Instead, they demanded closer Czech ties with the United States. One Czech writer described the possible result: "The decision of the State Department may theoretically be what diplomats of the old school used to call 'a healthy lesson,' but contrary to American intentions and the aim of Czechoslovakia, it may have a much more serious consequence, namely to push Czechoslovakia even further into the orbit of Russia and make her more deeply dependent on trade with the Soviet Union and the rest of the Slav bloc."[20]

Steinhardt and some State Department officers did not share this opinion. They believed that diplomatic leverage and United States influence in Czechoslovakia had increased as a result of the suspensions. James Riddleberger, chief of the Central European Division, thanked Steinhardt for providing useful advice on the question of United States aid to countries that "fail to show a proper recognition of its value and of the United States objectives in Europe." Washington had to "cool the Czechs off a bit" because of improved economic conditions there and because some Czech officials apparently believed "that they can get what they want from us and still play both sides of the street." "Our stiffened attitude" would strengthen the "Western-minded Czechs" against the Communists. American relations with Czechoslovakia were entering a new phase, he concluded, "a more hardheaded approach." As Riddleberger summarized that approach, no loan would be offered until Czechoslovakia *"shows concrete evidences of friendship towards the United States,* which would include *some reorientation in its general foreign policy* as well as an agreement on compensation and commercial policy questions."[21]

Indeed, there did seem to be some immediate favorable results from this policy. Steinhardt and Riddleberger were pleased that press attacks on the United States had subsided and that Gottwald and Beneš seemed more eager to settle grievances in American-Czech relations, including compensation.[22] On November 14, 1946, Czechoslovakia and the United States signed a commercial agreement endorsing the following principles: "the elimination of all forms of discriminatory treatment in international commerce, and the

---

[19] *Foreign Relations, 1946,* VI, 239-40 (italics added).
[20] Joseph Kodicek, "The Suspension of the American Loan," *Central European Observor,* XIII (Nov. 8, 1946), 353.
[21] Riddleberger to Steinhardt, Oct. 3, 1946, Box 50, Steinhardt Papers (italics added).
[22] *Ibid.,* Dec. 2, 1946; *Foreign Relations, 1946,* VI, 233-34, 238, 239.

reduction of tariffs and other trade barriers."[23] Compensation negotiations also began in Prague, and in early 1947 some claims were settled.[24]

Yet Steinhardt still advocated the "hard-headed approach." He urged more pressure, fearing that improved economic conditions in Czechoslovakia would decrease the Czech desire for a loan and hence limit the diplomatic effectiveness of economic power. He was also alarmed that compensation might encourage the State Department to grant credits: "I don't hold with the theory that just because things are going right temporarily we should start ladling out credits." Rather, "the hope of obtaining credits accomplishes much more for us than once the credits have been extended." Economic hardship, he added, would pressure Czech Communists to admit that "they *must have* credit from the United States." United States officials should continue to "drag our feet" on the loan because the Czech Communists would be weakened and the "moderates" shored up. A State Department officer informed Steinhardt that George F. Kennan and Charles Bohlen agreed with his assessment but that the policy should be carried out "in a nice way."[25]

It would appear that the United States reversed its policy on aid to eastern Europe when it issued an open call to all European nations to participate in the Marshall Plan in mid-1947. Czechoslovakia first accepted the invitation on July 8, then rejected it two days later, thus confirming many Americans in their belief that Czechoslovakia was already a Soviet satellite.[26] Yet the Marshall Plan, presented as it was as an American-dominated program aimed against the Soviet Union, could not have been accepted by Czechoslovakia without serious disruption of its delicate balance between East and West. There is evidence to suggest that the familiar story of Czechoslovakia giving in helplessly to the U.S.S.R. lacks sophistication and precision. For example, Stalin did not force a Czech delegation to depart suddenly for Moscow to hear his appeal against the Marshall Plan; a Czech-Soviet meeting on commercial questions had been planned earlier, and the Marshall Plan issue arose at the same time—which was certainly propitious for Russia. There is no question, however, that Stalin told the Czech delegation that acceptance of the invitation to participate did not jibe with Soviet wishes.[27]

James P. Warburg, a prolific foreign affairs publicist and friend of Jan

[23] U.S., Department of State, *Treaties and Other International Acts,* ser. 1569 (Washington, D.C., 1947), and 1560 (Washington, D.C., 1947); Diamond, *Czechoslovakia,* pp. 147-48.
[24] The claim of a wholly American-owned corporation (Montanwerte) was settled for $5 million. The Vitkovice claim (unidentified) was settled for $12.6 million, and the claim of ITT was nearing settlement. Steinhardt to Francis Williamson, May 21, 1947, Box 84, Steinhardt Papers. For progress on Socony-Vacuum's claims, see Steinhardt to Harold Sheets, May 7, May 20, and June 30, 1947, *ibid.*
[25] Steinhardt to Riddleberger, June 12, 1947, *ibid;* John H. Bruins to Steinhardt, Aug. 20, 1947, Box 54, *ibid.*
[26] Harold C. Vedeler, State Department, to Steinhardt, Aug. 12, 1947, Box 55, *ibid.*
[27] Korbel, *Communist Subversion,* p. 181; Claire Sterling, *The Masaryk Case* (New York, 1968), pp. 7-8, 77-78.

Masaryk, reports that Masaryk told him shortly after the Czech rejection of the Marshall Plan that actually it was the American interpretation of the original Czech acceptance as a rebuff to Russia that necessitated Soviet pressure and the Czech reversal.[28] Indeed, the official Czech statement read: "Czechoslovakia's participation would be interpreted as an act directed against our friendship with the Soviet Union."[29] The minister of foreign trade, Hubert Ripka, a member of the National Socialist Party, later explained that Czechoslovakia was unwilling to risk a break with Russia for the sake of United States aid, however badly needed, because most Czechs "have constantly in mind the German danger which has threatened them since the Middle Ages" and valued close ties with Russia.[30] Mikaly Karolyi, a Socialist Hungarian diplomat later driven into exile by the Communists, recalled that he agreed with the Communist position on the Marshall Plan: "It was inconceivable for either of our countries [Czechoslovakia or Hungary] to risk a break with the Soviets, the only safeguard against future German revival."[31] And a Catholic People's Party member of the Czech Parliament asked: "Is it worthwhile to risk the certainty of the Soviet-Czechoslovak alliance, which we need against Germany, for such an uncertainty as is a proposition by Mr. Marshall, made at some American university, which— similar to Wilson's League—may not even be approved by the U.S. Senate?"[32] As was evident in Byrnes's earlier 1946 policy statement and in the Truman Doctrine, the United States insisted that nations choose sides in international relations and that Czechoslovakia virtually repudiate its friendship with Russia for the sake of an ill-defined aid program.

After Czech renunciation of the Marshall Plan, but before the coup, Steinhardt was still arguing that Czech economic distress, aggravated by the withholding of American loans, would weaken the Communists within the government because they would realize that the United States, not Russia, was the valuable ally. In late 1947 he said boldly, "we have everything to gain and little to lose by standing back at this time and shutting our ears to the pleas for help that we may expect in the comparatively near future. Some of the people around this town have been playing a double game long enough. It is high time they were brought to their senses."[33] He complained that "all that is left of our position here as far as the Communist members of the

---

[28] Zdenek Fierlinger, Czech deputy prime minister in 1947, has concluded similarly that the Western misrepresentation of the Czech acceptance forced the Czech reversal. He feared Czech actions "might be interpreted as a blow against the Soviet Union." Zdenek Fierlinger, "Why Czechoslovakia Rejected the Marshall Plan," *Current Digest of the Soviet Press*, XV (Apr. 24, 1963), 17-19, 40; James P. Warburg, *Long Road Home* (Garden City, N.Y., 1964), pp. 237-40; Warburg, *Last Call for Common Sense* (New York, 1949), pp. 238-60.

[29] Senate, *ERP*, p. 47.

[30] Ripka, *Czechoslovakia Enslaved*, p. 59.

[31] *Memoirs: Faith without Illusion* (London, 1956), p. 340.

[32] Quoted in Duchacek, "Czechoslovakia," p. 198.

[33] Steinhardt to Francis Williamson, Oct. 29, 1947, Box 85, Steinhardt Papers.

government are concerned is their hope of either an Export-Import or International Bank loan. . . . They are still hoping for a loan."[34] But the State Department suddenly reversed its policy just before the coup, and Steinhardt announced Washington's willingness to grant $25 million to Czechoslovakia. As a former Foreign Affairs Ministry official later wrote: "It was not only too little and too late, but also ineffective in kind."[35]

Such economic diplomacy between 1945 and 1948 did not satisfy either Washington or Prague. Most American companies received no compensation. In April, 1949, the Czechs offered compensation in exchange for a loan and the withdrawal of United States export controls, but no bargain was consummated. The British-Czech arrangement of September, whereby British companies were compensated in exchange for a trade agreement, provided a sharp contrast.[36] Czech-American trade dwindled. The so-called Czech moderates were not strengthened. Indeed, as a former non-Communist officer of the Czech Foreign Ministry later observed: "The reaction in Czechoslovakia [to the 1946 loan suspension] was exactly that which the Communists and the Soviet government wished: shock, disappointment, a feeling that the West had failed to understand the country's problems in its struggle for independence."[37] More important, the United States failed to achieve its major goal of orienting Czech foreign policy toward the West. Soviet-Czech economic relations improved, Russia stepped in to supply Czech needs for cotton and wheat and granted Czechoslovakia $33 million in 1948. On December 4, 1947, Czechoslovakia and Russia entered into a five-year trade agreement, despite the ardent wish of Czechs of varying political beliefs before the coup to trade and to maintain pacific relations with the West.[38]

Was United States foreign policy vis-à-vis Czechoslovakia really important to that country's history from 1945 to 1948? Internal crises over control of the police, Communist fears of losses in forthcoming elections, and the resignation of non-Communist cabinet officers all help explain the coup.[39]

---

[34] *Ibid.,* Oct. 8, 1947. As a member of the International Bank, Czechoslovakia had applied for a $350 million loan, but the United States blocked it. Czechoslovakia withdrew from the Bank in 1954.

[35] Korbel, *Communist Subversion,* p. 213. After the coup, Steinhardt hoped to use the "bait of a cotton loan" to speed compensation, and in July, 1948, Washington surmised that it had one last bargaining tool, Czechoslovakia's portion of the German "gold pool." Dulles and Steinhardt successfully urged the State Department to postpone these gold deliveries. Steinhardt to John Bruins, Jan. 23, 1948, Box 86, Steinhardt Papers; Bruins to Congressman Karl Stefan, July 13, 1948, Box 57, *ibid.;* John Foster Dulles to Steinhardt, June 15, 1948, *ibid.*

[36] Dana A. Schmidt, *Anatomy of a Satellite* (Boston, 1952), pp. 354, 371-72.

[37] Korbel, *Communist Subversion,* p. 179.

[38] William H. Draper, Jr., "Memorandum re Czechoslovakia," Oct. 23, 1946, Box 50, Steinhardt Papers; Ripka, *Czechoslovakia Enslaved,* pp. 129-31, 311; Starr, *Communist Regimes,* p. 289; *Foreign Relations,* 1946, VI, 197; Dean, "Economic Trends in Eastern Europe-I," pp. 21-22; Robert B. Lockhart, "The Czechoslovak Revolution," *Foreign Affairs,* XXVI (July, 1948), 637; Diamond, *Czechoslovakia,* pp. 146-47.

[39] See Paul Zinner's study, *Communist Strategy and Tactics in Czechoslovakia, 1918-1948* (New York, 1963). Zinner gives almost no attention to the influence of

External issues, such as the schism between Yugoslavia and Russia, the festering disputes in Germany leading to the Berlin blockade, and the Marshall Plan, also had their impact on the political turmoil in Czechoslovakia, perhaps by prompting Russia to tighten control over its sphere of influence. It is not the argument here that United States loan policy was the controlling factor in Czech affairs, but there is some evidence that it made a difference in weakening the Masaryks and Ripkas and in augmenting Soviet influence.[40] In trying to draw Czechoslovakia from Russia to the West through economic pressure, the United States helped undermine Czech independence. American policymakers showed little understanding of the difference between an independent country influenced by the Soviet Union and housing a large Communist movement and a subjugated country with the same elements present. Facile and inaccurate labels were attached to Czech behavior, the Soviet presence in eastern Europe was exaggerated, a heated rhetoric was used which was often wanting in careful analysis, and Russia was constantly challenged in its sphere of influence through pressure on it or on its neighbors.

In early 1948 Jan Masaryk lamented that "Washington and London have failed completely to understand my position, and they are making a serious mistake in not granting my request for funds or material assistance." He added that "with the end of UNRRA and America's insistence on refusing help except in connection with the Marshall Plan, Czechoslovakia has become completely dependent upon the 300,000 tons of grain which the Soviet Union has promised to Gottwald." In short, "this policy has completely spoiled my changes for playing Gottwald on even terms." It was a disservice to his country, he concluded, for the United States to have thought in 1946 that Czechoslovakia lay behind an "iron curtain."[41]

Just a few months before the coup, in December, 1947, the journalist Alexander Werth interviewed Hubert Ripka. Ripka and Werth were friends and they talked frankly. "These goddam Americans," Ripka exploded when he described his appeal to Washington for wheat to help fend off a Czech famine. "And these idiots started the usual blackmail: 'Okay, you can have 200,000 or 300,000 or even 500,000 tons of wheat, but on one condition only—that you throw the Communists out of the Czechoslovak Government.'" Ripka said he tried to explain that the Czech people had voted a good number of Communists into office. "But they said they didn't care. At

---

foreign relations, ignores United States foreign policy, exaggerates Communist influence from 1945 onward, and too often bases sweeping generalizations—which he offers as fact rather than speculation—on scanty evidence.

[40] Alexander Werth is more certain than the author that the American actions were decisive: "The economic help for which the Czech government had asked Washington might, if granted, have delayed the Communist take-over in Prague. But the rejection by Washington of the Czech request made the change of regime in Czechoslovakia virtually inevitable." Alexander Werth, *Russia: The Post-War Years* (New York, 1971), p. 330.

[41] Quoted in Trygve Lie, *In the Cause of Peace* (New York, 1954), p. 233.

this point Gottwald got in touch with Stalin, who immediately promised us the required wheat. . . . And now these idiots in Washington have driven us straight into the Stalinist camp."[42]

In his book *Czechoslovakia Enslaved,* published in 1950, Ripka claimed that he had tried to establish cordial relations with both Russia and the United States and that American aid might have maintained a balance in internal Czech politics. He thought the suspension of the loan "extremely regrettable" because the assistance was "indispensable" and because the Communists reaped considerable propaganda from the decision. "We hoped that the Government of the United States would reverse its decision when it came to realize that Czechoslovakia was a country basically democratic, which must be helped against the Communist danger. Unfortunately our hopes were disappointed."[43] It is reasonable to argue, as did Warburg in the 1940s, that United States foreign policy toward eastern Europe—particularly Czechoslovakia—helped pull down the "iron curtain" from the American side.[44]

PRESSURE ON POLAND

There were similarities in United States economic foreign policy toward Czechoslovakia and Poland. In both countries ambassadors were eager to apply economic pressure. The goals of American foreign policy in both were the "open door," "democracy," compensation, fewer attacks by the press on the United States, a commitment to multilateralism, and a reduction of Soviet and Communist influence. There were credit suspensions in both countries. More generally, the United States sought to orient Poland and Czechoslovakia toward Washington and away from Moscow. But the major powers squabbled more vigorously in Poland over opposing interpretations of wartime agreements at Yalta and Potsdam and the American call for "free elections" echoed over Poland more than over any other nation. Poland was under considerable Russian influence immediately after the war and much less free to govern itself, yet it appears that United States reconstruction diplomacy helped reduce the degree of independence which it did have.

[42] Quoted in Werth, *Russia: Post-War Years,* pp. 328-29. (Professor Ronald Landa brought this interview to the author's attention.) Steinhardt stated, "we should let them know that as soon as they throw off the shackles they will get help from us." "Conference at Embassy with Ambassador and Staff, Prague, September 24, 1947," Box 93, H. Alexander Smith Papers, Princeton University Library.

[43] Ripka, *Czechoslovakia Enslaved,* p. 49. Beneš told Sir Robert Bruce Lockhart in 1947: "if the Americans were wise, they would realise that the best way of defeating Communism was to give a loan to Governments like the Czechoslovak Government in which the Communists, though strong, had not an absolute majority." Paraphrased by Lockhart in his *My Europe* (London, 1952), p. 97.

[44] For an account from a different point of view, see Walter Ullman, "Czechoslovakia's Crucial Years, 1945-1948: An American View," *East European Quarterly,* I (September, 1967), 217-30.

A State Department briefing book paper prepared for the Potsdam Conference advocated free elections in Poland; furthermore, "in assisting through credits and otherwise in the physical reconstruction of Polish economy, we should insist on the acceptance by Poland of a policy of equal opportunity for us in trade, investments and access to sources of information."[45] Harriman thought reconstruction aid would increase American influence in Polish politics.[46] The Export-Import Bank began preparations in mid-1945 for granting credits, and Ambassador Arthur Bliss Lane duly informed President Boleslaw Bierut that aid might be forthcoming if Poland adhered to the principle of nondiscriminatory world trade. Lane also determined to use economic assistance as a "lever" to obtain Polish acceptance of American interpretations of the Yalta and Potsdam agreements.[47]

This interest in aid to Poland began shortly after the successful diplomatic mission of Harry Hopkins to Moscow in May and June, 1945, where he secured Stalin's agreement to a broadened Polish government. Some Americans were hopeful that the Soviet concession would at last produce an acceptable Polish government and eliminate this deeply divisive issue. In June President Bierut appealed for American support in reconstructing Poland and indicated a willingness to "compromise" to satisfy the United States. Bierut asked more specifically for a commercial treaty to develop trade between the United States and Poland and for technical experts to rebuild Polish industry.[48]

But Poland remained under the strict tutelage of the Soviet Union, and Lane insisted that freedom of the press must be restored, American property protected, arrests by the security police ended, and American trade principles accepted before aid could be extended. He complained, too, that the Polish-Soviet trade agreement of July, 1945, was "along lines of Nazi and Fascist commercial policy and contrary to our foreign economic policy of encouraging free private trade among nations."[49] The State Department agreed with Lane but instructed him to discuss only economic matters with the Poles. Lane exceeded his instructions and "stressed my view that continuance of chaotic economic conditions as well as lack of personal liberty and danger to private individuals might eventually create serious situation in U.S. towards Poland." Bierut, like Beneš in Czechoslovakia, pointed out the country's precarious status as a neighbor of the Soviet Union, the importance of preserving some remnants of independence, and the considerable Soviet

---

[45] *Foreign Relations: Berlin*, I, 715.

[46] *Ibid.*, p. 786.

[47] *New York Times*, July 18, 1945; Lane, *I Saw Poland Betrayed*, pp. 226-27.

[48] *Foreign Relations, 1945*, V, 347-48.

[49] *Ibid.*, pp. 364-65 (Aug. 22, 1945). See also *ibid.*, pp. 361-63, 383-86, 390-92, 396-97; Lane, *I Saw Poland Betrayed*, p. 228; Lane to Elbridge Durbrow, Oct. 22, 1945, Lane Papers.

pressure on his country: "If, however, this pressure were resisted forcibly it would mean war and the extermination of Poland."[50]

Lane continued to press for his terms and advised Washington that financial assistance would be interpreted by the "Polish people" as acquiescence in the "nondemocratic and brutal practices which exist in Poland today." By late October he had acquired an ally in Elbridge Durbrow, chief of the Division of Eastern European Affairs. Together they succeeded in deferring action on a cotton credit and a reconstruction loan request of several million dollars. Lane's attitude also had a negative effect in Warsaw. Bierut, as Lane reported it, "replied somewhat heatedly that if Poland must accept an Allied Power's activity in the internal affairs of Poland as a price for economic assistance then Poland would prefer not to have such assistance."[51]

Another Polish leader, Vice-Premier Stanislaw Mikolajczyk, head of the anti-Communist Peasant Party, argued that United States aid was essential to Polish independence because it would convince Poles that the "West" was interested in their welfare and because the Soviet Union could not fulfill its promises of aid. He outlined special needs in heavy machinery and expressed some optimism that an election in the early part of 1946 would diminish the power of the Communists. It was this hope which encouraged him to plead for credits so that when non-Communists assumed power, they would have a sound economic base from which to work. On November 9, 1945, Mikolajczyk met with Truman, who seemed to indicate to him aid was in the offing.[52]

On the same day, Byrnes informed Lane that the Department of State was inclined to tie only economic questions—that is, Polish acceptance of multilateralism and divulgence of trade treaties with other nations—to a credit. Of course, he added, continued failure to meet the Yalta and Potsdam commitments could adversely affect the Polish application. Lane quickly protested that political questions were central because Poland was "not master in its own house." He held that free elections were an impossibility at that time and that the extension of large-scale aid would be interpreted as a relaxation of United States resistance to "despotic rule."[53] However, in late November Lane and Byrnes agreed that small credits for the purchase of surplus goods, the building of a "single outstanding reconstruction project" such as the restoration of a port, and the purchase of United States cotton would, while not "necessarily reducing Soviet influence in Poland," demonstrate Washington's concern without shoring up the prestige of the Communist regime. It was evident that Mikolajczyk's earnest pleas for help had

[50] *Foreign Relations, 1945,* V, 374-79; Lane's remark and his paraphrase of Bierut's comment appear on p. 379.

[51] *Ibid.,* pp. 388-89, 392, 415.

[52] *Ibid.,* pp. 400-409, 428-30. See also Lane, *I Saw Poland Betrayed,* pp. 216-17, 317-18.

[53] *Foreign Relations, 1945,* V, 411-14.

influenced the Department of State, although the Polish request for a substantial reconstruction loan was being shelved at that time.[54]

The question of aid moved slowly in the early months of 1946. Poland made specific requests for large credits ($480 million), but the Export-Import Bank found the figure too high and was disturbed that Poland intended to purchase cotton from Russia, not the United States.[55] Durbrow informed Lane that "cold water was thrown" upon the request.[56] The Polish government's decree of January 3, 1946, which nationalized all major industrial property, including that of American companies, and its reluctance to agree to a bilateral commercial aviation convention with the United States confirmed Lane in his opposition to substantial assistance.[57] At the same time the United States was increasingly tying "free elections" to credits and was frank in requiring Polish "conformity with the announced policies of the United States Government" with regard to world trade principles.[58]

In February, the State Department expressed its willingness to grant a credit in the range of $25 to $50 million, dependent on Poland's behavior in conducting elections, compensating American companies, and allowing American businessmen access to their property.[59] The next month Lane, whose opposition to small credits had now hardened, was disturbed to learn that a $50 million surplus credit for bulldozers and railway equipment had been offered to Poland. He urged unsuccessfully that it be stopped as a protest against repressive political measures.[60]

In late April, Poland and the United States exchanged notes on an Export-Import Bank credit of $40 million. The State Department was pleased because it had accomplished a number of key objectives. The credit was specifically for purchase of locomotives and coal cars, which would speed the flow of vital coal to western Europe. Poland agreed to hold "free and unfettered" elections within the year, to endorse the principle of non-discriminatory trade, to make adequate compensation to American business, to accord United States nationals and companies equal treatment under the law, and to reveal "full information . . . concerning the international economic relations of Poland."[61]

[54] *Ibid.*, pp. 419-20, 422-23.
[55] Memorandum, "Polish Request for Credits," Dec. 5, 1945, Lane Papers.
[56] Durbrow to Lane, Dec. 11, 1945, *ibid.* See also *Journal of Commerce*, Jan. 11, 1946.
[57] *Foreign Relations, 1946*, VI, 374-76; Lane, *I Saw Poland Betrayed*, pp. 230-31. For the United States desire for an aviation treaty, see F. Lestrade Brown, American Airlines, 1946, to Lane; Lane to Brown, May 31, 1946, Lane Papers; Lane, *I Saw Poland Betrayed*, p. 234; *Foreign Relations, 1946*, VI, 500-502, 521.
[58] *Foreign Relations, 1946*, VI, 376-79. Washington strongly denounced "political murder" in Poland and demanded free elections. *DSB*, XIV (Feb. 10, 1946), p. 209.
[59] *Foreign Relations, 1946*, VI, 393-95.
[60] *Ibid.*, pp. 413, 433-35; Lane, *I Saw Poland Betrayed*, p. 234.
[61] *DSB*, XIV (May 5, 1946), 761-62; Export-Import Bank, *Second Semiannual Report*, pp. 20, 23. Dean Acheson's law firm represented the Polish government in the transaction. McGeorge Bundy, ed., *The Pattern of Responsibility* (Boston, 1952), p. 10.

Lane vigorously opposed State Department approval of the credit. The notion that Poland would fulfill its commitments he dismissed because it had always shown "bad faith," and he again insisted that aid to the Polish government would serve as an endorsement of its "terroristic activities."[62] Secretary Byrnes replied on April 22, 1946, that of course the possibility of failure existed but that Polish coal was vital to western Europe, that at least the promise of elections and adherence to multilateralism represented progress, and, more important, that Polish leaders were aware that no further aid would be forthcoming if commitments were not met. "This gives us further means of pressure."[63] Lane could only conclude that Washington had little confidence in his advice and made plans to fly to the Paris Peace Conference the next month to consult with Byrnes.[64]

Lane's mission to Paris in May, coupled with Byrnes's difficult time there and Washington's belief that Poland was not fulfilling its commitments fast enough, initiated a confusing series of American actions and Polish responses. Because Poland had not published the notes exchanged on the Export-Import Bank credit and had not furnished the texts of its trade treaties, on May 6 Byrnes decided to stop all shipments of goods under the $50 million surplus property credit. Poland replied that no date had been set for publication of the trade treaties and that it would not feel compelled to produce them until the United States restored the surplus property credit. Washington also suspended the $40 million Export-Import Bank credit, the formal contract for which had not yet been signed.[65]

Polish-American relations chilled, but Poland did publish the notes and cleared up a question about censorship of American correspondents' reports. Warsaw further set about to give Lane the texts of trade treaties, especially the Polish-Soviet agreement of 1946. Lane was delighted with this "satisfactory development," which inflated his belief in a "strong stand" toward Poland.[66] The United States announced on June 26 that it had restored the surplus property credit, and on October 3, after Poland sent the texts of its trade treaties to Washington, the $40 million credit contract was finally signed.[67]

But about that same time, as we have seen, Byrnes established his policy of only aiding those nations which supported "the principles for which we stand." Poland would receive no further credits, and like Czechoslovakia, boycotted the Marshall Plan. The State Department, exercising its consider-

---

[62] *Foreign Relations, 1946,* VI, 431-32; Lane, *I Saw Poland Betrayed,* pp. 236-37, 318-20.

[63] *Foreign Relations, 1946,* VI, 432.

[64] *Ibid.,* pp. 436-37.

[65] Only $3.7 million in surplus supplies had reached Poland by May 6. *Ibid.,* pp. 448-53; Lane, *I Saw Poland Betrayed,* p. 239; Lane to Gerald Keith, May 6, 1946, Lane Papers.

[66] Lane, *I Saw Poland Betrayed,* p. 239; *Foreign Relations, 1946,* VI, 456-61.

[67] *Foreign Relations, 1946,* VI, 466-67, 489-90; *DSB,* XV (July 7, 1946), 33 (Aug. 8, 1946), 335.

able influence in the World Bank, effectively pigeon-holed the Polish application to that institution for $600 million after giving some thought to the idea that a loan be tied to the shipment of coal to western Europe. In 1950, unable to overcome the United States-imposed obstacle, Poland withdrew from the Bank. The United States also denied a cotton credit and refused to undertake a relief program for Poland.[68]

The absence of a compensation agreement and the repressive political conditions in Poland, where non-Communists were harassed and arrested before the election scheduled for January 19, 1947, further undermined Polish-American relations and any Polish hope for additional United States assistance.[69] The United States persuaded the Poles to accept a mixed commission to hear complaints and settle compensation claims, but it failed to reach agreement. As a reward for Polish acceptance of the commission, however, Washington freed Polish assets in the United States amounting to $37,700,000.[70] As observers expected, the Polish elections were hardly "free and unfettered." The Truman administration protested that the Polish government "employed wide-spread measures of coercion and intimidation against democratic elements. . . ."[71] Lane resigned his ambassadorship on March 31, 1947, and returned to the United States to become a leading critic of the Truman administration's "betrayal" of Poland through what he considered its unwillingness to stand more firmly against Soviet intrusions.

The Polish ambassador to the United States, Oskar Lange, commented in 1946, "if we cannot get help from the West we will obtain it from the Soviet Union," but, he added, "we would like and we need a balanced economy, not tied up exclusively with either the Soviet Union or the West."[72] Polish leaders of all political factions desired trade with the United States. Vice-Premier Wladyslaw Gomulka, for example, stated in early 1947 that "we consider an economic rapprochement and commercial exchange [with the United States] an essential factor for good relations."[73] But the opportunity to improve relations through commerce was not given, as both Moscow and Washington restricted Poland's freedom to trade. On terms more beneficial to

[68] *Foreign Relations, 1946,* VI, 504-6, 519, 530; Gardner, *Sterling-Dollar Diplomacy,* pp. 295-96; Emilio G. Collado to John W. Snyder, "Activities of the International Bank in the Loan Field," rept. no. 20, Oct. 25, 1946, IBRD folder 1, Snyder Papers; *DSB,* XXII (Mar. 27, 1950), 497, XVII (Aug. 3, 1947), 223-24.

[69] *Foreign Relations, 1946,* VI, 519, 522, 528-38, 541-44. Poland announced that some of the nationalized properties would not be compensated because they were run by Germans during the war, contributed to the German war effort, and therefore were defined as German property. *Nation's Business,* XXXIV (November, 1946), 18-19; Lane to Donald Russell, Jan. 15, 1947, Lane Papers; *New York Times,* Nov. 8, 1946; *Business Week,* Oct. 12, 1946, p. 109.

[70] Lane, *I Saw Poland Betrayed,* p. 231; *DSB,* XVI (Jan. 5, 1947), 28.

[71] *DSB,* XVI (Feb. 9, 1947), 251.

[72] *New York Times,* Aug. 18, 1946.

[73] *Ibid.,* May 23, 1947. See *Foreign Relations, 1946,* VI, passim, for Polish interest in commercial relations with the United States, and Hilary Minc's comments in Werth, *Russia: Post-War Years,* p. 275.

itself than to the Poles, Moscow gave assistance and trade and thus tied Poland more closely to it.[74] In March, 1947, Russia granted Poland a $28 million gold loan, less than a year later extended a $450 million commodity credit, and in 1950 granted $100 million. While United States export controls were inhibiting Polish-American trade in 1948, Russia was shipping machinery to Poland for its industrial development program. In 1947 Russia dropped its claim of 6.5 million tons of Polish coal provided in the German reparations arrangement.[75] The United States helped isolate Poland economically, making it easier for the Soviet Union to draw that country more deeply under its influence.[76] Finland was treated differently.

AN EXCEPTION: FINLAND AND NEUTRALISM

At the close of the war Finland became politically part of eastern Europe. Uncomfortably allied with Germany and defeated by Russia, Finland lay helpless in late 1944. It signed an armistice which required large reparations payments and the cessation and lease of territory to Russia. In the peace treaty of 1947 these provisions were reaffirmed, and Finland accepted severe limitations on the size of its military establishment. Russia set the reparations bill at $300 million, and many diplomats feared that Finland would lose its independence.

There were some early signs that the country would manage to preserve its independence despite the Soviet presence. Most Soviet troops departed in early 1945; elections in March produced only a 20 percent vote for the Communists. Under the cautious leadership of President Juho Paasikivi, Finland consciously established a foreign policy of "neutralism" in the growing Soviet-American confrontation and avoided decisions which might antagonize the Soviet Union. Finland was "friendly" toward Russia, an attitude necessitated by realism. United States representatives who arrived in Finland in early 1945 were impressed that the country was treated more leniently than Hungary and Rumania and that the Soviet-dominated Control Commission did not meddle overtly in Finnish politics or interfere with civil liberties.[77]

[74] Russia was apparently willing to allow United States trade with and aid to eastern European countries over which it had influence before 1947 (in part, because Russia could not meet their needs) so long as the economic activity was not dominating or exploitative. See n. 2 above, Chapter 5 above, and *Foreign Relations, 1946*, VI, 477.

[75] *Journal of Commerce,* Aug. 7, 1947; *New York Times,* Jan. 31 and Aug. 12, 1948; Starr, *Communist Regimes,* p. 289.

[76] For a similar use of economic diplomacy toward Bulgaria, Hungary, and Rumania, see *Foreign Relations, 1946*, VI, 80n, 102-3, 103n (Bulgaria). For Hungary, see *ibid.,* pp. 261, 287-89, 293-96, 310-12, 315-16, 342-45, 347-50; Nagy, *Struggle behind the Iron Curtain,* pp. 136, 226-30; *DSB,* XVI (June 15, 1947), 1166; *Business Week,* Mar. 11, 1950; Margold, "Economic Life," p. 66. For Rumania, see *Foreign Relations, 1946*, VI, 610, 619-20, 628, 645, 669-70, 671.

[77] *Foreign Relations, 1945,* IV, 605-6, 610-11, 613-15, 619; Annette Baker Fox,

Still, as U.S. Representative Maxwell M. Hamilton reported from Helsinki, "Finland exists as do other former satellite countries in the shadow of Soviet power and Soviet attitude is an important and ever present factor."[78] Some diplomats assumed that Finland was subjugated and therefore should be excluded from United States aid. Others pointed out that such assistance would in practice finance Finnish reparations to Russia and that, if Moscow thought Washington would give aid, reparations demands might be increased. The official advice in late 1944 was that, if the Finns asked for help, the United States should "assume a discouraging attitude. . . ."[79]

But the Finns insisted. Ake Gartz, the "hardheaded businessman" who served as minister of commerce and industry, appealed for aid with the argument that "without credits the game is up."[80] In April, 1945, the Finns asked for commodity agreements. Willing to trade wood products for American machinery, they hoped that such trade would revive industry and thus make it possible to meet reparations payments. Hamilton asked Washington: "Could this be arranged and how?"[81] He himself approved such arrangements and assumed a conciliatory attitude toward the Finns. The Export-Import Bank agreed to consider a commodity credit, but Washington decided to withhold announcement of its willingness until after the Finnish war crimes trials because "it would offend Soviets to announce our assistance at present juncture and would strengthen Finn attitude of independent defiance already too strong for Finland's good."[82] By early 1946, however, it appeared that the trials would go on indefinitely, so Finland and the United States on February 1 signed an agreement for a $35 million Export-Import Bank credit. Byrnes was emphatic that the credit had no "political implications," that it was solely a commercial arrangement to facilitate trade.[83] The United States intended, apparently, to maintain the public fiction that its assistance was not related to Finnish reparations payments to Russia, yet such credits shored up the Finnish economy, enabling it to meet those obligations.[84] Washington also invited Finland to open further loan discussions in December, 1946.

The results of the talks were immediate. On January 22, 1947, the Export-Import Bank granted a reconstruction loan of $37 million, and, less than a month later, another $2.5 million was added for the purchase of

---

The Power of Small States: Diplomacy in World War II (Chicago, 1959), pp. 70-77; Max Jakobson, "Finnish Foreign Policy," *International Affairs* (London), XXXVIII (April, 1962), 196-202.

[78] *Foreign Relations, 1945*, IV, 614 (Apr. 28, 1945).

[79] *Ibid.*, p. 634 (Dec. 19, 1945).

[80] *Ibid.*, pp. 636, 646.

[81] *Ibid.*, p. 647.

[82] *Ibid.*, p. 660n.

[83] *Ibid., 1946*, VI, 242. The United States also extended a $5 million cotton credit in December, 1945.

[84] Hamilton pointed out to Byrnes that democracy in Finland could be maintained by relieving Finland's economic burden—reparations. *Ibid., 1946*, III, 7-8.

American machinery. Since the reparations to be paid were mostly to consist of machinery, this assistance figured in Finnish efforts to send indemnity shipments to Russia. Finland extracted a $5 million cotton credit from Washington in November, 1947, $675,000 for the purchase of General Motors cars and bus chassis in May, 1948, and $10 million for American equipment and raw materials the following November. From 1944 to 1952, when Finland completed its reparations to Russia, the United States granted it some $100 million in credits and sold it $23 million in surplus property. The World Bank also helped with $38 million in the period 1949-1952. United States diplomats tried unsuccessfully at the Paris Peace Conference to reduce Finland's reparations bill from $300 million to $200 million, but Russia itself unilaterally cut the figure by half in mid-1948.[85] The Commerce Department made exceptions and allowed shipments of industrial equipment to Finland under its export control procedures. As Secretary Sawyer explained in 1948, "all agencies concerned expressed the feeling that it is important to strengthen the Finnish economy as well as the faith of the Finnish people in the Western democracies in order to maintain and increase their will to resist aggression."[86]

United States officials had an uncommonly sophisticated understanding of Finland's precarious postwar status and "friendship" with Russia. Although clearly opposed to Soviet influence, they avoided decisions which might antagonize Russia and thwart Finnish attempts to remain independent. The United States did not apply the political tests and standards there which it applied to other nations in the Soviet sphere. Washington seemed to respect Finnish "neutralism" and made no vigorous protest when Finland refused to join the Marshall Plan. The official Finnish statement was explicit: "the Marshall Plan having become the source of serious differences of opinion among the Big Powers, Finland, desiring to remain outside the areas of conflict in Big Power politics, regrets that it does not find it possible to participate. . . ."[87]

Why the Soviet Union pursued the comparatively moderate policy it did in Finland will remain unknown until Soviet archives are opened to scholars. Perhaps Russia wanted a showcase to demonstrate its tolerance of independent nations in eastern Europe. The stubborn Finnish resistance in World War II may have convinced the Russians that control of Finland after the war was impossible. Finland itself pursued a policy which was calculated to calm Soviet fears about its security, but it is also conceivable that it was the comparatively low-keyed United States policy (and rhetoric) toward Finland

[85] *Ibid., 1946*, VI, 249; Export-Import Bank, *Semiannual Reports to Congress, 1947-1949;* John H. Wuorinen, *A History of Finland* (New York, 1965), p. 468; *DSB*, XV (Oct. 27, 1946), 745; Jaakko Auer, "Finland's War Reparations Deliveries to the Soviet Union," in Finnish Political Science Association, ed., *Finnish Foreign Policy: Studies in Foreign Politics* (Helsinki, 1963), p. 74.

[86] Charles Sawyer to Senator Henry Cabot Lodge, June 21, 1948, Office of Secretary, GC 93126, Commerce Records.

[87] Quoted in Wuorinen, *History of Finland*, p. 453.

which had a calming effect. There were no noisy appeals for free elections, compensation (because Finland did not nationalize), protection of American corporations, and the "open door." To the Soviets, United States aid to Finland was not a threat but an assurance that the valuable reparations shipments would be sent. It also appeared that Finnish independence and Soviet security were compatible. In the case of Finland, Washington recognized the distinction between a satellite government and an independent government friendly to the Soviet Union and did not attempt to force Finland into its camp. Maxwell Hamilton was a far more cautious diplomat than either Steinhardt or Lane, and his reports to Washington were considerate of the beleagured Finnish position. Finland had a reservoir of goodwill in the United States, for it had been both anti-German 'and anti-Soviet in World War II, and many Americans had admired its heroic defense in the Winter War of 1939-1940. Then, too, unlike Poland, it was not a symbol of the Cold War: tempers were cooler, the rhetoric less strained, the policies more conciliatory. The Finns were tenacious in their pursuit of aid, and in this case Washington was willing to use its economic power to help maintain Finnish independence.[88]

ANOTHER EXCEPTION: YUGOSLAVIA AND INDEPENDENT COMMUNISM

United States policy toward Yugoslavia followed the pattern set in other eastern European nations (except Finland) until mid-1948. The enthusiastic Yugoslav support for Soviet foreign policy and restrictions on civil liberties convinced American officials that the country was a Soviet satellite. Yet conflicts between Yugoslavia and Russia were festering below the surface. Marshal Josip Broz Tito and the Yugoslav Communist Party, fresh from their wartime victories against the Germans, unassisted by the Russians, resisted Soviet attempts to direct Yugoslav foreign policy and frequently acted independently. In 1946, for example, Tito disapproved of the Russian agreement with the West to make Trieste a free territory; he wanted to create a Balkan federation, a desire Russia interpreted as competitive; and he aided the Greek revolutionaries against Stalin's advice. The growing schism became public in early 1948, when the Cominform dramatically expelled the Yugoslav Communist Party and applied political and economic sanctions.[89]

[88] John H. Wuorinen, "Finland," in Kertesz, *Fate of East Central Europe,* pp. 321-37; Albin T. Anderson, "The Soviets and Northern Europe," *World Politics,* IV (July, 1952), 468-87; A. J. Fischer, "The Finnish Scene," *World Affairs* (1947), p. 289.
[89] Phyllis Auty, "Yugoslavia's International Relations (1945-1965)," in Wayne S. Vucinich, ed., *Contemporary Yugoslavia: Twenty Years of Socialist Experiment* (Berkeley, Calif., 1969), pp. 156-63; Milovan Djilas, *Conversations with Stalin* (New York, 1962); U.S., Congress, Senate, Committee on the Judiciary, 87th Cong., 1st sess., *Yugoslav Communism: A Critical Study* (prepared by Charles Zalar) (Washington, D.C., 1961), pp. 149, 153, 159, 162-66; Dedijer, *Battle Stalin Lost.*

In 1945 Yugoslavia asked the United States for postwar aid, but Washington argued that the Italian-Yugoslav contest over Trieste had had an adverse effect on congressional opinion. The Yugoslavs replied that they might have to turn to Russia, "the only door open to them," yet the Truman administration turned down a $300 million request.[90] After Tito's pre-determined victory in the November, 1945, elections, Ambassador Richard C. Patterson, Jr., reported to Washington that "Belgrade is like the capital of a Soviet Republic and regime is hostile to America and Britain. . . ." Indeed, he suggested that the State Department close the American embassy. He noted, rather naively, that "when UNRRA aid ceases the regime may well be sufficiently in need of our support to be willing to conform to principles of Western democracy in order to gain our approval."[91] The nationalization of Socony-Vacuum oil properties, the continued tension over Trieste, and the downing of American planes over Yugoslav territory further delayed consideration of the aid request. When the State Department rejected a Yugoslav offer to discuss general relations and a loan in Washington in early 1946, the Yugoslav ambassador complained that his country would not give in to such pressure. As the State Department reported his response, "Yugoslavia could get along without a loan. It could wait. It would like to develop commercial relations with the United States, but it could wait if necessary."[92] The United States also waited, through 1947 and 1948, excluding Yugoslavia from post-UNRRA aid and refusing to release Yugoslav gold (taken to the United States in 1940 to avoid its seizure by Germany).[93] Tito asserted that "we were not humbly begging on our knees for charity, but . . . were asking for the help to which we were entitled." He further noted that Germany, against which he had fought, was receiving United States aid. When Yugoslavia rejected the Marshall Plan, Tito explained that "we cannot expect unselfish and frank help" from the United States.[94]

The open squabbling between Tito and Stalin in 1948 stimulated a re-evaluation of American policy. Tito asked Washington for increased trade. Truman hesitated but did release the Yugoslav gold in July. Yugoslavia successfully completed trade negotiations with the British and joined the Coal and Steel Community of Europe in November. Badly in need of coal and trade because the nations in the Soviet sphere had severed their economic ties with Yugoslavia and were obstructing its use of the Danube River and because

[90] Josip Broz Tito, *Selected Speeches and Articles, 1941-1961* (Zagreb, 1963), p. 13; *Foreign Relations, 1945*, V, 1210, 1229, 1233, 1235, 1266, 1277, 1290.

[91] *Foreign Relations, 1945*, V, 1292, 1293.

[92] *Ibid., 1946*, VI, 867-70, 886. Surplus property (valued at $1.25 million) had been sold to Yugoslavia on a cash basis in late 1945 and early 1946, and UNRRA aid continued, despite the U.S. wish to stop it.

[93] Campbell, *United States in World Affairs, 1945-1947*, p. 464; Dedijer, *Tito*, p. 308.

[94] Josef Korbel, *Tito's Communism* (Denver, Col., 1951), pp. 256, 281.

of bad harvests in 1948 and 1949, Tito again appealed to the United States in mid-1949.[95]

Washington now began to take action. In June, 1949, the Commerce Department relaxed export controls to permit shipments of machinery to Yugoslavia. As one official of the department put it, "foreign policy considerations brought out by the Department of State outweigh the strategic considerations. . . ."[96] The Truman administration saw in Belgrade's declaration of independence a setback for Russia and decided to encourage it through aid with no strings attached.[97] In September the Export-Import Bank extended $20 million to improve Yugoslavia's mining industry. In March of the next year the Bank added another $20 million and in August $15 million. The famine of 1950 prompted further American aid in grain and foodstuffs ($50 million). Washington began to supply Tito with military aid in 1951, although he refused to join NATO or endorse the intervention in Korea. But Yugoslavia did ship valuable raw materials (zinc, copper, and lead) for the United States rearmament program. The International Bank and International Monetary Fund also assisted Yugoslavia.[98]

Despite Mikoyan's remark that "Tito can be bought with a hundred million dollars,"[99] the evidence suggests that Tito could not be bribed. Although he toned down his criticisms of the United States and improved relations with Turkey, Greece, and Italy, he did not support American foreign policy and repeatedly asserted his commitments to socialism, nonalignment, and independent coexistence.[100] "We have never given anybody reason to hope that we would join the Western bloc, or any other bloc for that matter,"

[95] Millis, *Forrestal Diaries,* p. 456; Ernst Halperin, *The Triumphant Heretic: Tito's Struggle against Stalin* (London, 1958), p. 142; Auty, "Yugoslavia's International Relations," pp. 168-69.
[96] Thomas C. Blaisdell to Charles Sawyer, June 6, 1949, Office of Secretary, GC 93126, Box 752, Commerce Records.
[97] Auty, "Yugoslavia's International Relations," p. 170. Charles Zalar has suggested in Senate, *Yugoslav Communism,* pp. 169-70, that Tito closed the Yugoslav border to the Greek rebels as a precondition for American aid. There is little evidence at present for this interpretation, and the Tito-Stalin competition for control of the Greek Communist Party seems to have been a more important factor (see Chapter 9 below). For a view similar to Zalar's, see Halperin, *Triumphant Heretic,* pp. 140, 142-43.
[98] Export-Import Bank, *Semiannual Reports to Congress;* William A. Brown, Jr., and Redvers Opie, *American Foreign Assistance* (Washington, D.C., 1953), pp. 424-26, 496-99. In December, 1947, Yugoslavia asked the World Bank for $300 million. Negotiations broke down but were resumed in May, 1949. The result was a $2.7 million loan for timber equipment. In October, 1951, $28 million was granted, and in February, 1953, another $30 million. The Fund sold $9 million to Yugoslavia in 1949. International Bank for Reconstruction and Development, *Fourth Annual Report, 1948-1949* (Washington, D.C., 1949), p. 28, and *Eighth Annual Report, 1952-1953* (Washington, D.C., 1953), p. 27; International Monetary Fund, *Annual Report, April 30, 1950* (Washington, D.C., 1950), p. 76.
[99] In Auty, "Yugoslavia's International Relations," p. 170.
[100] *Ibid.,* pp. 171-72, 189-93; Tito, *Selected Speeches,* pp. 172-73.

he wrote in *Foreign Affairs* in 1957.[101] In 1951 he commented, "we appreciate the aid we have received particularly because the American Government had not attached any conditions, either of a political or any other nature, which might prejudice the authority and repute of our own people or, indeed, of the American people."[102] Although privately he was suspicious of American intentions, he publicly acknowledged the importance of such assistance.[103]

Students of Yugoslav foreign policy tend to agree that American aid was crucial to the independence of Tito's nation. Phyllis Auty has concluded that "if the West had refused all aid to Tito, starvation after the bad harvests of 1948, 1949, and 1950, and unemployment might have forced Yugoslavia to capitulate to Russia."[104] Although Tito took the initiative, and Washington took advantage of the fact of Soviet-Yugoslav animosity, the Truman administration demonstrated some flexibility when it seized the opportunity to support Yugoslav independence.

With the exception of Finland and Yugoslavia, the United States consistently attempted to use economic pressure in eastern Europe to achieve its goals. This active diplomacy further undermined the independence of the eastern European nations, already suffering from the Soviet presence. It is an intriguing question whether the United States could have helped alleviate the harshness of Soviet hegemony in eastern Europe in the early Cold War through a different loan policy. Franklin A. Lindsay, former chief of the military mission to Yugoslavia and a member of the United States delegation to the United Nations Atomic Energy Commission, gave an affirmative answer in early 1947. "We can never make liberals out of communists by making love to them with dollars," he asserted. "They would rather starve a portion of their population than compromise their political creed to gain economic assistance." But it did not follow, he went on, that the United States should abandon eastern Europe. Rather, it should "extend economic aid, within the limits of our capacity, to help rebuild terribly devastated areas. We will receive little or no thanks for such aid, and we can only hope that in the long run we will be helping to build an economic atmosphere in which the people will be able to slowly establish liberal institutions as a result of their own efforts." Eschewing the use of economic power for diplomatic pressure, Lindsay concluded, "we can lead the Balkan 'horse' to democratic 'water' by helping in the achievement of the necessary minimum economic prosperity, but we cannot make him drink by dollars, bayonets, or

---

[101] Josip Broz Tito, "On Certain International Questions," *Foreign Affairs*, XXXVI (October, 1957), 77.

[102] *Selected Speeches*, p. 121 (Aug. 11, 1951).

[103] See Ambassador George V. Allen to his parents, Mar. 5, 1950, George V. Allen Papers, Duke University Library.

[104] Auty, "Yugoslavia's International Relations," p. 169.

ballots. . . ."[105] Few American officials held such views in the early years of the Soviet-American confrontation, and most diplomats practiced a counter-productive reconstruction diplomacy in the Soviet sphere. They were more successful in the American sphere of influence.

[105] Franklin A. Lindsay, "American Foreign Policy in the Balkans," Jan. 9, 1947, part XI:1, Baruch Papers. Also see Lindsay's study for the State Department, "Developments in Yugoslavia, March-August, 1945," [n.d.], *ibid.*

PART II
Confrontation in the American Sphere

CHAPTER 7

INTERNATIONAL ORGANIZATIONS FOR AMERICAN
PURPOSES: THE BANK AND FUND OF BRETTON WOODS

"The question before us," Senator Robert Wagner of New York declared on behalf of the Bretton Woods Agreements in mid-July, 1945, "is whether by default we allow the world to repeat the tragic blunders of the 1920's and 1930's."[1] Troubled by the legacy of those interwar years and eager to shed the isolationist label, most Americans professed a new commitment to international organizations. Yet the United States participated enthusiastically only in those international institutions it could control and circumvented or weakened those which did not serve its purposes. We have already seen how the Truman administration abandoned UNRRA and set up its own relief program. Later chapters will show how the United Nations was bypassed when Truman launched his new "Doctrine" and how the Economic Commission for Europe (established on a European-wide basis in 1947) was similarly ignored when he organized the Marshall Plan.

The United States was no more evil or more noble in its relations with international organizations than Britain and Russia; each major power attempted to employ them for its own national purposes. But there was a difference; the United States held a distinct advantage in the International Bank for Reconstruction and Development and the International Monetary Fund and so added them to its arsenal of Cold War weapons. It manipulated these agencies to strengthen its sphere of influence; the Bretton Woods creations merged with the British loan, the Truman Doctrine, the Marshall Plan, and the rehabilitation of West Germany to shore up and tie together nations stretching from the Persian Gulf to the English Channel. As the major contributor to the Bank and Fund, the United States exerted the authority conferred by its economic power. Both Britain and Russia disliked such domination but expected it. It is nevertheless true that the United States control of the Bank and Fund enfeebled multilateralism and further divided the former Allies. Russia would not join the institutions even to obtain a loan.

[1] *Congressional Record,* XCI (July 16, 1945), 7557.

FORMATION AND RATIFICATION

The IBRD and Fund succumbed early to United States control. Forty-four nations sent delegates to a resort hotel in the White Mountains of New Hampshire to attend the Bretton Woods Conference of July 1-22, 1944. There they considered an Anglo-American proposal drawn up largely by Harry D. White, assistant secretary of the treasury, and John Maynard Keynes, the noted economist and adviser to the chancellor of the exchequer.[2] Britain and the United States had consulted Soviet officials in 1943-1944 about the proposed new international institutions to bring stability, commercial and financial, to the postwar world, and Moscow agreed hesitatingly to attend the conference. His advisers, it seems, at first convinced Stalin that Russian participation was undesirable, but after a personal appeal by President Roosevelt, Stalin changed his mind. Deputy Foreign Commissar A. W. Vyshinsky later quoted Stalin as having said that "this is very difficult for us. It involves a large amount of money. I do not understand it completely. It will take some time; but if you need it, and our commitment and signature must be added now, you can take this as my signature, and the answer is 'yes.' "[3]

Russia sent M. S. Stepanov, deputy commissar of foreign trade, and seventeen assistants to Bretton Woods, but they contributed little to the discussions. Keynes believed that the Russians "*want* to thaw and collaborate. But the linguistic difficulties and very poor interpretation are a dreadful obstacle. Above all, they are put in a most awkward, and sometimes humiliating, position by the lack of suitable instructions and of suitable discretion from Moscow."[4] The Russian delegates demonstrated no enthusiasm at the meeting. At one point, Secretary Morgenthau tried to attract Russia to the Fund by dangling a large American loan before Stepanov. As noted, one prerequisite for the loan was Soviet acceptance of the Bretton Woods institutions.[5] For whatever reason, the Soviet Union voted with the majority to submit the final agreements to the forty-four participating nations for ratification. Morgenthau left the meeting prematurely elated that he had been able "to work with Russia," and

[2] R. F. Harrod, *The Life of John Maynard Keynes* (New York, 1951), pp. 537-73, and Gardner, *Sterling-Dollar Diplomacy,* pp. 71-95, discuss the differences between the White and Keynes plans. In brief, the issues centered on the liquidity size of the Fund, the extent of freedom given to members to adjust their exchange rates, and limitations on the direct lending policy of the Bank. See also Blum, *From Morgenthau Diaries,* III, 229-38, 243-45.
[3] Stalin, quoted in diary journal of Joseph E. Davies, July 15, 1945 (at Potsdam), Box 18, Davies Papers. See also Raymond F. Mikesell, "Negotiating at Bretton Woods, 1944," in Raymond Dennett and Joseph Johnson, eds., *Negotiating with the Russians* (Boston. 1951), pp. 102-4; Blum, *From Morgenthau Diaries,* III, 245-46, 249, 250.
[4] Harrod, *Keynes,* p. 582. Also see Mikesell, "Negotiating," pp. 104-6; Blum, *From Morgenthau Diaries,* III, 258-64.
[5] See Blum, *From Morgenthau Diaries,* III, 263; Chapter 2 above.

especially pleased with the last-minute Soviet agreement to increase its subscription to the World Bank.[6]

The Articles of Agreement stated that the Bank intended to "assist in the reconstruction and development" of member nations, to "promote private foreign investment," and to "promote the long-range balanced growth of international trade. . . ." These goals would be achieved through its direct lending authority and guarantee of private loans. Member nations could obtain World Bank loans to finance reconstruction projects. The Fund was to "promote international monetary cooperation," to "facilitate the expansion and balanced growth of international trade," and to "assist in the establishment of a multilateral system of payments" through consultation and currency loans. Members were permitted to borrow from the Fund's pool of foreign currencies to meet their balance of payments problems.[7]

When the Roosevelt administration sent the Bretton Woods Agreements bill to Congress in February, 1945, it did so realizing that the debate would be prolonged and confusing. As a United Press correspondent in Washington put it, Bretton Woods was "so complicated that the burden of starting work on it is generally regarded with great reluctance on the Hill." Believing that Senator Robert A. Taft of Ohio and Harry D. White were the only men who understood the topic, journalist Allen Drury concluded that "everyone else is being swept along on the tide. The country has only the foggiest notion of what it is all about, and the same applies to the Senate."[8] Although Drury exaggerated the ignorance of the Senate, it is true that the debate was often listless and perhaps predetermined by the extensive government publicity campaign and the timidity of legislators who feared being tagged as isolationist if they spoke against the international organizations.

Seldom intimidated, Senator Taft led the attack. He and other critics underestimated American power in the new institutions, and he charged that the Fund would be controlled by the debtors, all eager for easy money. He joined Merwin K. Hart of the National Economic Council to suggest, without substantiation, that the Fund might be dominated by Communists. He further asserted that Bretton Woods would cost the United States too much. During the congressional debate in mid-July, 1945, Taft, perhaps recognizing his minority position, called for delay: "If we want to have established the proposed fund and the proposed bank, why not hold out the proposed contribution of $6,000,000,000 as a bargaining weapon in the final [peace]

---

[6] Blum, *From Morgenthau Diaries*, pp. 276-77; U.S., Department of State, *Proceedings and Documents of the United Nations Monetary and Financial Conference, Bretton Woods, New Hampshire, July 1-22, 1944*, 2 vols. (Washington, D.C., 1948), I, 1107-8, 1111-12; Harrod, *Keynes*, p. 580; J. Keith Horsefield et al., *The International Monetary Fund 1945-1965*, 3 vols. (Washington, D.C., 1969).
[7] Bank and Fund Articles of Agreement, in U.S., Department of State, *Treaties and Other International Acts* (Washington, D.C., 1946), ser. 1501-2.
[8] Allen Drury, *A Senate Journal, 1943-1945* (New York, 1963), pp. 364, 465.

settlement with other nations?"[9] Other opponents complained that the United States would be relinquishing control of its own economy to an international body, that the broken world economy should be patched up first, that loopholes in the Fund would permit members to continue bilateral practices in violation of American principles, and that the Bank's lending authority was too liberal.[10] W. Randolph Burgess, head of the American Bankers Association, which opposed the Fund but accepted the Bank, feared that the Fund would be financially burdensome and that members could use its sources to build military establishments hostile to the United States. Burgess did not want candy to be given to bad boys, as he put it.[11] Other critics feared that the Fund would be exhausted quickly because of the shortage of dollars abroad.[12] Most criticism centered on the Fund because the Bank seemed to have more safeguards against unsound lending. The United States held a veto over any Bank loans in dollars but did not have this power for Fund transactions. Thus the Association, like many opponents of the Fund, recommended that Washington accept the Bank but renegotiate the Fund according to less liberal banking and trade principles.[13]

Administration officials refuted every criticism and refused to alter the agreements in any way. Conscious of Wilson's mistake at Versailles, they had wisely included congressmen, senators, and a banker in the Bretton Woods delegation, and Senators Robert Wagner and Charles Tobey of New Hampshire returned from the conference committed to push legislation through their chamber.[14] The administration amassed a wide array of labor, business, banking, farm, and civic support and set forth its case in the rhetoric of "peace and prosperity." Acheson warned that rejection of Bretton Woods

[9] *Congressional Record*, XCI (July 17, 1945), 7625; also Gardner, *Sterling-Dollar Diplomacy*, pp. 130-31; Senate, *Bretton Woods* (June 21, 1945), pp. 370-71.

[10] J. D. Gelder, in *Wall Street Journal*, July 3, 1944; Gardner, *Sterling-Dollar Diplomacy*; pp. 130-33; Senate, *Bretton Woods* (June 20, 1945), p. 243, (June 28, 1945), pp. 594-97; House, Committee on Banking and Currency, *Bretton Woods Agreements Act* (Hearings), 79th Cong., 1st sess. (Mar. 22, 1945), p. 410; New York State Bankers Association, *Bretton Woods Proposals* (New York, 1945); *Nation's Business*, XXXIII (July, 1945), 18; Winthrop W. Aldrich (Chase National Bank) to Herbert Brownell, Jr. (chairman, Republican Party), Apr. 13, 1945, Box 34, Aldrich Papers; *Banking*, XXXVII (February, 1945), 40-41, 121-22; John Williams, "Currency Stabilization: The Keynes and White Plans," *Foreign Affairs*, XXI (July, 1943), 645-58.

[11] W. Randolph Burgess to John F. Neylan, Nov. 28, 1944, Box 37, John F. Neylan Papers, Bancroft Library, University of California; Senate, *Bretton Woods* (June 25, 1945), pp. 469-72.

[12] *Fortune*, XXXII (July, 1945), 200; L. M. Giannini to Congressman George E. Outland, Mar. 24, 1945, Bank of America Archives, San Francisco.

[13] Senate, *Bretton Woods* (June 20, 1945), p. 244; New York State Chamber of Commerce, *Monthly Bulletin*, XXXVII (May, 1945), 50.

[14] Other delegates were Representatives Brent Spence and Jesse Wolcott, Edward E. Brown (chairman, First National Bank of Chicago), Morgenthau, Fred Vinson (director, Office of Economic Stabilization), Acheson (assistant secretary of state), Leo T. Crowley (administrator, Foreign Economic Administration), Marriner S. Eccles (chairman, Federal Reserve System), Mabel Newcomer (professor of economics, Vassar College), and White.

would endanger the United Nations Organization itself; Morgenthau said the program "is definitely good business for the United States"; the Federal Reserve System Board of Governors concluded that it was "an important step in the restoration of world trade and in safeguarding the interests of the United States . . ."; the Congress of Industrial Organizations predicted that Bretton Woods would create five million jobs because of its favorable effect on export trade; and Harry A. Bullis, president of General Mills, found the Bank and Fund "part of a great program that is being designed to give all the world better incomes, better diets, and better hopes for the future, and thereby to promote peace."[15]

To the charge that the United States would relinquish decisionmaking and economic power to an international organization, Senator Tobey replied that the United States vote "will be close to a third of the total, and it is clear that a control of that much of the voting power is sufficient to prevent the adoption by the Fund of any course of action that would be prejudicial to the United States."[16] The Treasury Department spoke similarly of "the great weight of our voting power."[17] Proponents mentioned the nation's commitment to multilateralism and noted that, although the Fund allowed temporary trade restrictions for recovery purposes, no new controls could be introduced without its approval.[18] The benefits of American membership in the Bank and Fund, in short, were too important to pass up; world trade would be facilitated; the domestic economy would be invigorated; stability and peace would be stimulated; United States power would be exerted. Any risk had to be ventured. Burgess felt the pressure of the opposition in March, 1945: "We are having a great fight here. The government boys are putting in everything possible to put over the plan without dotting an i or crossing a t."[19] The Bretton Woods Agreements Act passed the House and Senate in

[15] Acheson is quoted in House, *Bretton Woods* (Mar. 8, 1945), p. 33; Morgenthau in *ibid.* (Mar. 7, 1945), p. 4; Bullis in *ibid.* (Mar. 23, 1945), p. 496; the Federal Reserve Board in *Federal Reserve Bulletin*, XXXI (April, 1945), 304. For other support, see *Congressional Record*, XCI (July 17, 1945), 7602-6; Committee for Economic Development, *International Trade, Foreign Investment and Domestic Employment Including the Bretton Woods Proposals;* Henry Morgenthau, Jr., "Bretton Woods and International Cooperation," *Foreign Affairs*, XXXIII (January, 1945), 182-94; Edward O'Neal (Farm Bureau Federation) to Wagner, June 13, 1945, Box 92, Charles Tobey Papers, Dartmouth College Library; Business and Industry Committee for Bretton Woods, letterhead, *ibid.* The latter group included Henry F. Grady (American President Lines), Charles Hook (American Rolling Mills), Henry Bristol (Bristol-Myers), C. H. Hilton (Hilton Hotels), and James H. Rand, Jr. (Remington-Rand), among many other prominent businessmen.

[16] "Senator Taft's Criticisms," July 18, 1944, Box 92, Tobey Papers.

[17] Fred M. Vinson, in House, *Bretton Woods* (Mar. 16, 1945), p. 174; U.S., Department of the Treasury, *Questions and Answers on the Fund and Bank* (Washington, D.C., 1945), p. 7.

[18] U.S., Department of the Treasury, *The Bretton Woods Proposals* (Washington, D.C., 1945); *DSB*, XII (Apr. 22, 1945), 740.

[19] W. Randolph Burgess to John F. Neylan, Mar. 8, 1945, Box 83, Neylan Papers.

mid-1945 by very comfortable margins.[20] The Bank and Fund soon entered a time of troubles as the United States began to mold the institutions into the shape of its foreign policy.

THE UNITED STATES AND BRETTON WOODS

The act of July, 1945, provided for close supervision of the Bank and Fund through the cabinet-level National Advisory Council on International Monetary and Financial Problems. According to one student of the arrangement, it "constituted a major departure from the original conception of a Fund and Bank managed by impartial financial experts rather than representatives of national governments."[21] The legislation required United States representatives to the Fund and Bank to consult with the Council on all questions affecting the United States—which meant, in essence, all questions. Morgenthau had argued that the two agencies would make loans on a nonpolitical basis, but his own insistence that the IMF and IBRD be permanently located in Washington increased the opportunities for United States interference.[22]

United States supremacy stemmed from the Washington location, occupancy of top offices by United States nationals, the large United States voting strength and rank as largest subscriber, and the critical importance of the dollar to world trade and finance. American domination could be seen as early as the organizing meeting of the Bank and Fund in Savannah, Georgia, during March, 1946. On his way to the conclave, Keynes stopped in Washington and reported his disapproval of the United States as the permanent location for the new organizations. Acheson insisted that "you fellows will have to give way on this matter," and Keynes recalled that Treasury Secretary Fred Vinson told him that the selection of Washington itself "was a final decision the merits of which they [Americans] were not prepared to discuss." The Truman administration, Vinson went on, was entitled to decide what location within the United States it preferred.[23] It wanted the agencies near the capitol and away from the somewhat hostile financial center on Wall Street.[24] This unilateral decision created ill will and

---

[20] The House by 345-18 (June 7) and the Senate by 61-16 (July 19). *Congressional Record*, XCI, 5723, 7780. For a fuller discussion of the debate see Alfred E. Eckes, "Bretton Woods: America's New Deal for an Open World" (Ph.D. dissertation, University of Texas, 1969).

[21] Gardner, *Sterling-Dollar Diplomacy*, p. 134.

[22] Senate, *Bretton Woods* (June 12, 1945), pp. 14-15; Gardner, *Sterling-Dollar Diplomacy*, pp. 265-67; Jack N. Behrman, "Foreign Aid as a Technique in Attaining United States International Objectives" (Ph.D. dissertation, Princeton University, 1952), p. 23.

[23] Quoted in Harrod, *Keynes*, pp. 679, 630.

[24] Raymond F. Mikesell, "The International Monetary Fund, 1944-1949: A Review," *International Conciliation*, No. 455 (November, 1949), 845.

suspicion, for a majority of the delegates at Savannah preferred New York. Keynes, who had defended the United States in Parliament during a heated debate over the Bretton Woods agreements, complained of "railroading" at Savannah: "I went to Savannah expecting to meet the world, and all I met was a tyrant."[25] However, he could not walk out in protest because the vital British loan was then before Congress.[26]

After Savannah it was obvious that Washington was the "piper" which would "call the tune."[27] The first president of the World Bank was Eugene Meyer, owner of the *Washington Post* and a former Federal Reserve Board member. Since then, the president has always been a United States citizen, and his influence within the organization has been decisive.[28] Meyer, it seems, resigned in something of a huff in December, 1946, after the Truman administration put pressure on the Bank to refuse loans to Poland, a member.[29] Wall Street bankers and others lacked confidence in the Bank, and hence Meyer was able to sell few of its securities in the American market.[30] John McCloy, a lawyer with Wall Street ties and a former assistant secretary of war, replaced Meyer and brought a new hierarchy with him.

[25] Harrod, *Keynes*, p. 639.

[26] *Ibid.*, p. 636. There was another testy issue at Savannah, resolved in favor of the United States. A seemingly insignificant debate over salaries for officers reflected the larger question of whether the Fund was to have continuously active or infrequently active directors. The United States preferred the former, seeing in the Fund an active instrument for tight control in currency matters. Britain saw the Fund as somewhat automatic and thus advocated weaker leadership. The decision was that each director was to be paid $17,500 annually for full-time service. See Mikesell, "International Monetary Fund," pp. 844-45; Gardner, *Sterling-Dollar Diplomacy*, pp. 259-60.

[27] *Manchester Guardian*, Mar. 23, 1946, quoted in Gardner, *Sterling-Dollar Diplomacy*, p. 267.

[28] James Morris, *The Road to Huddersfield* (New York, 1963), p. 70. Serving as vice-president was Harold Smith, former director of the budget; he died suddenly in January, 1947. The first executive director was Emilio G. Collado, an economist with service in the State Department from 1938 to 1946. After leaving the Bank in 1947, Collado joined Standard Oil of New Jersey as an officer. Chester A. McClain of New York was named general counsel of the Bank. The United States also had a member on the Board of Executive Directors of the Fund, which selected the managing director. Camille Gutt, an industrialist from Belgium, held the latter post. The executive director was Harry White; Andrew Overby replaced him in 1948. Many other Americans served the Fund in top positions.

[29] Meyer to Bernard Baruch, Sept. 3, 1946, part XI:1, Baruch Papers. For evidence of hostility to a loan to Poland, see below and Emilio G. Collado to John W. Snyder, "Activities of the International Bank in the Loan Field," IBRD folder 1, Snyder Papers. Collado resigned only three months after Meyer, and he had indicated his opposition to political loans to Will Clayton in a note of July 23, 1946, Greece folder, *ibid.*

[30] Several states obstructed the sale of Bank securities. The Wisconsin Banking Commission, for example, voted unanimously to forbid state banks and trust companies to invest in International Bank securities and as late as October, 1946, twelve states (including Ohio and Connecticut) did not recognize Bank securities. The change in Bank leadership, its anti-Communist proclivities, and its publicity campaign helped clear investment impediments, and by November of 1949, it had issued $250 million in bonds. *Business Week*, Nov. 2, 1946, p. 17, and Dec. 7, 1946, p. 18; *Journal of Commerce*, Dec. 3, 1946; Emilio G. Collado to John W. Snyder, Oct. 16, 1946, IBRD folder 1, Snyder

Robert L. Garner, a vice-president of General Foods, became vice-president; Eugene Black, vice-president of Chase National Bank, assumed the office of executive director and sat on the twelve-man executive board.[31] Under the new leadership the Bank became a reliable arm of United States foreign policy, and banks and insurance companies were soon purchasing IBRD bonds.

The voting strength of the United States in the Bank acted as another measure of control. Washington possessed one-third of the votes by virtue of its subscription of $3.175 billion to the total of $9.100 billion.[32] In the Fund the United States had one-third of the votes, subscribing $2.750 of $8.800 billion.[33] The world shortage of dollars created a demand by Bank members for dollar loans, the Bank could grant dollar loans only with the consent of the United States, and "because the bank must rely mainly upon the American capital market, the rest of the management will be loath to offend" the executive director, as one contemporary observer put it.[34]

BRETTON WOODS AND THE COLD WAR

Since Washington was so frank about the Bank and Fund as foreign policy instruments, it is hardly surprising that Russia, which attended the Bretton Woods Conference, never joined and soon attacked the United States for violating the principles of international organization. Russia was hesitant at the New Hampshire meeting because the Bank and Fund were oriented toward capitalist, private-trading nations. Indeed, as one commentator has written, "inextricably mixed up in its attitudes was a conviction that capitalism was the right way, that private enterprise was best, and, as a

---

Papers; William A. Sullivan (insurance commissioner, State of Washington) to L. M. Giannini, Dec. 24, 1946, Bank of America Archives; Antonin Basch, "International Bank for Reconstruction and Development, 1944-1949," *International Conciliation,* No. 455 (November, 1949), p. 801.

[31] Garner had served as vice-president and treasurer of Guaranty Trust from 1929 to 1943. Later he re-entered private banking. Black was with the Chase National Bank from 1933 to 1947; he stayed with the International Bank until 1962.

[32] Each member had 250 votes plus one vote for every $100,000 of its subscription. Thus the United States held 32,000 votes of a total of 95,000. Great Britain followed, with 15 percent of the vote, China with 7 percent, and France with 6 percent; the remaining votes were scattered. International Bank for Reconstruction and Development, *Second Annual Report, 1946-1947* (Washington, D.C., 1947), p. 35.

[33] The Fund's voting arrangement was similar to that of the Bank, except that a member's voting power increased as its currency was purchased from the Fund. Thus, with dollars in demand, the voting power of the United States at times increased beyond one-third.

[34] Henry C. Wallich, "Financing the International Bank," *Harvard Business Review,* XXIV (Winter, 1946), 175. For further discussion of the American domination of the IMF and IBRD, see Jack N. Behrman, "Political Factors in U.S. International Financial Cooperation, 1945-1950," *American Political Science Review,* XLVII (June, 1953) 447-52.

rule-of-thumb dogma, that the less State interference, the better."[35] The Articles of Agreement succinctly stated that the institutions were designed to encourage private investment.

As a state-trading nation, usually through bilateral arrangements, Russia found Bretton Woods uninviting and challenging. "The decisions made at Bretton Woods," concluded one Russian commentator, "are adapted to the capitalistic economy and are directed toward the settlement of the difficulties which are faced by the capitalistic countries. Many of the provisions are simply superfluous, with regard to the USSR, or inapplicable, due to the peculiarities of the economy of the USSR."[36] The Soviet Union, with its traditional passion for secrecy, disliked the requirement that members must furnish information on the Fund's operations, and because it was a large producer and holder of gold, it also disliked the requirement that members must report their annual gold reserves, production, imports, and exports. It was suspicious of the provision that Bank officials thoroughly investigate all loan-related projects for their feasibility, arguing that this requirement was unnecessary for state-planned economies. The Fund's chief function, currency stabilization, was not found relevant to the Soviet Union's managed money system. The ranking of Russia third, behind the United States and Britain, was also resented. Britain, Russian leaders pointed out, was a weak nation which should concede second place or at least give parity to Moscow. Finally, Russia was well aware of the all-pervading influence of the United States.[37] American leaders, for their part, were "vague" about Russian participation and never really studied the problem carefully.[38]

At the time of the Savannah conference, Russia had still not decided upon membership. The conference gave the Soviet delegation until December, 1946, to decide, but Russia never joined the Bank or Fund. Commercially and financially, of course, Soviet participation was not vital, for its percentage of world trade was minimal and the ruble was not an international currency. Politically, on the other hand, its membership might have alleviated some conflicts, however minor. Harry D. White commented that the "Fund

[35] Morris, *Road*, p. 43. See also William Y. Elliot et al., *The Political Economy of American Foreign Policy* (New York, 1955), p. 209.

[36] Quoted in Charles Prince, "The USSR's Role in International Finance," *Harvard Business Review*, XXV (Autumn, 1946), 125.

[37] Russia did like the concept of increased world trade, which aids a country seeking imports from capitalist nations—and applauded the provision that part of a member's subscription must be in gold because it interpreted this to mean that the large Soviet gold product would weigh heavily in international currency arrangements. *Ibid.*, pp. 112-14, 124; *Nation's Business*, XXXIV (January, 1946), 18; *Journal of Commerce*, Jan. 7, 1946; Walter C. Louckheim, Jr. (Securities and Exchange Commission), to Harry White, Apr. 27, 1944, part II:24, White Papers; "Meeting in Mr. White's Office, May 10, 1944," *ibid.*; Blum, *From Morgenthau Diaries*, III, 259, 261; Mikesell, "Negotiating," pp. 113-14; Ladislas Farago, "World Bank: Council of Securities," *United Nations World*, I (April, 1947), 20-23.

[38] Mikesell, "Negotiating," p. 102; Eckes, "Bretton Woods," p. 273.

needs Russia. I mean, you can't have a cannon on board a ship that isn't tied down because they can do a lot of harm if they are not in."[39] Consultation, loans and reconstruction, recognition of Russia as a great power, more Soviet involvement in international trade—Soviet membership in Bretton Woods would have meant an improvement upon the bifurcated world economy which developed. Yet officials like White and Morgenthau nurtured a contradiction; they wanted to tie down the Soviet cannon to the United States ship, binding the Russians to United States economic principles and to United States influence. Thus one could not expect, as George F. Kennan put it, that Russia would pay any more than "lip service" to the principles of the Bank and Fund.[40]

The assumption became popular in the United States that the rejection of the Bretton Woods Agreements was calculated to exacerbate international tension. To officials in control of the two agencies "the Soviets not unexpectedly assume an obstructionist role, which then confirms the Western powers' belief in the innate hostility of the Soviet Union toward international organizations." At the same time, "Western domination reinforces the Soviet belief" that such international bodies serve anti-Soviet purposes. "A self-fulfilling, circular pattern of attitudes and behavior is thus induced in the approach of each," Alvin Rubinstein concludes.[41]

Had Russia joined, it probably would have resigned later in protest against the blatant United States manipulation. "International" was a misnomer. The Bank forwarded all loan applications to the executive director, who dutifully submitted them to the National Advisory Council for decision. The Bank followed a policy of "strategic non-lending" in order to persuade borrowers to alter their economic systems in favor of private enterprise and private foreign investment. By screening proposed projects the Bank hoped to establish private undertakings.[42] There was no attempt to deny this policy: "It seems clear that the real measure of the Bank's effectiveness will be, not so much the number or amount of its loans and guarantees, significant as they may be, but rather its success in *influencing attitudes*—in promoting a realistic, constructive approach to development problems on the part of its members and in fostering a greater degree of confidence among investors."[43]

[39] Quoted from the Morgenthau diaries, Roosevelt Library, by Alfred E. Eckes, Jr., "Open Door Expansionism Reconsidered" (unpublished paper, 1970).

[40] This cable of February 22 later emerged as the "X" article, "The Sources of Soviet Conduct," *Foreign Affairs*, XXV (July, 1947), 566-82, and led to the addition of Kennan to the State Department Policy Planning Staff. *Foreign Relations, 1946*, VI, 703.

[41] Alvin Z. Rubinstein, "Soviet and American Policies in International Organizations," *International Organization*, XVIII (Winter, 1964), 51-52. See also J. W. Beyen, *Money in a Maelstrom* (New York, 1949).

[42] Behrman, "Foreign Aid," p. 40; David A. Baldwin, *Economic Development and American Foreign Policy, 1943-62* (Chicago, 1966), pp. 33-50; Senate, *ERP* (Jan. 16, 1948), pp. 539-40.

[43] International Bank of Reconstruction and Development, *Third Annual Report, 1947-1948* (Washington, D.C., 1948), p. 21 (italics added).

President McCloy indicated in 1947 that the Bank "will increasingly prove useful as an influence to prompt and perhaps to facilitate the taking of the necessary political steps to bring about economic stability."[44] The Bank justified its consideration of political questions (such as government ownership of industry, socialist organization, and friendship with Russia) by arguing that "political tensions and uncertainties" affected economic conditions.[45] The problem was, of course, that other members disagreed with the definition of "political uncertainty," "necessary political steps," and "constructive approach."

With the United States firmly in control and with the notion established that state-regulated and Communist economies were basically unsound, the Bank excluded Poland and Czechoslovakia, both members and subscribers, from loans.[46] In the fall of 1946 Poland notified the Bank that it would apply for $600 million over a three-year period. In October Secretary Byrnes called for delay: "Certainly we should give no financial assistance to Poland without absolute guarantees that a reasonable proportion of coal exports will be allocated to countries west of the iron curtain."[47] The World Bank had become "we" in Byrnes's mind. Acheson assured him that "we can discuss in greater detail what course of action we can pursue, in light of our commitments as a member of the International Bank and Fund, to achieve your objectives of *preventing or limiting assistance to countries opposing principles for which we stand.*"[48] Poland never got a loan, and McCloy explained in 1948 that Poland and Czechoslovakia had not received loans because "of the impact of the existing political tensions and uncertainties upon their economies and their credit."[49] Bank leaders abruptly shifted their definition of "political tensions and uncertainties" after Tito's break with Moscow; Yugoslavia, which had been denied loans until then, had received over $30 million by October, 1951.[50] Poland resigned its membership in 1950, Czechoslovakia in 1954. It was evident, according to the State

[44] International Bank for Reconstruction and Development, *Proceedings of the Second Annual Meeting of the Board of Governors* (Washington, D.C., 1947), p. 7.
[45] IBRD, *Third Annual Report*, p. 14; see also IBRD, *Second Annual Report*, p. 17.
[46] Czechoslovakia received $6 million from the Fund in 1948. International Monetary Fund, *Annual Report, April 30, 1949* (Washington, D.C., 1949), pp. 44, 102.
[47] *Foreign Relations, 1946*, VI, 504n.
[48] *Ibid.*, p. 506 (italics added).
[49] NFTC, *Report of 35th National Convention* (Nov. 8, 1948), p. 54. The Bank almost granted Poland a loan for the purchase of coal mining equipment in 1947 so that Polish coal could help speed recovery in western Europe, but terms could not be reached. See Richard M. Bissell, Jr. to Thomas C. Blaisdell, Jr., Oct. 18, 1947, General Areas folder, President's Committee on Foreign Aid Records; *Business Week,* Nov. 22, 1947, pp. 115-16.
[50] In 1949 Yugoslavia received $2.7 million to finance the purchase of equipment for timber production; in 1951 it received $28 million for power, mining, industrial, and other projects. International Bank for Reconstruction and Development, *Fifth Annual Report, 1949-1950* (Washington, D.C., 1950), p. 34; International Bank for Reconstruction and Development, *Seventh Annual Report, 1951-1952* (Washington, D.C., 1952), pp. 25-26.

Department, that the Polish resignation served the Kremlin's purpose of isolating its satellites from the "free world." The Department denied that the Bank or Fund was subservient to the United States and ignored the fact that the resignation was directly linked to its own policy, as reflected also in the Export-Import Bank, of isolating eastern Europe economically.[51]

In the two years prior to passage of the Economic Cooperation Act (Marshall Plan) in 1948, the World Bank had made only four loans, all to friends of the United States who could contribute to western European recovery.[52] It became evident after General Marshall's speech in 1947 that the Bank would focus its attention and resources on western European reconstruction—the Department of State, in fact, required it to do so.[53] The Bank and Fund consciously followed the lead of the Economic Cooperation Administration and reduced their activities elsewhere. Many developing nations joined Poland and Czechoslovakia in protesting the loan limitations.[54]

The Fund had to admit in 1949 that "dependence on bilateral trade and inconvertible currencies is far greater than before the war."[55] Indeed, Bretton Woods was a failure, in terms of its own goals, in the early Cold War. The Bank and Fund did not function as international institutions and did not contribute much to reconstruction, world trade, monetary cooperation or investment. They were used by the United States to develop its embryonic sphere of influence. Even one of the chief architects of Bretton Woods, Harry D. White, noting the exertion of United States authority at the Savannah conference, said that the insistence of the United States upon dominating the Bank and Fund "resembles much too closely the operation of power politics rather than of international cooperation—except that the power employed is financial instead of military and political."[56]

[51] *DSB*, XXII (Mar. 27, 1950), 497.

[52] $497 million to France, Holland, Denmark, and Luxembourg.

[53] U.S., Department of State, "Questions and Answers and Procedure Regarding U.S. Aid to a European Program of Economic Recovery," [n.d.], ERP folder 2, Clifford Papers; IBRD, *Second Annual Report*, p. 5; IBRD, *Third Annual Report*, pp. 7-21; IBRD, *Fourth Annual Report, 1948-1949* (Washington, D.C., 1949), pp. 14-15.

[54] See Baldwin, *Economic Development*. Point Four was launched in part to satisfy the developing nations; see Thomas G. Paterson, "Foreign Aid under Wraps: The Point Four Program," *Wisconsin Magazine of History*, LVI (Winter, 1972-73), 119-26.

[55] Gardner, *Sterling-Dollar Diplomacy*, p. 298. Also see Brian Tew, *International Monetary Co-operation, 1945-56*, 3d ed. (London, 1956), p. 86.

[56] White memorandum, May, 1946, White Papers, quoted in Gardner, *Economic Aspects*, p. 290.

CHAPTER 8

FRIENDLY PRESSURE: THE BRITISH LOAN

Shortly after the launching of the Bretton Woods organizations at Savannah, President Truman asked the House speaker to assist him in promoting another measure for peace and prosperity, the British loan of 1946. "Without this Agreement," he warned, "it will be difficult, if not impossible, to proceed with the United Nations program for international economic cooperation."[1] Bretton Woods and the British loan were fused in the American mind, but the latter aroused far more opposition in the United States.

The British loan, more so than Bretton Woods, created rancor between London and Washington, although it did help forge an uneasy Anglo-American coalition. Many Americans detested the British Empire, and the British were alarmed by the new United States interest in the Middle East and Mediterranean, which challenged that empire. Anglo-American squabbles during the war over the atomic bomb, civil aviation, trade competition and principles, and oil in the Middle East had threatened to divide the allies. Some Americans protested the Labour Party's assumption of power in Britain. The British were furious over what Winston Churchill called the "rough and harsh" decision to discontinue Lend-Lease so abruptly in August, 1945, and Americans were piqued that the British would respond with seeming ingratitude to their wartime aid. Overshadowing all other issues was the awareness on both sides of the Atlantic that the United States had emerged from the war a mammoth power, while Britain was weak, its empire collapsing, dependent upon American aid.[2]

---

[1] Truman to speaker, June 29, 1946, OF 212A, Truman Papers.

[2] Clemens, *Yalta*, pp. 99-102; M. A. Fitzsimmons, *The Foreign Policy of the British Labour Government: 1945-1951* (Notre Dame, Ind., 1954), pp. 17-20; Groom, "U.S.-Allied Relations and the Atomic Bomb in the Second World War"; *Foreign Relations, 1945*, VIII, 64-81 (civil aviation); Cushing Strout, *The American Image of the Old World* (New York, 1963), pp. 230-31; D. C. Watt, "American Aid to Britain and the Problems of Socialism," *American Review* (Bologna), II (March, 1963), 46-67; Hugh Dalton, *High Tide and After: Memoirs, 1945-1960* (London, 1962), pp. 255-56; Roy Harrod, "Hands and Fists across the Sea," *Foreign Affairs*, XXX (October, 1951), 63-76; Gardner, *Sterling-Dollar Diplomacy* p. 185; *Foreign Relations, 1945*, VI, 115 (Lend-Lease); Eric Estorick, *Stafford Cripps: Master Statesman* (New York, 1949), pp. 301-2.

But the unifying factors were potent enough to overcome the divisive ones. Great Britain and the United States had had a long history of amicable relations, as well as long-range mutual postwar diplomatic and economic interests. Relations during World War II were marked more by cooperation than by the discord that characterized Soviet-American intercourse. Anglo-American military affairs were supervised by a combined chiefs of staff, the United States did share atomic information with the British during the war, and British scientists helped develop the atomic weapon. Combined boards worked on the problems of raw materials and food allocation, and the possibility seemed to exist for postwar cooperation on these questions.[3]

A number of British and American leaders in fact believed that the two allies would continue their alliance in the postwar period. Shortly after the war, according to Prime Minister Clement Attlee, "the two English-speaking countries began to see that their close cooperation was essential to world peace and prosperity."[4] Presidential adviser Harry Hopkins wrote in 1945: "If I were to lay down the most cardinal principle of our foreign policy, it would be that we make absolutely sure that now and forever the United States and Great Britain are going to see eye to eye on major matters of world policy."[5] Finding more to agree upon than to divide over, the United States and Britain soon molded a coalition to face Russia, a coalition many considered natural because of the past. "The strategic interdependence of Great Britain and the United States," wrote one student of the major powers, "is so great that for many purposes it is permissible to speak of these Western democracies as if they constituted a single power-nucleus."[6] The British loan of 1946 symbolized and shaped that developing coalition, at the same time that it illuminated differences between the two competitors.

POSTWAR BRITAIN AND THE LOAN

As the war in Europe neared its end, American officials began to scrutinize Lend-Lease shipments to Britain more closely. They sought to reduce material which could be used to meet civilian needs and to funnel goods to the Far Eastern theater. Winston Churchill protested to Washington in May that Roosevelt had agreed at the Quebec Conference of September, 1944, that Lend-Lease goods for Birtish reconstruction purposes would continue to flow until Japan was defeated.[7] At that conference Roosevelt had prom-

---

[3] For World War II relations, see William McNeill, *America, Britain, and Russia* (London, 1953); Gaddis Smith, *American Diplomacy during the Second World War, 1941-1945* (New York, 1965); Kolko, *Politics of War.*

[4] Clement R. Attlee, *As It Happened* (New York, 1954), p. 239.

[5] Sherwood, *Roosevelt and Hopkins,* p. 922. See also Herbert Feis, "On Our Economic Relations with Britain," *Foreign Affairs,* XXI (April, 1943), 462-75.

[6] William T. R. Fox, *The Super-Powers* (New York, 1944), p. 73.

[7] Coakley and Leighton, *Global Logistics and Strategy, 1943-1945,* pp. 640-44, 664-70.

ised—at least the British considered it a promise—to give Britain $6.5 billion between V-E and V-J days in reconstruction aid. Yet within a few months, after pressure from the State and War departments, Roosevelt partially retreated from the offer, and denied that he had made any such commitment. This retreat was not adequately conveyed to the British, who continued to believe from May until August that the United States would use its vast economic power, either through Lend-Lease or another Rooseveltian "brainwave," to stimulate British recovery.[8] The decision in mid-August to kill Lend-Lease altogether on V-E Day was therefore a great shock. Even United States embassy officials in London were not informed about the abrupt cessation and were startled to hear the news on the radio.[9]

The sudden demise of Lend-Lease underscored a crucial postwar issue for the British—economic survival in the transition period from war to peace. "We have spent all we had," lamented Sir John Anderson, chancellor of the exchequer, and "we have gone almost to the limit of physical and economic strength. . . . We shall want help."[10] The country had lost one-quarter of its prewar national wealth and had been forced to liquidate one-half, or $8 billion worth, of its foreign investments, while its external debt had increased. By the close of 1944 British exports had dropped to one-third of their prewar volume. An increase of 50 to 75 percent in exports would be required to recoup these losses and to revive the economy, yet such a buildup would take at least three years, and during that period Britain would face a staggering balance of payments deficit of $5 billion.[11]

In the last few days of the Far Eastern war the critical British economic plight and the intense American desire for freer postwar trade stimulated discussions in London. Ambassador John Winant had warned Washington earlier that the British would place "serious obstacles" in the way of United States postwar commercial policy. Talks during the war had indicated that the British were not eager to remove trade privileges granted to members of the Empire or to embrace multilateralism enthusiastically.[12] For example, they had accepted reluctantly, and only after much debate, Article VII of the Lend-Lease Agreement (1942), which stated that Britain and the United States would cooperate to eliminate "discriminatory treatment in interna-

[8] Cordell Hull was upset that the president had not secured British trade concessions at Quebec, and other officials and some congressmen opposed using Lend-Lease as reconstruction aid. For the confusing story of Quebec and its aftermath, see Hull, *Memoirs*, II, 1613-14; Blum, *From Morgenthau Diaries*, III, 313-14, 320, 450-51; diary, Sept. 26, 1944, Box 5, Breckinridge Long Papers, Library of Congress; George C. Herring, Jr., "The United States and British Bankruptcy, 1944-1945," *Political Science Quarterly*, LXXXVI (June, 1971), 266-69.

[9] Will Clayton, "Reminiscences of William Lockhart Clayton," 1962, Oral History, Columbia University Library, pp. 166-69.

[10] Quoted in Pritchard, "Will Clayton," p. 211.

[11] *Journal of Commerce*, Aug. 15, 1945; Gardner, *Sterling-Dollar Diplomacy*, pp. 178-79; *Foreign Relations, 1945*, VI, 80-84.

[12] *Foreign Relations, 1945*, VI, 3, 19-20, 38.

tional commerce" and to reduce "tariffs and other trade barriers."[13] In July, 1945, United States officials requested Britain to send representatives to Washington to negotiate commercial and financial questions—that is, trade policy and a loan—simultaneously. A briefing book paper at Potsdam, where the offer of negotiations was tendered, stated frankly that American trade principles would be jeopardized without financial aid for the British.[14]

The State Department economic specialist, Will Clayton, was one of the most ardent and early advocates of postwar reconstruction aid for Britain. In mid-1945 he recommended a loan of $2 to $3 billion and argued that the "British financial problem is admittedly the greatest barrier to rapid progress towards free multilateral payments and relaxation of barriers to trade." He predicted that the British would hesitate to borrow at all. Recognizing Britain's key place in world trade, he believed Washington would have to grant generous terms, such as an interest rate of only 2 percent.[15] Instructed to prepare an agenda for the Washington talks, Clayton met with Keynes in early August and told him that the United States would insist on a reduction in tariffs, cartels, quotas, and trade discriminations before a loan of perhaps $3 billion could be granted.[16] The American bargaining stance hardened noticeably as Britain's economic plight became more conspicuous. Officials recognized that "the British are putting up a very determined front to cover a basically weak financial position with a very serious outlook."[17] The British naturally wanted loan and trade talks to be separate, but Clayton, under strong pressure from Washington to obtain commercial policy concessions, insisted upon combining the two questions.[18] Attlee recalled that the English "weren't in a position to bargain."[19] With both the British and the Americans aware of the American advantage and of the use of the loan as a potential diplomatic tool, negotiations officially began in Washington on September 11, 1945.

For almost three months, until the signing of the loan agreement on December 6, Keynes, Vinson, and Clayton wrestled with questions about the size and interest of a loan, commercial policy, Lend-Lease settlement, and currency.[20] The meetings were marked by Keynes' sarcastic sallies and Vinson's resentment at some of them, yet there was a minimum of bitterness in the debates. Without question, however, there was great division on the

[13] Quoted in Gardner, *Sterling-Dollar Diplomacy*, p. 59.

[14] *Foreign Relations, Berlin*, I, 810-14; II, 1184.

[15] *Ibid., 1945*, VI, 54-56. See also Clayton, "Reminiscences," pp. 168-69; Harrod, *Keynes*, pp. 593-94.

[16] *Foreign Relations, 1945*, VI, 79-87.

[17] Winant to secretary of state, Aug. 17, 1945, *ibid.*, p. 101.

[18] *Ibid.*, pp. 110, 116-17.

[19] Quoted in Francis Williams, *A Prime Minister Remembers: The War and the Post-War Memoirs of Rt. Hon. Earl Attlee* (London, 1961), p. 134.

[20] The following discussion is drawn from *Foreign Relations, 1945*, VI, 122-204; Gardner, *Sterling-Dollar Diplomacy* pp. 188-207.

issues. The British entered the conference with the hope that the Americans would recognize the recent common war effort and extend a grant-in-aid rather than an interest-bearing loan. The American negotiators, however, were wary of congressional and public critics who would not endorse a gift for the British and who were even skeptical of an interest-bearing loan. The British, on the other hand, were alarmed by reports from home that the cabinet resented Washington's attempts to impose its commercial policy and the lack of sympathy for a stricken ally.

The agreement was settled on United States terms, with the British request for $5 to $6 billion reduced to $3.75 billion. The loan was to be interest-free for five years, with a 2 percent interest rate for fifty years. A waiver of interest payments would be allowed if the United Kingdom encountered serious economic trouble. Included in the agreement was a Lend-Lease settlement whereby the United States erased Britain's $20 billion indebtedness. Washington also transferred to the British $6 billion in surplus and Lend-Lease property for only $532 million. Lend-Lease goods in the pipeline—on order or being delivered—were sold to the British for $118 million.[21] On the whole, the terms were generous.

The United States forced the British to make commercial policy concessions. They agreed to lift currency restrictions from the sterling bloc in order to allow members of the bloc to convert their large holdings of sterling into dollars.[22] To further stimulate world trade, the British accepted the trade goals of multilateralism and nondiscrimination as stated in the *Proposals for the Expansion of World Trade and Employment*.[23] But the British endorsement in this case was weak and noncommittal; they set no deadline for reducing trade preferences in the Empire. The joint Anglo-American statement noted only that the United Kingdom was "in full agreement on all important points in these proposals and accepts them as a basis for international discussion" and would work to reduce "trade barriers."[24] At

[21] U.S., Department of State, *Anglo-American Financial and Commercial Agreements* (Washington, D.C., 1945).

[22] The sterling area or bloc consisted of the United Kingdom, Eire, Australia, New Zealand, Union of South Africa, Egypt, Iceland, India, Burma, Iraq, and the British colonies and mandates. These countries agreed to deposit with London all non-sterling currency, including dollars. After the war, they held large amounts of blocked and nonconvertible sterling which could not be exchanged for dollars because of the dollar shortage in Britain. Blocked sterling amounted to $12.3 billion in July, 1945, and presented a barrier to American foreign trade. See U.S., Congress, Senate, *Anglo-American Financial Agreement* (March, 1946), pp. 105-6; Paul Bareau, *The Sterling Area* (London, 1948).

[23] See also U.S., Department of State, *Proposals for Consideration by an International Conference on Trade and Employment* (Washington, D.C., 1945), the original American document submitted to the Anglo-American talks.

[24] Department of State, *Anglo-American Financial and Commercial Agreements*. For interpretation of the agreement as weak on commitments to multilateralism, see McNeill, *America, Britain, and Russia*, pp. 682-84; Judd Polk and Gardner Patterson, "The British Loan," *Foreign Affairs*, XXIV (April, 1946), 429-40.

the most, the British had agreed to talk about trade questions in a future international conference; there was no binding commitment to multi-lateralism or nondiscrimination. Yet American officials apparently believed that they had significantly reduced bilateralism and imperial trade pref-erences, perhaps because the agreement aroused such a public outcry in Britain. Lord Keynes, after noting Clayton's determination to obtain British acquiescence in multilateralism, quipped that "the *Mayflower* must have been filled with theologians."[25] Later events, however, were to demonstrate the serious shortcomings of the commercial agreement.

The financial and commercial agreements went quickly to Parliament and were linked with the question of British membership in the Bretton Woods institutions. After short but heated debate, the House of Commons passed the package in late December by a vote of 343 to 100, with 169 abstentions. The abstentions represented a Conservative bloc led by Churchill, who appreciated the loan but was irritated by the fact that it carried interest.[26] In the United States, debate proceeded much more slowly. A long congressional holiday, hearings, and obstructive tactics such as the introduction of crippling and long-debated amendments, delayed action until mid-1946. The arguments over the loan pointed up the importance of foreign trade to the foreign policy and economy of the United States and the significance of Britain as an ally in the developing Cold War.

THE STAKES: THE CASE FOR THE LOAN

Truman administration leaders offered three major reasons why the United States should finance British reconstruction. First, Britain was one of America's best customers. Second, the British Empire accounted for a major segment of international trade and had to be persuaded to follow a course of multilateralism for the sake of peace and prosperity. The third reason was seldom publicly advocated by government officials but became prominent in the congressional debates: Britain was a valuable ally.

Truman expressed the first point in early 1946: "The British Loan agreement is an important step in rebuilding foreign trade and and in creating

[25] Quoted in William C. Mallalieu, *British Reconstruction and American Policy, 1945-1955* (New York, 1956), p. 23.

[26] There was some vigorous British criticism of the United States during the debate. Some saw the United States pressing for economic advances in a prostrate and helpless world. Others thought that the loan subordinated British foreign policy to that of the United States, and that a free grant was in order because of the sacrifices of World War II. A large group within the Labour Party criticized its leadership for "tying the economy of Britain with that of capitalist America." Quoted in Watt, "American Aid to Britain," p. 56. For British criticisms, see Senate, *Anglo-American Financial Agreement*, p. 20; Smith, *State of Europe*, p. 88; Harrod, *Keynes*, p. 617; Gardner, *Sterling-Dollar Diplomacy*, pp. 225-28; *Foreign Relations, 1945*, VI, 197-99.

jobs in America."[27] Secretary Vinson noted that, if the loan negotiations had collapsed, "it would have meant very bad business for us," and Eric Johnston predicted that in such a case "a depression is inevitable in my opinion."[28] The Committee on International Economic Policy, which spent over twenty thousand dollars lobbying for congressional approval of the loan and whose membership consisted of large corporations, argued that "every American should know that it is in our national interest to strengthen the financial position of our best customer. . . ."[29] Both government and business officials were alarmed by the possibility that the British dollar shortage would cause Britain to ignore American goods, and most took seriously the *Economist*'s warning that in case the United States failed to aid Britain, "we shall have to economize our dollars and buy elsewhere."[30] Clayton in fact believed that the best case for the loan could be made by explaining its importance to the economy; Dean Acheson simply called the loan "self-preservation" for the United States.[31] Clair Wilcox of the Department of State issued a summary statement: "The United States and Great Britain are the mainstays of the world's economy. Economically there is no other nation that is anywhere nearly as important to us. It is this fact that gives the Anglo-American understandings their peculiar significance."[32]

The Truman administration bombarded Congress with statistics showing that the United Kingdom was essential to prosperous foreign trade and to the economy in general. In the 1936-1938 period, the United States acquired 22.3 percent of its imports from the sterling area and shipped a total of 26.7 percent of its exports to that bloc; in 1937 the sterling area countries bought 77 percent of American tobacco exports, 29 percent of wood and pulp, 35 percent of metals, machinery, and vehicles, 20 percent of petroleum and petroleum products, and 27 percent of cotton.[33] In that period the United

27 Press release, Mar. 4, 1946, OF 275A, Truman Papers.

28 U.S., Department of State, *The British Loan—What It Means to Us* (Washington, D.C., 1946), p. 5 (Vinson); Johnston, in Senate, *Anglo-American Financial Agreement* (Mar. 13, 1946), p. 464.

29 Senate, *Anglo-American Financial Agreement* (Mar. 13, 1946), p. 343. For similar sentiment see *Journal of Commerce*, Feb. 20, 1946 (Wilbert Ward of National City Bank of New York); *Business Week*, Sept. 15, 1945, p. 124; *DSB*, XIV (Jan. 20, 1946), 55 (Vinson).

30 Quoted in *Nation's Business*, XXXIII (November, 1945), 88. For concern about losing markets, see *Journal of Commerce*, Aug. 28 and Sept. 25, 1945, Jan. 11, 1946 (Philip Reed, General Electric), and Feb. 13, 1946 (the vice-president of Alcoa Steamship Company); Clayton to Eugene Holman (Standard Oil), Sept. 12, 1945, chronological file, Clayton Papers; Senate *Anglo-American Financial Agreement* (Mar. 14, 1946), p. 390 (Acheson).

31 Pritchard, "Will Clayton," p. 233; Acheson, in Senate, *Anglo-American Financial Agreement* (Mar. 13, 1946), p. 314.

32 U.S., Department of State, *Why Lend to Britain?* (Washington, D.C., 1946), p. 9. See also "Problems Confronting the American Businessman Today," speech, Feb. 28, 1946, Barkley Papers.

33 Another 26.7 percent of U.S. exports went to countries having payments agreements with Britain, and another 22.3 percent of U.S. imports came from such countries. Senate, *Anglo-American Financial Agreement* (March, 1946), p. 105.

States shipped more goods to Great Britain than to any other country.[34]
During the war, Britain alone consumed almost one-third of United States
exports, and American businessman, optimistic about postwar trade with
Britain, hoped to maintain the trend.[35]

American companies not only traded extensively with Britain and the
sterling area but also invested heavily in British industry. After the war,
expectations for increased American investment in England were high, and
the results seemed to justify the excitement.[36] By October, 1946, over fifty
new American-built plants existed; Monsanto Chemical was operating a $10
million factory in Wales; General Foods expanded its operations after the war
and in early 1947 purchased the profitable Alfred Bird and Sons. From 1945
to 1953, sixty American firms began manufacturing in Britain; by 1950, 695
American enterprises, with a total investment of $847 million, were operating
in the United Kingdom. Such companies as Remington Rand, Cincinnati
Milling Machine, Champion Sparkplug, American Rolling Mills, Armco International, Proctor and Gamble, and Standard Brands were active, and between
1945 and 1955 Standard Oil of New Jersey and the Socony Vacuum
Company invested nearly $200 million. England welcomed American invest-
ment because it helped the balance of payments deficit by reducing costly
dollar imports and by expanding exports, and Englishmen were fond of many
American products, some of which had been introduced under Lend-Lease.[37]
Dean Acheson pointed out that the loan agreement would protect these
investments through its provision that Americans doing business in Britain
would receive dollars rather than blocked sterling.[38]

The second argument held that Great Britain's prominent rank in world
trade and its propensity to impose trade restrictions compelled aid. Should
Britain encounter economic distress, the interdependent world economy
would unravel, international economic cooperation would be unattainable,
and trade blocs would form. The *New Republic* was emphatic: "On the loan
depends the success of Bretton Woods and the UNO international trade body
[ITO]. It is not too much to say that on the loan depends the economic

[34] Amounting to $499,163,000, or 16.8 percent of all U.S. exports, this trade
represented more than that with all of South America ($274,097,000) or Asia
($498,544,000). Commerce, *Foreign Trade of the U.S.,* pp. 42, 46.

[35] *Ibid.,* p. 46; *Steel,* CXVIII (June 24, 1946), 62; *Business Week,* July 27, 1946.

[36] See, on such expectations, W. L. Clayton to Thomas C. Blaisdell, Oct. 19, 1945,
Blaisdell Papers, Truman Library; James S. Knowlson (Stewart-Warner Corporation) to
Thomas C. Blaisdell, Feb. 1, 1946, *ibid.;* Wilkins and Hill, *American Business Abroad,* p.
357.

[37] In 1943, U.S. investments in Britain amounted to $518 million; in 1955 the figure
stood at $1.420 billion, mostly in manufacturing and petroleum. John H. Dunning,
American Investment in British Manufacturing Industry (London, 1958), pp. 46, 48, 49,
52-53, 348-55; *Business Week,* Oct. 19, 1946, p. 107; General Foods, *Annual Report,
1946,* p. 6; C. M. Chester, *My Philosophy of Leadership for American Business*
(pamphlet published by General Foods, Apr. 12, 1944).

[38] U.S., Department of State, *The Credit to Britain and World Trade* (Washington
D.C., 1946), p. 14.

peace of the world.''[39] Vinson pointed out that "no other nation plays the part in world trade that Britain plays," and Truman listed the revival of international trade as a primary reason for the loan.[40] Henry Wallace defended the loan as a stimulant to world trade, which could be freer "only if we and Great Britain pull together in this world enterprise."[41]

Supporters of the loan amassed impressive statistics. The sterling area accounted for 29.3 percent of the world's imports in the 1936-1938 period. The figure for exports was 24.1 percent. Countries having payments agreements with Britain accounted for another 25.3 percent of world imports, and another 24.4 percent of world exports.[42] The chairman of the National Foreign Trade Council argued that the loan "will set the pattern by which nearly half the trade of the world is governed, thus providing a powerful fulcrum on which remaining problems could be balanced and resolved, and enable us to say with considerable assurance that the productive plant . . . will be fully employed for as long as reasonable men can predict."[43]

Defenders of the loan tied it to international economic organizations, such as the World Bank and International Monetary Fund. Paul Hoffman, later to head the Marshall Plan, called the loan "a first step toward international economic coordination. And international economic coordination is in turn a first step toward world peace."[44] One State Department official advocated passage because "we get participation by Britain in the International Monetary Fund and a consequent commitment that she will not take independent action to put our exporters at a competitive disadvantage by depreciating the pound."[45] The Truman administration made a strong case for the loan as an agent to speed the work of the Bretton Woods institutions, and the British realized that their adherence to the agencies would help in moving the loan agreement through Congress.[46]

Another important consideration was that the sterling bloc arrangement threatened to obstruct trade. Clayton noted that the sterling area was "anathema to all our businessmen because they lose business by it. They lose exports."[47] Wallace prophesied a "costly trade war" unless the trade

---

[39] *New Republic*, CXIII (Dec. 24, 1945), 856.

[40] Vinson, in Department of State, *British Loan—What It Means*, p. 14; *Public Papers: Truman, 1946*, p. 347 (July 15, 1946). See also New York State Bankers Association, *Bretton Woods Proposals*.

[41] Senate, *Anglo-American Financial Agreement* (Mar. 12, 1946), p. 266.

[42] Senate, *Anglo-American Financial Agreement*, p. 103.

[43] John Abbink, in *Journal of Commerce*, Feb. 19, 1946.

[44] Paul G. Hoffman, "The Survival of Free Enterprise," *Harvard Business Review*, XXV (Autumn, 1946), 24. See a similar statement by the State Department in *International Trade and the British Loan* (Washington, D.C., 1946), p. 1.

[45] Department of State, *Why Lend*, pp. 15-16.

[46] Dalton, *High Tide*, p. 72. For the Truman case see Gardner, *Sterling-Dollar Diplomacy*, p. 245; *Journal of Commerce*, Feb. 9 and Mar. 28, 1946; Pritchard, "Will Clayton," p. 212; *DSB*, XIII (Dec. 9, 1945), 912; National Advisory Council on International Monetary and Financial Problems, *Report* (Mar. 8, 1946), p. 17.

[47] Senate, *Anglo-American Financial Agreement* (Mar. 6, 1946), p. 129.

impediments of the area were reduced.[48] The Truman administration argued that the loan destroyed trade barriers (especially those of the British Empire). Yet the provisions relating to multilateralism and nondiscrimination were vague, and it may be that government officials oversold them in their drive to pass the loan. As Richard Gardner has written: "Whatever their temporary effect, the Administration's arguments were sowing dragon's teeth for an eventual harvest."[49]

The *Wall Street Journal* expressed the third argument: "without assistance Britain may have a very hard time holding her empire together and she may lose strength and prestige to the extent that Russia will sweep over western Europe and encompass the Mediterranean."[50] Ralph Flanders actually called the loan the "first skirmish" with the Soviet Union and Communism.[51] Secretary Vinson quoted approvingly an editorial from the *Arkansas Democrat* claiming that Britain "is our natural ally," and the Houston Cotton Exchange urged the government to "preserve Great Britain as a first-class power," for the British were "natural allies."[52] Former ambassador to London Joseph P. Kennedy favored an "outright gift" to the United Kingdom because it was the United States' best customer and because "the British people and their way of life form the last barrier in Europe against communism; and we must help them to hold that line."[53]

The view that Great Britain should be shored up as a bulwark against the Soviet Union came late in the congressional discussion in 1946, and Clayton, who handled the liaison with congressional supporters, did not use this argument so much as the political-economic logic of the peace and prosperity concept.[54] Yet Congressman John McCormack of Massachusetts reported that the most telling consideration was the suggestion that Congress would allow Russia to assume world leadership should the loan fail, a suggestion which became popular in the last few days of the debate.[55] Speaker of the House Sam Rayburn of Texas hammered away on the issue: "I do not want Western Europe, England, and all the rest pushed toward an ideology that I despise. I fear if we do not cooperate with out great natural ally that is what will happen. . . ."[56]

This anti-Soviet sentiment ensured passage. Multilateralism was not a very exciting issue, and trade and loan statistics were tedious, but the growing

---

[48] *New York Times*, Nov. 13, 1945.

[49] Gardner, *Sterling-Dollar Diplomacy*, p. 248.

[50] *Wall Street Journal*, Mar. 8, 1946.

[51] Senate, *Anglo-American Financial Agreement* (Mar. 14, 1946), pp. 391, 392.

[52] Editorial in Department of State, *British Loan—What It Means*, p. 19; J. W. Evans (Houston) to Robert Wagner, Feb. 1, 1946, Committee on Banking and Currency, Senate Records.

[53] *New York Times*, Mar. 4, 1946.

[54] Pritchard, "Will Clayton," p. 236; Gardner, *Sterling-Dollar Diplomacy*, pp. 248-53.

[55] "British Loan," McNaughton Report, July 13, 1946, Box 10, McNaughton Papers.

[56] Quoted in Gardner, *Sterling-Dollar Diplomacy*, p. 249 (July 12, 1946).

disputes with the Soviet Union in 1946 in eastern Europe, Iran, the United Nations, and the Foreign Ministers Meeting in Paris aroused opinion favorable to the British loan. Increasingly strained relations with Russia thus reinforced the widespread support of farm, labor, and business groups.[57] Clayton rallied business leaders behind the loan and used the directory of the Department of Commerce Business Advisory Council (125 names) to make personal appeals to such prominent executives as Paul Hoffman of Studebaker, Carle Conway of Continental Can, and Thomas J. Watson of IBM.[58]

THE OPPOSITION AND REBUTTAL

Vigorous opposition to the loan came from old Anglophobes and anti-imperialists like Senator William Langer of North Dakota, who castigated British imperialism and facetiously offered an amendment providing that the $3.75 billion be spent on a urinalysis of every person in the United States.[59] As Senator Edwin Johnson of Colorado put it, "The British loan is not to provide relief for starving people. It is to provide relief for a decadent empire. My slogan is 'Billions for the relief of starving children but not one cent of American taxpayers' money for the relief of Empires.' "[60] Walter White, of the National Association for the Advancement of Colored People, demanded that "none of the money . . . be used to perpetuate imperialism or to deny any colonials of British Empire full freedom and justice. Reported use of American war materials by British against Indonesian people constitutes one of greatest scandals and tragedies of contemporary history."[61] Many Irish- and Jewish-Americans also opposed the loan, the latter because of bitter hostility toward Britain over the Palestine issue.[62]

Senator Robert Taft denounced the notion that the United States had to help Britain or a world in economic trouble: "Well, I say that is baloney. It will ruin this country, that kind of doctrine. Every cent we give away must come from the American workingman."[63] He was unenthusiastic about the

[57] Support came from the American Federation of Labor, Congress of Industrial Organizations, Houston Cotton Exchange, National Farmers Union, and American Farm Bureau Federation. See the hearings in *Anglo-American Financial Agreement* and Committee on International Economic Policy, *We Quote: The Quality and Scope of Support for the Loan Agreement with Britain* (Washington, D.C., 1946).

[58] Pritchard, "Will Clayton," pp. 236, 250; for widespread business support see Paterson, "Economic Cold War," pp. 179-209.

[59] "British Loan," McNaughton Report, May 10, 1946, Box 9, McNaughton Papers.

[60] Quoted in Gardner, *Sterling-Dollar Diplomacy,* p. 238. Also *Congressional Record,* XCII (July 8, 1946), 8394, 8414.

[61] Walter White to Truman, Dec. 13, 1945, OF 212-A, Truman Papers.

[62] Westerfield, *Foreign Policy and Party Politics,* p. 229; *New Republic,* CXV (July 22, 1946), 63; "British Loan," McNaughton Report, July 3, 1946, Box 10, McNaughton Papers.

[63] Senate, *Bretton Woods* (June 13, 1945), p. 37. Taft proposed an amendment to give Britain $1.25 billion as a gift which had to be spent in the United States in 1946 through 1948, but it was defeated by a vote of 50 to 16.

claims made for multilateralism and argued further that the loan would have damaging inflationary effects.[64] Senator Robert M. LaFollette, Jr., agreed that the loan would burden an already troubled American economy, and other critics insisted that attention must first be given to domestic problems, that the agreement was full of loopholes, and that the United States could not keep the world from "going Communist" through political loans.[65] It was also argued that Britain could not possibly repay the loan, that it would encourage and subsidize British socialism, that other countries would want similar loans and a precedent would be set, that the United States would be financing a commercial competitor, and that the Bretton Woods institutions should handle Britain's economic problems.[66] Jesse Jones, former head of the Reconstruction Finance Corporation, noted perceptively that the question of multilateralism was really left to future consideration. He also suggested that it was "unbusinesslike" to give the British a loan when they held large securities-collateral in the United States which were unaffected by the terms of the agreement.[67]

To the charge that the United States would be financing British socialism, Willard Thorp of the State Department replied that the loan would in fact reduce pressure for socialist experimentation, because with it the British government could more easily fulfill its citizens' demands for goods. Philip Reed of General Electric agreed that refusal would push the British government toward even more extensive controls on the economy and further nationalization.[68] Actually, the issue of socialism never seriously disrupted Anglo-American relations; American government and business leaders learned to accommodate themselves to the British system.[69] Lord Keynes, in one of his less critical moods, praised the generosity of Americans and asked; "Has any country ever treated another country like this . . . for the purpose of rebuilding the other's strength and competitive position?"[70] Proponents of the loan, however, played down the threat of British competition. Philip Reed, among others, simply said that the United States could meet any competition, and that, at any rate, prosperous countries were better cus-

[64] Senate, *Anglo-American Financial Agreement* (Mar. 12, 13, 1946), pp. 282, 332-33.

[65] *Congressional Record*, XCII (Apr. 30, 1946), 4234-39, 4253; (May 1, 1946), 4269-70; (May 6, 1946), 4497; (July 11, 1946), 8699.

[66] *Ibid.* (Apr. 30, 1946), 4335; (May 7, 1946), 4536; (May 9, 1946), 4747; (May 10, 1946), 4791-4802; *Journal of Commerce*, Nov. 5, 1945, Jan. 3 and Mar. 28, 1946; Gardner, *Sterling-Dollar Diplomacy*, pp. 238-42; Pritchard, "Will Clayton," p. 215; *Foreign Relations, 1946*, I, 1417.

[67] *Houston Chronicle*, Apr. 16, 1946; Pritchard, "Will Clayton," p. 248.

[68] Thorp, in New York State Chamber of Commerce, *Monthly Bulletin*, XXXVIII (May, 1946), 50; Reed in Senate, *Anglo-American Financial Agreement* (Mar. 13, 1946), p. 368. See also *DSB*, XIV (Mar. 31, 1946), 540-41; Clayton to Bernard Baruch, Apr. 26, 1946, part XIII, Baruch Papers.

[69] Watt, "American Aid to Britain"; Clayton to Baruch, Dec. 16, 1946, part XIII, Baruch Papers; Wilkins and Hill, *American Business Abroad*, p. 367.

[70] Pritchard, "Will Clayton," pp. 230-31.

tomers and traders, or, as one committee put it, "You just don't find profitable markets among paupers."[71] Acheson stated his position succinctly: "It isn't *competitive* trade that we fear, it's *discriminatory* trade—trade hampered by high tariffs, exchange restrictions, quotas and so on."[72]

To the criticism that the loan would have an inflationary impact upon the American economy, Thorp argued that it would be spent over a five-year period, that Britain would buy some of her needed raw materials in other countries than the United States, and that the United States had safeguards against drains on items in short supply.[73] This argument was somewhat confused by the fact that other supporters were claiming that the British loan dollars would eventually return to their source through the purchase of American goods. Secretary Vinson, for example, had to agree with Senator Taft that the loan was "an easy way to give our businessmen the dollars,"[74] yet Vinson placed the burden elsewhere: "If we get dangerous inflation, it won't be because of the British loan. The causes will be a lot nearer home than that. It will be because we have failed to get our peacetime production rolling soon enough; or it will be because controls are lifted too soon."[75]

Most supporters of the loan stressed that the crucial question was not repayment, inflation, or competition. Rather it was whether Great Britain, a good customer, would be economically sound enough to buy American goods and to support American foreign policy. What was at stake, Vinson said, was a "healthy Britain and a healthy world trade."[76] The foreign lending program, Chester Bowles, director of the Office of Economic Stabilization, concluded, "is essential to our long-run prosperity and peace."[77] With arguments such as these behind it, the British loan agreement passed the Senate by a vote of 46 to 34 (May 10) and the House by 219 to 155 (July 13).

THE LOAN AND THE COLD WAR

Ambassador to Russia Walter Bedell Smith reported in July, 1946, that Russia was attempting to split up an existing "Anglo-American alignment."[78]

---

[71] Senate, *Anglo-American Financial Agreement* (Mar. 13, 1946), pp. 370-71 (Reed); Committee on International Economic Policy, *It's Up to You* (Washington, D.C., 1946).

[72] Department of State, *British Loan—What It Means*, p. 15.

[73] New York State Chamber of Commerce, *Monthly Bulletin*, XXXVIII (May, 1946), 51.

[74] Senate, *Anglo-American Financial Agreement* (Mar. 5, 1946), p. 15.

[75] Department of State, *British Loan—What It Means*, pp. 13-14. See also Winthrop Aldrich, "The Anglo-American Financial Agreement," address, May 17, 1946 (from the files of the Chase-Manhattan Bank, New York City).

[76] Department of State, *British Loan—What It Means*, pp. 13-14.

[77] Chester Bowles to Clayton, letter quoted in Senate, *Anglo-American Financial Agreement* (Mar. 13, 1946), p. 312.

[78] *Foreign Relations, 1946*, VI, 769.

Through 1945 and 1946 the Russians had watched uneasily as the United States and Britain cooperated more and more in international affairs, and although they continued to speak of Anglo-American differences, they introduced the word "bloc" to describe their two opponents.[79] Churchill's "iron curtain" speech of March, 1946, convinced Stalin, according to Smith, that "a definite alignment of Great Britain and the United States against the USSR" had formed.[80]

It is difficult to measure the impact of the British loan on the developing Cold War; the paucity of Soviet historical sources renders any judgment tentative. To the Russians it was probably just another sign of the existence of the hostile bloc, yet it angered them because at the same time, as we have seen, their own loan request was shelved. They could not have been unaware of the statements in Congress that the British loan was an anti-Russian instrument. The Anglo-American collaboration forced custodians of Stalinist ideology to shift from a thesis of inevitable conflict between Britain and America to the theme of bloc cooperation.[81] Senator Vandenberg may have been correct in December, 1945, that "if we grant a loan to England and then deny one to Russia (if she asks for it as she undoubtedly will) we have thereby made further cooperation among the Big Three practically impossible (which, incidentally, would be the end of UNO)."[82] Certainly the loan to Britain was evidence that the United States would use its economic power to help "friends" antagonistic to Russia. The loan also appeared to strengthen the United States economy and to divert depression because it ensured exports and trade with a major international trader. Finally, as William McNeill has observed, the British loan "sealed Anglo-American political solidarity in the postwar world."[83]

Whatever its influence in the Soviet-American confrontation, however, the loan failed to revive Britain's sagging economy and trade or to implant multilateralism. The exhaustion of the loan and the demise of the financial and commercial agreements was rapid. In the first quarter of 1947 the British withdrew $500 million and in the second quarter $950 million, and it looked as though the loan would be depleted by early 1948. (it was supposed to last until 1951). British trade leveled off, its dollar deficit grew, and the severe winter of 1946-1947 taxed British resources heavily. Occupation costs in Germany and Greece siphoned off considerable sums. Inflation in the United States meant that Britain had to pay more in dollars for American goods, and

    [79] See, for example, *ibid.*, pp. 684, 758, 773-74; *ibid., 1945*, II, 750-58; Clemens, *Yalta*, p. 96.
    [80] *Foreign Relations, 1946*, VI, 734-35. For Iran, see Chapter 9 below.
    [81] Eugene Varga, "Anglo-American Rivalry and Partnership: A Marxist View," *Foreign Affairs*, XXV (July, 1947), 583-95.
    [82] Vandenberg, *Private Papers*, p. 231. See also Wallace, "Path to Peace with Russia," p. 404.
    [83] McNeill, *America, Britain, and Russia*, pp. 652-53. See also Gardner, *Architects of Illusion*, p. 118.

this further pinched British funds. On July 15, 1947, the provision for convertibility of blocked sterling into dollars became operable. The result was disastrous for Britain's dollar supply; to meet the drain it drew upon the loan and had exhausted it by March 1, 1948. During the crisis Britain suspended the convertibility and nondiscrimination principles of the loan agreement; indeed, a new imports plan specifically discriminated against American goods. The loan failed, multilateralism suffered a blow, but at least economic disaster in Britain had been temporarily averted.[84]

The downfall of the loan called attention to Britain's difficulties in maintaining military commitments in Greece and Germany and thereby helped foster the Truman Doctrine and German bizonal arrangements. The failure also stimulated the Marshall Plan; it became obvious that uncoordinated, country-by-country, stop-gap aid would not rebuild the American sphere in Europe.[85] Britain revived under the Marshall Plan and became the junior partner in the Anglo-American coalition. It was a partnership the weak British grudgingly welcomed and the insecure Russians feared, as events in the Middle East, Turkey, and Greece would demonstrate.

[84] *Foreign Relations, 1947,* III (Washington, D.C., 1972), 1-94; Gardner, *Sterling-Dollar Diplomacy,* pp. 306-47; *Report of Activities of the National Advisory Council* . . . (Washington, D.C., 1948; 80th Cong., 2d sess., H. Doc. 501), p. 4; Dalton, *High Tide,* p. 221; Harrod, *Keynes,* p. 615.

[85] W. M. Scammell, "British Economic Recovery, 1945-51," *American Review* (Bologna), II (March, 1963), 94-95.

CHAPTER 9

EXPANSION AND CONTAINMENT IN THE NEAR AND MIDDLE EAST: THE TRUMAN DOCTRINE

As the rapid exhaustion of the loan demonstrated, Britain spent heavily to maintain troops in its vast but crumbling empire. By early 1947 its efforts to quell a Greek civil war had proved expensive and futile. Communist-led rebels steadily and successfully challenged the repressive regime in Athens. When London appealed for direct American assistance to crush the insurgents in February, 1947, Washington was not unprepared, and on March 12 President Truman asked Congress for major military and economic aid for Greece and also for Turkey. At the same time, he seized the opportunity to launch a grand summary doctrine quickly popularized as the "containment" of Communism. Behind the Truman Doctrine lay years of expanding United States activity in the Near and Middle East, those strategic areas rimming the Mediterranean Sea and the Soviet sphere of influence. Likened in importance to the Monroe Doctrine (no foreign domination of areas vital to United States security) and Roosevelt's Lend-Lease speech of 1941 (foreign aid for United States defense), the Truman Doctrine became the simple guide for foreign policy in the Cold War.[1]

Evident in the Truman Doctrine were the inseparable components of the peace and prosperity ideology—economic and political stability, anti-Communism, quest for raw materials, open door and free trade, and security. The Doctrine assumed that eastern Europe was already lost to the Soviet Union. Iran, Greece, and Turkey, wracked by crises, were to be drawn into the United States sphere of influence. Using the rotten-apple-in-the-barrel metaphor, Under Secretary Dean Acheson told congressmen that instability in these countries would invite Soviet penetration of the Mediterranean. Then, he insisted, South Asia, Africa, Italy, and western Europe would be vulnerable to Communist and Soviet engulfment. The question was a global one indeed. To Acheson, who had a taste for hyperbole, Russia was "playing one of the greatest gambles in history. . . . We and we alone were in a position to break up the play."[2]

---

[1] For the comparison, see James Reston in *New York Times*, Mar. 13, 1947; for the endurance of the Truman Doctrine, see Paterson, *Containment and the Cold War.*

[2] Acheson, *Present at the Creation*, p. 219.

The other side of the coin from containment was expansion, and, at least from World War II onward, both elements coexisted in American foreign policy.[3] Before World War II the United States had participated comparatively little in the affairs of the Near and Middle East, for it was assumed they were part of a British sphere of influence,[4] but the global ramifications of the war stimulated new interest in these areas, an interest which alarmed Britain, France, and Russia alike. It appeared that the United States would no longer be a "mere spectator" in those regions.[5]

Americans watched warily in 1944 and 1945 as a Greek civil war flared up and then, temporarily, died down. Although highly critical of the heavy-handed British domination of Greece, Washington, in its desire for stability, gradually came to support the British presence there. As early as March, 1945, Harold Macmillan promised in Athens that Britain would back General Nicholas Plastiras' government "with the assistance of America in economic and other matters."[6] A State Department memorandum of mid-1945 suggested that the United States might "take an active and benevolent interest in Greece at this time" because such interest "offers one of the most practical means of demonstrating this Government's determination to play an international role commensurate with its strength and public commitments."[7]

American interest in the Middle East also intensified, as its oil resources and strategic location caught the attention of policymakers. Herbert Feis recalled that Washington feared oil shortages: "In all surveys of the situation, the pencil came to an awed pause at one point and place—the Middle East."[8] American oil companies expanded with governmental encouragement. The Arabian-American Oil Company (Aramco) began to tap Saudi Arabia's large

[3] Robert W. Tucker has written: "By a dialectic as old as the history of statecraft, expansion proved to be the other side of the coin of containment. To contain the expansion of others, or what was perceived as such, it became necessary to expand ourselves. In this manner the course of containment became the course of empire." Tucker argues that expansion grew from containment, yet it can be argued that American postwar power permitted the expansion so traditional to American history and that containment grew from that expansion, because in order for the United States to expand it had to restrict the power of others. Robert W. Tucker, *The Radical Left and American Foreign Policy* (Baltimore, 1971), p. 109.

[4] John A. DeNovo, *American Interests and Policies in the Middle East, 1900-1939* (Minneapolis, Minn., 1963).

[5] Loy Henderson, in *Foreign Relations, 1945*, VIII, 11 (Nov. 10, 1945).

[6] *Ibid.*, p. 120. The British apparently noted and de-emphasized the standard by which Washington vigorously opposed the Soviet-imposed government in Rumania but endorsed the British-imposed government in Greece. See *ibid.*, pp. 119, 156, 205.

[7] *Ibid., Berlin*, I, 651.

[8] Herbert Feis, *Three International Episodes: Seen from E. A.* (New York, 1946; rpt. 1966), p. 102. For this interest in Middle East oil, see *DSB*, XIII (Aug. 5, 1945), 175; "Statement of the Navy's Position with Relation to a National Oil Policy," [n.d.], Box 5, Special Committee Investigating Petroleum Resources, Senate Records; "The Protection of the American Position in the Middle East Oil Picture," Headquarters, U.S. Army Forces in Middle East, Jan. 1, 1944, Box 24, *ibid.*; *Wall Street Journal*, Mar. 22, 1944; *American Petroleum Institute Quarterly*, XV (April, 1945), 13; Michael Brooks, *Oil and Foreign Policy* (London, 1949).

holdings in 1939 with a 440,000-square-mile concession. American companies also secured concessions in Bahrein, Ethiopia, Iraq, and Kuwait. By 1944 these corporations controlled 42 percent of the "proved" oil reserves of the Middle East, a nineteen-fold increase since 1936.[9] In Iran during the war Lend-Lease goods were channeled to Russia, and by 1943 thirty thousand American troops were stationed there to oversee the program. The British-owned Anglo-Iranian Oil Company dominated the country's oil, but American influence grew. The Standard-Vacuum and Sinclair oil companies, invited by Iran and urged on by Washington, applied for oil concessions in 1944 and set off an international scramble for oil.[10] Secretary Stettinius predicted that year that "Iran is perhaps the most important area of the world where inter-Allied friction might arise," and Byrnes added in 1945 that a stabilized Iran "will serve to lay a sound foundation for the development of American commercial, petroleum, and aviation interests in the Middle East."[11]

Britain, which controlled the oil of Iran, Iraq, and Kuwait and had military forces stationed in the first two countries, saw the Mediterranean and Persian Gulf as vital links in its Empire. France came out of the war with special privileges in Lebanon and Syria and a stake in Iraqi oil. Russia alone had little influence, but the joint occupation of Iran by Russian, British, and United States troops during the war offered Russia an opening. The initial antagonism to American expansion into the area came from the British, who were fighting a "stubborn rearguard action" in the Middle East and who protested loudly as the United States, under the principle of the "open door," nibbled away at their interests.[12] When Roosevelt informed Churchill that America would not deprive the British of their stakes in the Middle East, the suspicious Prime Minister replied: "Thank you very much for your assurances about no sheeps [sic] eyes at our oilfields in Iran and Iraq. Let me reciprocate by giving you fullest assurance that we have no thought of trying to horn in upon your interests or property in Saudi Arabia. . . . On the other hand, [Britain] will not be deprived of anything which rightly belongs to her. . . ."[13] However, Britain realized that its power was waning and, fearing Soviet expansion, cooperated with Washington more and more.

[9] Raymond F. Mikesell and Hollis B. Chenery, *Arabian Oil: America's Stake in the Middle East* (Chapel Hill, N.C., 1949), pp. 48-54, 98, 181; Arabian-American Oil Company, *Arabian Oil and Its Relation to Oil Needs* (1948); George Kirk, *The Middle East in the War* (London, 1952), p. 25n; George Lenczowski, *Oil and State in the Middle East* (Ithaca, N.Y., 1960), pp. 17-19, 21.

[10] George Lenczowski, *Russia and the West in Iran, 1918-1948: A Study in Big Power Rivalry* (Ithaca, N.Y., 1949), pp. 263-83; Arthur C. Millspaugh, *Americans in Persia* (Washington, D.C., 1946).

[11] Stettinius, in Jacob C. Hurewitz, *Middle East Dilemmas: The Background of United States Policy* (New York, 1953), p. 25; Byrnes, in *Foreign Relations, 1945*, VIII, 534.

[12] Kirk, *Middle East in the War*, pp. 368-69. For examples of British-American tension, see *Foreign Relations, 1945*, VIII, 14, 42-46, 69, 71-72, 77-80, 956; Benjamin Shwadran, *The Middle East, Oil and the Great Powers*, rev. ed. (New York, 1959), pp. 320-32.

[13] *Foreign Relations, 1944*, III, 103.

Britain, the United States, and Russia collided in Iran. When a British company applied for a new oil concession in southeast Iran in the spring of 1944, Washington-backed American companies requested a concession too. In order not to be excluded from a nation on its borders, Russia followed with a concession request in September. Although the Iranian government appeared favorable to the American application, the Russian overture startled it, and Iran announced postponement of all oil concession questions until after the war. The Soviets were angry, especially after Washington notified the Kremlin that it respected this Iranian decision.[14] Kennan reported in 1944 that the "basic motive of recent Soviet action in northern Iran [where Soviet troops were aiding the revolutionary Tudeh Party] is probably not the need for oil itself but apprehension of potential foreign penetration in that area...."[15] Indeed, both the United States and Russia sought new influence in Iran at the expense of the British, who were persuaded to cooperate with Washington against Moscow. The chief of the State Department Petroleum Division confirmed in mid-1945 that "petroleum policy toward the United Kingdom is predicated on the *mutual recognition* of a very extensive *joint* interest and upon a control, at least for the moment, of the great bulk of the free petroleum resources of the world."[16]

The Anglo-American Oil Agreement of August 8, 1944, constituted one sign of that joint interest, although the accord was vague in its call for the open door in oil, cooperative oil trade, respect for existing concessions, and an International Petroleum Commission managed jointly by Britain and America. Although the United States never ratified the agreement because of domestic opposition from small independent oil companies, its timing was probably important. It signified to Russia increasing Anglo-American cooperation in the Middle East and may have helped stimulate the Soviet concession request the next month. Herbert Feis commented that Russia could join the agreement after Anglo-American ratification, but he was uncertain: "This may have been a mistake. No one will ever know what would have happened had a more comprehensive group, including the U.S.S.R., been invited into these first conferences."[17] This early failure of the great powers to cooperate foreshadowed the Iranian crisis of 1945-1946.

THE IRANIAN CRISIS: PRELUDE TO THE TRUMAN DOCTRINE

The traditional account of the controversy over Iran depicts a ruthless and aggressive Russia intent upon subjugating Iran by force, determined to

[14] *Ibid., 1943*, IV (Washington, D.C., 1964), 625-28; *ibid., 1944*, V, 445-97; Lenczowski, *Russia and the West in Iran*, pp. 216-23; N. S. Fatemi, *Oil Diplomacy: Powderkeg in Iran* (New York, 1954), 229-60.

[15] *Foreign Relations, 1944*, V, 470.

[16] *Ibid., 1945*, VIII, 54 (italics added).

[17] Herbert Feis, "The Anglo-American Oil Agreement," *Yale Law Journal*, LV (August, 1946), 1178. See also Feis, *Three International Episodes*, pp. 134-82; Mikesell and Chenery, *Arabian Oil*, pp. 95-100; Lenczowski, *Oil and State*, pp. 169-73.

overthrow a stable government by fomenting revolution in northern Iran (Azerbaijan). Louis Halle describes a "wanton course of political and military aggression," and John Spanier, in a recent widely read history of the Cold War, concludes that the "Soviets sought to convert Iran into a Soviet satellite."[18]

Such assessments ignore the conspicuous Anglo-American presence, the Anglo-American requests for oil concessions, the British domination of Iranian oil, the anti-Soviet, foreign-influenced Iranian government, and the strategic importance of Iran to Russia. There is little evidence that Russia intended to make Iran a "satellite"; there is more evidence that the Iranian crisis was a classic case of competition for spheres of influence. Britain, the United States, and Russia must share responsibility for the crisis, and there is little doubt that the United States triggered some reprehensible Soviet actions. Expansion and containment merged in the United States interest in Iran.

There were four central questions in 1945-1946: foreign troops, postponed oil concession requests, Anglo-American political influence in Teheran, and Soviet influence in northern Iran. After the Iranian decision to defer consideration of concessions, Russia encouraged the Communist-dominated Tudeh Party of northern Iran to challenge the Teheran regime. Teheran responded by arresting a number of Tudeh leaders. During this turmoil, Washington notified Moscow that it accepted the Iranian decision to postpone, which led Moscow to believe that the United States had engineered the postponement.[19] In August, 1945, the Tudeh Party openly rebelled and demanded autonomy for Azerbaijan. Although Russia had obviously aided the rebellion and had hampered the movement of Iranian troops to squelch it, there were serious indigenous complaints about the failure of the Iranian ruling elite to alleviate what the United States ambassador called Iran's "deplorable" social and economic conditions.[20]

Although Iran, Britain, and the United States asked Russia to remove its troops, they came up against the undeniable fact that Russia (and Britain) had the right, under a 1942 treaty, to remain until March 2, 1946. Moscow insisted on staying and denied any Soviet interference in Azerbaijan. The denial persuaded no one, and at the Moscow Conference of Foreign Ministers in December, 1945, Byrnes repeatedly questioned Stalin about Iran, suggesting that its sovereignty and integrity were threatened. Stalin calmly replied that Soviet troops were there legally and that it was necessary to maintain them until March because the Teheran government was hostile to

[18] Halle, *Cold War as History*, p. 99; John Spanier, *American Foreign Policy since World War II*, 4th ed. (New York, 1971), p. 29.

[19] Lenczowski, *Russia and the West in Iran*, pp. 221, 223; John G. Geilfuss to Secretary Forrestal, "State Department Dispatches," Apr. 9, 1946, Box 101, Forrestal Papers.

[20] *Foreign Relations, 1945*, VIII, 418.

the Soviet Union and because saboteurs might attempt to destroy the Baku oil installation near the Iranian border. Furthermore, he asked, why did not the United States protest the presence of British troops on Iranian soil as well? Byrnes had no satisfactory rejoinder: he contented himself with warning that Iran might make a noisy issue of the matter at a forthcoming meeting of the United Nations. Stalin was unmoved and refused to agree to any statement on Iran. The declaration by Azerbaijan in December that it had established an independent government further antagonized Washington as it attempted to counter the seemingly improved Soviet position in Iran.[21]

On January 17, 1946, the Security Council opened its first session, and two days later Iran asked the body to investigate charges of Soviet meddling in Iranian affairs. The Soviets quickly responded by asking the Council to· investigate the presence of British troops in Greece and Indonesia. Syria and Lebanon did not help the British image by requesting that both British and French forces depart their countries. Byrnes had, in essence, encouraged the Iranians to take their case to the Security Council. Soviet delegate Andrei Y. Vyshinsky told his colleagues that Russia and Iran would settle the northern Iranian issue outside the United Nations through bilateral talks, and on January 30 the United States accepted the compromise resolution that Iranian-Soviet "direct negotiations" proceed but that the Iranian issue remain on the Council agenda.[22]

Meanwhile, events in Iran seemed to provide opportunities for an agreement. By January, 1946, American troops had withdrawn, although advisers remained behind, and British forces were evacuating (all were gone by March 2). The Soviets could no longer use the argument of a double standard in Iran. On January 26 a new Iranian government was formed under Prime Minister Ahmad Qavam, who had pledged to seek negotiations with the Russians. But March 2 came and went without an accord, and the Soviets announced that their troops would remain until a settlement was reached. It became evident that they would not leave until granted an oil concession and that the Iranians would not negotiate until they departed. Washington protested the open defiance of the 1942 treaty, and there was even more alarm when a series of overexcited cables were received from the vice-consul in Tabriz, Azerbaijan, in early March charging that Soviet troops were marching toward Turkey and Teheran. Upon hearing the news on March 7, Byrnes slammed his fist into his open hand and asserted, "Now we'll give it to

[21] Radio broadcast by James F. Byrnes, State Department press release, Dec. 30, 1945, Folder 555, Byrnes Papers; James F. Byrnes, "Report," October, 1950, Folder 573, *ibid.*; Robert Rossow, Jr., "The Battle of Azerbaijan, 1946," *Middle East Journal*, X (Winter, 1956), 17-32; George V. Allen, Memoirs (unpublished [n.d.]), George V. Allen Papers, Truman Library; *Foreign Relations, 1945*, VIII, passim; *ibid.*, II, 685-86, 750-52, 808.

[22] *Foreign Relations, 1945*, VII, 289-326; Campbell, *United States in World Affairs, 1945-1947*, pp. 85-91, 522-23; Rossow, "Battle of Azerbaijan"; Allen, Memoirs, ch. 1.

them with both barrels."[23] Despite this private outburst, the official note to Moscow the next day could be read as a mild reproach which left the Soviets a "graceful way out," as Acheson put it.[24]

The Soviets ignored the note, and the issue again shifted to the United Nations. The Soviet Union requested that the Security Council postpone its debate scheduled for March 26 until April 10. Byrnes himself led the United States delegation and helped deny the request. Apparently at this time (around March 25) Qavam and the Soviets were near an agreement, and the Iranian ambassador to the United States was instructed by Teheran to temper his forthcoming comments on the Council floor. Ambassador Hossein Ala consulted closely with United States officials and decided to ignore his instructions. George V. Allen, a State Department expert on Iran (who was appointed ambassador to Teheran in April), recalled that when he handed a copy of Ala's speech to Byrnes: "Mr. Byrnes asked, jocularly, whether I had written it. I said I hadn't but I suspected an American hand had been in it. The Secretary commented, dryly, that every man was entitled to his lawyer. From that time on, however, Mr. Byrnes frequently referred to me as 'Ala Allen.' "[25] Unable to keep the Iranian issue off the agenda, the Soviets walked out of the Security Council on March 27.

In late March, Russia and Iran reached a mutual agreement. Announced on April 5, the accord provided for the withdrawal of Soviet troops within six weeks and the establishment of a joint Iranian-Soviet oil company, the latter step to be ratified by the Iranian parliament within seven months. The night before the announcement Stalin complained sharply to the United States ambassador, Walter Bedell Smith, that Washington and London had placed obstacles in the way of the Soviet oil concession and had been unreasonable in opposing the Soviet request for postponement of Security Council discussion.[26] The Iranian crisis appeared settled, but the friction it had produced would trouble Soviet-American relations for months.

The State Department accepted the April agreement as the best that could be arranged without force. Not pleased with the oil concession, it nevertheless applauded the evacuation of Soviet soldiers. It then set about to influence Iranian foreign policy and internal affairs in a subtle and patient way. Byrnes was even irritated when a United States official asked Qavam if he was now ready to negotiate an oil concession for American companies. He reprimanded the official for jeopardizing the Iranian-Soviet settlement and for possibly giving the Soviets a pretext for staying in the country.[27]

The new ambassador to Iran, George V. Allen, quickly created fruitful

23 For the Tabriz reports see Rossow, "Battle of Azerbaijan," and *Foreign Relations, 1946*, VII, 340, 342-43, 344-45 (the quotation appears on p. 347).

24 *Foreign Relations, 1946*, VII, 347.

25 Allen, Memoirs, p. 12. See also citations in nn. 22-24 for early 1946 events.

26 *Foreign Relations, 1946*, VI, 734.

27 Much of the following is derived from *ibid., 1946*, VII, and the Allen Memoirs.

relations with Qavam; indeed, it was soon Qavam's "custom" to seek advice from American diplomats. Allen also developed contacts with the vehemently anti-Soviet Shah, who increasingly served as a check on Qavam. Allen constantly discouraged Qavam from any expressions of friendship for Russia. After one interview he informed Washington that it would have a "salutary effect, at least in letting Qavam know that American reaction must be reckoned with, and that he will be more mindful of this factor in the future." Allen and the British ambassador, "every day, in every way we can think of," urged Qavam to take a "firmer line against Tudeh and against Russians. . . ." The State Department cautioned that joint Anglo-American representations were anathema because "they may give rise to [the] impression that US and UK are forming [a] bloc in Middle East opposed to Russia."[28]

In September, 1946, Qavam contemplated a "sharp change of policy," as he put it, and asked for military and financial assistance from the United States to challenge the Tudeh Party and to effect economic reforms. A week later the director of the Office of Near Eastern and African Affairs recommended that the State Department encourage Iran to hope for aid. The Joint Chiefs of Staff added that a Russian sphere of influence in Iran would threaten the United States: "They hold the view that the oil fields in Iran, Saudi Arabia, and Iraq are absolutely vital to the security of this country." With the Shah putting more and more pressure on Qavam, in mid-October, Iran asked for $10 million (a figure suggested by Allen), and shortly thereafter Qavam dramatically ousted the four Tudeh Party members from his cabinet, an action for which Allen claimed credit. In mid-November Washington assured Iran of $10 million in combat materiel. Later that month Qavam decided to send troops against Azerbaijan, and Allen publicly stated that the decision was "normal and proper." The Iranian army was advised by Major General Robert W. Grow of the United States Army. Government troops easily routed dissidents in Azerbaijan. The presence of American correspondents in an American military vehicle, clearly marked with an American flag, even sparked rumors that United States forces were spearheading the invasion. Before and after the expedition, the Soviets warned Iran in the strongest terms that Russia could not stand idly by while military action was conducted so close to its border. Yet the bold move, conceived in part by the Shah and encouraged by Allen, was ingenious. Russia wanted the oil concession, and through it big power influence, more than it wanted Azerbaijan. The northern Iranian rebels quickly learned that Soviet assistance would not be forthcoming.[29]

In Teheran, the Iranian Cabinet thanked Allen for the critical American support, and the Shah toasted the United States, proclaiming that the Iranian

---

[28] Allen, quoted in *Foreign Relations, 1946*, VII, 460, 497, 499, 502.
[29] Qavam is quoted in *ibid.*, p. 518, the Joint Chiefs of Staff in *ibid.*, p. 524, and Allen in *ibid.*, p. 549. See Allen, Memoirs, ch. 4, for an interesting account of the "battle" of Azerbaijan.

victory represented the "turn of the tides against Soviet aggression through-out the world." Ambassador Smith agreed that the collapse of the "Azer-baijan house of cards" meant a major triumph for the United Nations and for a "firm policy" toward Russia. Meanwhile, the Iranian parliament had not yet ratified the oil agreement. Indeed, elections for the assembly were not held until early 1947, and the parliament was supposed to have acted upon the agreement by October of the previous year. The Soviets were furious, and American diplomats quietly advised Iranians against ratification. In large part because of American influence, the parliament in October, 1947, rejected the agreement by a vote of 102 to 2. Moscow had been dealt a diplomatic blow—both Azerbaijan and the oil concession had been denied to the Russians, not just by Iran but by the United States.[30]

Several years later, Truman told a news conference and wrote in his *Memoirs* that in 1946 he had sent an ultimatum to Moscow to pull out of Iran. Truman's memory "played him false," as Allen later put it.[31] No ultimatum was sent, although one may have been contemplated. But this long-standing myth is indicative of the "lesson" Americans drew from the crisis: the Soviets had been contained through confrontation; aggression had been stopped. "Getting tough with the Russians" became a popular slogan. Few observers pointed out that Washington had denied to Russia what it and London already had in Iran: oil and influence.[32] United States expansion in Iran, on a Soviet border, which might have affected Russian decisions, was rarely mentioned, although Arthur C. Millspaugh, former United States financial adviser to the Iranian government, did comment that "Iran's geographic relation to the Soviet Union is roughly comparable to the relation of Mexico or Canada to the United States."[33] Moscow must have wondered about "accommodation" in the future, since it was evident that its with-drawal from Iran and its inaction during the Azerbaijani expedition were not read as contributions to accommodation but as victories for the United States.

The "lesson" of Iran was significant for the development of the contain-ment theory and the Truman Doctrine, as well as for the United States response to the immediate crises in Greece and Turkey. Drafters of the Truman Doctrine speech frequently alluded to Iran; and Iran, Greece, and

[30] The Shah is quoted in *Foreign Relations, 1946*, VII, 563; Smith is quoted in *ibid.*, p. 566. For American influence in the Iranian decision to reject the oil agreement, see *Foreign Relations, 1947*, V (Washington, D.C., 1971), 890-972; Fatemi, *Oil Diplomacy*, pp. 324-26.

[31] For the myth of the ultimatum, see *Foreign Relations, 1946*, VII, 348-49; Allen, in Allen to Alexander George, June 4, 1969, Allen Papers.

[32] In December, 1946, the Anglo-Iranian Oil Company conceded to two American oil companies the marketing of 20 percent of the company's annual production for twenty years. George Kirk, *The Middle East, 1945-1950* (London, 1954), p. 9.

[33] A. C. Millspaugh, "Memorandum on Recent American Diplomacy in Iran," Sept. 8, 1948, Box 20, Snyder Papers.

Turkey merged in American thinking as areas susceptible to Soviet probing. In early 1946, in speaking of Iran, Byrnes used language similar to that found later in the Truman Doctrine speech when he warned against "political infiltration," "aggression," "threat of force," and "coercion." This speech was included in the working papers when writers put together the president's March 12, 1947, address.[34] The experience in Iran gave officials the confidence to push forth United States interests more aggresively and to take a bold stand against Soviet diplomacy.[35]

GREECE: AID BEFORE THE TRUMAN DOCTRINE

Greece, too, was a testing ground for a firm policy toward the Soviet Union. Like most countries occupied by the German army, Greece faced serious economic crisis in the postwar period. Nearly one-third of its villages were destroyed or damaged, and its railroads and oceangoing fleet were crippled. World War II cost the Greeks at least $20 billion in materials, lost productive capacity, and government expenses.[36] When the Germans pulled out of Greece in 1944, much of the countryside was controlled by resistance fighters (the ELAS, or National Popular Liberation Army) and their political organization (EAM, or National Liberation Front), which included Communists. But the British had formed another government under Prime Minister George Papandreou, who arrived from Egypt in October with his cabinet. Greece was soon wracked by political struggle, and in December violence broke out between the EAM and a government heavily dependent upon the British for its survival. Churchill pledged "no peace without victory" against this leftist challenge to the Papandreou regime. The fighting was vicious until the rebels accepted an agreement in February of 1945 to lay down their arms in favor of elections. Except for the Athens-Piraeus area, the insurgents were the dominant force.[37]

With British encouragement, the Athens government and rightwing terrorist groups began to repress EAM members and their sympathizers through arrests and violence. At the same time the Athens regime approached Washington for economic assistance. On August 20, 1945, it asked for a $250

[34] *DSB*, XIV (Mar. 10, 1946), 355-58; Jones, *Fifteen Weeks*, p. 54.

[35] Lenczowski, *Russia and West in Iran*, p. 311; Halle, *Cold War as History*, p. 100; Cabell Phillips, "U.S. Interest in Middle East Oil Is Strategic," *New York Times*, Apr. 6, 1947, sec. 4, p. 5; Jones, *Fifteen Weeks*, ch. 2; Ulam, *Expansion and Coexistence*, p. 428.

[36] UNRRA, European Regional Office, *Post-War Public Finance in Greece* (London, 1947), pp. 1-2; *Foreign Relations, 1945*, VIII, 233-34.

[37] John O. Iatrides, *Revolt in Athens: The Greek Communist "Second Round," 1944-1945* (Princeton, N.J., 1972). This thorough study documents well the high degree of British influence and the absence of Soviet involvement. Churchill is quoted on p. 208.

million credit from the Export-Import Bank and submitted a catalog of needs. United States officials thought the figure too high but were prepared to grant $25 million. Concurrently, Byrnes instructed Ambassador Lincoln MacVeagh to meet confidentially with the Greek regent to persuade him to change the electoral schedule. When the armistice was signed in early 1945 the EAM and Greek regime had agreed that general elections would follow a plebiscite on the issue of the return of the monarchy. Byrnes and the British wanted the general elections first, the regent agreed, and the British warned the Greeks that they would withhold aid unless the new arrangement was accepted.[38]

The Export-Import Bank began processing the $25 million loan in the fall of 1945, at a time when MacVeagh's reports were becoming alarmist. The Greek economy was deteriorating, and the British were not granting enough aid. Washington clearly disliked the Athens government because of its repressive measures and ineptitude, but it feared the EAM more, believing that it was tied to Moscow. So Washington decided to press the Greeks for reforms with foreign aid as the pressure device. The State Department began to insist to the Greek ambassador that intensive internal efforts must be made to alleviate disunity and economic dislocation. The ambassador, harping on a theme that was to recur frequently thereafter, blamed the disorder not on actions of the Greek government but on outside influences from Yugoslavia, Albania, Bulgaria, and Russia, which, he alleged, were encouraging discontent.[39]

During November, 1945, reports of a possible political collapse in Greece increased. Byrnes spoke of the "gravity" of the situation, criticized Greek leaders for continued governmental incompetence, but also mentioned that the State Department was considering "strong action to help Greece save herself and avert financial and economic chaos." Allied military leaders in Greece were advocating joint Anglo-American aid to stop what Lieutenant General William D. Morgan, the supreme Allied commander in the Mediterranean theater, called the "Red Tide." Alexander C. Kirk, Morgan's political adviser, told the secretary of state that the British could no longer manage Greece alone and that Greece's neighbors might stir up border trouble. He also reported that the Greek government had been notified that as of January 1, 1946, it must pay for the maintenance of its army (the notification was later suspended pending further discussion). He appealed for American aid.[40]

---

[38] Greece received $81,321,000 in Lend-Lease aid during the war. UNRRA assistance to Greece totaled $362 million, a major proportion of which originated in the United States. Commerce, *Foreign Aid, 1940-1951*, p. 88; *DSB*, XVI (May 4, 1947), 858 (supplement); Stephen G. Xydis, *Greece and the Great Powers, 1944-1947: Prelude to the "Truman Doctrine"* (Thessaloniki, 1963), pp. 97-98; *Foreign Relations, 1945*, VIII, 150-51, 179-82, 232-37.

[39] *Foreign Relations, 1945*, VIII, 173, 178-79, 181-82; Xydis, *Greece and the Great Powers*, p. 146.

[40] *Foreign Relations, 1945*, VIII, 251-54; also pp. 256-57.

In the State Department, Loy Henderson surveyed the "critical" problem, insisted on internal reforms, and warned that "a weak and chaotic Greece is a constant invitation to its unfriendly neighbors on the north to take aggressive action and constitutes a menace to international peace and security."[41] When Byrnes suggested sending American technical experts to Greece, the British endorsed the suggestion. The Greek government requested a joint Anglo-American technical mission, but the United States chose a unilateral mission. MacVeagh asked non-Communists to join together against the EAM to "establish stable government" and persuaded the regent not to resign.[42]

Both the British and Greek governments urged Washington to speed up the $25 million credit. The British noted that a loan would shore up the confidence of the faltering Greek government, especially since Britain could not assist in the reconstruction effort. MacVeagh wrote in mid-December of Greek fears of attacks from northern neighbors controlled "almost completely by USSR" and from internal Communists trained and directed from Moscow. He warned that the Greek army could not withstand a "Russian-supported invasion." The conclusion was obvious: Greece might become a "Soviet puppet." Shortly before this cable was sent, the United States indicated its concern by ordering the *U.S.S. Providence* to visit Pireus. Meanwhile, the $25 million loan awaited official approval by the Export-Import Bank, which was inopportunely caught in a personnel shift requiring congressional approval. Dean Acheson assured Ambassador John Winant in London that the "Secretary has also recently expressed especial desire for strenuous measures to assist Greece in its economic difficulites."[43]

In early January, 1946, Greece and the United States finally concluded terms for the $25 million loan. MacVeagh released a letter to the Greek press strongly suggesting that the credit was an initial step in an expanding aid program. One historian has labeled this letter a "pre-election message," designed to influence the upcoming March general elections in favor of a stable non-EAM government.[44] When the State Department announced the loan, it also cautioned the Greek government to undertake internal economic reforms. Acheson told a press conference that Greece could not begin the necessary reforms until it received financial aid, "but we are giving them a very strong statement here that something is called for from them." He noted further that the "situation is moving too fast."[45]

[41] *Ibid.*, pp. 263-65. See also the depressing report on Greek transportation in "A Report Covering the Interim Conclusions of the Joint Transport Facilities Mission to Greece (U.S. Section), February 1, 1946," HR 80A-7.3, Foreign Affairs Committee, House Records.

[42] *Foreign Relations, 1945*, VIII, 168-69, 183-84, 266, 270-71, 276-77, 289.

[43] *Ibid.*, pp. 278, 284-88, 289, 297, 298 (MacVeagh is quoted on p. 286, Acheson on p. 297); William H. McNeill, *The Greek Dilemma: War Aftermath* (Philadelphia, 1947), p. 258; Xydis, *Greece and the Great Powers*, p. 143.

[44] Xydis, *Greece and the Great Powers*, pp. 148-49.

[45] Acheson news conference transcript, Jan. 11, 1946, Folder 556, Byrnes Papers; *DSB*, XIV (Jan. 20, 1946), 78.

In early January the British dipped further into their meager resources to assist Greece with an interest-free loan of $40 million for the stabilization of currency and a waiver of repayment for $182 million loaned during the war. Ernest Bevin, the foreign secretary, reporting the agreement to the House of Commons, stated that the United States had given "the utmost help and support" in the negotiations and that its officials had been present at all the meetings. Bevin assumed that Washington would offer more aid after the March elections.[46]

United States officials generally considered the Greek elections of March 31 a success and took further steps to assist the Athens government. The EAM refused to participate, and the royalist, conservative Populist Party and its allies secured 231 of the 354 parliamentary seats. The parliament favored close cooperation with Britain and the United States, and Gardner Patterson, an economist formerly with the Treasury Department, soon joined the Greek Currency Control Committee, an agency of the Greek government (comprising one American, one Englishman, and two Greeks) charged with supervising the financial system.[47]

At this point both Greek and British leaders were interpreting United States aid and interest as indicators of a commitment to support and defend the regime. Indeed, the British cabinet undertook an important reassessment of its policy toward Greece. In March, 1946, Prime Minister Clement Attlee recommended that Britain disengage from areas where a clash with Russia was possible, especially the Middle East and Greece, and concentrate its defenses in Africa. Chancellor of the Exchequer Hugh Dalton agreed. Bevin himself said shortly after the Greek elections that he was eager for British troops to leave Greece as soon as possible.[48] This sentiment, which became accepted by late 1946, was based on the assumption that the United States would replace the British in those critical areas. To the knowledgeable observer, it must have appeared that Washington was already playing that role, as its influence grew in Iran, Greece, and seemingly in Britain itself (with the British loan). As *Fortune* magazine remarked in early 1946: "In the Greek situation, where Russia has missed no chance to raise the cry of 'fascism,' it is too often forgotten that the U.S. bears a responsibility almost

[46] Xydis, *Greece and the Great Powers*, p. 151. Quietly within the Truman administration Forrestal gathered support for his plan to send more warships to the Mediterranean. One day after Churchill's iron curtain speech, the State Department announced that the *U.S.S. Missouri* would sail to that sea. Vincent Davis, *Postwar Defense Policy and the U.S. Navy, 1943-1946* (Chapel Hill, N.C., 1966), p. 224; Xydis, *Greece and the Great Powers*, pp. 159, 169.

[47] Xydis, *Greece and the Great Powers*, pp. 152, 181, 184, 591; William H. Taylor and Edward H. Foley to Secretary Synder, "Information on Greek Delegation," Oct. 1, 1946, Greece folder, Synder papers.

[48] Dalton, *High Tide and After*, p. 105; Xydis, *Greece and the Great Powers*, p. 184.

as great as Britain. The U.S. has underwritten Greek reconstruction."[49]

The aid rendered was slow to produce results. By August, 1946, the inefficient regime had not used the $25 million loan, and food shortages were acute. Nevertheless, Washington, convinced that the EAM was not an indigenous movement but an arm of Soviet power, clung to the government, especially after the civil war flared up again in May. In that month the United States extended a $10 million surplus property credit and promoted a United Nations Food and Agriculture Organization mission.[50] On April 10 the *U.S.S. Missouri* anchored at Athens. The Greek press was well aware of the significance of this visit, and the pro-West, royalist newspaper *Ethnos* declared that the *Missouri* was a "sedative" to the "warlike neurosis" engulfing the world. The ultra-royalist *Akropolis* went even further: "Around us and over the Balkans hovers the great Russian shadow. So America comes here too, to tell us: Hold tight, and you may be sure we are with you."[51] Later, when questioned about the movement of the Sixth Fleet into the Mediterranean, Fleet Admiral William ("Bull") Halsey stated baldly that "It's nobody's damn business where we go. We will go anywhere we please."[52]

In mid-July, 1946, Greece announced that it would send a new economic mission to Washington to discuss further assistance. The State Department only reluctantly approved the mission because of the fact that the original $25 million had not yet been spent. The delegation, headed by Sophocles Venizelos, a center party leader, arrived in August and appealed for another $175 million. President Truman praised the visitors for their wartime struggle against fascism, again stressed the need for internal reforms in Greece, and seemed to encourage them to think that the United States would help resolve Greek economic problems.[53] The Export-Import Bank shared the irritation

---

[49] *Fortune*, XXXIII (March, 1946), 83. Also see William H. McNeill and Elizabeth McNeill, *Report on the Greeks* (New York, 1948), 74-76; Library of Congress, European Affairs Division (prepared by Floyd A. Spencer), *War and Postwar Greece* (Washington, D.C., 1952), p. 99.

[50] Xydis, *Greece and the Great Powers*, p. 449; Campbell, *United States in World Affairs, 1945-1947*, p. 476.

[51] Quoted in Xydis, *Greece and the Great Powers*, pp. 187-88.

[52] Quoted in *Journal of Commerce*, Aug. 28, 1946.

[53] *Foreign Relations, 1946*, VII, 182, 187-88; William H. Taylor and Edward H. Foley to Secretary Snyder, "Information on Greek Delegation," Oct. 1, 1946, Greece folder, Snyder Papers; Xydis, *Greece and the Great Powers*, pp. 261-62. Substantially increased trade with Greece was another sign of support. United States exports to Greece climbed in the early Cold War: the average for 1936-38 was $6,683,000; for 1942-45, $30,291,000; for 1946, $143,826,000; for 1947, $116,607,000; for 1948, $238,462,000; for 1949, $186,634,000. In 1946 one-third of all Greek imports came from the United States (much of them in the form of UNRRA supplies). Greek imports to the United States were minimal: the average for 1936-38 was $14,269,000; for 1942-45, $153,000; for 1946, $23,651,000; for 1947, $16,631,000; for 1948, $19,480,000; for 1949, $15,723,000. American investments in Greece were very small: $8.5 million in 1936, $9.6 million in 1943, and $5.9 million in 1950. Commerce, *Foreign Trade, 1936-49*, pp. 42-43; Commerce, *Foreign Investments of the United States*, p. 48.

in Washington over the lethargy of the Greek government. American officials alternately criticized and aided the Greek regime, and encouraging words from such individuals as Truman, Clayton, Acheson, Forrestal, and John Snyder weakened their demands for reform. The Greek government could not have been unhappy with the State Department's parting words that it was its "earnest desire" to see economic stability in Greece and to "render effective assistance" to that end.[54]

September and October, 1946, represented months of re-evaluation in United States policy toward Greece. Twenty-eight thousand British troops proved unable to crush the Greek insurgents, and although the plebisite of September 1 on the monarchy returned the king, there was little political stability. In September, in the same cable in which he ordered loans cut from Czechoslovakia and urged aid to "friends of the United States," Byrnes specifically mentioned Greece and Turkey as "friends" who needed assistance because of a menacing Russia. It was time, concluded Byrnes, to establish "new outlines of policy on Turkey, Greece, and Iran, the three Near and Middle Eastern nations we consider most seriously affected by present developments."[55] Earlier, in the late summer at Paris, he had agreed with the British that henceforth the British would sponsor military aid and the United States economic aid to Greece.[56] The re-evaluation was in essence an extension of that agreement and of the placement of Greece in the general perspective of the Soviet-American confrontation. MacVeagh kept the notion alive that the Soviet Union was responsible for the continued strife in Greece.[57]

Loy Henderson's memorandum regarding Greece dated October 21 was approved by the secretary of state as a summary of American policy. Greece "is becoming a focal point in strained international relations," and during the next few months its status "may be a deciding factor in the future orientation of the Near and Middle East." The memorandum discussed the deteriorating condition of the Greek economy, the intransigence of the royalist regime, the disruption caused by a Communist-dominated minority supported by the U.S.S.R., and Greece's troubled relations with her neighbors. It was an alarmist document which stated directly that Russia was trying to absorb Greece into its sphere of influence. If Greece fell, Turkey would fall next; then "we will have allowed to go unchecked another step of Soviet aggression aimed at exclusive domination of the Eastern Mediterranean." "Lest it come too late," the United States had to increase its political and economic support

[54] *DSB*, XV (Sept. 1, 1946), 426; *Foreign Relations, 1946,* VII, 190-91, 201.
[55] *Foreign Relations, 1946,* VII, 209, 223-24, 235n, 857 (the quotation appears on p. 225).
[56] *Ibid.,* pp. 245n, 262.
[57] *Ibid.,* pp. 226-27 (Sept. 30, 1946). MacVeagh cited provocations from "Soviet puppets" on the Greek border, "secret Soviet control of Greek Communist party," and the Soviet veto in the United Nations of the investigation proposal. The Soviets, he believed, wanted control of the north Aegean.

of Athens.[58] Greece, Turkey, and Iran were identified as bulwarks against Soviet aggression and as outposts of containment and United States influence.

New naval demonstrations, appeals for reform, missions, and aid were the tools of this policy. In late September, Secretary Forrestal announced that the United States would maintain a permanent naval force in the Mediterranean, including cruisers, destroyers, and an aircraft carrier. That same month the *U.S.S. Roosevelt* visited Greece.[59] In late September the United States awarded Greece $35 million in surplus property, and the Federal Reserve Bank (New York) granted Greece a $10.8 million credit.[60] In late October, the United States gave Greece a detailed list of measures the government might pursue to bolster the economy. Greece replied with a request for more American aid to implement the program.[61] In November and December Greek operators purchased over one hundred surplus liberty ships. Early in December Washington announced that an economic mission headed by Paul A. Porter, former head of the Office of Price Administration, would be sent to Greece to study reconstruction problems. At the same time, the *U.S.S. Randolph* stopped off at Athens, after having visited Turkey.[62] Yet vicious fighting between guerrilla bands and government forces continued.

With the encouragement of the British, Prime Minister Constantine Tsaldaris departed for the United States in December, 1946, on a new economic mission. He filed requests for a variety of loans and relief funds. The Export-Import Bank was again unenthusiastic because the Athens regime had managed to spend only $3.4 million of the original loan. Acheson decided that the United States would delay a decision on the requests until the Porter mission had reported, but Byrnes apparently led Tsaldaris to believe that a helping hand was about to be extended, for Tsaldaris asked for $1.246 billion before he departed. He later contended that the State Department comminiqué concerning his visit served as the basis of the Truman Doctrine. In this release, the Department confirmed that further aid was under study, and it renewed "assurances of support, in accordance with the principles of the United Nations, for the independence and integrity of Greece." Years later Tsaldaris remarked that he had not been surprised by the president's Truman Doctrine address because "I was sure that he was going to do this, because of what he said to me, as well as Byrnes and Acheson, and

[58] *Ibid.,* pp. 240-45.
[59] Davis, *Postwar Defense Policy,* pp. 224-25; *New York Times,* Oct. 1, 1946; *New York Herald Tribune,* Oct. 14, 1946.
[60] *Foreign Relations, 1946,* VII, 232; Xydis, *Greece and the Great Powers,* p. 378.
[61] *Foreign Relations, 1946,* VII, 250-55.
[62] Xydis, *Greece and the Great Powers,* p. 425; *Journal of Commerce,* Nov. 29 and Dec. 5, 1946; "U.S. Economic Mission to Greece," [n.d., but early 1947], Box 1, Joseph Jones Papers; Robert G. Albion and Robert H. Connery, *Forrestal and the Navy* (New York, 1962), pp. 185-89.

other people of the State Department. We had a very long conversation in December of 1946."[63]

If Tsaldaris was optimistic about United States aid, there was little else for him to be sanguine about. The EAM was conducting raids from Yugoslav and Albanian bases. An UNRRA report found Greece in "critical condition" with the future "dark." Only about 5 percent of the roads in the country were usable. UNRRA was terminating its food program. The government had almost exhausted its foreign assets. One United Nations report estimated that $708 million was needed for reconstruction. MacVeagh pressed Washington for a speedup in assistance.[64] Britain and the United States seemed to face a major crisis in Greece, which they perceived as part of a Soviet onslaught.

ANOTHER COMMITMENT: TURKEY BEFORE 1947

The State Department Division of Near Eastern Affairs concluded in October, 1946, that "Turkey constitutes the stopper in the neck of the bottle through which Soviet political and military influence could most effectively flow into the eastern Mediterranean and Middle East."[65] Because of Turkey's strategic position and control of the Dardanelles, the major powers sought to draw that country into their spheres of influence. Counting on strong anti-Soviet sentiment in Turkey, the United States was unwilling to compromise on a question of prime interest to the Soviets—the Straits. Turkey, like Iran and Greece, was eventually fastened to the American sphere of influence, and the Soviet Union once again protested American expansion into a bordering state.

During the war Turkey had shipped strategic goods to Germany and had closed the Dardanelles to Russian and Allied vessels but had permitted access to German ships. At Yalta, Stalin insisted that he could no longer "accept a situation in which Turkey had a hand on Russia's throat."[66] Everybody seemed to agree that the Montreux convention needed revision, but in mid-1945 when the Soviets explained their terms, United States officials became more cautious and began speaking of Soviet threats to Turkish independence.[67] Russia demanded "real" guarantees about joint control of

---

[63] Transcript, Constantine Tsaldaris interview, May 4, 1964, ERP Project, Truman Library; *DSB*, XVI (Jan. 5, 1947), 29; *Foreign Relations, 1946*, VII, 286-88; Xydis, *Greece and the Great Powers*, pp. 445-50.

[64] UNRRA, European Regional Office (prepared by William Diamond), *Foreign Trade in Greece* (London, 1946), pp. 32, 37; *Foreign Relations, 1946*, VII, 282-83; Xydis, *Greece and the Great Powers*, pp. 392, 449.

[65] *Foreign Relations, 1946*, VII, 895 (Oct. 21, 1946).

[66] *Ibid., Yalta*, p. 903.

[67] The Montreux convention of 1936, signed by the U.S.S.R. and Britain, among others, provided that if Turkey were a belligerent, it could determine unilaterally what warships could pass through the Straits. If Turkey were not at war, other warships could pass on a limited basis. Turkey could also fortify the Straits. Kirk, *Middle East in War*, pp. 21-44, 444, 464.

the Straits, a possible base on Turkish soil, and revision of the Turkish-Soviet boundary. At Potsdam, Churchill and Truman rejected the request for a base as a violation of Turkish soveriegnty, as it surely was. Truman, as he had done with the Danube, appealed for the open door in all international waterways. Months of bitter Turkish-Soviet relations followed, and the United States increasingly argued against Soviet participation in the postwar control of the Straits. In November, 1945, Washington urged free navigation for all commercial vessels. But only Black Sea warships (including Russian) could use the Straits. A United Nations agency (with United States membership) would be created to govern the vital waterway.[68] Russia did not consider these proposals protective of Soviet security. Despite the many Soviet protests, however, as Harriman pointed out in the fall of 1945, the "U.S.S.R. remained remarkably inactive with regard to Turkey."[69]

Yet Russia persisted in its demands for more control over the strategic Dardenelles and moved troops near the Turkish border in early 1946. United States Ambassador to Turkey Edwin C. Wilson drew a grand conclusion about Soviet intentions. The Soviets, he reported in March, wanted to install a friendly government in Ankara, build a security belt from the Baltic to the Black Sea, and put to an end "Western influence in Turkey. In short, domination of Turkey."[70] Although historians cannot precisely determine whether the Soviet objective in Turkey was the creation of a satellite, previous and subsequent events would suggest that Wilson, like United States officials in Iran and Greece, exaggerated the extent of the Soviet "threat."

State Department records indicate that American and Turkish diplomats exchanged ideas and support frequently, thus contributing to the Soviet belief that the United States itself was seeking a base in Turkey (as well as Iran). Certainly in 1945 and 1946 United States actions contributed to Soviet alarm. In April, 1946, the battleship *Missouri* stopped at Istanbul, in August the *Roosevelt* entered the Mediterranean, and in November the *Randolph* followed. Two Export-Import Bank loans in September, 1945 ($3.060 million for airport equipment), and October, 1946 ($25 million), and the sale of surplus ships demonstrated United States interest in the area. In 1946 Turkey also received a $45 million surplus property credit. The American presence was also noticeable in direct investments of $25 million, largely in oil and tobacco.[71]

[68] *Foreign Relations, 1946,* VII, 801-4; *ibid., 1945,* VIII, 1260-81; Kirk, *Middle East, 1945-1950,* pp. 21-27; Millis, *Forrestal Diaries,* p. 71.
[69] *Foreign Relations, 1945,* V, 901-2.
[70] *Ibid., 1946,* VII, 818-19. See also p. 821.
[71] Xydis, *Greece and the Great Powers,* pp. 176-77, 424; Byrnes, *Speaking Frankly,* p. 128; Kirk, *Middle East, 1945-1950,* pp. 32-34; House, *Assistance to Greece and Turkey,* p. 352; Commerce, *Foreign Investments of the United States,* p. 48; *Foreign Relations, 1946,* VII, 901n, 915. In 1946 the United States replaced Germany as the most important country in Turkish trade, taking 20 percent of Turkey's exports and supplying 31 percent of its imports. Commerce, *Foreign Trade, 1936-1949,* p. 44.

In the late summer and early fall of 1946, when United States officials were becoming more active in Iran and Greece and withdrawing aid to eastern Europe, the State Department began to toughen its stand on Turkey and the Straits. On August 7, the Soviet Union summarized its position in a note to the Turkish government. The note cited a number of wartime incidents in which German vessels had passed through the Dardanelles and engaged in naval operations against the Soviet Union. Then the Soviets accepted some of the principles suggested earlier by the United States: that the Straits be open to all merchant vessels and to the warships of Black Sea powers but closed to warships of non-Black Sea nations. But the Russians insisted that control over the Straits come under the authority only of Black Sea countries, not of an international agency. Furthermore, the note went on, Turkey and the Soviet Union should "organize joint means of defense" so that "hostile" countries could not utilize the waterway. Nothing was said specifically about bases on Turkish soil.[72]

Discussion in Washington proceeded at a fast pace. G. Lewis Jones, assistant chief of the Division of Near Eastern Affairs, made a lengthy case against the Soviet note two days later. He argued that the Soviets were ignoring the United Nations and would deny the United States and other Western powers authority over the Straits. Furthermore, the United States could not accept a fortified Dardanelles. Jones recommended that Washington stick to its position of international control. Although the Turks themselves thought the Soviet requests surprisingly moderate and Stalin let it be known that he would not attack Turkey, officials in Washington, supported by Ambassador Wilson's repeated cables from Ankara that Russia was plotting to make Turkey a satellite, decided that a vigorous reply was needed to demonstrate that the United States would not be excluded from influence there.[73]

As Jones recalled, "it was simply a matter of taking out old discarded memos and re-writing them."[74] On August 15, Acting Secretary Acheson, War Secretary Forrestal, and other top officials conferred with the president. Acheson presented Truman with a strongly worded memorandum charging Moscow with aggression. "The primary objective of the Soviet Union is to obtain control of Turkey," it concluded. If Turkey were to fall to the Soviets, "it will be extremely difficult, if not impossible, to prevent the Soviet Union from obtaining control over Greece and over the whole Near and Middle East." Furthermore, "when the Soviet Union has once obtained full mastery of this territory, which is strategically important from the point of view of resources, including oil, and from the point of view of communications, it

---

[72] *Foreign Relations, 1946,* VII, 827-29 (Aug. 7, 1946).
[73] *Ibid.,* pp. 834-40.
[74] Quoted in John Jay Iselin, "The Truman Doctrine: A Study in the Relationship between Crisis and Foreign Policy-Making" (Ph.D. dissertation, Harvard University, 1964), p. 181.

will be in a much stronger position to obtain its objectives in India and China." Turkey's status had global implications. The United States, the memorandum continued, should deter the Russians by emphasizing that it would meet aggression with "force of arms."[75] The president liked Acheson's firm language and said, according to Forrestal, that "we might as well find out whether the Russians were bent on world conquest now as in five or ten years."[76] Washington thereupon informed Moscow that it stood firm in its position that the Straits should be controlled internationally, not just by Russia and Turkey, that the United Nations should be the governing regime, and that Turkey alone should be responsible for the defense of the Dardanelles. It made clear that the United States would have an influental role in control over the Straits—if not directly, through Turkey. Once again, expansion and containment went hand in hand.[77]

Through the fall of 1946 note and counter-note passed between Ankara, Moscow, and Washington, but no minds were changed. At the end of the year the Straits issue was deadlocked. There was no Soviet military attack of any sort nor any evidence of Soviet intention of world conquest. It would appear that Russia was primarily concerned with its security, not with the subjugation of Turkey. As Joseph Davies had noted in September, "the Dardanelles is Russia's 'Panama Canal,' is her 'Suez Canal,' is her 'Gibraltar,' vital to the security of her lifeline through the Black Sea."[78] Certainly, a double standard was evident: a Soviet request for "international" control of the Panama Canal and for sole Panamanian authority over the defense of the waterway would have been met with the sternest of objections from the United States. In the case of the Straits, the label "aggression," if applied to Russia, must also be applied to Washington. The United States got the influence it wanted, but also acquired an obligation: Ambassador Wilson wrote in late December that Turkey's large military establishment was placing a strain on the economy, which was arousing political discontent, and that more extensive economic aid from the United States might be necessary.[79]

A "FITTING MOMENT": LAUNCHING THE TRUMAN DOCTRINE

The dramatic announcement of the Truman Doctrine in March, 1947, was not a new departure or revolution in foreign policy, but rather a summary statement. As we have seen, before 1947 the United States had firmly committed itself to the expansion and preservation of its influence in the

[75] *Foreign Relations, 1946*, VII, 840-42. See also Clark Clifford's similar report (in September) in Krock, *Memoirs*, p. 226.
[76] Millis, *Forrestal Diaries*, p. 192. For another account of the White House meeting, see Smith, *Acheson*, p. 34.
[77] *Foreign Relations, 1946*, VII, 847-49.
[78] Undelivered speech by Joseph E. Davies, Sept. 20, 1946, OF 539, Truman Papers.
[79] *Foreign Relations, 1946*, VII, 899.

Near and Middle East through economic assistance, naval demonstrations, missions, and military advisers. In the American perception, Iran, Greece, and Turkey were vital links in the "chain of events" which explained a single-minded, aggressive, and global Soviet thrust.[80] As a draft speech prepared for Dean Acheson put it less than two months after Truman's address, "in its wider context the President's policy means that it is this government's intention to seek through a judicious use of its economic resources to lay a basis for political stability in the world." Indeed, the "use of economic power ... to achieve broad political ends is no new policy."[81] Expansion and containment were again partners in the Truman Doctrine—not the expansion of narrow economic self-interest but a "way of life" Truman summarized so often as "peace and prosperity." The Soviet Union and/or Communism had to be contained because they challenged the conception of a world open to the intertwined ideals and interests of the United States. The Truman Doctrine became enshrined as a grand statement of the country's postwar foreign policy.

What precipitated the Truman speech were two British notes delivered to the State Department on February 21 (formally presented three days later). One note recalled the 1946 Anglo-American agreement that Britain would supply military assistance and the United States economic aid to Greece. London could no longer meet its obligation; Washington would have to assume the whole assigment after March 31. The second note depicted a weak Turkey incapable of resisting aggression, in dire need of outside help. Since Britain lacked resources to bolster Turkey, that burden too would have to shift to the United States.[82] British leaders had long contemplated cutting their expenses abroad. The Bevin-Byrnes agreement of late summer, 1946, reflected steady movement toward that goal. Truman's address of March must be read as the acceptance of a more active American role whose development was well-advanced by the time the British notes arrived.

Events in early 1947 help to explain the timing. Since the liberation of Greece from German occupation the United States had given it $181,500,000 in assistance, but the impact of the aid had been minimal.[83] The Porter mission arrived in Greece on January 18, just as UNRRA aid was being phased out. Members of the delegation found economic conditions worse than they had anticipated.[84] A few days later, a new government—a coalition cabinet of seven non-Communist parties—was organized. Washington on a number of occasions had called for just such a broadening of

---

[80] For one example of the theory that countries were linked, meaning that the collapsed one would topple all (later called the "domino theory"), see draft speech by Loy Henderson, [n.d. but 1947], Box 1, Joseph Jones Papers.

[81] Draft speech by Joseph Jones, April, 1947, *ibid.*

[82] Jones, *Fifteen Weeks*, pp. 3-7.

[83] U.S. delegation to the United Nations, press release, statement by Ambassador Warren Austin, Mar. 28, 1947, Box 1, Jones Papers.

[84] "U.S. Economic Mission to Greece," *ibid.*

representation as a step toward political stability.[85] The premier, Demitrius Maximos, quickly offered amnesty to the rebels and welcomed a United Nations commission, which arrived in Athens on January 30 to investigate Greek charges that bordering countries were keeping the civil war alive. The United States had been the chief advocate of the U.N. commission. In February the commission members interviewed captured insurgents, who revealed that they had been trained in Yugoslav camps. It was welcome evidence to those people who blamed Greece's problems on "outsiders." On February 12, in accordance with Porter's recommendations, the number of government ministries was cut from thirty-one to fifteen to impose efficiency on the regime. That same day Ambassador MacVeagh appealed for American economic aid because he believed British support was faltering.[86] Eight days later, one day before the British notes arrived, the ambassador cabled Secretary of State George C. Marshall that he considered Greece's independence so precarious that "no time should be lost in applying any remedial measures. . . ." The words "imminent" and "collapse" stood out in the cable.[87] The next day, just before the British notes were handed to State Department officers, Marshall instructed Acheson to prepare a bill providing for a direct loan to Greece and to plan for the transfer of military equipment.[88] In essence, the British had seized the opportunity presented by events in Greece and the jittery United States attitude, all of which presaged a stepup in United States assistance.

Crises in England itself also explain the timing. On January 27 Hugh Dalton cut the defense budget. The cabinet agreed that troops stationed in Greece had to be brought home by March 31, and the Greeks were so informed on February 19.[89] The British military retrenchment was forced by the state of the domestic economy. By early 1947 the British loan had not worked its magic, and the dollar deficit persisted. Military spending for overseas forces accounted for the entire budget deficit of 1946. On January 20 the British exposed their economic illness to the world in a White Paper. By mid-February many of the country's essential industries were crippled by a coal shortage. Heavy blizzards aggravated the crisis. On February 21 another White Paper stunned even the London *Times*, which found it the "most

---

[85] Secretary George C. Marshall applauded the new government and spoke of American assistance to maintain Greek "independence and territorial integrity." *New York Times,* Feb. 15, 1947.

[86] Department of State, "Background Material," [n.d.], Box 65, George Elsey Papers, Truman Library; Xydis, *Greece and the Great Powers,* pp. 400-405, 464, 470.

[87] *Foreign Relations, 1947,* V, 28-29 (Feb. 20, 1947). Also on February 18 Mark Ethridge, a United States delegate to the U.N. Commission, informed Washington that Greek Communists were ready to seize the country. Xydis, *Greece and the Great Powers,* p. 472.

[88] Jones, *Fifteen Weeks,* p. 131. See also *Foreign Relations, 1947,* V, 29-31.

[89] Dalton, *High Tide,* pp. 193-94, 197-98, 206-7; Xydis, *Greece and the Great Powers,* pp. 453, 474.

disturbing statement ever made by a British government."[90] Thus events in Greece and Britain coincided in February, convincing the British to approach Washington for considerably more assistance in the Near East.

United States officials responded with uncommon alacrity. Their expanding activities in late 1946 and early 1947 left little doubt that they would accept the challenge, but there was one worry of some proportions: how could Congress be persuaded that the United States would have to act alone and to spend so heavily? Bipartisanship prevailed, but the Republican Congress did not appear to be in a spending mood. The speedy preparation of the Truman Doctrine speech is explained by the administration's awareness that the atmosphere of crisis would carry Congress with it. To ensure that the message be most convincing, White House and State Department drafters put together lofty statements summarizing the global perspective of the United States. No longer could Republican charges of administration indecisiveness be hurled; no longer could it be said that the United States lacked a defined foreign policy. The February crisis enabled Truman to snatch the anti-Communist banner from the Republicans (it was also in March that Truman initiated a new loyalty program at home) and to ensure that his reconstruction diplomacy would continue to be funded.[91] This was an opportune moment to clarify the nation's foreign policy, which Truman, a few days after his speech, said he had wanted to do for several months but had waited for a "fitting moment."[92]

Truman himself participated only minimally in the actual preparation of the speech. When the first draft was completed on March 3 by Joseph Jones of the State Department, the president was standing before an audience in Mexico City espousing the good neighbor policy. When the March 6 draft emerged from Jones's busy typewriter, Truman was telling a Baylor University crowd in Waco, Texas, that "our foreign relations, political and economic, are indivisible." He spoke of the interrelationship of "freedom of worship—freedom of speech—freedom of enterprise." Citing the lessons of history, he declared that "peace, freedom, and world trade" were inseparable.[93] It would be evident on March 12 that the drafters of the Truman Doctrine speech had had a hand in the March 6 address.

[90] Gardner, *Sterling-Dollar Diplomacy*, pp. 307-9; Jones, *Fifteen Weeks*, pp. 78-82 (the *Times* is quoted on p. 81); Mallalieu, *British Reconstruction and American Policy*, pp. 42-43.

[91] Warren L. Hickman, *Genesis of the European Recovery Program: A Study of the Trends of American Economic Policies* (Geneva, 1949), pp. 238-39; Athan Theoharis, "The Rhetoric of Politics: Foreign Policy, Internal Security, and Domestic Politics in the Truman Era, 1945-1950" and "The Escalation of the Loyalty Program," in Bernstein, *Politics and Policies*, pp. 196-268; Bernard Weiner, "Truman Doctrine: Background and Presentation" (Ph.D. dissertation, Claremont Graduate School, 1967), pp. 138-39; Richard M. Freeland, *The Truman Doctrine and the Origins of Mc-Carthyism: Foreign Policy, Domestic Politics, and Internal Security, 1946-1948* (New York, 1972).

[92] Interview with Arthur Krock, *New York Times*, Mar. 23, 1947.

[93] *Public Papers, Truman, 1947*, pp. 167-72.

Although Truman remained somewhat aloof from the hurried writing of the speech, he had confidence in Dean Acheson and Clark Clifford, who commanded the joint State Department-White House effort. On March 3 Acheson collected a number of drafts from various members of the department. He liked Joseph Jones's best, and instructed him to draft the message. Jones worked steadily for hours, after listening for some time to Acheson's suggestions. During the next three days Acheson called Near Eastern experts to his office, and they together dissected Jones's drafts sentence by sentence. On March 7 Acheson carried a polished draft to the White House. Clifford and his staff revised it on March 10, and Acheson then joined Clifford for a late-afternoon session to iron out minor differences in wording. Throughout the drafting process, it was the sense of the participants that the speech should play down the role of Britain, military aid, the United Nations, and the corruption of the Greek regime, and should emphasize in straight-forward terms the global confrontation between "democracy" and "totalitarianism." Acheson told Jones: "If F. D. R. were alive I think I know what he'd do. He would make a statement of global policy, but confine his request for money right now to Greece and Turkey." The Truman Doctrine speech was approved by the president on March 11, and he delivered it before a joint session of Congress the next day.[94]

The president presented his case very simply on March 12, in only eighteen minutes. He spoke of "the gravity of the situation which confronts the world today," the depressed Greek economy, and the precariousness of a "free" and independent Greek government beseiged by a "militant minority," i.e., Communists. He briefly described the British decision to withdraw and stressed the need for United States aid "to build an economy in which a healthy democracy can flourish." He repeatedly implied that the Greek regime was "democratic" and "free," or was becoming so. As for Turkey, "the future of Turkey as an independent and economically sound state is clearly no less important to the freedom-loving peoples of the world than the future of Greece." Turkey's "integrity" had to be upheld: "That integrity is essential to the preservation of order in the Middle East." The United States had demonstrated in World War II, and would again in 1947, that countries must be allowed to exist "free from coercion." But "we shall not realize our objectives . . . unless we are willing to help free peoples to maintain their free institutions and their national integrity against aggressive movements that

[94] The consensus in Washington, according to Jones, was that the United States could now "take action on a broad enough scale to prevent the Soviet Union from breaking through the Greece-Turkey-Iran barrier." Jones, *Fifteen Weeks*, pp. 133-34. The many drafts, with marginal notes, are easily located in the Jones (Box 1) and Elsey (Box 17) Papers, Truman Library. Of particular help in following the drafting are Joseph Jones, memorandum for the file, Mar. 12, 1947, Box 1, Jones Papers; "Chronology, Drafting of the President's Message of March 12, 1947," [n.d.], *ibid*. (Acheson is quoted in the latter document.) For early discussion, see "SWNCC Subcommittee on Foreign Policy Information Meeting, 2/28/47," *ibid*.

seek to impose upon them totalitarian regimes." He mentioned Soviet coercion in eastern Europe and throughout his speech clearly suggested that the Greek-Turkish question was Hitler and World War II all over again. He went on to describe the world as divided into two "ways of life," the American and the Communist way. Every nation, he said, must make a choice between them. Then came global policy: "I believe that it must be the policy of the United States to support free peoples who are resisting attempted subjugation by armed minorities or by outside pressures." He pointed to the strategic position of Greece to Europe and to the Middle East and urged "immediate and resolute action," in the form of assistance amounting to $400 million for Greece and Turkey. Congress was also asked to authorize the dispatch of economic and military personnel to supervise the aid. Only the United States could help; it was a precious opportunity. "If we falter in our leadership, we may endanger the peace of the world—and we shall surely endanger the welfare of this Nation."[95]

It was a moving speech, filled with echoes of battles against Hitler's Germany and homespun oratorical clichés, with special emphasis on the word "free." Nowhere did the president specifically mention the long-standing Greek civil war, the ineptitude and social conservatism of the Greek regime, the absence of democracy in either Greece or Turkey, the relationship between United States interest in the Middle East and oil,[96] the Iranian crisis, the British role, or the traditional squabble between Turkey and Russia over the Dardanelles. He said that the United States had received an "urgent appeal" from the Greek government; Washington actually wrote the Greek request. It was a message containing little analysis, not designed to educate but to be taken at face value, expressed in the language of crisis, panic, panacea, traditional American values, and the peace and prosperity theme. It

[95] *Public Papers, Truman, 1947,* pp. 176-80.
[96] Concern for raw materials (especially oil) and the Middle East was deleted from the March 10 draft at Acheson's request because he did not want the issue singled out. The March 10 draft read: "If, by default, we permit free enterprise to disappear in the other nations of the world, the very existence of our own economy and our own democracy will be gravely threatened. . . . This is an area of great natural resources which must be accessible to all nations and must not be under the exclusive control or domination of any single nation. The weakening of Turkey, or the further weakening of Greece, would invite such control." Draft of Mar. 10, 1947, Box 17, Elsey Papers. For other evidence of interest in the importance of raw materials, see James Forrestal to Paul Smith, Mar. 19, 1947, Box 91, Forrestal Papers; Forrestal and Paul Shields, telephone conversation, Mar. 20, 1947, *ibid.*; *Business Week,* Mar. 8, 1947, p. 103; *Wall Street Journal,* Mar. 17, 1947; UNRRA, *Foreign Trade in Greece,* pp. 4-5, 22-23; Frances C. Mattison, ed., *A Survey of American Interests in the Middle East* (Washington, D.C., 1953), p. xiv; Bernard Brodie, *Foreign Oil and American Security* (New Haven, Conn., 1947); Walter L. Wright, Jr., "Our Near Eastern Policy in the Making," *The Annals of the American Academy of Political and Social Science,* CCLX (January, 1948), 93-104; A. C. Sedgwick, "The Plot against Greece," *Foreign Affairs,* XXVI (April, 1948), 486-96; William Reitzel, *The Mediterranean: Its Role in America's Foreign Policy* (New York, 1948), pp. 116-17; *New York Times,* Mar. 5, 1947. For the removal of references to the Middle East and raw materials from the speech, see Jones, *Fifteen Weeks,* p. 156, and Draft of Mar. 10, 1947, Elsey Papers.

was the "most important thing that had happened since Pearl Harbor," the drafters agreed.[97]

PRESIDENTIAL MASTERY OF THE DEBATE

Within the Truman administration there were a few critics of the speech and the alarmist way in which it presented foreign policy issues. Presidential assistant George Elsey told Clark Clifford that "there has been no overt action in the immediate past by the U.S.S.R. which serves as an adequate pretext for the 'All-out' speech. The situation in Greece is relatively 'abstract;' there have been other instances—Iran, for example—where the occasion more adequately justified such a speech and there will be other such occasions—I fear—in the future." Another reason why Elsey thought the timing inappropriate was that it would divide the American people and wreck the Moscow Foreign Ministers Conference, about to convene.[98] George F. Kennan, whose own cables from Moscow and as yet unpublished article, "The Sources of Soviet Conduct," had helped shape official opinion on containment, objected to the openendedness of an early draft shown him, the "sweeping language," the "universal policy," and the recommendation for military aid to Turkey.[99] But neither Elsey's nor Kennan's objections were vigorous or persuasive enough to alter Acheson's conviction that a hard-hitting message was what was needed. Secretary Marshall received the text of the speech on his way to Moscow. Charles Bohlen, who accompanied him, recalled that "we were somewhat startled to see the extent to which the anti-Communist element of this speech was stressed." Although Marshall questioned this aspect of the text, he apparently was satisfied with Truman's reply that "from all his contacts with the Senate, it was clear that this was the only way in which the measure could be passed."[100]

The bill to aid Greece and Turkey passed Congress with surprising ease, largely because of its alarming language and a president's ability to shape public opinion by using the language of crisis. Congressional hearings and debates and public discussions took place, and the critics suggested alternatives, but their effect was essentially insignificant. The dramatic tone of the speech made it difficult for critics to be heeded or for congressional doubtfuls to vote "no." Truman's language left little doubt that the United States would be shirking its duty if it turned the bill down. Few politicians with an ·

---

[97] Jones, Memorandum for the file, Jones Papers. See the useful article by William Neumann, "How To Merchandise Foreign Policy, I," pp. 183-93, and "SWNCC Subcommittee on Foreign Policy Information Meeting, 2/28/47," Jones Papers, for ways to "sell" the Truman Doctrine.

[98] George M. Elsey to Clark Clifford, Mar. 7, 1947, Greece folder, Clifford Papers.

[99] Kennan, *Memoirs*, pp. 320-21. See also Paterson, *Containment and the Cold War*.

[100] Charles E. Bohlen, *The Transformation of American Foreign Policy* (New York, 1969), p. 87.

eye to their careers, aware of the presidentially initiated consensus, dared rebel. Republicans feared that a negative vote would call their own anti-Communism into question. South Dakota Congressman Francis Case frankly told the president that supporters of the bill were not enthusiastic. "The situation was regarded as an accomplished fact. You had spoken to the world." Case reported that he would have voted against passage "had it not been that we thought it would be like pulling the rug out from under you. . . ."[101]

As the *St. Louis Post Dispatch* noted, "Congress may ponder and debate, but the President's address has committed the nation to all-out diplomatic action."[102] Actually, there was little congressional debate. Truman had laid the groundwork with Congress before he delivered his speech. On February 27 he met with Vandenberg, Charles Eaton (chairman of the House Foreign Affairs Committee), and Senator Styles Bridges (chairman of the Appropriations Committee), among others. After Acheson had regaled them with a highly colored picture of the aggressive Soviets sweeping over one region after another, they left the meeting supporters of the President's policy. They did tell him to give a straightforward speech so that the American people would also be convinced.

The Senate did not begin debate upon the Greek-Turkish aid bill until April 8, as it was caught up in the controversy over David Lilienthal's confirmation as chairman of the Atomic Energy Commission. Before that date both houses conducted brief public hearings. An audience of three hundred jammed into the caucus room of the House Office Building on March 20 to hear Acheson. Bothered by the glaring lights and condescending toward the congressmen, Acheson antagonized many observers. As one reporter described the scene, "Acheson's manner was clipped, precise, and as he progressed through the hearing, it became somewhat acid. He didn't exactly tell the committee to go to hell, but his attitude in some instances bespoke it." Apparently realizing that his "acidosis" might damage the bill's chances, Acheson changed his style the next day and became more conciliatory.[103]

The Senate Foreign Relations Committee, chaired by Vandenberg, spent only four days in public hearings, and a large part of that time was devoted to the testimony of administration figures like Acheson, Clayton, and Forrestal, who had actually answered most questions in earlier executive sessions.[104] Vandenberg opened debate in the Senate on April 8 with a speech laced with

---

[101] Francis Case to Truman, May 10, 1947, Box 1278, OF 426, Truman Papers. See also Weiner, "Truman Doctrine," pp. 202, 248, 251; Iselin, "Truman Doctrine," pp. 383-86, 442-43; excerpts from telephone conversation between James Forrestal and James Reston, Mar. 13, 1947, Box 1, Jones Papers.

[102] Quoted in *U.S. News*, XXII (Mar. 21, 1947), 28.

[103] McNaughton Report, Mar. 20 and Mar. 21, 1947, Box 11, McNaughton Papers.

[104] For the executive session, see U.S., Senate, Committee on Foreign Relations, *Legislative Origins of the Truman Doctrine* (Hearings, March-April, 1947; made public Jan. 12, 1973).

references to Munich and appeasement, as Acheson sat approvingly in the gallery. Two weeks later Vandenberg spoke of a "Communist chain reaction from the Dardanelles to the China Sea and westward to the rim of the Atlantic. . . ." With business, labor, and newspaper support, with a Gallup poll shortly after the president's speech indicating that about 75 percent of the population had heard of the aid program and that most applauded it, the bill passed the Senate on April 22 by a vote of 67 to 23. Seemingly hemmed in by the president and the Senate, the House followed suit on May 8 with a vote of 287 to 107. A revised bill emerged from conference and passed on May 15 by voice vote. Truman signed the act on May 22.[105]

The critics had made few gains. A group of strange bedfellows, they included Senators Robert Taft, Kenneth Wherry, and Claude Pepper, Henry Wallace, James P. Warburg, Walter Lippmann, and Congressman Vito Marcantonio (American Labor Party). Taft and Wherry complained of the high cost, but Taft, who vigorously opposed military escalation in the Cold War, also feared bloc solidification and war with Russia. "If we assume a special position in Greece and Turkey," he said, in pointing out a double standard, "we can hardly . . . object to the Russians continuing their domination in Poland, Yugoslavia, Rumania, and Bulgaria."[106] Lippmann, in a series of widely read columns later published as *The Cold War*, questioned the vagueness of the doctrine and the administration's bypassing of the United Nations machinery. He further argued that containment left little room for negotiations or for selective intervention abroad. America would be locked into a policy of global intervention.[107] Pepper and Wallace also disapproved of the deliberate side-stepping of the United Nations and protested military aid to a corrupt regime. Pepper asked for evidence, which he never got, that the Soviet Union was masterminding the Greek civil war. Marcantonio considered the policy imperialist, and others smelled oil.[108] Wealthy publicist Warburg, a constant and sensible critic of the Cold War and a friend of policymakers, asked: "What is so urgent that we must act alone, without consultation, without knowing how far our first step will carry us, and in such a way as to undermine the very structure of peace, which we have

[105] Vandenberg, in *Congressional Record*, XCIII (Apr. 22, 1947), 3772-73; for business support, see Paterson, "Economic Cold War," pp. 384-91; for the press and the polls, Jones, *Fifteen Weeks*, pp. 172-73, 179, editorial, *New York Times*, Mar. 13, 1947, *Washington Post*, Mar. 13, 1947; for labor, Senate, *Assistance to Greece and Turkey*.

[106] Henry W. Berger, "Senator Robert A. Taft Dissents from Military Escalation," in Paterson, *Cold War Critics*, pp. 167-204 (the quotation appears on p. 177).

[107] Lippmann, *The Cold War*, passim; Bernstein, "Lippmann and the Early Cold War."

[108] Thomas G. Paterson, "The Dissent of Senator Claude Pepper," in Paterson, *Cold War Critics*, pp. 114-39; Henry Wallace, "The Truman Doctrine—Or a Strong UN," *New Republic*, CXVI (Mar. 31, 1947), 12-13, and "The Truman Doctrine" (editorial), *ibid.* (Mar. 24, 1947), 5-6; Norman Kaner, "Towards a Minority of One: Vito Marcantonio and American Foreign Policy" (Ph.D. dissertation, Rutgers University, 1968); Robert W. Dunn, "Oil and the Truman Doctrine," *Soviet Russia Today*, XVI (June, 1947), 9; "Is Mid East Oil So Necessary," *The Christian Century*, LXIV (May 21, 1947), 643; Bernard Baruch, in Krock, *Memoirs*, p. 266.

struggled so hard to erect?"[109] On the whole, the dissenters opposed the military emphasis of the aid doctrine, its jilting of the United Nations, its ill-defined global implications, and its assistance to a right-wing government.

Without question it had a military emphasis, for only $128,150,000 of the $400,000,000 consisted of economic aid. Supporters beat back amendments to reduce military aid. Without question it neglected the United Nations, but this neglect was remedied superficially by a Vandenberg amendment, drafted in cooperation with the State Department, stating that the United Nations was weak and without the necessary resources to undertake a Greek-Turkish aid program. But the United States would terminate its program if the Security Council or General Assembly requested it. It was a harmless addition, for Washington had the votes to cripple any United Nations opposition.[110] The Vandenberg amendment, recalled Acheson, "was window dressing and must have seemed either silly or cynical or both in London, Paris, and Moscow. Nevertheless, it was a cheap price for Vandenberg's patronage...."[111] Clearly, too, the United States was helping an inefficient and undemocratic regime. Truman admitted in his speech that the Greek government had "made mistakes," and officials tried to explain away its character and behavior by suggesting that it was becoming democratic and would be encouraged on that path by United States aid. Anyway, there was a

[109] Warburg, in Fleming, *Cold War and Its Origins*, I, 453. See also William Berman, "James Paul Warburg: An Establishment Maverick Challenges Truman's Policy toward Germany," in Paterson, *Cold War Critics*, pp. 54-75.

[110] Truman had explained in his address that the United Nations was weak and that "it is of the utmost importance that we supervise the use of any funds made available to Greece...." *Public Papers, Truman, 1947*, p. 177. Perhaps remembering the UNRRA experience, he wanted an American-oriented program. Acheson admitted to Pepper that Washington had not consulted the United Nations about a role for that organization. Indeed, Dean Rusk, director of the Office of Special Political Affairs (concerned with State Department relations with the United Nations), did not participate in the development of the Truman Doctrine. Barnet, *Intervention and Revolution*, p. 120; Senate, *Assistance to Greece and Turkey*, Mar. 27, 1947, pp. 45-46. It is an open but important question whether the United Nations could have been utilized to help reduce or end the civil strife in Greece through economic improvements or policing the borders. The Truman administration did not wait for the U.N. commission report (completed in June) which called for an international force along the Greek border to halt Yugoslav, Bulgarian, and Albanian aid to the rebels, nor did it consider the Food and Agriculture Organization of the United Nations as an alternative. Russia was not a member of the FAO, and there was no major-power veto in that body, so the Soviets could not have obstructed such a program. In May, 1946, an FAO mission had been sent to Greece, many of whose members were United States irrigation, economics, and hydro-electric experts on loan from the Department of Agriculture. In a comprehensive report of September, 1946, the mission recommended a variety of industrial and agricultural improvements and suggested a U.N. mission to replace the British and United States missions. United Nations, Food and Agriculture Organization, *First Annual Report of the Director-General to the FAO Conference* (Washington, D.C., 1946), pp. 3-4, 11, 14, 16; FAO Mission for Greece, *Preliminary Summary of Findings and Recommendations* (Washington, D.C., 1946); United Nations, *Report of the FAO Mission for Greece* (Washington, D.C., 1947).

[111] Acheson, *Present at the Creation*, p. 224. See also Vandenberg, *Private Papers*, p. 346; Ross to Austin, memorandum, Apr. 3, 1947, general correspondence, Warren R. Austin Papers, University of Vermont Library.

distasteful job to be done, and critics should not ask for perfection. Finally, Lippmann was right in calling containment ill-defined. If the new policy had any geographical or chronological limitations, they went unnoticed. Acheson and Truman considered the new doctrine global, which left policymakers a great deal of flexibility.[112]

The Truman administration never responded to the criticism that the Greek turmoil was largely an internal civil war waged by leftist rebels against a British-supported conservative government, and not a Soviet-inspired and Soviet-financed aggressive operation against the "West." Influenced by the Iranian crisis and the noisy verbal attacks upon Turkey, Washington assumed that Russia had charted a path of aggression through the Near and Middle East with ultimate destinations in other parts of the world. The popular "chain of events" theme and the common use of the label "aggression" indicate that it was believed that the EAM was aided and manipulated by Moscow. One of the first working papers for the Truman Doctrine speech concluded, "in the opinion of veteran U.S. representatives EAM is not a 'friend' or ally of the U.S.S.R.: it is an instrument of Soviet policy."[113] Indeed, many conservative Greeks, especially members of the Populist (royalist) Party, unwilling to admit that their own shortcomings and repressive measures had encouraged the civil war, popularized the impression that the EAM was synonymous with Moscow.[114]

Leaders in Washington also adhered to this simple assumption. Because the EAM had many Communist officials and sympathizers, because bordering Communist nations had given aid to the rebels, and because the Soviets were verbally hostile to the British-dominated Athens government, American diplomats assumed a significant Soviet involvement and predicted that both Greece and Turkey would become "Soviet puppets" after a "Soviet conquest."[115] Yet the Soviet Union gave little, if any, aid to the EAM, ignored the Greek Communists, and even tried to persuade Yugoslavia to do the same.[116] The historian can understand how American leaders came to think as they did but may also question why they abandoned careful and complex analysis in favor of soothing and distorting simplicity.

---

[112] See Paterson, *Containment and the Cold War.*
[113] "Background Memorandum on Greece," Mar. 3, 1947, Box 1, Jones Papers.
[114] Geoffrey Chandler, *The Divided Land: An Anglo-Greek Tragedy* (London, 1959), p. 81. Chandler was a British officer flown into Greece in September, 1944, to work with the EAM-ELAS. In March, 1946, he joined the British embassy in Athens. His book depicts well the depth of hostility between the left and right in Greece and the cruelties committed by both sides. He himself presents no evidence of Soviet involvement.
[115] *Foreign Relations, 1947* (Washington, D.C., 1972), V, 51. See also Central Intelligence Group, "Revised Soviet Tactics in International Affairs," Jan. 6, 1947, Folder 596, Byrnes Papers.
[116] Iatrides, *Revolt in Athens,* pp. 53, 74-76, 101, 107, 110, 123-24, 129, 141, 164n, 165, 174, 221-24, 248, 253, 279-80; Stephen G. Xydis, "Greece and the Yalta Declaration," *American Slavic and East European Review,* XX (February, 1961), 7; Churchill, *Triumph and Tragedy,* p. 293.

When the ELAS-EAM organized its resistance against the German army in 1941-1942 it had no ties with Moscow, and a large proportion of its membership was non-Communist. Not until mid-1944 did a team of ten Soviet military officers visit ELAS headquarters, and they were not convinced that the organization deserved support. By 1944 the resistance fighters had occupied a major part of Greece, yet Russia remained aloof. The violence which erupted in December was not Moscow-directed; indeed, the Soviet Union's attitude was still one of "gloomy disinterest."[117] A few months later, Ambassador MacVeagh, although still believing that the EAM would someday link up with the Soviet Union, concluded that the EAM leaders had "waited in vain for Russia to support them in their revolt. . . ."[118] As Anglo-American criticism of Soviet actions in eastern Europe increased in 1945-1946, Moscow stepped up its own criticisms of the British-American role in Greece. After the March, 1946, elections in Greece, which the royalists won handily under less than democratic conditions and which the EAM boycotted in protest, the EAM again engaged the Athens regime in civil war. Although Bulgaria, Albania, and Yugoslavia helped the rebels with supplies and provided a sanctuary, Moscow did not order the new outbreak of violence, and Yugoslavia, the major source of support, acted independently on its own initiative.[119] The Russians watched and waited while verbally lashing the Greek government. Shortly after the Truman Doctrine announcement, they withdrew their ambassador from Athens but continued to withhold assistance from the EAM.

Increasingly the EAM turned to Tito for help, setting off a struggle between pro-Tito and pro-Stalin factions within the organization. The majority decided to rely on Yugoslavia, and Russia refused to recognize the revolutionary government proclaimed in December, 1947. In early 1948 Stalin attempted to convince the Yugoslavs to cease their participation in the Greek civil war, telling them that the "uprising in Greece has to fold up."[120] He wanted no part of the revolt because it might prompt a confrontation between Russia and the Anglo-American coalition and because the Greek Communists were aligning with his arch-foe Tito.[121] The Greek rebels

[117] Edgar O'Ballance, *The Greek Civil War, 1944-1949* (New York, 1966), p. 78; C. M. Woodhouse, *Apple of Discord: A Survey of Recent Greek Politics in Their International Setting* (London, 1948), pp. 198-99; Iatrides, *Revolt in Athens*, pp. 74-76 (the quotation appears on p. 221).

[118] *Foreign Relations, 1945*, VIII, 117 (Mar. 10, 1945). See also Sir Reginald Leeper, *When Greek Meets Greek* (London, 1950), pp. xvi-xvii. For MacVeagh's belief that the EAM and Moscow would eventually draw together, see Iselin, "Truman Doctrine," and Iatrides, *Revolt in Athens*, both of which make extensive use of the MacVeagh Papers.

[119] Phyllis Auty, *Tito: A Biography* (New York, 1970), p. 251.

[120] Stalin, quoted in Djilas, *Conversations with Stalin*, p. 181. See also Iatrides, *Revolt in Athens*, p. 224n; Barnet, *Intervention and Revolution*, pp. 110-12; Weiner, "Truman Doctrine," p. 89-118.

[121] Djilas, *Conversations with Stalin*, pp. 181-83; Dedijer, *Tito*, pp. 321-22.

became victims of the open schism between Russia and Yugoslavia in mid-1948. They began to shift toward Stalin as resentment grew over Tito's apparent attempt to influence the EAM, which by now was largely Communist. When the Greek Communists denounced Tito in mid-1949, he retaliated by closing his border to the insurgents, making it possible for United States-directed Greek regulars to trap them. With supplies and an important escape route closed to them, and with no Soviet assistance, the rebellion collapsed. On October 16, 1949, the EAM declared a cease-fire, and the civil war once again ended.

It was not the Truman Doctrine alone, with its economic and military aid and advisers,[122] which "saved" Greece's "freedom," as Truman later claimed. Greek guerrillas numbered between twenty-two and twenty-five thousand in late 1948, whereas in late 1947 there were only fifteen to eighteen thousand. What crushed the Greek revolution was the combination of Stalin's nonsupport, Anglo-American intervention, and Tito's decision to seal off the border.[123] Yet American leaders have continued to argue that the Truman Doctrine stopped Communist-Soviet aggression in the Near East and have cited Greece as a precedent for containing "Communism" elsewhere. As one student of this response to revolution in Greece concluded: "The fifth-column analogy from World War II dominated official thinking. The possibility that men had taken to the hills for reasons of their own and not as agents of a foreign power was never seriously considered."[124]

"Democracy" and "economic stability" never implanted themselves in Iran, Greece, or Turkey after 1945, despite the outpouring of millions of dollars in United States aid and the efforts of hundreds of military advisers. Yet these countries were drawn into the American sphere of influence. The results of this postwar policy in the Near and Middle East were embittered relations with the Soviet Union, continued support for anti-reform governments, instability, military alliances, and the acquisition of raw materials.[125] The aid

---

[122] Over three hundred and fifty American officers accompanied the Greek army in its campaign against the EAM in 1947-1949. Lieutenant General James A. Van Fleet advised the Greek general staff. By the spring of 1952 the United States had expended over $500 million to build up Greek military forces. In Turkey, United States advisers helped Americanize that country's army. Both Greece and Turkey joined NATO in 1952, and a year later the United States obtained military bases in both countries. Library of Congress, *War and Postwar Greece*, pp. 112, 127; U.S., Department of State, *President's Eighth Report to Congress on Assistance to Greece and Turkey* (Washington, D.C., 1949); Barnet, *Intervention and Revolution*, pp. 125-27; Bickham Sweet-Escott, *Greece: A Political and Economic Survey, 1939-1953* (London, 1954), p. 105; Kirk, *Middle East, 1945-1950*, pp. 38-56; Theodore A. Couloumbis, *Greek Political Reaction to American and NATO Influences* (New Haven, Conn., 1966); Hurewitz, *Middle East Dilemmas*, pp. 200-206.

[123] Weiner, "Truman Doctrine," pp. 110-18.

[124] Barnet, *Intervention and Revolution*, p. 121.

[125] Economic improvement in Greece and Turkey took hold very slowly, the Greek government's ineptitude and corruption continued, and the leadership in both countries initiated repressive measures to silence domestic critics. The Greek regime became largely dependent on American aid: in 1950, for example, one-quarter of the country's national

to Greece and Turkey and the implementation of the Truman Doctrine solidified developing blocs. The Truman Doctrine probably accelerated the subjugation of Hungary and the tightening of Soviet control over eastern Europe in 1947. In exaggerating the Soviet threat against Iran and Turkey and in misinterpreting the Greek civil war, the United States exerted its economic power in such a way as to further divide the world. Yet aid to Greece and Turkey provided Americans with another "lesson." As Truman explained it in 1952, "We helped the Greeks to defeat a Communist invasion of their soil, and our aid has kept Turkey free and independent."[126] The vaguely defined containment doctrine served as the rationale for American intervention on a global scale thereafter. But in 1947 there was still the recovery of western Europe and West Germany to worry about.

---

income derived from the Marshall Plan. With this aid the United States gained influence so extensive that it interfered in Greek politics and, of course, in the Greek economy. Paul R. Porter, "Report of the Chief, Special Mission to Greece Economic Cooperation Administration, September 1949 to November 1950," Nov. 11, 1950, briefing book (in his possession, Washington, D.C.); C. A. Munkman, *American Aid to Greece: A Report of the First Ten Years* (New York, 1958), p. 58; Barnet, *Intervention and Revolution,* pp. 125-26; Stephen Rousseos, *The Death of a Democracy* (New York, 1968), pp. 81-87; Couloumbis, *Greek Political Reaction,* pp. 31-32, 53-68. The United States did realize some economic benefits from the Near and Middle East. By 1949 Turkey was its largest supplier of chromium and had increased its production of manganese ore. In 1954 an international oil consortium was established in Iran, with British-Dutch interests amounting to 54 percent, American interests 40 percent, and French interests 6 percent. The Soviet Union was noticeably absent from the arrangement. New American oil concessions were obtained elsewhere in the Middle East, and by 1953 American companies were producing 70 percent of the Middle East's oil. Greece and Turkey, the chairman of the Commission on Foreign Economic Policy reported in 1954, were among a handful of nations which had revised their corporate laws to attract American capital investment. Minutes, President's Materials Policy Commission, Mar. 29, 1951, Box 5, Records of President's Materials Policy Commission, Truman Library; Hurewitz, *Middle East Dilemmas,* pp. 33, 43-45, 229; Randall, *Foreign Economic Policy,* p. 29; Commerce, *U.S. Business Investments,* p. 92; Lenczowski, *Middle East in World Affairs,* pp. 184-89; Lenczowski, *Oil and State,* pp. 10-11; Mattison, *Survey of American Interests,* p. xi; "U.S. Share in Suez Traffic Mounts in 1947-1948," *Foreign Commerce Weekly,* XXXV (June 27, 1949), 10; Mikesell and Chenery, *Arabian Oil,* pp. 57, 131. See also the Soviet complaints that the United States was using Iran as a "strategic base," in Hurewitz, *Middle East Dilemmas,* p. 29; I. Korobeinikov and I. Shatalov, "The Grasping Policy of British and American Imperialism in Iran," *Voprosy Ekonomiki* (1951), in *Soviet Press Translations,* VII (Jan. 1, 1952), 3-10.
    [126] Speech, Oct. 9, 1952, Box 53, Elsey Papers.

CHAPTER 10

RECOVERY CRISIS AND COORDINATION:
THE MARSHALL PLAN

Many prominent Americans were dismayed in March of 1947 that the president had delivered an alarmist speech filled with warnings of imminent crisis and global confrontation, but mentioning aid only for Greece and Turkey, a speech which appeared to be both negative and hastily prepared. Even before Truman handed a somewhat resentful Congress his fait accompli, administration figures had begun to discuss long-range coordinated aid to other countries. After the address, publicists Walter Lippmann and Marquis Childs, congressmen, and Dean Acheson, among others, demanded to "see the whole picture at once."[1] They wanted a comprehensive aid program to meet the world's reconstruction needs, especially to alleviate economic disorder and political unrest in countries like Italy and France, the homes of large Communist parties. Americans became confident that a unified aid program closely supervised by Washington would achieve peace and prosperity— economic recovery, political stability, weakened Communist parties, healthy multilateral world trade, and American economic well being and security. By 1947 they had come to realize that the foreign aid (in excess of $9 billion) furnished to western Europe by the United States since the end of the war had been too haphazardly given in a variety of emergency loans, grants, surplus sales, and international assistance, and had not fulfilled its goals.[2] But the European Recovery Program (ERP) or Marshall Plan would be different; it would also be the "Truman Doctrine in Action."[3]

---

[1] *Foreign Relations, 1947,* III, 197-204 (the quotation by Sherman Sheppard of the Bureau of the Budget, April 7, appears on p. 200); Walter Lippmann, "Today and Tomorrow," *Washington Post,* Mar. 13, 1947; Marquis Childs, "Washington Calling," *ibid.*

[2] Commerce, *Foreign Aid, 1940-1951,* pp. 16-17. The International Bank also issued $250 million to France (May 9, 1947), $191 million to the Netherlands (Aug. 7, 1947), $40 million to Denmark (Aug. 22, 1947), and $12 million to Luxembourg (Aug. 28, 1947). The participants in the ERP constituted "western Europe," in the American mind: Austria, Belgium, Denmark, France, Greece, Iceland, Ireland, Italy, Luxembourg, The Netherlands, Norway, Portugal, Sweden, Turkey, the United Kingdom, Trieste, and West Germany.

[3] Handwritten notes by George Elsey, Nov. 29, 1947, Box 19, Elsey Papers.

Less than three months after the dramatic Truman Doctrine speech, on June 5, 1947, Secretary of State George C. Marshall stood before a Harvard commencement audience and asked for a new foreign aid plan for Europe. After the address, which lacked specifics, United States and western European committees formulated the European Recovery Program (ERP), a four-year, United States-directed program of grants and loans under a new agency of the United States government called the Economic Cooperation Administration (ECA). With West German but without Soviet or eastern European participation and outside the United Nations Economic Commission for Europe (ECE), the ERP helped shape and reflect the Cold War schism. This format grew from the deliberate manner in which the United States presented and shaped the Marshall Plan and ignored the ECE and from an uncompromising Russia which read the ERP as an aggressive anti-Soviet undertaking. As one commentator has noted, "with the Marshall Plan the cold war assumes the character of position warfare. Both sides become frozen in mutual unfriendliness."[4] Both Russia and the United States attempted to forge mutually exclusive recovery programs for their spheres; the confrontation seemed to be institutionalized by the Marshall and Molotov Plans.

APPROACHING THE WATERFALL

George C. Marshall alone did not conceive the Marshall Plan, although as secretary of state he encouraged and guided its preparation. His famous speech represented the collective thinking of his department over several months. Dean Acheson, as with the Truman Doctrine, was a chief architect, for while Marshall and Under Secretary Clayton were absent from Washington attending international conferences, he ran the State Department. The grand overseer was Harry S. Truman, who had allied his administration unequivocally with the goals of European recovery, anti-Communism, and expanded world trade. The continued crisis in Greece, further deterioration of Soviet-American relations as exemplified by the inconclusive foreign ministers meetings, Communist electoral and trade union strength in Italy and France, a serious European dollar shortage, and an unusually hard winter, disruptive to already sick economies, provided the immediate stimulants.

Before and after the Truman Doctrine speech, new committees began to tackle the problem of enlarging United States aid in a more systematic way. On March 11 a special group within the State-War-Navy Coordinating Committee (SWNCC) began its study, and Dean Acheson established a special foreign aid committee within the State Department. They were instructed to hurry.[5] The SWNCC subcommittee responded with a lengthy document on

---

[4] Ulam, *Expansion and Coexistence*, p. 437.
[5] *Foreign Relations, 1947*, III, 197-99.

April 21. Admittedly a "hasty analysis," this report recommended "a well-considered comprehensive world-wide program" to enable the United States to "take positive, forehanded, and preventative action in the matter of promotion of U.S. national interests. . . ."[6] Several countries were in "urgent" need of United States aid, and others would be needy later.[7] The nation's economic power should be used to "support economic stability and orderly political processes throughout the world and oppose the spread of chaos and extremism." Echoing the words of the Truman Doctrine speech concerning resistance to militant minorities, the report again combined the themes of expansion and containment. The United States would "orient foreign nations toward the U.S." (and toward the United Nations) and would "prevent the growth" of hostile foreign power. Sources of raw materials, the report went on, must be kept in "friendly hands," military collaboration abroad must be continued for American security, and American exports must be financed to head off a business depression.[8] It was a persuasive document which found its way into other speeches and reports, including the Harvard address. Although it did not establish a dollar figure, it did articulate the rationale for a massive new foreign aid effort. Less emotional than Truman's speech, the report nevertheless conveyed a sense of urgency and crisis.

One week after the filing of the SWNCC report, Marshall returned to Washington from an exasperating Foreign Ministers Conference with the Russians over the rehabilitation of Germany. Convinced that the Soviets were waiting eagerly for western Europe to collapse, Marshall reported in a radio message to the nation that the "recovery of Europe has been slower than has been expected. Disintegrating forces are becoming evident. The patient is sinking while the doctors deliberate." Action on the part of the United States was required immediately.[9] Marshall himself moved quickly; on April 29 he called George F. Kennan, then a lecturer at the War College, to his office and ordered him to establish a Policy Planning Staff to study the crisis in Europe and to make recommendations within two weeks. A harried Kennan scurried about to find a staff and put his team to work on May 5. He agreed with his chief that the Soviets were exploiting weak economies through Communist parties with the goal of subjugation and that western Europe ranked first in America's list of priorities.[10]

The pace further quickened when Acheson traveled to Mississippi on May 8 to address the influential Delta Council, a group of leading businessmen of

[6] *Ibid.*, pp. 205-6.

[7] In "urgent" need and in order of priority: Greece, Turkey, Iran, Italy, Korea, France, Austria, and Hungary. Note that the bill to aid Greece and Turkey had not yet passed and Hungary had not yet had its Communist coup. Less urgent were the needs of China, Great Britain, Belgium, Luxembourg, the Netherlands, the Philippines, Portugal, Czechoslovakia, and Poland. *Ibid.*, p. 206.

[8] *Ibid.*, pp. 208-11.

[9] *DSB*, XVI (May 11, 1947), 924.

[10] Kennan, *Memoirs*, pp. 325-29; *Foreign Relations, 1947*, III, 220n.

one of the world's richest agricultural regions. Joseph Jones was again the primary speechwriter, and Acheson told him to "elaborate our Greco-Turkish program into a more comprehensive statement of foreign policy."[11] The speech on the seriousness of the European crisis was straightforward. Americans, Acheson declared, may see peace or anarchy in Europe depending on the quantities of food and fuel available there. His figures were startling. In 1947 the United States would export $16 billion worth of goods and services, yet the nations of the world would be $8 billion short in payment. Much of the deficit would be closed through American loans, grants, and private investments abroad. "But what of next year, and the year after that?" Although he presented no plan, he did conclude that new American aid would have to be concentrated in areas where economic instability threatened political order, that Germany and Japan would have to be reconstructed, and that the president would need the authority to control exports: "It is necessary if we are to preserve our own freedoms and our own democractic institutions. It is necessary to our national security. And it is our duty and our privilege as human beings." As Acheson recalled in 1953, "the skiff was approaching the waterfall."[12] Obviously stung by Walter Lippmann's criticisms of the Truman Doctrine and appeals for a comprehensive program, Jones sent Lippmann a copy of the Delta speech the day before it was delivered. This speech, Jones insisted, was "positive."[13]

Kennan was working his staff hard. With remarkable speed, it produced an important memorandum dated May 23. Communist activities, it began, were not at the root of western European problems; they stemmed from the war which had so disrupted European life. American aid should be aimed not at combating Communism but at correcting the economic maladjustment "which makes European society vulnerable to exploitation by any and all totalitarian movements and which Russian communism is now exploiting." Using words to appear later in the Harvard address, Kennan's report suggested strongly that Europe itself initiate a new joint program. "With the best of will, the American people cannot really help those who are not willing to help themselves." The Economic Commission for Europe might initiate the project as a general European-wide (not just western European) effort, but "it would be essential that this be done in such a form that the Russian satellite countries would either exclude themselves by unwillingness to accept the

[11] Memorandum, [n.d.], Box 1, Jones Papers. For background on the speech, see memorandum of conversation with Senator Eastland, Apr. 8, 1947, *ibid.*; notes on Acheson speech of May, 1947, *ibid.*

[12] See *DSB*, XVI (May 18, 1947), 991-4, for the speech. The Acheson statement of 1953 is quoted in Price, *Marshall Plan*, p. 24n. See also Acheson, *Present at the Creation*, pp. 227-30, and Jones, *Fifteen Weeks*, pp. 199-207. The day after Acheson's speech, Marshall sent a letter, the text of which was made public, to Philip D. Reed of General Electric. It too linked political harmony to economic stability. *DSB*, XVI (May 18, 1947), 996.

[13] Joseph Jones to Walter Lippmann, May 7, 1947, Box 1, Jones Papers.

proposed conditions or agree to abandon the exclusive orientation of their economies." Russia would not be permitted to block the new program. At this point, Kennan's report was less than lucid; his working principle had been that a plan was needed for western Europe, but now he appeared to be opening the door to eastern European participation. Revealing his own dissatisfaction with the Truman Doctrine, Kennan closed the memorandum with a plea for eradicating two misconceptions arising from the Truman Doctrine: first, that the United States would only react defensively to Communist pressure and would not attempt to restore devastated economies unless a Communist menace were present; second, that Washington would give aid to any nation threatened by Communism. In short, Kennan sought some limitations on the anti-Communist crusade, while he wanted it known that the United States was waging a self-defined and self-interested war against economic instability.[14]

Kennan's document, soon to be discussed at the highest levels, was joined by another from the shaky hand of Under Secretary Will Clayton. Clayton had spent much of April and May in Europe establishing the ECE and negotiating tariffs at Geneva; he returned weakened by bronchial pneumonia, yet determined to talk about the European crisis. Europe, he recorded in his influential memorandum of May 27, "is steadily deteriorating. The political position reflects the economic." He outlined food and coal shortages and a $5 billion balance of payments deficit. America would have to save Europe, "not from the Russians" but from "starvation and chaos." He specifically recommended an aid program of $6 to $7 billion a year for three years. This program would not be another UNRRA. *"The United States must run this show."*[15]

The State Department meeting of May 28 was decisive. Clayton and Kennan brought their memoranda. Marshall and Acheson were accompanied by the various directors of offices. Clayton opened the discussion with a stirring account of misery in Europe and warnings that severe disintegration there would lead to a depression in the United States. A firm believer in the interlocking components of the peace and prosperity theme, Clayton so

[14] *Foreign Relations, 1947,* III, 223-30. See also Kennan, *Memoirs,* pp. 335-42. On May 23, 1947, Marshall released a statement criticizing the House for increasing duties on wool at a time when Clayton was in Geneva attempting to reduce tariffs. In his message, Marshall pointed out that expanding trade would help the United States to export and Europe to recover. Truman vetoed the Wool Act on June 26. *DSB,* XVI (June 8, 1947), 1137; *Public Papers, Truman, 1947,* pp. 309-10.

[15] *Foreign Relations, 1947,* III, 230-32. See also William L. Clayton, "Gatt, the Marshall Plan, and OECD," *Political Science Quarterly,* LXXVIII (December, 1963), 493-503. Clayton prepared a terse memorandum on March 5, 1947, which he kept to himself but which contributed to his report of May 27. In the earlier version he wrote that Europe faced disaster: "If Greece and then Turkey succumb, the whole Middle East will be lost. France may then capitulate to the Communists. As France goes, all Western Europe and North Africa will go." Complete memorandum in Ellen Clayton Garwood, *Will Clayton: A Short Biography* (Austin, Tex., 1958), pp. 115-18.

moved the conferees with his story that he is often credited with getting the Marshall Plan launched. Both the Clayton and Kennan staff memoranda emphasized a joint European program, and few questioned the point. But quickly a major problem arose—whether to include or exclude eastern Europe. Clayton was emphatic that western Europe did not need eastern Europe in the program. Kennan said "play it straight," and it was agreed that the plan should be presented in such a way as not to exclude the eastern European countries, but to let them exclude themselves. The conditions laid down would be difficult for them to meet: abandonment of state-trading practices and Soviet influence in their economies. As Kennan recalled, "we would not ourselves draw a line of division through Europe." The tenor of the meeting would suggest that few thought the countries in the Soviet sphere would participate.

Kennan successfully drove home his point that the initiative for a new program should come from Europe, although others stated that American pressure would have to be applied. The role of the ECE was also discussed; Clayton dominated the topic with a strong statement that the ECE was "completely unusable as a forum" because he thought the U.S.S.R. would block constructive action in it. Dean Rusk replied that the American public might not be enthusiastic about another program which bypassed the United Nations. The question of the ECE was left unresolved. Finally Acheson addressed the major problem of timing. He recommended that over the next four to six months the administration prepare Congress and the public for new foreign aid legislation, which might be presented in the special fall session of Congress or in the new session beginning in January, 1948. At this time Washington could also open talks with other governments. These recommendations were generally followed. The morning meeting of May 28 had been productive; the next step was up to Marshall, who apparently listened and said little during the discussion.[16]

That noon, Dean Acheson lunched with a dozen senators, who seemed eager for information about American policy toward the European crisis. Senator Brien McMahon of Connecticut announced firmly that he would vote against another fait accompli handed him by the administration. Acheson was impressed and quickly informed Marshall of this attitude. He urged him to begin to court the favor of Senator Vandenberg and to make a speech on the problem in Europe. He suggested that "solutions" be announced later.[17] The next day Marshall decided to confirm his tentative acceptance of a speaking engagement at Harvard and, against the advice of Acheson, who feared that a commencement address would draw little news coverage, to use the occasion

[16] *Foreign Relations, 1947,* III, 234-36; "Meeting of May 28, 1947," Box 1, Jones Papers; Kennan, *Memoirs,* p. 342; Acheson, *Present at the Creation,* pp. 230-32; Jones, *Fifteen Weeks,* pp. 247-49; Dean Acheson, *Sketches from Life of Men I Have Known* (New York, 1961), p. 157; Bohlen, *Transformation,* p. 91.

[17] *Foreign Relations, 1947,* III, 232-33.

for his major speech. He instructed his special assistant Charles E. Bohlen to draft a speech; Bohlen drew heavily upon Clayton's memorandum and the Policy Planning Staff report for the text.

The Harvard speech was indeed a summary of widespread thinking in the administration. Calmly, in less than fifteen hundred words, Marshall described a distraught Europe barely recovering from the war's destruction. Machinery needed replacing; fields needed plowing; food and fuel were scarce. Europe must have help to face "economic, social and political deterioration of a very grave character." He called upon the European nations to agree together on their requirements, for the initiative for a joint program must come from Europe. He offered no plan, but said simply that the United States would help. His message skirted the issue of eastern European participation, and he did not mention Russia specifically. But some words were directed at Moscow: "Any government that is willing to assist in the task of recovery will find full cooperation, I am sure, on the part of the United States Government. Any government which maneuvers to block the recovery of other countries cannot expect help from us."[18]

Marshall had ordered the State Department not to publicize his speech, and newsmen were given no advance notice of its importance. He apparently feared public disapproval of a dramatically announced new foreign aid expenditure. Truman's news conference comment that the coup in Hungary was an "outrage" actually received greater press coverage the next day. However, to make certain that the British understood the significance of the speech, on June 4 Acheson called in three top British correspondents, revealed its import, and told them to send the text to their editors, who should bring it to the immediate attention of Foreign Minister Ernest Bevin. In retrospect, this seems a strange way to conduct diplomatic affairs, but Washington wanted to avoid public criticism about another shocking crisis, to have it appear that Europeans were appealing to the United States, and to place the burden for any failure on the Europeans themselves.[19]

THE EUROPEAN RESPONSE

Bevin soon acquired a copy of Marshall's address, but it came from one of the British newsmen, not from the British embassy. There was immediate

---

[18] *DSB*, XVI (June 15, 1947), 1159-60. Bohlen gives his account in *Transformation*, pp. 88-91. See also Acheson, *Present at the Creation*, pp. 232-34, and Jones, *Fifteen Weeks*, pp. 254-56. For other studies on the preparation of the Marshall Plan, see Charles P. Kindleberger's memorandum of July 22, 1948, Document 23, "Correspondence . . . Not Part of the White House Central Files," Truman Papers, and his "The Marshall Plan and the Cold War," *International Journal*, XXIII (Summer, 1968), 369-82; William C. Mallalieu, "The Origins of the Marshall Plan: A Study in Policy Formulation and National Leadership," *Political Science Quarterly*, LXXIII (December, 1958), 481-505.

[19] Bohlen, *Transformation*, pp. 89-90; typescript, Leonard Miall (BBC) interview, European Recovery Project, June 17, 1964; Jones, *Fifteen Weeks*, pp. 255-56; *Public Papers, Truman, 1947*, p. 265; *Foreign Relations, 1947*, III, 235.

consternation in the Foreign Office. Bevin decided not to ask Marshall what he meant for fear that "if you ask questions, you'll get answers you don't want. Our problem is what *we* do, not what *he meant.*"[20] On June 7 French Foreign Minister Georges Bidault directed his ambassador in Washington to alert Marshall to France's interest. On June 14 Bevin asked Bidault to meet with him to discuss Marshall's proposal, and Bidault informed the Soviets that France desired to exchange views on the Marshall speech with both Britain and Russia.

The Bevin-Bidault exploratory talks of June 17 and 18 were at first icy. The French were worried about the reaction of the Communist Party, which at the time was effectively exploiting the issue of the American rebuilding of West Germany. Bidault also expressed some feeling to Jefferson Caffery, the United States ambassador to France, that Bevin was stealing the "show." The joint communiqués simply welcomed the idea of a European recovery program, in liaison with appropriate U.N. agencies, and invited V. M. Molotov to join the two ministers in discussion the following week. Privately Bidault and Bevin hoped Molotov would not accept. Bidault worried that Russia would be obstructive and that the United States did not have enough money to go around. Both expected the ECE, which would hold another session in July, to figure in the program, but their attitude toward the ECE was guarded.[21]

The Marshall speech and the invitation must have deeply troubled Soviet leaders, although the lack of Soviet documents makes an assessment difficult. Certainly, the apparent openendedness of the Marshall proposal and the ever-present suspicions of a capitalist trap must have produced vigorous discussions, at a time when the Soviets had hardly completed their diatribes against the Truman Doctrine and the developing Anglo-American coopera- tion. *Pravda*'s comments less than two weeks after the Harvard speech were not friendly: "Mr. Marshall's plan is, not withstanding its apparent novelty, only a repetition of the Truman plan for political pressure with the help of dollars, a plan for interference in the domestic affairs of other countries." *Pravda* argued perceptively that it would be contradictory for the United States to include eastern Europe in an American undertaking, in the light of its hostile policy toward that area, and that Marshall was attempting to make it appear that Russia and eastern Europe "are excluding themselves. . . ." *Tass* added on June 19 that it was reasonable to think that the Bevin-Bidault talks were "nothing less than an attempt to make a deal behind the back of the

[20] Acheson, quoting Bevin from memory, in Robert H. Ferrell, *George C. Marshall* (New York, 1966), p. 112.

[21] *Foreign Relations, 1947*, III, 251-60, 262-63; Paul E. Koefod, *New Concept in the Quest for Peace: Marshall Plan, Aspect of Power Politics* (Geneva, 1950), pp. 115, 119, 123-27; Kindleberger, "Marshall Plan and Cold War," p. 337; Ferrell, *Marshall*, pp. 113-14; Georges Bidault, *Resistance: The Political Autobiography of Georges Bidault* (New York, 1967), p. 150.

Soviet Union and other European countries," and "what are the political considerations involved?" Yet Russia surprised many by announcing on June 22 that it would send a delegation to a Paris meeting with France and Great Britain. The announcement betrayed some irritation over the talks by stating that Russia was uninformed about any "conditions" the United States might impose and about any "measures" thus far discussed by the two Foreign Ministers.[22]

Meanwhile, Clayton went to London on June 24 to begin two days of intense talks with Bevin and the British Cabinet. The topics were wide-ranging, but the discussion usually came back to the economic plight of the British. Bombarding Clayton with gloomy statistics and reminders of the failure of the British loan, the British appealed for special treatment, "some temporary interim solution," so that they could participate in a European-wide program later. Clayton was unimpressed with the argument that Britain was different from the rest of Europe because it was an empire with global responsibilities and heavy occupation expenses in Germany and had to contribute more than most nations to Europe's economic revival. British leaders at first balked at the idea of British membership in a European "pool" or of economic integration. Clayton replied that the United States would not tolerate "piecemeal assistance"; the British would have to join in a European solution. At times the discussion was vigorous, especially during the American criticism of Britain's economic performance and of the delay of several months in giving the American embassy adequate facts about that performance. The British, for their part, were annoyed that Clayton carried no "plan" with him and could often respond in only the vaguest manner to questions about procedures and organization. In the final meeting of June 26 the touchy issue of the Soviet and eastern European relationship to European recovery was raised by Bevin. Clayton probably reinforced the British hostility to Soviet participation by stating that unless there was a major change in Soviet foreign policy the American people would not approve financial assistance for Russia. Bevin was encouraged to go ahead with the "Marshall program" if the Russians remained outside it.[23]

Molotov arrived in Paris for talks with Bevin and Bidault on June 27, and it is an open question whether he came with predetermined orders to obstruct a cohesive European program. On the eve of the conference *Pravda*'s columns were more conciliatory and complimentary than they had been, and nobody knew what to expect from the Soviets except suspicion and hard bargaining. Indeed, almost immediately upon his arrival, Molotov asked Bidault what the British and French "had done behind his back." Ambassador to Russia Walter Bedell Smith was convinced that the Russians were going to Paris for

[22] Quoted in Koefod, *New Concept*, pp. 120-21. See also *Foreign Relations, 1947*, III, 294-95.

[23] *Foreign Relations, 1947*, III, 268-93. See also Ferrell, *Marshall*, pp. 114-18.

"destructive" purposes, and Bevin believed that the one hundred advisers in the Soviet delegation were really spies sent to agitate among French Communists. Yet, as Bevin recalled to Acheson, it was not until well into the discussions that Molotov was handed a note which, from the change in his tone and pained expression, probably consisted of Moscow's rejection of a joint program.[24]

Bevin and Bidault began the conference cool toward the Russians and determined, if not to exclude Russia, at least to proceed without her should agreement be difficult. Backstage, United States diplomats listened and conferred. The British and French gave Caffery detailed accounts of the Bevin-Bidault-Molotov meetings, which he cabled to Washington.[25] At the first gathering, as indicated by Molotov's question, quoted above, it was clear that the Russians were suspicious of the previous Bevin-Bidault meeting and Clayton's talks in London, and Molotov, seemingly to expose any prior agreements, proposed that the delegates ask Washington the exact sum the United States would grant to a program and whether Congress would appropriate the money. Both Bevin and Bidault rejected the idea, lecturing Molotov on the uncertainties of the American political system, the need to come up with an integrated plan first, and the humility with which debtors should approach creditors. There the first meeting closed. Caffery reported to Washington that Molotov was probing, cautious, and affable and Bevin insistent that the Soviets not be allowed any obstructionist or delaying tactics.[26]

Molotov opened the second meeting (June 28) by rejecting a closely organized program. He argued that each nation should inform the United States of its needs for credits or supplies. Molotov agreed that there should be collaboration, but only to the extent that a joint list of needs be presented to Washington. Demonstrating a long-standing, if unreasonable, Soviet fear of divulging economic statistics, he stated that it was not the task of the conference to collect data on the resources of each needy country—that would be a violation of sovereignty. There was also disagreement on which nations should participate. Molotov desired to include ex-enemy states only in a "consultative capacity," but the French and British insisted that Germany, because of its coal, was essential to European recovery and should

[24] Maurice Peterson, *Both Sides of the Curtain* (London, 1950), p. 272; Acheson, *Present at the Creation*, pp. 234-35; Ferrell, *Marshall*, pp. 118-19; Koefod, *New Concept*, p. 122; *Foreign Relations, 1947*, III, 266, 296.

[25] For the reports see *Foreign Relations, 1947*, III, 297-307; letters in the Will Clayton Papers, Rice University Library; and Koefod, *New Concept*. For other accounts of the Paris meetings, see Senate, *ERP: Basic Documents*, pp. 152-56; Kenneth Ingram, *History of the Cold War* (New York, 1955), pp. 60-63; Warburg, *Long Road Home*, pp. 237-40; Smith, *State of Europe*, p. 98; typescript, Clayton interview, Marshall Plan Project, pp. 30-31, Ellen Garwood Papers, Truman Library; Northedge, *British Foreign Policy*, p. 44.

[26] *Foreign Relations, 1947*, III, 297-99.

be an integral part of the program. There was not much to arouse optimism after the second day. Bidault believed that the Russians showed restraint and suspected that the United States was trying to acquire influence in Europe but that they were "in no hurry" to conclude the conference. Bidault remarked to Caffery that Russia's "satellites" were putting pressure on Russia to participate, and Bevin added, "Molotov is dragging his feet. However Bidault and I gave him to understand yesterday we were determined in one way or another to go ahead with this with or without him."[27]

The conferees made no progress toward agreement at the third meeting on June 30. The debate was similar to that of the second day, but more divisive. Molotov propounded the Soviet position again, asking more specifically for a "committee of assistance" to catalog the needs of European states, for subcommittees to study food, fuel, and equipment, for specific requests for American aid, and for some ties with the ECE. The question, then, was the degree of coordination, and the Soviets sensed that the higher the degree, the more influence the United States could exercise over the program. Bevin-Bidault replies that an integrated program would not impinge on a nation's sovereignty, that Germany had to be included, and that Russia was asking America for a "blank check" did not convince a more contentious Molotov. It was during this exchange that Molotov was handed a partially decoded message from Moscow, which apparently directed him to reject a United States-dominated program. At the close of the session, Bevin was both angry with the Russians and pleased with himself: "This conference will break up tomorrow," Caffery reported the Foreign Minister's words. "I'm glad cards have been laid on the table and the responsibility will be laid at Moscow's door. They've tried to sabotage it in the conference room from the beginning, as I knew they would."[28]

The fourth meeting on July 1 was a curious and destructive session. The French presented a "compromise" statement that no nation would be forced to participate and that no nation would have to modify its internal economic system to receive aid, but the statement was submitted not because the French thought agreement was possible or because it changed the French-British position, but because it would mollify French public opinion and disarm the French Communists—the Soviets would appear as the obstructionists. Apart from Molotov's queries about the German role in European recovery, there was no substantive discussion in the fourth meeting.[29]

At the fifth and final session on July 2, Molotov accused France and Britain of plotting with the United States to dominate Europe. Seeing a challenge to the Soviet sphere of influence, he complained, "Today pressure

[27] *Ibid.,* pp. 299-301; Lewis Douglas to secretary of state, June 29, 1947, Clayton Papers; Koefod, *New Concept,* pp. 130-31.
[28] *Foreign Relations, 1947,* III, 301-4; Koefod, *New Concept,* pp. 132-33.
[29] *Foreign Relations, 1947,* III, 304-6.

may be exerted on Poland to make her produce more coal, even at the cost of restricting other Polish industries, just because certain European countries may be interested in it; tomorrow it will be said that Czechoslovakia must be asked to increase her agricultural output and curtail her machine-building industry. . . ." Bevin labelled Molotov's statements a "complete travesty." The next day Molotov abruptly departed for Moscow, and Bevin and Bidault settled down more comfortably and invited all European nations (with the exception of Spain and Russia, but including Turkey) to attend another Paris meeting scheduled for July 12.[30]

The expected, and on the part of some, the desired, had happened. The answer to the question of whether there ever was any chance of Soviet participation lies partly in Soviet fears about American intentions, especially after the abortive American loan, the curtailment of UNRRA, the Truman Doctrine, numerous anti-Soviet statements by leaders like Acheson, and the obvious British and French coldness toward Soviet participation. Russia also read an integrated program as a return to the *status quo ante bellum*; that is, western Europe would be the industrial center and eastern Europe the supplier of raw materials, especially grains and coal. The Russians feared this subordination of the agricultural East to the industrial West. Eastern European countries, with Russian prodding, had developed plans for industrialization. They were essentially undeveloped nations, and their economic difficulties had been augmented by the destruction of the war. As Vera Michales Dean noted in 1948, "experts on Eastern Europe believe that only through industrialization accompanied by modernization of agriculture can the countries of this region solve their rural overpopulation problems, and ultimately raise their standards of living."[31] A student of the area has added: "It is also understandable that the new regimes would wish, from a general feeling of patriotism, to diminish their countries' dependence on foreign countries."[32] Indeed, United States diplomats did expect the Russian participation to provide raw materials to help recovery in the West.[33] Finally, Soviet influence in or control over eastern Europe was not firm or decided in mid-1947, and a massive influx of American dollars into the region would certainly have challenged the Soviet position. Hence Russia put considerable pressure on Poland and Czechoslovakia, which were both eager to join, to reject participation. Kennan and other State Department officials have suggested that the Czech coup of February, 1948, in part represented the Soviet "defensive reaction" to the Marshall Plan.[34] It would have been difficult for Russia to accept a place in a program so conspicuously

[30] *Ibid.*, pp. 306-7; Molotov, *Problems of Foreign Policy*, p. 466; Caffery to secretary of state, July 2, 1947, Clayton Papers.

[31] Dean, "Economic Trends in Eastern Europe–II," p. 38.

[32] Hugh Seton-Watson, *East European Revolution* (New York, 1956), p. 254.

[33] Price, *Marshall Plan*, p. 24.

[34] Kennan, *Memoirs,* p. 379; State Department, "Weekly Review," Mar. 3, 1948, Box 20, Elsey Papers. See also Shulman, *Stalin's Foreign Policy Reappraised,* pp. 14-15.

dominated by the United States and geared more toward western than eastern Europe. One can only wonder, with Arnold Toynbee, whether, if the Marshall Plan had preceded the Truman Doctrine, Russia would have accepted membership.[35]

Perhaps the invitation to Russia to join a European recovery program was not terribly critical anyway. It would have been the utmost of illogic and contradiction for Congress to approve funds for the Soviet Union so shortly after it had been persuaded to pass the anti-Soviet Truman Doctrine. James P. Warburg was frank in asking whether people could "really assume that President Truman believed that the Congress, which he himself had indoctrinated with the spirit of an anti-Soviet crusade, would consent to a plan which made American dollars available to the Soviet Union and its satellites."[36] Then, too, some congressmen were still resentful about UNRRA, while others were calling for restrictions on Soviet-American trade.

Kennan had said "play it straight," so Marshall agreed to let the answer come from Moscow—an answer he and most State Department officials expected to be in the negative. It may have been Henry Wallace who prompted the State Department not to exclude Russia. Both State Department staffman Joseph Jones and Ambassador to Great Britain Lewis Douglas have mentioned as a relevant factor Wallace's early 1947 speeches advocating a massive European reconstruction plan with substantial assistance going to Russia.[37] Yet there was really no gamble in offering Russia access to a recovery program. Russia would shun any American-dominated program directed in large part against it, and the United States would not compromise on control. The invitation, then, was a diplomatic gesture intended to place the burden of rejection of the Marshall Plan and of the division of Europe on the Soviet Union.[38] Its propaganda value was immense: Americans and growing numbers of Europeans became all the more convinced that Russia was the obstructionist in Europe. Furthermore, as Kennan told Marshall, the Soviet position had strained Soviet relations with eastern Europe and with Communist parties in the West. "Events of past weeks the greatest blow to European communism since termination of hostilities," read Kennan's notes.[39]

The obstructionist image was further reinforced when Russia denounced the new Committee of European Economic Cooperation (CEEC), which was organized at a Paris meeting of sixteen nations in mid-July. During the

[35] Peter Calvocoressi, *Survey of International Affairs, 1947-1948* (London, 1952), p. 6.

[36] James P. Warburg, *Germany: Key to Peace* (Cambridge, Mass., 1953), p. 57. See also Masaryk's similar point in Werth, *Russia: Post-War Years*, p. 270.

[37] Joseph Jones to Dean Acheson, Apr. 24, 1947, Jones Papers; typescript, Douglas interview, Garwood Papers; Henry Wallace, *Toward World Peace* (New York, 1948), pp. 11-12.

[38] The Marshall Plan Project interviews with leading participants, housed in the Garwood Papers, reveal the same theme.

[39] *Foreign Relations, 1947,* III, 335 (July 21, 1947).

summer months the United States closely watched over the work of the CEEC subcommittees, warning them against depending too much on outside help and against asking for too large a sum. Clayton, for example, told Sir Oliver Franks that the tentative CEEC figure for four years of $28.2 billion in American aid "was out of the question." Clayton was blunt in informing Washington that the CEEC had to be told what to do: "I am convinced there is no other way to deal with this situation than to impose certain necessary conditions. If we fail to do so we are going to be presented with a bill which I don't think our people should or will meet."[40] United States officials were also irritated that the sixteen nations placed strong emphasis on national sovereignty and seemed to be preparing "shopping lists" of needs.[41] Just before the CEEC's final report of September 22, Clayton, Douglas, and Caffery helped revise this "European" document with an eye to its persuasiveness when put before the American people and Congress.[42] The final report was rather vague on the extent of cooperation in a European recovery program. The countries agreed to increase production, to reduce tariffs, and "to organize together the means by which common resources can be developed in partnership."[43]

Russia not only vehemently attacked the developing machinery for the Marshall Plan but it took organizational action of its own. Following the collapse of the tripartite Paris meetings, the Soviet Government laid the onus for that failure on the United States because it refused to give any information about its intentions. "Instead, the United States urges the appointment of a master committee . . . ," which would interfere in the internal affairs of nations by controlling trade and would, in this way, "make the economy of these countries dependent on the interests of the United States."[44] The language became harsher, but the message remained the same. The Soviet press and Soviet representatives at meetings of the ECE, the United Nations, and the Council of Foreign Ministers denounced the Marshall Plan as an imperialist venture dangerous to Europeans because of a potential depression in the United States and the uncertainty of congressional appropriations.[45]

This verbal assault was reinforced by the formation of the "Molotov Plan" and the Cominform. The Molotov Plan was never a carefully organized program but rather a series of trade treaties, signed in July, August, and September, 1947, between Russia and her eastern European neighbors,

[40] *Ibid.,* p. 379 (Aug. 25, 1947).
[41] *Ibid.,* pp. 372-75 (Aug. 24, 1947), 397 (Sept. 4, 1947).
[42] *Ibid.,* pp. 425-28 (Sept. 12, 1947).
[43] Committee of European Economic Co-operation, *General Report,* 2 vols. (Washington, D.C., 1947).
[44] July 8, 1947, in Robert E. Summers, ed., *Economic Aid to Europe: The Marshall Plan* (New York, 1948), pp. 113-14.
[45] "Economic Commission for Europe Convenes," *United Nations Bulletin,* III (July 15, 1947), 85; Keofod, *New Concept,* pp. 194-98; Carlyle, *Documents, 1947-1948,* pp. 58-59 (Vishinsky), 138 (Malenkov); Molotov, *Problems of Foreign Policy,* p. 487.

designed to halt any diversion of eastern European products to Marshall Plan nations, to draw the states more closely to Russia, and, probably, to alleviate the chagrin of the eastern European countries over having to boycott the ERP. The Cominform acted as a propaganda agency of the eastern European, French, and Italian Communist parties; it was organized in September specifically to undermine the Marshall Plan. General Andrei A. Zhdanov, founder of the Cominform, charged that the Truman Doctrine and the Marshall Plan were "an expression of a single policy, they are both an embodiment of the American design to enslave Europe." And he claimed, not inaccurately, that the "cornerstone of the 'Marshall Plan' is the restoration of the industrial areas of Western Germany...."[46]

MAKING ECONOMIC SENSE: THE DEBATE IN THE UNITED STATES

The noisy Soviet reaction made it easier for the Truman administration to convince Congress to underwrite the ERP. Interim aid of $597 million for Austria, China, France, and Italy, especially "to give the peoples of Europe the strength to hold out" until the ERP began, was authorized in December, 1947.[47] But the task of cultivating public support for the multi-billion-dollar ERP was more difficult. As late as November, 1947, according to a poll, 40 percent of the American people had never heard of the Marshall Plan.[48] A combination of shrewd government tactics and propaganda, pressure group organization, and shocking events in Europe had dissipated that ignorance by early 1948, the time at which the administration hoped Congress would pass Marshall Plan legislation.

United States officials had repeatedly instructed European leaders and the CEEC that their requests and reports had to be drafted in such a way that they would appeal to the "economic sense" of the American people.[49] Washington also took steps to ensure that the message of "economic sense" and national interest spread widely in the public mind. With the help of the State Department, several prominent Americans, including Dean Acheson, recently retired from the State Department, organized the Committee for the Marshall Plan to Aid European Recovery. Former Secretary of War Robert Patterson joined Acheson in its leadership, and former secretary Henry L. Stimson served as honorary president. The organizing meeting took place in

[46] Carlyle, *Documents, 1947-1948*, pp. 129-30 (Nov. 10, 1947).

[47] *Public Papers, Truman, 1947*, p. 493. The vote margins were large: in the Senate, 83 to 6; by voice in the House; the conference report passed by voice in Senate and by 313 to 82 in House. The appropriations bill amounted to $522 million. See Senate, *Interim Aid* and *Foreign Relations, 1947*, III, 470-84.

[48] American Institute of Public Opinion poll, cited in Pritchard, "Clayton," p. 350.

[49] See, for example, *Foreign Relations, 1947*, III, 317 (July 10, 1947), 356-60 (Aug. 14, 1947).

October 30, 1947, in New York City, only a few days after a White House
conference on the ERP attended by a group of prominent businessmen.[50] At
the organizing meeting held at the Harvard Club, Patterson, Arthur Page (a
New York businessman), Hugh Moore (Dixie Cup Company), Philip Reed
(General Electric), Herbert Swope (General Electric), Herbert Feis, James
Carey (CIO), and Herbert Lehman, among others, established a committee
which later ran full-page newspaper advertisements, circulated petitions,
organized speaker forums, initiated letter campaigns directed at Congress, and
prepared testimony for organizations like the Farmers' Union which appeared
before congressional committees.[51] The stature of the committee members,
its close cooperation with the State Department, and its diligent effort to
reach audiences ensured it a considerable influence in the Marshall Plan
debate.[52] Presidential assistant Richard E. Neustadt has concluded that the
committee was "one of the most effective instruments for public information
seen since the Second World War. . . ."[53] Standing with the almost solid front
of business leadership in endorsing the Marshall Plan were the American
Federation of Labor, the Congress of Industrial Organizations, Americans for
Democratic Action, Veterans of Foreign Wars, and the American Farm
Bureau Federation.[54]

A significant ally of the administration was one of the leading exponents
of bipartisanship, Senator Arthur Vandenberg. Shortly after Marshall's Harvard address, Vandenberg had informed the president that he would not
support a new European program unless Truman appointed a committee of
distinguished citizens to study it. In late June Truman named a high-level
bipartisan committee, headed by Secretary of Commerce W. Averell Harriman, after close consultation with Vandenberg.[55] This President's Committee

[50] "List of Persons Who Attended White House Conference, October 27, 1947," OF
426, Truman Papers; John Steelman to George Marshall, Oct. 16, 1947, ibid.; T. S.
Repplier to Steelman, Oct. 28, 1947, ibid.
[51] "Minutes of the Organizing Meeting of Committee for the Marshall Plan To Aid
Europe," Oct. 30, 1947, Box 2, Committee for Marshall Plan Records; Harold Stein
interview, Aug. 7, 1952, Price Oral History Project, Truman Library. For the numerous
petitions, see the Foregn Affairs Committee, 80A-H5.5, House Records.
[52] For the impressive membership list, see Senate, ERP, pp. 747-53. Acheson gives
examples of his busy speaking tour in Present at the Creation, pp. 240-41.
[53] Richard E. Neustadt, Presidential Power: The Politics of Leadership (New York,
1960), p. 49.
[54] For the support of various interest groups, see the hearings, Senate, ERP. For
business in particular, see Paterson, "Economic Cold War," pp. 399-421.
[55] The members were Hiland Batcheller (president, Allegheny-Ludlum Steel), Robert
Earl Buchanan (dean, Graduate College, Iowa State College), W. Randolph Burgess
(vice-chairman, National City Bank of N.Y.), James B. Carey (secretary-treasurer, CIO),
John L. Collyer (president, B. F. Goodrich), Granville Conway (president, Cosmopolitan
Shipping), Melvin F. Coolbaugh (Colorado School of Mines), Chester C. Davis (president,
Federal Reserve Bank, St. Louis), R. R. Deupree (president, Proctor & Gamble), Paul G.
Hoffman (president, Studebaker), Calvin B. Hoover (dean, Graduate School, Duke
University), Robert Koenig (president, Ayrshire Collieries Corporation), former Senator
Robert M. LaFollette, Jr., Edward S. Mason (dean, Graduate School of Public
Administration, Harvard University), George Meany (secretary-treasurer, AFL), Harold

on Foreign Aid shared information and ideas with two other groups charged by the president with analyzing the European recovery crisis and its impact on the United States and making public recommendations: a Department of the Interior committee headed by Julius Krug and the Council of Economic Advisers, chaired by Edwin G. Nourse. These committees issued reports in the fall of 1947 which argued, in the peace and prosperity vein, that a European recovery program was vital to the wellbeing of the United States and feasible, given the country's economic power, although some controls in the domestic economy would be necessary to avert strain.[56]

The majority of the members of the governmental committees and the diplomatic corps concerned with foreign trade and foreign aid were business-men.[57] Vandenberg assured his congressional colleagues that the new program would be a "business" venture and, as Secretary Forrestal put it, under "business management."[58] In December, 1947, the Michigan senator also recommended to the State Department that it line up "four or five top-level business executives of the country" to serve as "aggressive witnesses" before congressional committee hearings.[59] Many congressmen assumed that the administrator of the program would be a businessman. When the White House asked the Committee for the Marshall Plan to suggest candidates in early 1948 for ERP administrator, it submitted nine names. One was Clayton's; another was that of Lewis Douglas, ambassador to Britain, both men with successful business backgrounds. Acheson was on the list; he had rejoined his prestigious law firm of Covington, Burling, Acheson, and Shorb. Another in the group was Paul Porter, a former lawyer with the Columbia Broadcasting Company and a man who had held a number of government posts, and former senator Robert M. La Follette, Jr., who had completed his last term in early 1947. Philip Reed of General Electric, Eric Johnston of the Motion Picture Association of America and former president of the United States Chamber of Commerce, Charles E. Wilson of General Motors, and Paul Hoffman of Studebaker were also candidates.[60] Truman's first choice was Acheson, but Acheson himself warned the president that Vandenberg would probably disapprove, and he instead recommended Hoffman, one of the

G. Moulton (president, The Brookings Institution, Washington, D.C.), William I. Myers (dean, New York State College of Agriculture, Cornell University), Robert Gordon Sproul (president, University of California), and Owen D. Young (honorary chairman of the board of directors, General Electric).

[56] The findings of the three committees are integrated into Chapter 1. Their reports are: President's Committee on Foreign Aid, *European Recovery and American Aid* (Washington, D.C., 1947); Department of Interior, *Natural Resources and Foreign Aid* (Washington, D.C., 1947); Council of Economic Advisers, *The Impact of the Foreign Aid Program upon the Domestic Economy* (Washington, D.C., 1947).

[57] See ch. 1 of Paterson, "Economic Cold War," for a discussion of the reliance of the Truman administration on businessmen for ideas and personnel.

[58] Vandenberg, *Private Papers*, p. 383; Millis, *Forrestal Diaries*, p. 268.

[59] Vandenberg, *Private Papers*, p. 383.

[60] John Hammond to Donald Dawson, Mar. 25, 1948, ECA-Public Advisory Board folder, Friedman Files, Truman Papers.

senator's "aggressive witnesses," a well-respected businessman and one of Vandenberg's Michigan constituents. Truman agreed, consulted Vandenberg, and appointed Hoffman administrator in April, 1948.[61]

Considerable debate arose over the question of the Marshall Plan's administrative structure. An interdepartmental steering committee, chaired by Under Secretary of State Willard Thorp, gathered together the various committee reports, including those of the House Select Committee on Foreign Aid,[62] and helped Truman prepare his important message to Congress of December 19, 1947. Truman appealed in his speech for an ERP, estimated the total cost from 1948 to 1952 at $17 billion, and recommended that Congress appropriate $6.8 billion for the first fifteen months of the program (beginning April 1, 1948). He also asked for the creation of the Economic Cooperation Administration, whose administrator would work closely with the State Department, would be directly responsible to the president, and would be subject to Senate confirmation.[63] This administrative arrangement was a compromise.

Many legislators, mostly conservative Republicans, distrusted the State Department and wanted an independent agency to handle the Marshall Plan. After a meeting of twenty senators, including William Knowland of California, Kenneth Wherry of Nebraska, and Clyde Reed of Kansas, Reed urged that the role of the State Department "be severely limited." He desired instead "a strong competent organization of industrialists and scientists" who would apply "our 'know how'. . . ."[64] The Bureau of the Budget proposed a new agency within the State Department; the Select Committee of the House, the National Association of Manufacturers, and Winthrop Aldrich of Chase National Bank recommended a new public corporation with a bipartisan board of directors. These proposals did not satisfy Vandenberg and the leadership of the Republican 80th Congress, which insisted on closer supervision of monies and appointees. Vandenberg commissioned the Brookings Institution to resolve the conflict. Brookings produced the formula which Truman included in his message to Congress. By accepting an administrative structure (the ECA) which had links with both the executive and legislative branches and which reduced the influence of the State Department, the administration silenced some critics, but, still suspicious of the Democratic president and the State Department, the Congress set up a joint "watchdog" committee to review foreign aid programs.[65]

61 Acheson, *Present at the Creation,* pp. 241-42; Vandenberg, *Private Papers,* pp. 392-94; David E. Lilienthal, *Journals: The Atomic Energy Years 1945-1950* (New York, 1964), II, 329, 337; Price, *Marshall Plan,* pp. 71-72.

62 The House Committee was established in July, and Congressman Christian Herter of Massachusetts chaired it. After visits to Europe, it issued several reports, including *Final Report,* 80th Cong., 2d sess., H. Rept. 1845 (Washington, D.C., 1948).

63 *Public Papers, Truman, 1947,* pp. 515-29.

64 Memorandum by Clyde Reed, Jan. 13, 1948, Kenneth Wherry Papers, University of Nebraska Library (from the notes of Professor Robert Griffith).

65 George C. Marshall to James Webb, director, Bureau of the Budget, Nov. 7, 1947, Box 4, Clifford Papers, Truman Library; Westerfield, *Foreign Policy and Party Politics,*

Passage of ERP legislation was not in doubt, and the administration had not expected congressional action before early 1948, when the second session of the 80th Congress assembled. It was early recognized that several months would be required to make the necessary studies, gather information from and organize the European nations, popularize the Marshall Plan, and lobby in Congress, and that interim aid would meet the short-term needs of key European countries.[66] But the amount of aid requested by Truman for the ERP was never treated by congressmen as a fixed figure, and the administration made minor compromises downward to avoid the hefty cuts suggested by Senator Robert Taft. The Senate Foreign Relations Committee sent S. 2202 unanimously to the floor, where Vandenberg, on March 1, supported it in a nine-thousand-word speech of sweeping patriotic generalities. "If it succeeds," he concluded, "our children and our children's children will call us blessed." Vandenberg had convinced Truman to ask for an appropriation for one year instead of fifteen months, thereby reducing the initial request to $5.3 billion and permitting the new 81st Congress an earlier opportunity to review the program. On March 13 the Senate passed the Economic Cooperation Act by a vote of 69 to 17. On March 31 the House agreed, by a count of 329 to 74, after reducing the figure to $4.3 billion. A conference report passed both houses on April 2. The actual appropriations, passed in an omnibus bill in June, were spread over several programs. The ERP got $4 billion, $1.3 billion went to occupied areas (especially Germany), $400 million to China, another $225 million to Greece and Turkey, $71 million to the International Refugee Organization, and $35 million to the United Nations International Children's Emergency Fund (UNICEF). The administration campaign for a major new effort of "friendly aid" had paid off handsomely in the massive sum of $6 billion.[67] Soon after the establishment of the Economic Cooperation Administration Truman created the ECA Public Advisory Board as a means of perpetuating public support and aligning interest groups with the program, but Hoffman paid only lip service to the Board, and it essentially served a propagandistic function.[68]

The administration lobbying with Congress was made considerably easier

pp. 277-79; "Recommendations of the NAM," [n.d., but presented to the president on Nov. 10, 1947], OF 426 Misc.-N, Truman Papers; *Business Week,* Oct. 11, 1947, p. 26.

[66] *Foreign Relations, 1947,* III, 236, 326, 360-63, 402-3, 470-84.

[67] Vandenberg, *Private Papers,* pp. 383-92 (quotation, p. 392); Congressional Quarterly, *Evolution,* pp. 6-7. For other accounts of the national debate over the Marshall Plan, see Westerfield, *Foreign Policy and Party Politics,* pp. 274-95; Price, *Marshall Plan,* pp. 55-70; Ferrell, *Marshall,* pp. 123-30; Joseph Barber, ed., *The Marshall Plan as American Policy: A Report on the Views of Community Leaders in Twenty-One Cities* (New York, 1948); Harold L. Hitchens, "Influence on the Congressional Decision To Pass the Marshall Plan," *Western Political Quarterly,* XXI (March, 1968), 51-68.

[68] David S. Brown, "The Public Advisory Board in the Federal Government: An Administrative Analysis of Several Boards with Particular Attention to the Public Advisory Board of the Economic Cooperation Administration and the Mutual Security Program" (Ph.D. dissertation, Syracuse University, 1954), pp. 106-8, 154. See, for example, ECA, *Ninth Report for the Public Advisory Board* (Washington, D.C., March, 1949).

by alarming events in Europe. Elections in Italy were scheduled for April, and some congressmen joined administration figures in believing that passage of the Marshall Plan as soon as possible might reduce the projected large vote for the Communist Party.[69] The publication of the Nazi-Soviet documents of 1939 by the State Department in late January, the Czech coup of February, the growing crisis over Germany, which eventually led to the Berlin blockade, the knowledge that Germany would be included in the ERP, and Soviet pressure on Finland to sign a treaty of friendship all combined to spur passage. American military leaders, it became known, were thinking that a serious and sudden conflict with the Soviet Union was possible, and a war scare seemed to grip the country in March, 1948.

These crises afforded the Truman administration the opportunity to insist that the Marshall Plan was needed quickly to save Europe. Within the administration, however, there was disagreement on whether the president should go to Congress with a special message of alarm. Secretary Marshall opposed such a venture, fearing that the world was a "keg of dynamite" which might be ignited by Truman. Bohlen made Marshall's case with the White House, arguing that the president should avoid "tough" and intemperate language and simply state the facts. But Clark Clifford and George Elsey dissented from Marshall's "timid approach" and called for a "blunt" message, in part because Marshall and Vandenberg were receiving all the credit for the Marshall Plan and the president had to retrieve his leadership image. They were supported by Budget Bureau Director James E. Webb, who urged Truman to "scare" the country. On March 15, Clifford and Elsey persuaded Truman to deliver a strong speech, and the president agreed that Marshall's more restrained draft speech "stank." Truman addressed a joint session of Congress on March 17 to plead for a temporary selective service, universal military training, and the ERP. The speech was carried over radio nationwide and sounded as though the country were preparing for war.[70]

This combination of tactics and crises overwhelmed the badly divided and outnumbered critics who thought, variously, that the Marshall Plan would excerbate the Cold War, weaken the American economy through inflation, encourage European socialism, ignore the United Nations, and attempt to resurrect a Europe that was beyond saving. Wallace called it the "Martial Plan" and suggested an alternative United Nations Reconstruction Fund, and Senator Robert Taft unsuccessfully introduced an amendment to trim the first year's

[69] Congressman John Davis Lodge to Truman, Mar. 9, 1948, OF 233-Misc., Truman Papers; "McNaughton Report," Mar. 5, 1948, Box 13, McNaughton Papers; H. N. Morgan to Matthew J. Connelly, Apr. 13, 1948, OF 233, Truman Papers.

[70] *Public Papers, Truman, 1947,* pp. 182-86; Westerfield, *Foreign Policy and Party Politics,* p. 286; William L. Neumann, "How To Merchandise Foreign Policy, II: From ERP to MAP," *American Perspective,* III (October, 1949), 235-50; Adler and Paterson, "Red Fascism," pp. 1058-59; Freeland, *Truman Doctrine and Origins of McCarthyism,* pp. 269-87. For the debate within the administration and the quotations above, see handwritten notes by George Elsey, [n.d., but March, 1948], Box 20, Elsey Papers.

appropriation by over $1 billion.[71] The administration had had to conduct an intense domestic campaign, but, in the end, it did not find Congress all that difficult to persuade.

A SLENDER BRIDGE: THE ECONOMIC COMMISSION FOR EUROPE

The Economic Commission for Europe was almost forgotten in the hectic days of early 1948 when the Marshall Plan was facing its congressional test, yet in the spring and summer of 1947 it had been mentioned as a possible vehicle for implementing the ERP. Thereafter it declined in favor, despite Executive Secretary Gunnar Myrdal's urgent appeals that it be utilized. The ECE represented all of Europe, including Russia and its sphere, as well as the United States, but the major powers bypassed their creation.

In September, 1946, the United States, with British and Polish endorsement, proposed the establishment of the ECE in the United Nations Economic and Social Council in order to assist and coordinate European reconstruction. It was designed in part to absorb the work of three emergency committees: the European Coal Organization, the European Central Inland Transport Organization, and the Emergency Economic Committee for Europe. The Soviets questioned the proposal, asking why another agency was needed when UNRRA existed and why the new commission would not be given aid funds to dispense. At the December meeting of the General Assembly a resolution establishing the ECE passed unanimously, with the Russians now voting in the affirmative, for they knew that UNRRA would not be continued. The Economic and Social Council then shaped the new commission in early 1947. The Soviet Union tried unsuccessfully to introduce amendments which would keep contact between the ECE and Germany to a minimum. They feared a revived Germany, and, failing in their attempt, simply abstained from the final vote. The ECE began operations in March.[72]

At the ECE's first session in May delegates from the United States, western and eastern Europe, and Russia, sixteen nations in all, plodded through the adoption of procedural rules.[73] The only energetic debate erupted over the

---

71 For criticism, see Senate, *ERP* hearings; Paterson, *Cold War Critics;* Department of State, "Chief Arguments against the European Recovery Program," [n.d.], Tray 18822, Committee on Foreign Affairs, House Records; Henry A. Wallace, "My Alternative for the Marshall Plan," *New Republic*, CXVIII (Jan. 12, 1948), 13-14.

72 David Wightman, *Economic Co-Operation in Europe: A Study of the United Nations Economic Commission for Europe* (London, 1956), pp. 5-24; "Rebuilding Devastated Europe," *U.N. Bulletin*, I (Sept. 25, 1946), 13-17.

73 Belgium, Byelorussia, Czechoslovakia, Denmark, France, Greece, Luxembourg, the Netherlands, Norway, Poland, Sweden, Turkey, the Ukraine, the U.S.S.R., the United Kingdom, the United States, and Yugoslavia. Iceland was a member but was not represented at the first session. Albania, Austria, Bulgaria, Finland, Hungary, Ireland, Italy, Portugal, Rumania, and Switzerland as non-members of the United Nations were not full-fledged members of the ECE but participated in its work after the first session.

ECE's relationship to occupied Germany.[74] In the second session of July 5-16, 1947, however, the delegates took verbal potshots at each other. It convened, of course, shortly after Molotov's departure from the tripartite Paris conference and its last days overlapped the succeeding meeting of European nations. Executive Secretary Myrdal was confident that, through the transfer of economic experts to the ECE, his agency could deal competently "both with technical problems and the satisfactory distribution of any materials provided either by the United States or by European countries on a basis of self-help."[75] But none of the major powers asked for the help of the ECE in European recovery. The ECE continued to develop, nevertheless, largely along lines desired by the United States. The Soviets wanted a two-thirds majority vote on certain issues; the American proposal for a simple majority carried. Over strong Soviet objections, the conferees instructed Myrdal to continue his liaison with military authorities in Germany. Technical committees on electric power, coal, industry, and other problems were founded to conduct most of the commission's work, reducing the need for frequent general assemblies.[76]

United States officials had always been hesitant about the ECE. They thought it could be useful to American goals in Europe, but they also wanted direct control over their foreign aid funds. Kennan's Policy Planning Staff had at first contemplated a leading role for the ECE, but urged caution because the Soviets might try to block the recovery program there. The outlook for the infant organization further darkened when Clayton, back from its first session, told a story of Soviet bad behavior. He was emphatic that the ECE was unworkable because undoubtedly the Soviets intended to be disruptive. Marshall's Harvard address did not mention the ECE, although Jones has recorded that "all concerned in the State Department assumed the ECE would carry the ball." Jones certainly exaggerated State Department sentiment. American thinking at this point was undecided but was leaning away from the ECE. Washington was not yet willing to rule out the agency altogether because the Europeans might ask that it be utilized. As Marshall noted on June 12, "it would seem desirable to avoid any implication of commitment to use any one exclusive channel. . . ." The question remained open, but only slightly.[77]

[74] United Nations, Economic and Social Council, Official Records, 2d year, 5th sess., suppl. 3, Report of the Economic Commission for Europe (New York, 1947), Doc. E/451; "Work for European Reconstruction: Economic Commission Concludes First Session," U.N. Bulletin, II (June 3, 1947), 601-4.

[75] U.N. Bulletin, III (July 8, 1947), 66.

[76] Economic and Social Council, Report of the Economic Commission for Europe; "Economic Commission for Europe Convenes," U.N. Bulletin, III (July 15, 1947), 83-85; "How ECE Will Operate," ibid. (July 29, 1947), pp. 150-51; Gunnar Myrdal, "Prospects of the Economic Commission for Europe," ibid., pp. 147-49.

[77] Foreign Relations, 1947, III, 221 (May 16, 1947), 228 (May 23, 1947), 236 (May 28, 1947), 250-51 (June 12, 1947); Kennan, Memoirs, pp. 339-41; Wightman, Economic Co-Operation, pp. 29-30. The Jones quotation is from Fifteen Weeks, p. 254; the Marshall quotation is from Foreign Relations, 1947, III, 251.

In mid-June the deputy to the American ambassador to the United Nations talked separately with Byron Price, the Assistant Secretary General, James T. Shotwell of the Carnegie Foundation, and Clark Eichelberger of the American Association for the United Nations. Price complained that the Truman administration seldom mentioned the ECE and wanted to know "whether as in the case of the Greek-Turkish Aid Program initially, the United States intended to abandon the Economic Commission for Europe in favor of direct action." Price indicated that Secretary General Trygve Lie was quite concerned about the matter, and he admitted that large American funds were required for reconstruction. "If Norway or the Soviet Union were in the same position, there is very little practical doubt that those countries would also want to have a controlling voice in where and how funds were spent." Shotwell interjected that Myrdal "is one of the very best men in the world" and that "the 'realists' would say that Russia could always delay action in a United Nations body. . . ." Yet he asked the United States at least to try the ECE and urged Secretary Marshall to issue a statement supporting its work. Eichelberger had similar fears about American "bypassing" of the United Nations.[78]

These views did not find a sympathetic hearing, nor did Myrdal's statement in late June that the ECE was quite ready to undertake the solution to Europe's economic troubles.[79] Both the British and French were leary of the ECE and wished to work with the Russians as little as possible. Clayton, frequently in conference with Bevin and Bidault, probably had much to do with shaping this attitude, although the Policy Planning Staff and Marshall himself by July had largely ruled the ECE out because of the possibilities of Soviet obstructiveness. Polish, Swedish, and Norwegian pleas nothwithstanding, Washington decided to father a new and more malleable organization, the Organization of European Economic Cooperation.[80]

There was little in the Soviet attitude to encourage utilization of the ECE. Russia was a member, but it cautiously shunned the technical committees, and at the tripartite Paris meeting Molotov did not urge an active role for the ECE. Bevin had expected him to do so, but Molotov was noncommittal: "It is also necessary to consider the relations which should be established with the

[78] Memorandum of conversation by John C. Ross, June 17, 1947, general correspondence, Austin Papers; memorandom of telephone conversation by John C. Ross, June 16, 1947, *ibid.*

[79] Andrew W. Cordier and Wilder Foote, eds., *Public Papers of the Secretaries-General of the United Nations* (New York, 1969), I, 80-81; Koefod, *New Concept,* p. 128. For favorable opinion toward ultilization of the ECE for the Marshall Plan, see Senate, *ERP* (Jan. 26, 1948), 927 (National Farmers Union); Henry Wallace, "What We Must Do Now," *New Republic,* CXVII (July 14, 1947), 13-14; Jane Bedell, "United Nations News—Money Matters," *ibid.,* CXVII (July 21, 1947), 31; Michael J. De Sherbinin, "Planning without Headlines," *The Nation,* CLXV (Dec. 27, 1947), 701-2.

[80] *Foreign Relations, 1947,* III, 255, 296, 309, 321, 388, 395; Clayton to Clair Wilcox, June 16, 1947, Clayton Papers; Ernest H. van der Beugel, *From Marshall Aid to Atlantic Partnership: European Integration as a Concern of American Foreign Policy* (Amsterdam, 1966), p. 80; Beloff, *United States and Unity of Europe,* p. 24.

European Economic Commission." And on June 29, during the conference, Moscow radio broadcast that "the Soviet Delegation does not . . . insist that the U.N. Economic Commission be given the task of receiving and collating estimates. It prefers that it should be done by special European committees in which Allied countries should be given first place."[81] The Soviets were obviously wary of the ECE because of American membership. Later the Soviets charged (a blatant distortion) that they remained outside the Marshall Plan because the United States had bypassed the ECE. Not until European planning in the CEEC was well advanced and the ECE was functioning with remarkably few signs of Cold War schism did Moscow adopt a more favorable attitude toward the ECE by asking that foreign aid be funneled through that agency and that East-West trade be encouraged. In early 1948, when this shift occurred, neither London nor Washington read it as sincere, and, at any rate, they were too far down the path toward a western European recovery program at that point to turn back.[82]

Once Washington had decided that the Marshall Plan would be an United States-dominated program without Soviet participation, it became extremely difficult for the ECE to make a case for itself. Ignored by the major powers, the ECE nevertheless proved that it was a viable institution, "the most bumptious, the most business-like, and the least dreamy of any branch of the U.N.,"[83] that it was no threat to any nation's sovereignty, that it could gather statistics and report effectively, and that East and West could cooperate on practical questions without indulging in propagandizing. The CEEC drew heavily from ECE-compiled material, and the ECE's *Survey of the Economic Situation and Prospects of Europe,* published in March, 1948, with annual volumes thereafter, was widely respected. The Soviets gradually came to work with the ECE technical committees.[84]

Myrdal pointed out in early 1948 that the ECE was functioning well in its technical committees, especially coal, inland transportation, and timber. Other observers in 1948 were impressed with its ability to avoid corrosive East-West divisions. Its success lay in the fact that meetings were secret, to reduce the temptation to use them as a political forum, that only those countries really interested sent delegates, and that decisions were made by general consensus rather than by divisive votes. Although there were obvious ECE failures and disagreements, there were a number of noteworthy successes. Its Coal Committee, for example, collected data on the coal import

[81] Quoted in Wightman, *Economic Co-Operation,* p. 42; Koefod, *New Concept,* p. 141.

[82] "Expansion of Europe's Trade Discussed: Debate on Relations Between ECE and ERP," *U.N. Bulletin,* V (Aug. 15, 1948), 650-52; Molotov, May 9, 1948, quoted in Carlyle, *Documents,* p. 157; Harold K. Jacobson, "The Soviet Union, the UN, and World Trade," *Western Political Quarterly,* XI (September, 1958), 678-79.

[83] Michael L. Hoffman, "They Show That Nations Can Cooperate," *New York Times Magazine,* Sept. 12, 1948, p. 7.

[84] Wightman, *Economic Co-Operation,* p. 42; John H. Williams, "The Task of Economic Recovery," *Foreign Affairs,* XXVI (July, 1948), 619.

needs of European countries based upon war damage, the prewar level of consumption, improvements in hydroelectric power, requirements under trade treaties, and indigenous coal supplies. The Coal Committee also determined the availability of coal in Europe, including western Germany. On the basis of this information it allocated coal to European countries. Although the chances for disagreement were great, ECE allocation recommendations were always accepted unanimously. The committee stuck together, and Poland, a coal-exporting nation, cooperated effectively because it was interested in securing European markets; at the same time, the United States encouraged the flow of coal from Poland to western Europe to spur recovery. Western Germany collaborated in this successful and massive system of coal allocation: of the 60 million tons of coal allocated from April, 1948 to September, 1950, 42.6 million tons derived from western Germany. Russia did not obstruct the work of the Coal Committee despite its often-stated opposition to links between the ECE and Germany. Year after year it accepted, however, reluctantly, arrangements between ECE technical committees and western Germany.[85] The ECE proved itself to be one of the few postwar institutions in which the Soviet-American confrontation was tempered. The question of whether earlier great power participation in and respect for the ECE might have made possible an all-European recovery program is an intriguing one. As it was, the ECE came to represent a "slender bridge" between the two spheres in the Cold War.[86]

SUCCESSES AND SHORTCOMINGS

The Marshall Plan gave the United States its coordinated foreign aid program and a more cohesive sphere of influence, toward which Washington had been working since World War II, and the ERP revived the western European economy. Truman himself boldly concluded in 1956 that "without the Marshall Plan it would have been difficult for Western Europe to remain free from the tyranny of Communism," and Robert H. Ferrell agrees: "Americans could congratulate themselves that because of the Marshall Plan they did not have to spend even more in an enormous war in Europe."[87] Indeed, it is a popular conviction that the Marshall Plan prevented an aggressive Russia from sweeping over western Europe, either through revolution or overt

---

[85] "ECE Achieves Concrete Results," *U.N. Bulletin,* IV (Feb. 1, 1948), 104; J. Alvarez Del Vayo, "East-West Cooperation," *The Nation,* CLXVII (Sept. 11, 1948), 278-79; Hoffman, "They Show That Nations Can Cooperate," pp. 7ff.; Gunnar Myrdal, "Twenty Years of the United Nations Economic Commission for Europe," *International Organization,* XXII (Summer, 1968), 620; Wightman, *Economic Co-Operation,* pp. 73-91; United Nations, *ECE in Action* (New York, 1949); United Nations, *The Economic Commission for Europe* (Geneva, 1954).

[86] Wightman, *Economic Co-Operation,* p. 259.

[87] Truman, *Memoirs,* II, 119; Ferrell, *Marshall,* p. 134.

military action. The basic premise that Russia intended to seize western Europe has never been substantiated and is increasingly being questioned by scholars. Certainly western Europe benefited immensely from the ERP, but it is quite doubtful that that region was saved from an "enormous war" or the "tyranny of Communism" by it.[88]

When the European Recovery Program ended in mid-1952, the United States had dispensed $13 billion to the member countries, as well as several billions more to the members of NATO. These expenditures shored up both its own and the western European economy and created a sense of military security. The Korean War shifted the emphasis to military assistance, and by 1952 80 percent of United States aid to western Europe consisted of weapons. At the close of the Marshall Plan, industrial production in the ERP countries had risen 35 percent above the prewar figure, agricultural production 10 percent. The dollar gap had been reduced, West Germany had been rebuilt and partially integrated into the western European economy, and the goal of currency stabilization was partially achieved. The percentage of American exports going to the ERP countries was maintained at about 33 percent, with over half of United States exports to western Europe financed with ECA funds by the second quarter of 1949.[89] A guarantee program for investments allowed United States businessmen to convert profits in local currencies into dollars, and, in part because of this protection, companies like Ford, General Motors, Standard Oil, and Goodyear expanded their plants and investments in Europe.[90] Under the ECA the American stockpiling program accelerated, as the United States gave special attention to scarce raw materials from ERP sources. By 1950, almost $57 million in rubber, platinum, industrial diamonds, bauxite, and graphite had been acquired under the ECA.[91] On the whole, the Marshall Plan helped avert economic depression in both western Europe and the United States, and thereby, in the American mind, contributed to more pacific international relations by curbing Communism and the Soviet Union.

But contemporaries did point out some shortcomings which commentators more distant from the actual events have tended to overlook. Washington was not pleased with the Marshall Plan's meager contribution to European economic integration and stable, non-subsidized, multilateral, non-discrimatory trade. In 1950 the White House expressed alarm over the continued "dollar gap" in Europe, and noted that ERP's termination "will create tremendous economic problems at home and abroad unless vigorous

[88] This suggestion is based on the writings of Adam Ulam and George Kennan, among many others, who have questioned the premise that Moscow intended to subjugate western Europe.

[89] Ferrell, *Marshall,* p. 133; Price, *Marshall Plan,* p. 399; Commerce, *Foreign Aid, 1940-1951,* p. 46; ECA, *Fifth Report to Congress* (Washington, D.C., 1949), pp. viii-ix.

[90] By 1951 the ECA had executed guarantee contracts worth over $40 million. Commerce, *Foreign Aid, 1940-1951,* p. 62; ECA, *34th Report for the Public Advisory Board* (Washington, D.C., 1951), p. 54. See also *Business Week,* June 19, 1948, p. 117, Feb. 25, 1950, p. 129; *Fortune,* XXXIX (January, 1949), 22, XLI (April, 1950), 22.

[91] ECA, *Eighth Report to Congress* (Washington, D.C., 1950). pp. 66-68.

steps are taken both by the United States and foreign countries."[92] "Vigorous steps" were not taken, and United States trade with Europe depended for many years upon foreign aid. Will Clayton complained to Walter Lippmann in early 1952 that "economic nationalism" persisted and that western Europe appeared to be living "on the bounty of the United States." He added that "Russia tells her satellites over and over that all Western Europe lives by United States charity. . . . There is just enough truth here to put us squarely on the defensive."[93] William Draper, United States special representative in Europe, told the president in 1952 that "the existing 'dollar gap' threatens not only our own export trade, but if not reduced may unfavorably affect the mutual defense effort as well."[94] In 1954, in his *A Foreign Economic Policy for the United States,* Clarence B. Randall reported that world trade was approaching "a shaky balance, but this equilibrium is more apparent than real" because of restrictions on East-West trade and heavy American expenditures for defense.[95] By 1952, Harry B. Price concludes, "the continent was far more healthy than in 1948, but it had not yet acquired the dynamism needed for accelerated growth independent of external aid."[96] Nor had economic integration—which some Americans believed to be crucial to economic stability—succeeded.[97]

There was little restructuring of European industry or economic and social institutions. American aid tended to perpetuate the status quo, and the objective of non-Communist political stability through economic recovery was not achieved. Deflationary money policies and high unemployment rates undermined American goals. *Fortune* editorialized in 1951: "Thus the standard of living of French industrial workers . . . remained as low or lower than before the war, and they have little more stake in France's economic present or future than they had in 1788."[98] The Marshall Plan did not eliminate Communism from western Europe, Hans Morgenthau has noted. The seed of Communism continued to fall on fertile ground because the Plan left the western European "economic, social, and political structure by and large intact. The dangers to the stability and strength of Western Europe which have grown in the past from the defects of that structure have continued to grow because those defects were not repaired. The Marshall Plan almost completely lost sight of those roots of instability and unrest which

92 Press release, Apr. 3, 1950, OF 275A, Truman Papers.

93 Will Clayton to Walter Lippmann, Feb. 26, 1952, Clayton Papers.

94 "Report to the President from Ambassador Draper, U.S. Special Representative in Europe," Aug. 22, 1952, OF 3296, *ibid.*

95 Clarence B. Randall, *A Foreign Economic Policy for the United States* (Chicago, 1954), pp. 13-14.

96 Price, *Marshall Plan,* p. 400.

97 John H. Williams, "End of the Marshall Plan," *Foreign Affairs,* XXX (July, 1952), 593-611; Gunnar Myrdal, *An International Economy: Problems and Prospects* (New York, 1956), pp. 56-71; Beloff, *United States and Unity of Europe,* p. 68; Thomas B. DiBacco, "American Business and Foreign Aid: The Eisenhower Years," *Business History Review,* XLI (Spring, 1967), 21-35.

98 The editors of *Fortune* and Russell W. Davenport, *U.S.A.: The Permanent Revolution* (New York, 1951), p. 250.

antedated the emergency and were bound to operate after it was over."[99] The United States probably could not and should not have made political and social reform a condition for aid—reform was always a secondary concern in the Marshall Plan—but there is no doubt that the goals of economic stability and anti-Communism were only partially fulfilled at its close.

The thirst for raw materials represented in the Marshall Plan also contributed to European exploitation of colonial areas and nourished instability in the non-developed world. Belgium, for example, used some of its ERP aid to expand Congolese production of raw materials, and by mid-1951 France had spent $287 million in ECA funds for the purchase of equipment for its foreign territories. In 1950 Europe's dependent areas had provided the United States with, among other materials, 82 percent of its bauxite, 68 percent of its cobalt (critical to the manufacture of jet engines), 51 percent of its tin, and 23 percent of its manganese ore.[100] This exploitation, with few important economic returns to colonial peoples, helped to perpetuate the conditions of social and political unrest which the peace and prosperity theme was dedicated to eliminating. The Marshall Plan, then, in the long run, produced neither world stability nor world prosperity, especially as the Soviet-American confrontation moved into developing regions in the 1950s.

The exertion of American economic power through the ERP was successful in that the immediate recovery of Europe was achieved, but it created a deeper rift between the United States and Russia. When Moscow could not accept American conditions for aid, Washington put the blame for heightened Cold War tension almost solely on it. Its Molotov Plan was read as another plot to disrupt peace rather than as a defensive move to shore up its own sphere of influence. The Marshall Plan knitted together as never before the American sphere of influence in western Europe and was partially responsible for dividing the world in other ways. It encouraged restrictions on East-West trade, as export controls were instituted to direct products away from eastern Europe to western Europe. By drawing western Germany, as we shall note in the next chapter, into the western European economy, it aroused profound Soviet fears of a revived German power. The ERP, presented and formulated as an American offensive in the Cold War, was interpreted by the Soviets in 1947-1948 as a threat to their tenuous position in eastern Europe. The coup in Czechoslovakia may be evidence of that perceived threat, as the Soviets decided to consolidate their sphere of influence in the most repressive manner.[101] It may be true, as Adam Ulam has suggested, that Stalin feared the Marshall Plan more than the United States monopoly of the atomic bomb.[102] Certainly Moscow was alarmed at the Plan's rehabilitation of its nemesis, western Germany.

[99] Hans J. Morgenthau, *The Impasse of American Foreign Policy* (Chicago, 1962), pp. 264-65. See also Price, *Marshall Plan*; pp. 397n, 400; Ulam, *Expansion and Coexistence*, p. 435; Kolko, *Limits of Power*, pp. 428-52.

[100] Price, *Marshall Plan*, pp. 149-51, 263.

[101] Shulman, *Stalin's Foreign Policy Reappraised*, pp. 14-15.

[102] Ulam, *Expansion and Coexistence*, p. 455.

CHAPTER 11

VITAL CENTER: THE REHABILITATION OF
WESTERN GERMANY

As State Department officials in the spring and summer of 1947 prepared for a massive assault on the European economic crisis, they stressed Germany's pivotal station. It was widely assumed that Germany, because of its key economic role in the prewar period—its production of coal and heavy industrial goods and its consumption of products—was the "vital center" of Europe. Without a healthy Germany Europe could not be reconstructed, and the embryonic Marshall Plan would be jeopardized.[1] "Are we going to try to keep Germany a running boil with the pus exuding over the rest of Europe," Secretary Forrestal asked not long after the Truman Doctrine speech, "or are you going to try to bring it back into inner society?"[2] In 1947 the answer was clear: the western zones of Germany had to be substantially rehabilitated and, even more significant, had to be tied closely to western Europe and the United States sphere.

The Office of Military Government, of course, had begun reconstruction in the United States zone soon after the surrender.[3] But the Soviet-American failure to reach a peace settlement for Germany at the Moscow Foreign Ministers Conference in March-April, 1947, and the launching of the Marshall Plan in June-July prompted Washington to undertake a full-scale rehabilitation of the economy of western Germany and its merger with western Europe in the ERP. The trend since 1945 had been in that direction, but French and Russian opposition and American caution, both fostered by fears of a revived Germany and, in the American case, by debate within the administration over

[1] See, for example, *DSB,* XVI (May 11, 1947), 919-24; Allen W. Dulles, "Alternatives for Germany," *Foreign Affairs,* XXV (April, 1947), 421; Clinton P. Anderson to the president, July 18, 1947, Anderson Papers, Truman Library; CEEC, *General Report,* I, 39, 69-71; Stimson and Bundy, *On Active Service,* p. 572; Jones, *Fifteen Weeks,* p. 221; Senate, *ERP,* pp. 375, 1184; minutes, 35th Annual Meeting, Apr. 28-30, May 1, 1947, Chamber of Commerce Library, Washington, D.C.; *Foreign Relations, 1947,* II, 165, 229, III, 220n, 221, 249, 332, 388.
[2] "Excerpts from Telephone Conversation between Forrestal and James Reston," Mar. 13, 1947, Greece folder, Clifford Papers.
[3] See Bruce Kuklick, *American Policy and the Division of Germany: The Clash with Russia over Reparations* (Ithaca, N.Y., 1972); John H. Backer, *Priming the German Economy: American Occupational Policies, 1945-1948* (Durham, N.C., 1971).

the degree of rehabilitation, delayed a coordinated program. In December, 1946, Britain and the United States created "Bizonia," evidence that Washington had decided to proceed in Germany if necessary without Russian cooperation.

Both Russia and the United States insisted in 1945 that Germany be reconstructed in such a way that it would never again threaten the world with war. Although the Allies agreed that it should be stripped of its war-making machine, their other goals conflicted. Russia sought large German reparations to rebuild its own economy and to sap Germany of its potential for war. The United States wanted a Germany which could stand on its own economic feet, contribute to international economic stability and barrier-free commerce, and aid European reconstruction. Between 1945 and 1947 United States leaders came to believe that sizeable reparations shipments to Russia would be an obstacle to these goals, especially if German unification were not achieved first. The Soviets (and the French) complained futilely that the United States was giving German recovery a higher priority than that of the former Allies. Plans for the level of German industry, reparations, and the "unity" of Germany caused bitter conflict, and Russia and the United States gradually drew their respective zones into their spheres. The July, 1947, directive to the American military governor well summarizes Washington's position in the peace and prosperity idiom. It declared that "an orderly and prosperous Europe requires the economic contributions of a stable and productive Germany as well as the necessary restraints to insure that Germany is not allowed to revive its destructive militarism."[4]

A "CONSTRUCTIVE" OR "CORRECTIVE" PEACE?

The notion that Germany was essential to European prosperity did not go unchallenged, for in the United States (especially for 1944 and 1945) and in France and Russia some officials held that the "restraints" should be emphasized more than a "productive Germany"—that indeed the two goals were incompatible. The quarrel between those who advocated "constructive" measures in Germany (rehabilitation, German economic unity, and integration into the European economy) and those who stressed "corrective" measures (strict reduction in industry, large reparations, and a decentralized economy) was intense both within the Roosevelt and Truman administrations and among the Allies.[5]

At the center of the controversy was Secretary of the Treasury Henry Morgenthau, Jr., an advocate of a "hard" or corrective peace. In the fall of 1944 he began to record and disseminate his ideas for the treatment of

[4] Directive of July 11, 1947, in *DSB*, XVII (July 27, 1947), 186.
[5] The terms are used by Arnold Wolfers, *United States Policy toward Germany* (New Haven, Conn., 1947), p. 3.

postwar Germany. As a close associate of the president, he was able to take his proposals to the very top, where they were influential for a time. He foresaw a humbled Germany despoiled of any industries conducive to military strength and reparations to ensure removal of such industries. On September 4, 1944, he appealed to the president for extensive restrictions in the coal- and iron-rich Ruhr area. "Here lies the heart of German industrial power. This area should not only be stripped of all . . . existing industries but so weakened and controlled that it cannot in the foreseeable future become an industrial area."[6] Roosevelt carried Morgenthau's memorandum to the second Quebec Conference that month, and the Morgenthau formula seemed to have been accepted. "This programme," read a memorandum initialed by Churchill and Roosevelt, "for eliminating the warmaking industries in the Ruhr and in the Saar is looking forward to converting Germany into a country primarily agricultural and pastoral in character."[7] Morgenthau had been called to Quebec by the president and, with instructions from Churchill, helped prepare that statement. Treasury officials considered the meeting a victory for Morgenthau's ideas, but historians have wondered why Churchill accepted a statement so different from his own ideas. Apparently a bargain was struck at Quebec; Churchill accepted the Morgenthau scheme in exchange for the promise of a postwar American loan.[8]

Cordell Hull complained that Morgenthau had wasted his bargaining power at Quebec by failing to get a trade liberalization agreement. He also believed that too harsh a peace imposed on Germany would be disastrous to the European economy and to his vision of a world of open multilateral trade. Joining him in condemning the vague "Morgenthau Plan" was Secretary of War Henry L. Stimson, who strongly opposed reducing Germany to a "ghost territory" or "dust heap" when it sat at the center of an industrialized Europe. "Sound thinking teaches that prosperity in one part of the world helps to create prosperity in other parts of the world," Stimson told Roosevelt. "It also teaches that poverty in one part of the world induces poverty in other parts."[9] The Department of State added, "if we advocate a

[6] Memorandum in Morgenthau's *Germany Is Our Problem* (New York, 1945). For the development and demise of the Morgenthau Plan, see Blum, *From Morgenthau Diaries*, III, chs. 7 and 8; Paul Y. Hammond, "Directives for the Occupation of Germany: The Washington Controversy," in Harold Stein, ed., *American Civil-Military Decisions: A Book of Case Studies* (Birmingham, Ala., 1963), pp. 314-460. Morgenthau claimed in 1946 that his critics had exaggerated the extent to which he would reduce German industry. Morgenthau, "Postwar Treatment of Germany," *The Annals of the American Academy of Political and Social Science*, CCXLVI (July, 1946), 127. For one of his public critics, see Heinz Eulau, "Should Germany Be De-Industralized: Mr. Morgenthau's Panacea," *New Republic*, CXIII (Oct. 8, 1945), 457-60; "Germany Cannot Be Agricultural," *ibid.*, CXII (Oct. 15, 1945), 493-95; "German Industry and Europe's Trade," *ibid.*, CXIII (Oct. 22, 1945), 522-24.
[7] Quoted in Stimson and Bundy, *On Active Service*, p. 577.
[8] See Chapter 8 above.
[9] Stimson Diary, Sept. 8, 1944, in Stimson and Bundy, *On Active Service*, p. 572, and Henry Stimson to the president, Sept. 15, 1944, Box 100, Forrestal Papers.

'wrecking program' as the best means of assuring our security, we may face considerable European opposition on account of its effect on the European economy. . . ."[10]

The Treasury Department prepared for rebuttal, with Harry D. White as Morgenthau's chief defender. A White memorandum of September, 1944, backed the secretary's plan and held, contrary to widespread opinion, that Germany was not essential to European prosperity. German exports of steel and coal before the war (in 1938), he noted, were "trivial in comparison with the increased industrial potential of the U.S. alone." Britain and the United States could meet European coal needs. "Therefore the treatment to be accorded to Germany should be decided upon without reference to the economic consequences upon the rest of Europe."[11] The night before Roosevelt's death, Morgenthau talked with the president and reiterated that "a weak economy for Germany means that she will be weak politically, and she won't be able to make another war. . . ."[12]

On September 22, 1944, Roosevelt approved an interim Joint Chiefs of Staff directive (JCS/1067) to the United States commander in Europe. Behind this directive lay weeks of debate among officials in the State, War, and Treasury departments. As it turned out, War and Treasury joined against the first to gain acceptance of JCS/1067. Morgenthau dominated the exchange, using his special access to the president as leverage; Secretary Hull, who was planning to retire in November, protested only feebly. The War Department, which agreed with the State Department on the need for a constructive peace, was willing to cooperate with Morgenthau because he endorsed its plea for independence for the zonal commander in Germany and a short-term military role in postwar German reconstruction. The State Department, on the other hand, argued for a long-range program conducted by military authorities, as well as a constructive peace. By exploiting the differences between State and War over the role and length of military management of German affairs, Morgenthau secured in JCS/1067 many elements of a hard peace.[13] The political, financial, economic, and relief components of the directive sought to prevent Germany from ever again becoming a threat to world peace through programs of denazification and demilitarization, a new financial system, just enough relief to prevent disease and disorder, and a controlled economy. And "you will take no steps looking toward the economic rehabilitation of Germany nor designed to maintain or strengthen the German economy."[14]

[10] Quoted in Hull, *Memoirs*, II, 1606.
[11] Memorandum, Harry White, "Is European Prosperity Dependent upon German Industry?" Sept. 7, 1944, II:22, White Papers.
[12] Blum, *From Morgenthau Diaries*, III, 419.
[13] For the intra-administration debate, see Walter L. Dorn, "The Debate over American Occupation Policy in Germany in 1944-45," *Political Science Quarterly*, LXXII (December, 1957), 481-501.
[14] *Foreign Relations, Yalta*, p. 153. For the entire directive of September 22, 1944, see pp. 143-54.

Roosevelt retreated from the position expressed in JCS/1067 rather fast. On September 29 he informed Hull that "no one wants to make Germany a wholly agricultural nation again" and "I wish we could catch and chastise" the person who gave the press such faulty information.[15] Apparently, he was discovering that there were not many people who thought like Morgenthau. The State Department, however, still fearful that Roosevelt would succumb to Morgenthau's arguments, prepared numerous counter-reports, some of which were carried to the Yalta Conference. Although the Big Three at Yalta agreed to divide Germany into zones and to extract reparations, no operative plans were devised. The conference results could not be called a victory for either faction because the question of postwar Germany was, for the most part, postponed.[16]

After Yalta the State Department gradually moved the president away from JCS/1067, and on March 10 it gained Roosevelt's assent to a memorandum which essentially repudiated the directive. The Treasury Department once again asserted itself in favor of tougher economic restraints and found support from annoyed War Department officials: the Department had not been consulted by State about the new memorandum and found it too much of an infringement on the zonal commander's authority. Ten days later, as confusion mounted, the president revoked the State Department memorandum entirely and ordered a high-level discussion to resolve the conflict. A new memorandum, dated March 23, was accepted by the three departments (with only Treasury enthusiastic) and by the president. After Roosevelt's death and Truman's approval, it became the final draft of JSC/1067 (dated April 26, 1945) sent to General Dwight D. Eisenhower, the American commander in Europe. It was more detailed than the interim directive, and Morgenthau's economic views were quite evident. Industries like iron and steel, chemicals, and machine tools were to be shut down; scientific research laboratories were to be closed; and facilities would be converted to light consumer goods. The Germans were to be made aware of their own responsibility for their suffering. Truman signed the directive without enthusiasm, for he himself questioned the wisdom of a hard peace which might embitter the Germans.[17] Lewis Douglas, Military Governor Lucius Clay's financial adviser, complained that JCS/1067 had been "assembled by economic idiots."[18] Morgenthau had seemingly achieved a victory out of the administrative confusion.

Some of the president's hesitancy found its way into the Potsdam Conference agreements. Certainly the spirit of the directive was incorporated

[15] *Ibid.*, p. 155.
[16] Hammond, "Directives," pp. 409-14; Blum, *From Morgenthau Diaries*, III, 396-97.
[17] Dorn, "The Debate"; Hammond, "Directives," pp. 414-28; Blum, *From Morgenthau Diaries*, III, 451-61; Herbert Feis, *Between War and Peace: The Potsdam Conference* (Princeton, N.J., 1960), p. 57; Gaddis, *United States and Origins of Cold War*, pp. 120-24. The final version of JCS/1067 is printed in *DSB*, XIII (Oct. 21, 1945), 596-607.
[18] Quoted in Murphy, *Diplomat*, p. 251.

into the protocol of the Potsdam Conference, yet the protocol included "constructive peace" statements which reflected both State and War Department positions. The document assigned authority to the military governor of each zone, thereby giving him considerable discretion; levied an unspecified amount of reparations; allowed for improvements in the German living standard; and provided for rehabilitation of transportation, coal production, agriculture, housing, and utilities. Germany "shall be treated as a single economic unit."[19] As Paul Y. Hammond has concluded, the Potsdam Conference "left the treatment of Germany in fundamental ambiguity," with the tension between restraints and rehabilitation still not clearly resolved.[20]

What ensured the retreat from Morgenthau's formula was General Lucius D. Clay's conviction, as military governor, that Germany could not be permitted to languish economically and the work of lower-echelon officers who were concerned with "making things go."[21] In April, 1945, Clay commented that large reparations would impede "order" in Germany; Washington would have to revise its thinking on dismantling plants and contemplate rehabilitating industries.[22] As he wrote later, "fortunately the provisions of JCS/1067 were in some respects general in nature, so that the degree of application was left to the judgment of the military governor and some of its more drastic economic and financial provisions were tempered by the agreements reached in Potsdam."[23] Clay's reading of discretionary flexibility and his determination to get Germany on its feet by reviving it and uniting it economically undercut JCS/1067, spurred rehabilitation, disrupted reparations shipments from the American zone, and increased conflict with Russia and France.

REVIVING GERMAN INDUSTRY

The Potsdam protocol stated that "the amount of equipment to be removed from the Western Zones on account of reparations must be determined within six months from now at the latest."[24] Thus a German "level of industry" had to be determined so that plant capacity over that level could be removed as

[19] The protocol is found in *Foreign Relations, Berlin,* II, 1478-98 (the quotation appears on p. 1484).

[20] Hammond, "Directives," p. 436.

[21] See the discussion in Kuklick, *American Policy,* pp. 186-90.

[22] Quoted in John Gimbel, *The American Occupation of Germany: Politics and the Military, 1945-1949* (Stanford, Calif., 1968), p. 6.

[23] Lucius D. Clay, *Decision in Germany* (Garden City, N.Y., 1950), p. 19. Richard Scandrett, a member of the Pauley reparations commission, recorded a conversation with Clay in June, 1945, which further documents Clay's intention to use his own judgment: ". . . my overall impression is very strong that his chief concern is to prevent starvation in the American zone of occupation; that he feels that the directives are not realistic and are likely to be laid on ice for a considerable period of months." "Conservations with Lt. General Clay, June 15 and 16, 1945," Scandrett Papers.

[24] *Foreign Relations, Berlin,* II, 1486.

reparations. The complexity of this task was immense, for related to the level of industry question was not only reparations but decartelization, decentralization, exports and imports, and the larger problem of German economic viability and unity. Setting the level of industry and actually carrying out the dismantling of plants was a slow and troublesome process. When the State Department published the American position in December of 1945, the statement demonstrated how far the United States had moved from JCS/1067. The document approved reparations and the destruction of war industries but said that the United States would not "wantonly" destroy "German structures and installations" which could be used for peacetime purposes. Furthermore, the reparations and level of industry policy would be guided by the principle that Germany must have a reasonable standard of living, that the German people should develop their own resources toward that goal, and that Germany must export enough to pay for imports. Enough manufacturing plants should be left intact to ensure a viable German economy, and military authorities should begin repairs of industries like coal and electrical utilities.[25]

General Clay's staff began to study the level of industry in the fall of 1945, and the Coordinating Committee of the Allied Control Council discussed the problem. Friction between Russia and the United States quickly appeared, but France also clashed with the United States. Discussions with the French, British, and Soviets on steel and electrical power indicated that the six-month deadline for reparations would not be met. For German steel, Britain recommended an annual production of 9 million tons, the United States recommended 7.8 million, France 7 million, and Russia 4.6 million. The Soviets argued that anything higher than their figure would leave Germany capable of waging war, to which Clay replied facetiously that "it could not be a very big war." Irritated over the prolonged squabble, on December 31 Clay warned the Russians that "pending agreement on the steel figure and on the general level of industry, further progress on reparations would not be possible," yet he worked diligently to achieve a compromise figure for steel. On January 10, 1946, steel production capacity was set at 7.5 million tons, but the allowable annual production could not exceed 5.8 million tons without approval of the Control Council. It was a confusing resolution because the range between lower and upper limits invited differing interpretations.[26]

There were major differences over production levels to be set for other industries, with the French, British, and Americans usually close in their

<hr />

[25] "The Reparation Settlement and the Peacetime Economy of Germany," Dec. 12, 1945, *DSB*, XIII (Dec. 16, 1945), 960-63.

[26] B. U. Ratchford and William D. Ross, *Berlin Reparations Assignment: Round One of the German Peace Settlement* (Chapel Hill, N.C., 1947), pp. 103-30; *Foreign Relations, 1945*, III, 1485-86, 1499-1502 (Clay is quoted in *ibid.*, pp. 1486, 1501); *ibid., 1946*, V, 482-88, 498-99. Ratchford and Ross were economic advisers in the Office of Military Government in Germany in late 1945 and early 1946.

figures and the Soviet figures much lower. Russia wanted lower levels and more dismantling so that plants could be distributed as reparations. In copper, the three western powers wanted a limit of 160 million tons, Russia 80 million. In electrical power, the three set figures of about 35 billion kilowatt hours; the Soviets asked for 24 billion. The American figure for one of Germany's most valuable resources, coal, was 155 million tons, the British 190 million tons (reflecting the British desire for exported German coal), the French 169 million tons, and the Soviets 140 million tons. A compromise figure of 155 million tons was reached after the French were assured that German mining equipment would be exported to them and after the British were assured that 45 million tons would be sent to Britain. Step by step, but with the six-month deadline past, agreements were reached for most remaining industries, including automobiles and rolling stock. The minutes of the negotiations indicate that the discussion was tedious and punctuated by sharp differences over figures. At last, on March 28, 1946, the four Allies announced a plan for reparations and for the level of the postwar German economy in accordance with the Berlin protocol. This plan reduced German industry to about 70 percent of its 1936 level, limited some industries, and provided for elimination of industrial capital equipment used in the production of ball bearings, heavy tractors, heavy machine tools, war chemicals and gases, radio transmitting equipment, and synthetic gasoline, oil, and rubber, among others.[27]

The number of plants to be dismantled under this new plan remained imprecise, for the conferees set no figure. Guesses ranged from fifteen hundred to two thousand. The absence of a precise timetable also posed an obvious problem. The process of dismantling was slow; committees designated plants only after careful review, and the actual breaking up and shipping of the factories required considerable time. However, Clay was not eager for the dismantling program to proceed quickly. He, like most American officials, believed that a weakened German industry would impede European recovery and cost the United States too much in aid. He also wanted to delay the process to keep diplomatic pressure on Russia. In early May, 1946 (as discussed below), Clay halted dismantling operations and reparations shipments from the American zone to encourage the Russians to participate in German "economic unity" and rehabilitation. At the time of his decision, only 24 civilian industrial plants had been allocated for reparations. By August an additional 132 plants in the American zone had been marked for reparations, yet by September the Americans had completely dismantled only 7 of the original 24.[28] To Soviet protests against

[27] Ratchford and Ross, *Berlin Reparations,* pp. 131-82, 225-30. For examples of the hard bargaining see "Minutes of 34th Meeting of the Allied Control Authority, Directorate of Economics, March 1, 1946" (DECO/M 46 14), Manuel Gottlieb Papers, Littauer Library, Harvard University; *Foreign Relations, 1946,* V, 520-23.

[28] Gimbel, *American Occupation,* pp. 177, 306; Ratchford and Ross, *Berlin Reparations,* p. 194. Also, by September 1, 1946, 74 war plants had been designated for dismantling or destruction, and 55 had been completely dismantled.

this lethargy and Clay's "illegal policy" in suspending dismantling and reparations, he replied that he would continue his policy as long as Russia placed "illegal obstacles" in the way of economic unity.[29]

The Soviets also reassessed their policy in the first months of 1946. In their eagerness to acquire reparations for reconstruction in 1945, they had often hurriedly and crudely dismantled plants in their zone. They paid little attention to blueprints for reassembly and to the difficulties of shipment from Germany. The waste was extensive; parts of factories lay rusting beside railroad tracks; in Russia the results of speedy and careless dismantling could be seen in piles of unassembled machinery. With the Soviet zone "transformed into something like the Klondike during the Gold Rush," as one Russian put it, officials in Moscow began to debate the pros and cons of dismantling. Minister of Foreign Trade Anastas I. Mikoyan led the critics, and by mid-1946 he succeeded in changing Soviet policy. Henceforth, Russia—like the United States—would emphasize the economic recovery of its German sector. But unlike the United States, the Soviets would foster this recovery so that "current production," rather than dismantled plants, would flow to Russia as reparations. Dismantling activity dropped markedly in the Soviet zone, and by October two hundred Soviet-dominated corporations had been organized to oversee economic recovery and reparations.[30] The danger of a resurgent Germany, in the Soviet view, was reduced by the reparations drain and tight economic controls.

This shift to current production in the Soviet zone accompanied a shift in its attitude in the fall of 1946 toward dismantling in the Western zones. While continuing to denounce the United States and Britain publicly for their delay in dismantling, the Soviets quietly suggested that dismantling be played down in the American zone too so that current production could be forwarded to Russia as reparations. The American response was critical; the suggestion was called a "major modification of Potsdam. . . ."[31] The chargé in Moscow, Elbridge Durbrow, read the request as evidence of Soviet economic weakness, and Robert Murphy concluded that "the Russian need for commodities out of German production is so urgent and apparent that we would be well-advised to use the opportunity to obtain very definite commitments from them on the subject of the introduction into the Soviet zone of occupation of our form of democratic methods." Murphy was explicit in recommending diplomatic pressure: "This may be our last opportunity to use such a potent bargaining position in Germany for this purpose."[32] The

[29] *Foreign Relations, 1946*, V, 630-31. The Soviets also protested British slowness. "Minutes, Allied Control Authority, Coordinating Committee, 73rd Meeting, August 28, 1946" (CORC/M 46 44), Gottlieb Papers.

[30] The Soviets discuss their policy in Germany in Robert Slusser, ed., *Soviet Economic Policy in Postwar Germany* (New York, 1953). For dismantling and reparations see pp. 14-61 (the quotation, by Vladimir Rudolph, appears on p. 20).

[31] *Foreign Relations, 1946*, V, 593-94.

[32] *Ibid.*, pp. 602-3, 621-25. The United States chargé in the Soviet Union (and the British chargé) questioned whether any "lasting political concessions" could be realized in the Soviet zone. *Ibid.*, pp. 628-29, 632-33, 650-51.

United States refused to accept the Soviet suggestion, and its seeming eagerness to use the question to diplomatic advantage further impeded resolution of the tangle. Besides diplomatic pressure, United States officials also believed that current production should be used as much as possible for exports to pay for imports; otherwise the United States would have to continue to pump millions of dollars into Germany to maintain it even at a minimum standard of living. Then, too, the shipment of current production from Germany to the U.S.S.R. might spawn close economic ties between the former enemies, and those German goods might compete with American exports.[33]

In 1947 the United States, like Russia, continued to be unenthusiastic about dismantling, but for a different reason—the increasing importance of Germany to the economic reconstruction of western Europe. Many congressmen, prominent Americans like Herbert Hoover, businessmen interested in investments in Germany, and German leaders like Konrad Adenauer wanted to shelve the dismantling program altogether and increase the level of industry figures. Adenauer was constantly urging military authorities to revamp the program, gloomily predicting a Communist takeover of all Germany because of continued economic dislocation. He considered dismantling the "most important of all" questions, and appealed for the economic integration of Germany as a stimulant to cooperation in western Europe.[34] In February, 1947, Hoover chaired the President's Economic Mission to Germany and Austria, and his tour of Germany reinforced his earlier prejudice against restrictions on that country's economy. His report argued that the "whole economy of Europe is interlinked with German economy through the exchange of raw materials and manufactured goods" and warned: "We can keep Germany in these economic chains but it will also keep Europe in rags." Germany's heavy industry was "Europe's first necessity for recovery."[35]

The desire of the United States that the level of industry figures be revised upward was evident at the Moscow Council of Foreign Ministers meeting in March and April, 1947. At that conference, Secretary Marshall engaged in often bitter exchanges with the Soviets, who doggedly argued for reparations from current production. The Russians asked that the new level for steel be set at 12 million tons—a marked shift from their position in 1945—so that such increased production could be shipped out as reparations. Marshall, although he also favored a higher level of industry, held fast against the concept of payment of reparations from current production. Molotov asserted that the Yalta accords permitted such reparations, but Marshall

---

[33] Kuklick, *American Policy,* pp. 173-74, 222.
[34] Konrad Adenauer, *Memoirs* (Chicago, 1966), pp. 35-36, 58, 81 (the quotation appears on p. 57).
[35] See Herbert Hoover, *An American Epic,* 4 vols. (Chicago, 1964), IV, 245-56, for report. Also see Lewis Brown, *Report on Germany* (New York, 1947); Gustav Stolper (a Hoover assistant), *German Realities* (New York, 1948).

responded that Potsdam did not and that the United States would not retreat from Potsdam to Yalta. The Crimean agreement did indeed state that one form of reparations would be "annual deliveries from current production," but the Potsdam agreement did not mention current production at all. Furthermore, Marshall argued, the United States could not be expected to support the German economy indefinitely. The conference ended in stalemate, and Marshall came home, as we have seen, to advocate a European recovery program with German participation.[36]

In July, 1947, a new directive (JCS/1779) replaced the long-neglected JCS/1067. It called for German contributions to European recovery through its revived economy.[37] At about the same time, Clay's negotiations with the British for a revised level of industry came to fruition. In December, 1946, the British and American zones had been merged into "Bizonia" as a first step toward a unified German economy. The British and Americans worked more and more in concert in Germany, although certainly not without disagreements; the French and Russians frequently complained of this collaboration. When Clay was about to announce the revised level of industry plan in mid-1947, agitated protests by the French persuaded the British that they should be brought into new discussions. The French put forth their case that French security would be jeopardized by a rehabilitated Germany and that the United States was placing German recovery before French recovery. As they did so often, they demanded that the Ruhr be politically independent of Germany and placed under an international regime which would manage its economy. The United States had long believed that the Ruhr must remain part of Germany. In August, still opposing this French position but wishing to allay British fears of a deep split with the French, Washington invited France to join the other two powers in discussions in London.[38]

General Clay threatened to resign if the French were brought in to undermine his new plan. He was overruled by Washington, but his threat made United States negotiators less willing to compromise with the French. The Soviets also asked to be included, but American officials replied aloofly that they had tried for two years to create economic unity in Germany, that the Soviets had obstructed their plans, and that the U.S.S.R. could work with the United States in the future, if it wished to.[39] The three-power talks in London were polite but intense, with the French requesting a reduction in the level of certain industries like machine tools. The Anglo-American negotiators made few concessions but did issue a carefully worded com-

[36] *Foreign Relations, 1947,* II, passim; Ratchford and Ross, *Berlin Reparations,* pp. 197, 252-55; *Foreign Relations, Yalta,* p. 979. Manuel Gottlieb has suggested that in essence, the French, British, and Americans were already taking reparations from current production by underpricing German exports of coal and timber. Manuel Gottlieb, *The German Peace Settlement and the Berlin Crisis* (New York, 1960), pp. 68, 74n.
[37] *DSB,* XVII (July 27, 1947), 181-93.
[38] For the French protests and the new three-power talks, see *Foreign Relations, 1947,* II, 986-1072.
[39] *DSB,* XVII (Sept. 14, 1497), 530-31.

muniqué on August 28 to help the French government save face with or conciliate its people. The new level of industry permitted 100 percent of 1936 production by increasing production of metals, machinery, chemicals, and many others. The steel level was raised to 10.7 million tons (almost double the March, 1946, figure). In mid-October these new figures were translated into plants to be dismantled for reparations. In Bizonia, the dismantling list now included only 682 plants, 186 of them in the American zone. Independently, the French announced that they would dismantle 176 factories in their zone. With the addition of one more plant, the working number became 859, quite a drop from the 1946 estimate of fifteen hundred to two thousand.[40]

Harriman applauded the revised plan and told the president that the decartelization program, or decentralization of German business, "reaches the point of impractical pulverization."[41] His sentiment was shared by many others who feared that the subdivision of large corporations would impede German rehabilitation and the Marshall Plan. Along with the reduction in the dismantling program, then, came a slowdown in decentralizing the giant companies. Clay wrote in 1950 that the "decartelization group was composed of extremists, sincere but determined to break up German industry into small units regardless of their economic efficiency,"[42] and Americans sought

[40] Ibid., XVII (Sept. 7, 1947), 467-72 (communiqué); ibid., XVIII (Feb. 8, 1948), 185-90 (the French figure); Foreign Relations, 1947, II, 1126-27 (the announcement of the new list); U.S. High Commissioner for Germany, Report on Germany (Cologne, 1952), p. 123 (summary). See also Adenauer, Memoirs, pp. 97-99; "Minutes, 15th Meeting of Bipartite Board, August 7, 1947" (BIB/M[47] 11), Gottlieb Papers, in which Clay even asked that the United States and Britain buy back ballbearing machines already allocated as reparations to other countries.

[41] Harriman to the president, Aug. 13, 1947, Harriman Papers.

[42] Clay, Decision, p. 331. Clay has maintained that he set out early to break up German cartels and cites the decentralization of I. G. Farben and the big six banks. Ibid., pp. 325-30. Yet his record is quite mixed. He refused to decentralize VKF ball bearings and Henschel and Sohn Machines. Clay's slow pace in decartelization is evidenced by the resignation of members of his staff in March, 1948, and the reduction of the decartelization branch from twenty-five to nine members, with the possibility of a further reduction to three in April, 1948. G. W. Lawson, Jr., to Mr. Shepard, memorandum, Apr. 27, 1948, Foreign Aid folder, Frederick J. Lawton Papers, Truman Library. Then, too, a committee headed by Garland Ferguson of the Federal Trade Commission visited Germany in December, 1948, and early 1949, and it issued a report critical of the military government's laxity in decartelization. The committee urged the military government to carry out Law No. 56—to reorganize any firm found to be an "excessive concentration of economic power." James S. Martin, All Honorable Men (Boston, 1950), p. 276. This report troubled Truman, and he expressed his concern to John McCloy, who had replaced Clay in May, 1949, as high commissioner. But Louis Johnson, secretary of defense, reassured the president that decartelization was proceeding well, that slowness was necessary because the question was tied to the whole German economy, and that Clay had recombined some industrial firms in the interest of economic recovery. Louis Johnson to the president, July 15, 1949, OF 198, Truman Papers. See also Tracy S. Vorhees to Secretary of the Army Gray, June 24, 1949, ibid.; Martin, All Honorable Men, p. 203; Foreign Relations, 1946, V, 625-27, 642-43; Adenauer, Memoirs, pp. 377-78.

efficiency, especially after launching the ERP, in most aspects of German economic life.

In early 1948 congressional leaders joined Truman administration officials in growing sentiment for a rebuilt Germany and a revision of the new dismantling list.[43] Marshall's Republican adviser, John Foster Dulles, was more blunt than most: "I think the matter should be dealt with purely on an economic basis of that sort, not feeling bound in any way by the commitments of Potsdam and the so-called level-of-industry agreements reached at Berlin."[44] But there was division within the administration. Clay, Paul Hoffman, Harriman, Interior Secretary Julius Krug, Treasury Secretary John Snyder, and Forrestal favored more reductions in the dismantling program, but the State Department was cautious. It feared that the Soviet Union would seize upon the notion, for propaganda purposes, saying that the United States was giving German revival a higher priority than that of the nations which had defeated the Nazis. Truman himself wanted to avoid an outright rejection of the Potsdam agreements.[45]

Lethargy still controlled the dismantling process in Bizonia. The Department of State informed an inquiring speaker of the house that only 80 plants had been removed from Bizonia and that 91 plants had been completely dismantled by January, 1948. Another 169 were in various stages of disassembly, but work had not begun at all on the other 342 (out of a total of 682).[46] The next month, Truman appointed a Cabinet Technical Mission to study the dismantling program. The State Department wanted this new committee to add one plant for every one stricken from the list, but, in a more extreme position, Krug and Commerce Secretary Charles Sawyer called for a complete halt to dismantling. After spending several weeks in Germany, the technical mission compromised, recommending that approximately 300 plants be excised from the three-zone total of 859 because they were essential to European recovery and because steel factories were the "keystone" to that recovery.[47]

[43] *DSB*, XVIII (Feb. 8, 1948), 185-90; *Foreign Relations, 1947*, II, 1133-37; Gimbel, *American Occupation*, p. 178.

[44] Senate, *ERP* (Jan. 19, 1948), p. 612.

[45] Edwin Pauley wrote earlier that "Communist propaganda based on allegations that the United States intends to rebuild Germany into the economic overlord of Europe has made a greater impression in all of Europe than any other simple propaganda 'line.' " "Paper on Reparations," Nov. 17, 1947 (in Pauley's possession). For the debate within the administration and the State Department's caution, see Millis, *Forrestal Papers*, pp. 378-79; Robert Lovett to Charles Eaton, Dec. 6, 1947, 80A-F7.8, Committee on Foreign Affairs, House Records; "Meeting on Report of Technical Mission," N. H. Collisson to Julius Krug, July 2, 1948, Box 66, Krug Papers; *DSB*, XVIII (Feb. 8, 1948), 185-90.

[46] Senate, *ERP* (Jan. 24, 1948), p. 505; *DSB*, XVIII (Feb. 8, 1948), 186.

[47] Julius Krug and N. H. Collisson (mission leader), telephone conversation, Feb. 18, 1948, Box 49, Krug Papers; Collisson to Krug, "Dismantlement of German Industries," memorandum, Mar. 3, 1948, Box 66, *ibid.;* Collisson to Krug, May 20, 1948, *ibid.;* Cabinet Technical Mission, "Dismantlement of Industrial Plants in the Three Western Zones of Occupation of Germany," July, 1948, Tray 172, Committee on Foreign Relations, Senate Records.

Meanwhile, Paul Hoffman, at the urging of Congress, appointed an impressive special committee headed by George Humphrey of the Hanna Company.[48] After visiting Germany in October, 1948, this committee advised that 167 plants scheduled for dismantling remain intact in Germany. It was this recommendation, reduced to 159, which became the agreement of November, 1949, between France, Britain, and the United States. The new plant list contained only 700 names, and the dismantling of factories in steel, synthetic gasoline, and rubber was halted.[49] An upward revision of the ceiling for steel production grew out of a report prepared by a group of U.S. Steel Corporation officers headed by George W. Wolf, serving as a subcommittee of the Humphrey committee. The Wolf group recommended that no steel factories be "destroyed, dismantled or shipped to other countries" because German steel was vital to the ERP.[50]

This agreement constituted the last revision of the dismantling program in Germany. High Commissioner John McCloy considered the program "at an end" in 1952, when only 668 plants had been totally dismantled in the three Western zones.[51] All four occupying powers ultimately retreated from their wartime and postwar agreements and preserved substantial numbers of heavy industrial factories—factories which in 1945 had seemed to both America and Russia to be a potential threat to peace—in their rebuilt zones. The two major powers drew their German sections into their respective spheres of influence, and each began to look upon the revived German industry as some assurance of security against the other. The Russians realized economic contributions from eastern Germany in the form of current production, and the United States gained western German participation in a more united western European economy which was eager for German steel and coal. Lewis Brown, a close student of postwar Germany and head of the Johns-Manville Company, summarized the United States position succinctly for the Senate Foreign Relations Committee in early 1948: "It is time we quit seeing ghosts. Western Germany is economically and militarily, irretrievably tied to the west."[52]

REPARATIONS AND THE QUEST FOR ECONOMIC UNITY

The level of industry (dismantling) issue was closely intertwined with the question of reparations. There could be no significant reparations unless the

[48] Other members included John L. McCaffery of International Harvester, Gwilyn A. Price of Westinghouse Electric, Frederick V. Geier of Cincinnati Milling Machine, and Charles Wilson of General Motors.

[49] High Commissioner for Germany, *Report on Germany*, pp. 123-24; *DSB*, XXI (Dec. 5, 1949), 863a-64a.

[50] United States Steel Corporation, "Steel Mission," *Recommendations for Increasing German Steel Production in Bizonia* (New York, 1948).

[51] High Commissioner for Germany, *Report on Germany*, p. 126; Gottlieb, *German Peace Settlement*, p. 241.

[52] Senate, *ERP* (Jan. 31, 1948), p. 1184. Brown authored *Report on Germany* (New York, 1947), which appealed for a revived Germany.

occupying powers dismantled German industry and shipped it out or unless reparations were drawn from current production. Since the United States would not assent to current production as reparations from western Germany and reduced the disassembly of plants, reparations shipments to Russia were accordingly restricted. Along with export controls, reduced trade, and the halting of relief and loans, the curtailment of reparations from western Germany to Russia was calculated to place economic pressure on Russia. In the case of the cutback in reparations, this pressure was designed specifically to draw the Russian zone closer to the West in order to achieve German economic unity and, more generally, to gain Soviet acceptance of American postwar goals.

Months before General Clay decided to discontinue reparations shipments, a number of United States officials had recommended the action. In September, 1945, for example, Robert Murphy, political adviser for Germany and a chief counsel to Clay, told Secretary Byrnes that reparations paid in the form of German plants were disturbing German production and therefore perpetuating economic chaos throughout Europe.[53] But at that time Washington believed that dismantling and reparations would not impede European reconstruction. German reparations, replied Byrnes, would spur the recovery of nations heavily destroyed by the Nazi armies. The United States at the same time, of course, would permit Germany to reach a reasonable standard of living so that it would not retard that reconstruction.[54] Reparations Ambassador Edwin Pauley agreed with Byrnes but chided the State Department for not moving reparations along even faster to provide equipment for European recovery.[55]

The notion prevailed in 1945, then, that reparations in the form of factories would transfer industrial power to western Europe for its recovery, temporarily limit German economic growth, and thereby reduce Germany's ability to wage war in the foreseeable future. One governmental committee stated early that reparations were designed "primarily as a means of speeding physical reconstruction in the United Nations. . . ."[56] The president of the Federal Reserve Bank of Boston, Ralph E. Flanders, argued, in some widely circulated reports, that "the European economy must not be too seriously disarranged by the postwar settlement with Germany." To avoid such a disarrangement and to ensure the German contribution to the European economy, Flanders recommended that German heavy industry be moved to France, Belgium, Luxembourg, Poland, and Czechoslovakia, where these factories would continue to function as "integral parts of the European economy." He saw a number of advantages to his proposal. First, the

[53] *Foreign Relations, 1945*, III, 1320-21.

[54] *Ibid.*, pp. 1342-43; Department of State, "The Reparation Settlement and the Peacetime Economy of Germany," released Dec. 12, 1945, *DSB*, XIII (Dec. 16, 1945), 960-63.

[55] Edwin Pauley to W. L. Clayton, Sept. 12, 1945, Box 10, Lubin Papers.

[56] "Final Report of the Interdivisional Committee on Reparations, Restitution, and Property Rights," pt. 2, June 24, 1944, *ibid.*

European economy would not suffer from limitations on German industry; contiguous nations would simply absorb Germany's prewar role in the economy. Second, there would be no need for policing German industry. Third, moving these plants would allow the most modern and efficient practices in rebuilding. Last, the considerable French fears about a revived Ruhr and German industrial centralization would be assuaged enough to allow Germany "to exist as a political and economic unit." "Putting it bluntly," Flanders concluded, "we have to determine whether to assist the Germans or our Allies," and he, like most United States leaders at that time, favored using reparations to contribute to western European reconstruction.[57] There was little or no enthusiasm for reparations shipments to the Soviet Union.

For Russia, reparations were a symbol of victory and revenge, as well as assistance crucial to its crippled economy. At the Yalta Conference Stalin had asked for $20 billion in German reparations with half of this amount to go to Russia. No absolute figure was set, although the United States agreed to use the Russian figure as a basis for future discussion. The Russians apparently departed from the meeting believing that Washington had in essence committed itself to the figure. The Potsdam protocol clarified the matter only slightly; it provided for percentages but still no absolute number. Under the Potsdam agreement, all four occupying powers were entitled to reparations from their own zones, and Russia was also to get 25 percent of reparations (industrial equipment) from the Western sectors. Russia was required to pay for 15 percent of the 25 percent by shipping food, coal, potash, zinc, timber, and other products to the Western zones over a five-year period. Reparations from the Western zones to Russia were scheduled for completion within two years. The provision that each nation take reparations from its own zone was essentially an admission that the Allies had failed to reach a significant reparations agreement. The reciprocal percentage bargain could be fulfilled only with four-power agreement on Potsdam's call for "economic unity," a highly unlikely prospect, given the complexities of reconstruction and France's absence from Potsdam and utter abhorrence for a unified and reconstructed Germany. And, of course, without an absolute figure for reparations, percentages meant little.[58]

At Yalta the Allied Reparations Commission was created to determine the amounts and methods of reparations payments, and the agreement stated that the "Commission will work in Moscow." In March, 1945, President Roosevelt appointed an economist, Dr. Isador Lubin, as his representative (with the rank of minister) to the new body. Lubin organized a staff of specialists and prepared for negotiations in Moscow. Roosevelt's death interrupted his work,

[57] Ralph E. Flanders, "The Post-War Treatment of Germany," May 14, 1945, *ibid.;* Flanders, "Some Suggestions for the Postwar Control of Germany," Jan. 8, 1946, Box 35, Aldrich Papers.
[58] For Yalta and Potsdam, see Clemens, *Yalta*; Feis, *Between War and Peace.*

and Truman, who wanted a "tough bargainer," replaced Lubin with Edwin Pauley, distinguished for his oil wealth and contributions to the Democratic Party.[59] Lubin stayed on as second in command, and Pauley officially became the United States representative on the Allied Commission on Reparations with the rank of ambassador. Pauley added several friends to the delegation, many of whom had little time to study the complex reparations question before departing for Moscow in June.[60] Pauley was clearly instructed that German potential for military resurgence was to be destroyed and that any reparations plan must proceed under the assumption that the United States would not finance German reparations. In short, Washington was insisting that Germany had to pay for its own imports before reparations could be paid. Exports had to be sold, not given away as reparations, until the nation became self-supporting. The American taxpayer, as United States officials said so often, should not be asked to finance German reconstruction or its reparations.[61]

In the Moscow reparations conference the initial clash came over procedure, which reflected larger issues of substance. The Russians, reminding the Pauley mission of the American commitment to reparations and the agreement to discuss a $10 billion figure for Russia as spelled out in the Yalta accords, sought to fix an absolute amount first. Pauley balked, essentially disregarded Yalta, and asked that the Allies determine the German ability to pay before amounts were discussed. The Soviets angrily accused Pauley of delaying tactics to avoid meeting the terms set at Yalta. The antagonists managed to establish a steering committee, but the work of this body was not discussed because only one plenary session was held during the entire conference. At that one plenary meeting, on June 22, Pauley denounced the Russians for "looting" Germany. One of his staff members recorded that "there was not the slighest pretence of attempting to assess what plant or other assets could be made available for reparations."[62] In the face of strong Soviet opposition, as well as the terms of the Yalta agreement, Pauley decided to move the negotiations to Berlin. Demonstrating little sensitivity for Russian suffering in the war and their intense desire for reparations, he was apparently most concerned about his public image at home and thus eager to score points against the Russians. His overall antagonism toward the Soviet Union contributed much to the breakdown of discussions, although Washington officials had evidenced no eagerness for reparations to Russia. The Russians also proved stubborn, especially in the climate encouraged by Pauley, and postponed meetings, which further increased Pauley's hostility.

[59] Truman, *Memoirs*, I, 308.

[60] Richard Scandrett (member of the Pauley delegation), "Summary of Procedure of Allied Commission on Reparations," [n.d.], Scandrett Papers.

[61] *Foreign Relations, Berlin*, I, 502n; Kuklick, *American Policy*, p. 134.

[62] Richard Scandrett, "1945: Reparations Commission," [n.d.], Scandrett Papers. For Pauley's decision and actions, see *Foreign Relations, Berlin*, I, 510-11, 519-23, 530-31.

Despite the obvious stalemate, however, Pauley's reports to Washington, were "optimistic."[63]

Pauley's reluctance to negotiate was certainly not a personal matter. Washington officials, under Harriman's prodding, had increasingly come to believe that Russia was so desperate for reparations that the United States could gain Soviet concessions on diplomatic issues. As with the Russian loan, Harriman grasped at an opportunity for diplomatic pressure and urged Washington to delay the departure of the reparations delegation for Moscow. "The Russians have shown little willingness to implement a number of the Crimea decisions," Harriman wrote the secretary of state, "and I therefore see no reason why we should show eagerness in expediting decisions on reparations, which is one subject to which the Soviet Government is most anxious to get us committed."[64] Before the Moscow conference had begun, Russia and the United States had tangled over the membership of the Reparations Commission. Russia wanted to add Yugoslavia and Poland, but Washington rejected them. In turn, the Soviets rejected the American request that France be included. It was a bad start, and Harriman's espousal of diplomatic pressure matched and reinforced Pauley's own inclination. It might be suggested that Harriman's arguments, coupled with Truman's toughening position toward the Russians in mid-1945, prompted the president to select a man like Pauley. At the same time Truman was taking Harriman's advice that action on the Soviet loan request be delayed. A number of times in late April and early May Morgenthau spoke with the president about Germany, reparations, and the "Morgenthau Plan." On May 9 he quoted Truman in his diary as saying, "I have got to see Stalin and Churchill, and when I do I want all the bargaining power—all the cards in my hands, and the plan on Germany is one of them. I don't want to play my hand before I see them. . . ."[65] Although the evidence is not conclusive, it does suggest that Truman was unwilling to make any binding decisions on postwar Germany and reparations to Russia until, during, or after the Potsdam Conference.

[63] Scandrett noted: "The suddenness and force of the criticism [on looting] coming from the official representative of an allied nation little more than a month after the fighting in Europe had ceased, was understandably difficult for the Russian people and their army and Government to comprehend in terms other than in terms of unfriendliness. Their cities and homes had been destroyed. . . . Here in Byelorussia the German army had had official instructions 'to exterminate' the population. . . . No matter how Pauley may regard removal of property from Germany, it is easy to understand that the people here cannot look at it as anything more than getting back a small part of what had been taken from them." Memorandum, July 4, 1946, Scandrett Papers. See also Scandrett to Robert A. Taft, Jan. 2, 1946, *ibid.;* Ratchford and Ross, *Berlin Reparations,* pp. 41-42; *Foreign Relations, Berlin,* I, 527-28, 530. The Lubin Papers contain numerous documents indicating the divisiveness of the issue of moving the site from Moscow to Germany, although earlier (May, 1945), Molotov had suggested that Russia would not be adverse to moving the talks to Germany after preliminaries in Moscow. *Foreign Relations, 1945,* III, 1209.

[64] *Foreign Relations, 1945,* III, 1186. See also pp. 1195, 1210-12, 1214-15, 1220.

[65] Blum, *From Morgenthau Diaries,* III, 459. See pp. 452-60.

After the debacle at Moscow, Pauley journeyed to Potsdam, where he regaled the president and secretary of state with dramatic tales of Soviet "organized vandalism" in Germany. He believed that goods unrelated to the German war machine were being removed and predicted "ghastly and costly results. . . ." When General G. K. Zhukov retorted that the United States and Britain had removed railroad cars, locomotives, scientific data, and scientists from the Soviet zone, Pauley's staff dismissed these acts as "trivial" compared to those of the Soviets.[66] Pauley's remonstrances, and the evidence of American and Soviet removals, contributed to the American decision at Potsdam that each occupying power take reparations from its own zone, or as Kennan remarked, "catch as catch can."[67] The Soviets obviously were trying to remove as much as possible from Germany before a reparations plan was completed—a plan which might not be acceptable. They were encouraged to grab for reparations early in part because of the hesitancy and delay caused by the United States and because of Washington's lack of enthusiasm for the Russian loan.[68]

Strangely enough, Pauley informed General Clay after the Potsdam Conference that the "major responsibility of the Allied Commission on Reparations have [sic] been discharged" and that the Control Council and Clay could handle reparations thereafter.[69] The Potsdam protocol did provide that the Council, with approval of the zonal commanders, would determine the amount and character of reparations, but it also stated that the determination be made under policies set by the Commission. Clay himself was puzzled for months and frequently asked Washington for clarification of his relationship to the Allied Reparations Commission. The vague reply was that the Commission and Control Council should cooperate in Berlin. With Pauley's departure from Berlin, leaving a small staff behind, and with the State Department's conviction after Potsdam that agreement on reparations must await Allied treatment of Germany as an "economic unit," it was evident that the United States did not consider the Commission an important institution. Confusion and delay persisted, and Russia became more embittered.[70]

In the spring of 1946 Clay and the Soviets argued vigorously over German

---

[66] *Foreign Relations, Berlin,* II, 873-76, 888-92, 895, 902-3, 904-12 (quotations pp. 889, 905). See Clarence G. Lasby, *Project Paperclip: German Scientists and the Cold War* (New York, 1971), for the removal of scientists; also Gimbel, *American Occupation,* p. 9, for American removals of West German coal.

[67] Kennan, *Memoirs,* p. 260.

[68] For a solid discussion of the negotiations at Potsdam, see Kuklick, *American Policy,* ch. 6.

[69] *Foreign Relations, 1945,* III, 1241. In September, Pauley told the secretary of state that "I have completed my task" and would next consider Japanese reparations. *Ibid.,* pp. 1291-93.

[70] *Ibid.,* pp. 1280-82, 1283-85, 1346-47; Gimbel, *American Occupation,* pp. 27-28. For continued conflict over reparations until May, 1946, see *Foreign Relations, 1945,* III, 1295-1506, and *ibid., 1946,* V, 515, 532-33, 559. The United States, over Soviet protests, organized an Inter-Allied Reparation Agency.

"economic unity" and reparations. On April 8 he threatened that unless the Allies agreed to a common import-export program the United States would "insist on revision of reparation plan," and a few weeks later he stated that Germany was costing the American taxpayer too much and that unless the Soviets accepted a central economic administration United States authorities "might now find it necessary to interrupt work of some 16-17 thousand persons engaged in dismantling machines for reparations deliveries."[71] On May 3, during another discussion of German economic unity through central administration, Clay warned the Soviet delegate that economic unification had to be established before any determination of reparations. Until that time the United States was halting dismantling for reparations purposes. In the American zone work would continue only on those twenty-four plants already scheduled for reparations delivery.[72] Clay apparently made this decision without formal instruction from Washington, although it was certainly within the framework of current administration thinking about the need for economic unity to reduce American expenditures and its refusal to subsidize German reparations to Russia.[73] At the time, the halt was more a symbolic than a real and immediate slap at the Russians because the dismantling program had been so slow that the curtailment did not mean much in practice.

The Department of State was quick to applaud Clay's decision. It was interpreted as another form of pressure on the Soviets.[74] In the first State

[71] *Foreign Relations, 1946*, V, 538 (Apr. 8, 1945), 547 (Apr. 26, 1945).

[72] *Ibid.*, pp. 547-48; Clay, *Decision*, p. 122.

[73] Kindleberger, "Marshall Plan and Cold War," p. 372n; Ratchford and Ross, *Berlin Reparations*, p. 193.

[74] John Gimbel, in his impressive *American Occupation*, based on War Department documents, emphasizes French-American antagonism more than Soviet-American friction and argues that Clay's decision was directed more against the French, who also blocked economic unity. There is no question that France was as much, if not more, an obstructionist in Germany; yet the documentation suggests that Americans responded to the schism with Russia over German unity more intensely than to the conflict with France and considered the French opposition less critical because of the small size of the French zone. The events which prompted the May decision grew largely out of debate with the Soviets, and Clay's statements and the State Department reaction would suggest that the halt in reparations was directed against Russia. The United States seemed to think that Soviet obstruction would continue with or without French obstruction, and that the Russians were conveniently using the less important French obstruction to justify their own major failure to seek economic unity. Then, too, even if the decision was not anti-Soviet, the result was clearly so. It is probable that the Soviets believed the United States supported French positions, especially given anti-Soviet French sentiment, American aid to France, and the virtual absence of strong public American criticism of France. (See, for example, *Foreign Relations, 1946*, V, 506, 517, 555.) For American opposition to French policy toward Germany, see *ibid., 1945*, III, 879, 884, 885, 890, 893, 909, 911, 913, 914, 916, 917; *ibid., 1946*, V, 537, 540. See also A. W. DePorte, *DeGaulle's Foreign Policy, 1944-1946* (Cambridge, Mass., 1968); Alexander Werth, *France, 1940-1955* (London, 1956), pp. 305-10; Kuklick, *American Policy*, pp. 195-98, 214-15; John Gimbel, "On Implementation of the Potsdam Agreement: An Essay on U.S. Postwar German Policy," *Political Science Quarterly*, LXXXVII (June, 1972), 242-69.

Department communication on the question, Acheson explained to Byrnes that "unless Russians give convincing demonstration they are prepared to adopt and implement common economic policies now" there would be no assurance of economic unity and Germany would need outside assistance for years.[75] Clay's cessation order must also be viewed in the larger context of western European recovery and a stable international economy, for German reconstruction through economic unity was intended to contribute to that goal. Clay himself, however, was far more pessimistic than Washington about the importance of German industry to immediate European recovery.[76]

The Potsdam protocol provision for the treatment of Germany as an "economic unit" became the American answer to both the Russians and French on reparations questions. The United States sought four-power cooperation through centralized administrations in export-import trade, finance, transportation, communication, dismantling, and reparations. By economic unity Washington also meant Soviet fulfillment of the reciprocal shipments under the Potsdam agreement. Russia insisted that America first determine the 25 percent figure (as well as precise shipments) before reciprocity could be effected.[77] Yet the Potsdam agreement was not the lucid document that both the Russians and the Americans claimed it to be. In the American position there was a real contradiction. Potsdam certainly called for economic unity, but it also provided that each power take reparations from its own zone—a provision which did serious damage to the principle of unity. Then, too, when the United States spoke of unity it usually meant on its terms of drawing Germany toward western Europe and subordinating the Soviet zone to the other three. It appears that there were few illusions in Washington about success in uniting all of Germany in 1946 and that Washington was leaning toward the merger of the Western zones to get what unity it could.[78] There was little effort to compromise with the Soviets over reparations or economic unity.

Secretary Byrnes summarized the policy toward Germany in his Stuttgart speech of September 6, 1946. Clay later told Byrnes that the speech had become his "Bible" for Germany—a curious comment, since in it Byrnes had drawn heavily upon a policy paper written by Clay himself on July 19.[79] Byrnes delivered the Stuttgart speech for a number of reasons. It was intended as a reply to Molotov's widely circulated July 10 speech in Paris, in which he had opposed "annihilating" or "agrarianizing" Germany because such action would "undermine the economy of Europe." The words sounded much like those uttered so often by American diplomats and struck a positive

[75] Foreign Relations, 1946, V, 550-51.
[76] Clay, Decision, pp. 73-78.
[77] See Foreign Relations, 1945, III, 1308, 1310, 1331, 1337, 1352, 1480-81; ibid., 1946, V, 540; "Minutes of 95th Meeting of Allied Control Council Coordinating Committee," Dec. 19, 1946 (CORC/M [46] 66), Gottlieb Papers.
[78] Kuklick, American Policy, pp. 155-63.
[79] Lucius Clay to James F. Byrnes, May 11, 1947, Folder 651, Byrnes Papers.

note. Molotov also had advocated German unity and insisted that the blame for its absence did not rest with the Soviet Union. Above all, Molotov concluded, a new German government must ensure the delivery of reparations.[80] Apart from replying to Molotov, Byrnes hoped that his speech would provide some leverage to American officers who had proposed that German politicians in the American zone take the lead in uniting Germany politically. His last purpose was to move Germany closer to economic unity.[81]

In the Opera House, amidst military pagentry and a select audience of German officials and United States occupation personnel, Byrnes delivered a speech which was simultaneously translated and broadcast over German radio. If there was any doubt left that the United States had opted for a constructive peace, that doubt was now to be removed. He appealed for economic revival and unity through the obliteration of zonal boundaries, although he reiterated that war criminals would be punished and the German war machine destroyed. He asked for an upward revision of the level of industry so that Germany could become self-supporting and made frequent references to the Potsdam agreement and to a balanced, unified economy. After noting that the British had agreed to merge their zone with the American, he declared, "if complete unification cannot be secured, we shall do everything in our power to secure the maximum possible unification." He criticized the Control Council for failing to govern properly and went on to argue that Germany should be turned over to the Germans under a central government. As protection against a resurgent militarism, he proposed a twenty-five-year (or longer) major-power treaty to enforce the continued demilitarized status of Germany through inspections. He touched on many other questions, all with the theme of unification. Speaking of economic revival, he noted that "Germany is a part of Europe, and European recovery, particularly in Belgium, the Netherlands and other adjoining states will be slow indeed if Germany with her great resources of iron and coal is turned into a poor house." Flanked by Senators Vandenberg and Tom Connally and accompanied by the sounds of "The Star Spangled Banner," Byrnes departed the Opera House aware that his message had been well received and confident that he had placed France and Russia on the defensive. In essence, the speech indicated that the United States and Britain would proceed toward unification as they wished whether or not the other powers acquiesced.[82]

In the first months of 1946, Clay petitioned Washington for approval to

[80] Molotov, *Problems of Foreign Policy*, pp. 63-69.

[81] See Gimbel, "On the Implementation of the Potsdam Agreement." I do not agree with Gimbel's conclusion that the United States still regarded four-power cooperation in Germany as conceivable in September, 1946. The considerable discussion in the first eight months of 1946 over the merger of the British and American zones would suggest that such cooperation remained little more than a hope. Byrnes invited the Allies to unite their zones on July 11, 1946, realizing that the only serious possibility was Anglo-American cooperation.

[82] *DSB*, XV (Sept. 15, 1946), 496-501. Also see Clay's account of the speech in *Decision*, pp. 79-81.

begin talks with the British about merging their zone with the American sector. That invitation was extended by Byrnes in July with the intent, he said, of expediting economic unity. After extensive negotiations, the Anglo-American zones were merged as "Bizonia" in December, 1946.[83] The Soviets and French balked at this arrangement, although in the following year French began to rethink their opposition to a revived Germany. Bidault in late 1947 hinted that France would begin talks on an "evolutionary" merger of the French zone with Bizonia.[84] The Soviets castigated United States leaders and "monopolists" for creating an economic empire in Germany through Bizonia, but Secretary Marshall replied that the Soviets were responsible for the merger because of their obstructionism: "Certainly some progress towards economic unity in Germany is better than none."[85]

The Anglo-American relationship in Germany, Clay told Byrnes, was not a "bed of roses." There were constant squabbles, with Clay and other officials quite irritated with British "socialization" or nationalization in their zone. But despite this difference over "economic ideologies," Clay pointed out in 1948 that "we do have the same objectives and thus can pursue many things in common with harmony."[86] After difficult discussions over technical matters relating to finance, appropriations, control over coal, and the degree of centralization for Bizonia, Washington and London learned to work together. But the British, watching the rapid decline of its loan from the United States, appealed for a larger American share of the occupation costs of Bizonia, insofar as dollars were concerned, and in December, 1947, the United States accepted a substantial portion of the British dollar commitments in the merged zones.[87] Throughout 1947 and 1948 the Truman administration kept pressure on the French by arguing that German reconstruction was essential to the ERP. Finally, France attached its zone to Bizonia (now Trizonia) in late 1948 (not official until April, 1949), which allowed for new economic measures and a new West German government, the Federal Republic of Germany, created in 1949.[88]

The Berlin blockade (from June, 1948 to May, 1949) threatened to interrupt the long-desired German unity and West Germany's integration in the Marshall Plan. In late June, 1948, Western authorities initiated a new

[83] Clay, *Decision*, pp. 77-78; *Foreign Relations, 1946*, V, 578-81, 585-86, 589, 594-95, 606-7, 613-21, 635-38, 639-40, 644-45, 647.

[84] *Foreign Relations, 1947*, II, 738, 756, 813, 828-30. Ambassador Caffery reported in August, 1947, that the French would probably compromise in Germany, but could not be pushed publicly by the United States because of French public opinion. *Ibid.*, p. 349.

[85] Soviet attacks in *ibid.*, pp. 256, 749; Marshall in *DSB*, XVI (May 11, 1947), 921.

[86] Lucius Clay to James F. Byrnes, Sept. 18, 1948, Folder 683, Byrnes Papers. For complaints against "socialization," see, for example, *Foreign Relations, 1947*, III, 273, 909-77.

[87] For talks on technical issues consult *Foreign Relations, 1947*, III, 909-77. For the American assumption of the British dollar obligations, see *ibid.*, pp. 47, 89, 277, 324, 1141.

[88] Gimbel, *American Occupation*, pp. 197-99; Clay, *Decision*, pp. 407-9.

currency for their zones. The United States and Britain had sought currency reform to help stabilize the German economy and to end the hoarding encouraged by the discredited mark. At Stuttgart Byrnes had mentioned currency reform as part of the larger issue of German unification. In late 1947 Secretary Marshall told Bidault that a sound currency would rehabilitate western Germany "so that she could play her part in assisting European recovery."[89] All four powers had indicated interest in currency reform, but the Soviets rejected the American position that all the new marks be printed in the American zone in Berlin, where a minting factory already existed. Negotiations reached an impasse; the Soviets wanted some printing in Leipzig, in the Soviet zone, but the Americans would not accept minting in both cities until there was a central German finance agency. The issue of "economic unity" was once again disruptive.[90] In mid-1948 the Western zones went their own way, and the Soviets responded with the crude and unsuccessful blockade of Berlin, broken eventually by a dramatic airlift.

Yet the blockade represented more than Soviet anger over the sole issue of currency reform. Moscow saw the Americans moving farther and farther from the Yalta and Potsdam agreements in their drive to rehabilitate western Germany and western Europe. The slowness in dismantling, rejection of current production as reparations, cessation of reparations, creation of Bizonia, upward revisions in the level of industry, and the Marshall Plan, as well as movement toward a new western German government, were to the Soviets evidence of Washington's determination to impose its terms on Germany. The currency reform was just one point of disagreement, but the Soviets apparently decided to force a showdown over the issue. It appears that a mirror image existed: that is, the Americans believed that the Soviets were deliberately, by designed plan, obstructing reasonable German rehabilitation and attempting to move all of Germany into the Soviet sphere of influence. The Soviets, on the other hand, believed that the United States had the conscious intent of tying Germany to western Europe.[91] Because the Moscow archives are still closed to scholars, we cannot be sure of Soviet intentions; American intentions, however, were read correctly by the Soviets. The United States was intent upon rehabilitating western Germany in the interests of western European recovery, which in turn was vital to global peace and prosperity, and economic pressure on the Soviets was used as a means to this end. But American policy was not always systematically organized or administered. There were times of indecision and confusion, and

[89] *Foreign Relations, 1947*, II, 814 (Dec. 17, 1947). See also p. 273.

[90] *Ibid.*, pp. 876-77, 879-81. See also Lucius D. Clay to James F. Byrnes, Sept. 18, 1948, Folder 683, Byrnes Papers.

[91] *Foreign Relations, 1947*, II, 141; Gimbel, *American Occupation*, pp. 201-6; Feis, *Between War and Peace*, p. 251; Howard S. Ellis, *The Economics of Freedom: The Progress and Future of Aid to Europe* (New York, 1950), pp. 175-238, on "Western Germany and European Recovery," and H. C. Hillmann, "American Aid and the Recovery of Germany," *American Review*, II (March, 1963), 124-42.

the Soviets did often delay action. Yet the goal of rehabilitation was consistent, and Soviet delaying tactics, it would appear, were often a response to the American insistence that Germany be restructured on American terms. General Clay saw one advantage in a revived Germany: "If we can produce a reasonably certain stable economy we can push Communism back beyond the Elbe."[92]

Stalin's observation in early 1948 that "the West will make Western Germany their own, and we shall turn Eastern Germany into our own state" aptly summarized the results of this clash in postwar Germany.[93] Russia went its own way in Germany. A repressive political system, Russian-dominated companies, reparations from current production, and a pro-Soviet East German government represented the Soviet counterpart of British-French-American actions tying the Western zones to western Europe. Temporary divisions became permanent, and vigorous Soviet denunciations of the close links between the ERP and West Germany well illustrate the bitterness of the Cold War confrontation. Charging that the Marshall Plan would make Europe dependent upon the United States, Molotov added that the "development in Bizonia of such industries as iron and steel and coal mining creates the prerequisites for exploiting Western Germany as a strategical base for the reckless and aggressive plans of American imperialism."[94] The zonal lines across Germany remain as conspicuous evidence that the United States, despite its use of economic power in diplomacy, failed to achieve its goal of an open world of peace and prosperity.

[92] "Daily Summary, Smith-Bundt Committee, Berlin, Germany, September 23, 1947," Box 93, H. Alexander Smith Papers.

[93] Djilas, *Conversations with Stalin,* p. 153.

[94] Molotov, *Problems of Foreign Policy,* p. 553 (Dec. 31, 1947). For western Germany in the ERP, see Price, *Marshall Plan.*

CHAPTER 12

CONCLUSION: RECONSTRUCTION AND THE
ORIGINS OF THE COLD WAR

The national security and economic wellbeing of countries touched by the destructive force of World War II depended upon a successful recovery from its devastation, and the most conspicuous fact in the postwar period was that the United States alone possessed the necessary resources—the economic power—to resolve the recovery crisis. American military and atomic power also existed, but their influence on international affairs after the war was limited, whereas there was no doubt about the exceptional economic power of the United States. It seemed an unusual opportunity for Americans to fulfill their dream of a political and economic open world, a world so different from that of the depression years. Few international leaders underestimated the power of the United States, and most expected it to be used for diplomatic advantage. The question was how—whether as a diplomatic tool to reach mutually satisfactory agreements or as a weapon to compel compliance with American positions on international issues.

The question was quickly answered. Coercion characterized United States reconstruction diplomacy, and the Russians, British, and French, among others, resented it. It is obvious that the reconstruction crisis and diplomatic use of American economic power cannot alone explain the origins of the Cold War. Important factors were the long-standing Soviet anti-capitalist and American anti-Communist sentiments dating from 1917, the troubled relations before and after diplomatic recognition of the Soviet Union in 1933, and the strained alliance between the two in World War II. In 1945 and after, Soviet expansion into eastern Europe and rude diplomatic conduct aroused understandable hostility in Washington, Yet, as the evidence in this book has suggested, United States diplomatic maneuvers helped trigger some reprehensible Soviet actions, and United States diplomats exaggerated the impact of many others. Because the United States was maneuvering from an uncommonly powerful position and on a global scale, its foreign policy often was haughty, expansionist, and uncompromising. Washington attempted to exploit Europe's weaknesses for its advantage and must share a substantial responsibility for the division of the world into competing blocs. This is not to ignore or excuse the Soviet grip on eastern Europe, but as the preceding discussion has indicated, Soviet policy was flexible in the immediate postwar years. Use of economic power as a weapon served to encourage further Soviet intrusions and thereby reduced the independence of the eastern European nations.

All of Europe groaned under the burdens of reconstruction. Economies were paralyzed, populations uprooted, helpless millions left hungry, communications severed, and governments tottering. The mass bombings, scorched-earth campaigns, and deliberate destruction of people and property left much of the continent dazed and dependent. After six years of war thirty million Europeans were dead. Russia suffered most, with fifteen to twenty million killed. Poland lost 15 percent of its population, or 5.8 million. Germany counted 4.5 million dead, France 600,000, Czechoslovakia 415,000, and the United Kingdom 400,000. Another sixteen million displaced persons were wandering in unfamiliar lands.

The survivors' prospects were dreary. Major cities had been reduced to heaps of rubble; 75 percent of the houses in Berlin were uninhabitable, and twenty-five million Russians were homeless. Food shortages were acute. European grain harvests in 1945 were half those of 1939. Across Europe industrial plants were closed and would require new machinery, raw materials, and extensive repairs. The Rhine was blocked by collapsed bridges, and everywhere telephone lines, canals, and railroads were unusable. Both Russia and Britain had lost one-fourth of their prewar wealth. Europe was an appalling picture of ruin.[1]

The postwar picture of the United States provided a stark contrast. Its wartime death count of approximately 300,000 appeared merciful when set against European figures. Its countryside untrampled by armies and its economy booming, it had become an "economic giant," as President Truman proudly noted.[2] "For most Americans World War II spelled neither hardship nor suffering but a better way of life," Richard Polenberg has recently concluded.[3] During the war the gross national product climbed from $91 billion to $166 billion; industry grew in "hothouse fashion," sending Lend-Lease goods valued at $30 billion to the Allies.[4] Observers spoke of the performance as a "production miracle."[5] Such economic power, combined with European reconstruction needs, afforded an unprecedented opportunity to influence postwar international affairs, and United States diplomats knew it. As early as March, 1944, Ambassador Averell Harriman informed the State

---

[1] Gordon Wright, *The Ordeal of Total War, 1939-1945* (New York, 1968), pp. 263-67; F. Roy Willis, *Europe in the Global Age: 1939 to the Present* (New York, 1968), pp. 180-84.

[2] *Public Papers, Truman, 1947*, p. 168.

[3] Richard Polenberg, *War and Society: The United States, 1941-1945* (Philadelphia, 1972), pp. 131-32.

[4] Wright, *Ordeal of Total War*, p. 265.

[5] Peter F. Drucker, *The Concept of the Corporation*, 2nd ed. (New York, 1964), p. xi; Frederick Lewis Allen, *The Big Change* (New York, 1952), pp. 165, 286.

Department: "I am impressed with the consideration that economic assistance is one of the most effective weapons at our disposal to influence European political events in the direction we desire. . . ."[6]

By denying a postwar loan, abruptly terminating Lend-Lease, limiting Russian-American trade, severing eastern Europe from loans and trade, and halting UNRRA relief supplies to eastern Europe, White Russia, and the Ukraine, the United States tried to force Soviet concessions on American terms, but failed to orient eastern Europe toward the United States. Reconstruction diplomacy was more successful elsewhere. Britain and western Europe were drawn closer to American foreign policy positions. Western Germany was rehabilitated as the "vital center" of a revived western Europe, and Greece, Turkey, and Iran became bulwarks against the Soviet Union and Communism. The World Bank, International Monetary Fund, and United Nations became instruments of American diplomacy. The Truman Doctrine established the guiding principle and the Marshall Plan the model for foreign aid. The developing American sphere of influence in the Near East, the Middle East, and western Europe did rebuild. The United States had sought world peace and prosperity, but the world of 1947 resembled that of the 1930s more than Americans wished to admit.

Interwoven in the fabric of American diplomacy were several strands which together explain this determination to use United States power assertively. The outward-looking ideology of peace and prosperity, with its stress on foreign trade, and the very existence of great power itself were prominent. Another strand was the American reading of history. The Bolshevik Revolution of 1917 and the turmoil of the decade leading to World War II cast long shadows. Communism and Nazism were historical evils which had been in large part responsible for the twentieth-century cycle of war and peace, at least so Americans believed. When the postwar period brought tension rather than peace, an explanation was drawn from history: Soviet Russia was replacing Nazi Germany as the major disrupter of a stable, pacific international order. Therefore, the United States must isolate the evil and avert the cyclical recurrence of war. As Gaddis Smith has described Dean Acheson's historical understanding, "only the United States had the power to grab hold of history and make it conform."[7]

The particular style and personality of Harry S. Truman and many of his advisers constitutes another strand in the diplomatic fabric. The president's impatient "get tough" and "give 'em hell" style complemented and reflected the power he represented. His acerbity and quick temper seemed all the more dramatic and meaningful because he could back up his tough language. He, Harriman, Byrnes, and Acheson, as well as diplomats like Lane and Steinhardt, were in agreement that lecturing the Russians was a proper procedure because the Soviets understood only assertiveness and direct

---

[6] *Foreign Relations, 1944,* IV, 951.
[7] Smith, *Acheson,* p. 416. See also Adler and Paterson, "Red Fascism."

pressure. Giving Molotov a "straight 'one-two to the jaw' " meant more than a verbal lashing in 1945; it united Truman's hard-hitting style and a national awareness of unmatched power.[8] The president's frequently extreme and alarmist statements also helped garner support from Congress for his foreign aid legislation. His White House assistants believed that Truman was at his best and most persuasive when "he's been mad," and they cited the Truman Doctrine speech as a prime example.[9]

A sense of moral superiority and a conviction of the universality and attainability of American ideals also played a part. "Most nations, probably all," Stephen Ambrose has written, "believe in the moral goodness of their ideals, but few have had the conceit to imagine, much less constantly proclaim, that their particular ideals are universal."[10] Thus a double standard was created which often obscured the disparity between professions of political democracy and the open door behavior. American expansion into Iran, for example, buttressed world peace, while Soviet attempts to gain influence there were tagged "aggression." Because United States goals were noble and "right," its exercise of power could not be naked or raw, despite what many foreigners might believe. When President Truman reminisced in 1948 that American diplomacy stood as "a record of action in behalf of peace without parallel in history,"[11] he was not being deliberately deceitful: he was espousing the truth as the nation defined it.

What made American foreign policy so exceptional in the postwar period was the combination of these factors—the peace and prosperity ideology, the presence and awareness of power, "get tough" leaders, a particular reading of history, and the notion of American superiority. American diplomacy was not accidental or aimless: rather, it was self-consciously expansionist. An essential element in that expansion, expressed in the peace and prosperity ideology, was economic: the growth of foreign trade and investments and the acquisition of raw materials. But there was more to this expansionism than its economic aspects, nor can it be explained simply as a singular effort to sustain capitalism at home and to reform it abroad. The United States was capitalist, but it was also arrogant, Christian, militarist, racist, highly technological, chauvinistic, and industralized. To argue that these traits all stem from capitalist roots is to make the term "capitalist" so elastic and all-encompassing as to be meaningless. It should be kept in mind, truism though it may be, that the United States had become a world power of uncommon dimensions, not just a capitalist power, and behaved like other great powers through history—it exploited opportunities. Although Washington preferred a capitalist world, it learned in the postwar period that it could

[8] Quoted in Gaddis, *United States and the Origins of the Cold War*, p. 205.

[9] Elsey, handwritten notes, Mar. 2, 1948, Box 20, Elsey Papers.

[10] Stephen Ambrose, *Rise to Globalism: American Foreign Policy, 1938-1970* (Baltimore, 1971), p. 118. Also see Tucker, *Radical Left and American Foreign Policy*, p. 148.

[11] *Public Papers, Truman, 1948*, p. 337.

live securely and profitably with a socialist government in Britain, feudal Middle Eastern sheikdoms, and a Communist regime in Yugoslavia. What seems to describe United States expansionism best is the "will to dominate," which is motivated by the strands discussed above.[12]

There was bound to be conflict in the postwar period, but whether the Cold War, with its strident rhetoric, simplistic analyses, sacred myths, ideological battles, rigid alliances, military competition, blocs, and interrupted trade relations, was inevitable is questionable. Washington was free to make different choices or, at the very least, to pursue its reconstruction policies less coercively. To suggest that Americans (and Russians) could not have acted otherwise is to blind oneself to the options available, some of which were exercised (as, for example, in the treatment accorded Finland as opposed to Czechoslovakia). Many alternatives were ignored or rejected because Washington decided self-confidently to use its power to expand.

Few restraints inhibited the exercise of American power. Fears of a postwar depression, uncertainty about the magnitude of the plight of western Europe, and alarm about the "Russian menace" caused great concern in the United States. The bureaucracy at home did not always function smoothly; State and Treasury tangled over Germany, and the Export-Import Bank often moved slowly, for example. The Truman administration had to deal with a Congress which harbored a few recalcitrant isolationists, parsimonious budget-watchers, and many Republicans, and "public opinion" had to be marshaled behind Truman's foreign aid programs. Yet despite all this, Washington acted with a remarkable degree of confidence and cohesion, and one could suggest that their fears and anxieties actually encouraged Americans not to "retreat" from problems in foreign affairs but to "solve" them. It should further be noted that objects which can be easily moved or bypassed cannot be labeled restraints. The phrase "public opinion" suggests that the "people," or at least a majority of them, express opinions on most issues. Yet studies have demonstrated that only a small number of voting Americans (no more than 25 percent) in the early Cold War years were attentive to foreign policy questions. The real "foreign policy public" or "opinion leaders" were a minority, most of them professional people, businessmen, and members of organized interest groups. Evidence from the period 1945 to 1950 indicates that these people, especially businessmen, labor leaders, journalists, intellectuals, and citizens' groups, substantially endorsed Truman's foreign policy.[13] Most foreign policy debates centered on

[12] Barnet, *Intervention and Revolution*, p. 17. For a differing view, see Kolko, *Limits of Power*.
[13] See Ernest R. May, *American Imperialism: A Speculative Essay* (New York, 1968), pp. 21-24; James N. Rosenau, *National Leadership and Foreign Policy* (Princeton, N.J., 1963), p. 42; James N. Rosenau, *Public Opinion and Foreign Policy* (New York, 1961); Bernard C. Cohen, *The Influence of Non-Governmental Groups on Foreign Policy Making* (Boston, 1959); Ronald Radosh, *American Labor and United States Foreign Policy* (New York, 1969); Paterson, "Economic Cold War"; congressional hearings such as U.S., Congress, Senate, Committee on Foreign Relations, *European Recovery Program*, 80th cong., 1st sess. (1948).

how much to spend, not whether to spend. When United States diplomats told foreign officials that they could not make a certain decision because the "American people" would not countenance it, such statements often served more as diplomatic ploys than as expressions of real apprehension.

In masterful fashion the Truman administration quieted or isolated most critics of its foreign policy. The historian must be impressed by the president's ability to shape the "public opinion" he wanted to hear and to discredit the opposition. Henry Wallace, for one, was successfully identified by Truman and his advisers as "pro-Soviet," if not actually a Communist. Conservative critics feared the isolationist label, with its negative connotations from the rejected 1930s. Administration-backed citizens' groups like the Committee for the Marshall Plan generated widespread support. Truman's technique of presenting Congress with an accomplished fact while arousing patriotic fervor through inflammatory public pronouncements undercut his critics. Dissenters could develop only small followings. Most Democratic liberals joined the anti-Communist crusade at home and abroad by forming the Americans for Democratic Action. The Socialist Party and the peace movement were weak, and even Norman Thomas frequently applauded Cold War diplomacy.[14]

As for the Congress, at times it made Truman work hard for his legislation, but it trimmed budgets only slightly and usually left him free to exercise American power as he wished in the early Cold War years. Bipartisanship characterized the Congress until 1948. Senator Arthur Vandenberg congratulated himself on its maintenance, as did John Foster Dulles, a respected Republican adviser to the State Department. In both 1944 and 1948 Dulles was able to prevent conservatives from shaping the foreign policy platform of the Republican Party. Not until after the 1948 Republican debacle did bipartisanship begin to erode. During the 1948 campaign foreign policy was only marginally debated and Truman's effective explanations for the Czech coup and the Berlin Blockade helped gain him support. Vandenberg had persuaded leading Republicans to refrain from an open attack on the Truman administration's diplomacy. For most of the early Cold War years Dean Acheson took pride in his ability to flatter and manipulate Vandenberg into doing the administration's bidding.[15] Vandenberg himself told a Detroit

[14] Paterson, *Cold War Critics;* Barton J. Bernstein, "America in War and Peace: The Test of Liberalism," in Bernstein, ed., *Towards a New Past* (New York, 1968), pp. 309-10; Athan Theoharis, "The Rhetoric of Politics: Foreign Policy, Internal Security, and Domestic Politics in the Truman Era, 1945-1950," in Bernstein, *Politics and Policies of the Truman Administration,* pp. 221-222; Allen Yarnell, "Liberals in Action: The Americans for Democratic Action, Henry Wallace, and the 1948 Presidential Election" (unpublished paper presented at the annual meeting of the American Historical Association, December, 1971); Lawrence Wittner, *Rebels against War: The American Peace Movement, 1941-1960* (New York, 1969). For the view that domestic opinion was frequently decisive, see Gaddis, *United States and the Origins of the Cold War.*

[15] For discussions of congressional-executive relations and bipartisanship, see Smith, *Acheson,* pp. 142-43, 252, 332, 407-9; Louis Gerson, *John Foster Dulles* (New York, 1967), pp. 52-53; Michael A. Guhin, *John Foster Dulles: A Statesman and His Times* (New York, 1972), pp. 54-55; 160-61; Westerfield, *Foreign Policy and Party Politics;*

audience in early 1949 that "during the last two years, when the Presidency and Congress represented different parties, America could only speak with unity.... So-called bipartisan foreign policy provided the connecting link. It did not apply to everything—for example, not to Palestine or China. But it did apply generally elsewhere. It helped to formulate foreign policy before it ever reached the legislative stage." He concluded, "our Government did not splinter. It did not default. It was strong in the presence of its adversaries."[16]

Governed by bipartisanship and Vandenberg's commitment to it, aroused by Truman's alarmist appeals, disarmed by faits accomplis, and influenced by opinion leaders who applauded American diplomacy, Congress voted the president his requests. Although there was always some congressional opposition in this period, the Senate votes on Bretton Woods (61 to 16), on Truman Doctrine assistance to Greece and Turkey (67 to 23), on Interim Aid (86 to 3), and on the Marshall Plan (69 to 17) demonstrate its acquiescence in administration policy. There were exceptions: the vote on the British loan (46 to 33) was close, and Truman had to veto the Wool Act of 1947, which was embarrassing in view of his appeals for multilateral trade. But, on the whole, Truman got what he wanted from Congress, and Congress did not control foreign policy. When its reaction was very critical, as over the issues of UNRRA and Soviet-American trade, that criticism itself paralleled existing administration thinking. It may be that Truman spoke to Congress in alarmist tones and simplified the issues not necessarily because he had to persuade a reluctant legislature to his point of view but simply because this style had worked political magic for him throughout a long career.

In these years immediately after the war foreign aid became an integral part of the United States arsenal of weapons. American interests were world-wide, and the Truman Doctrine offered a principle by which the new global responsibilities could be understood. The crushing of the Greek civil war became a much-cited precedent to justify intervention in other countries. The Marshall Plan's place in history has been assured by those foreign aid advocates who point to the success of the ERP in combating Communism. The manipulation of international organizations became a feature of the Cold War. The declining influence of Congress on diplomacy and the curtailment of the debate at home on foreign policy were features of the early Cold War experience which have also persisted. The quest for raw materials, investments, and markets has been pursued vigorously, especially after attempts to create an open world had failed and trade blocs had been formed. Notions of American superiority and arrogance toward weaker states have dogged American diplomacy and have continued to obscure the gap between ideals and actions.

Robert Dahl, *Congress and Foreign Policy* (New York, 1950), pp. 226-32; Robert A. Divine, "The Cold War and the Election of 1948," *Journal of American History*, LIX (June, 1972), 90-110; Athan Theoharis, "Roosevelt and Truman on Yalta: The Origins of the Cold War," *Political Science Quarterly*, LXXXVII (June, 1972), 211.

[16] Vandenberg, *Private Papers*, pp. 550-51.

The most significant survival from this period is Washington's disdain for diplomacy as a means of solving disputes and avoiding confrontations. Walter Lippmann sensed this new attitude when he pointed out the shortcomings of the containment doctrine in 1947.[17] There seemed to be little faith in negotiations with the Soviet Union, especially after the breakdown of the Yalta agreements and the inconclusive Foreign Ministers meetings in the fall of 1945. Convinced that their interpretations of international agreements were alone the correct ones, depicting Stalin as Hitler's replacement, and fearful of charges of "appeasement," United States officials attempted to fulfill their goals through the unilateral application of the power they knew they possessed. Reconstruction would proceed on their terms. The tragic result of this attitude was the division of the world into hostile spheres and the emasculation of the goal of peace and prosperity that postwar Americans so eagerly hoped to fulfill.

[17] Lippmann, *The Cold War*. See also Smith, *Acheson;* Adler and Paterson, "Red Fascism."

BIBLIOGRAPHY

Any historian necessarily draws upon the work of others. My indebtedness to the many important books and articles by other scholars is demonstrated by the footnote citations. These secondary sources are too numerous to be listed here. Primary sources, both American and foreign, have provided the bulk of research material for this study. I have made extensive and systematic examinations of popular magazines and newspapers, congressional hearings and debates, governmental agency and departmental documents, reports of international and regional institutions, memoirs, speeches, and business and other special interest group publications, particularly for the 1945-1950 period. These sources are cited in the footnotes. Of special value to this book have been the manuscript collections and oral history project interviews housed in depositories across the United States. Their richness and magnitude are discussed below. Because of the recent availability of historical materials, research on the origins of the Cold War has entered a more fruitful and exciting stage of scholarship.

GOVERNMENT OFFICIALS

The *George V. Allen* Papers at the Harry S. Truman Library, Independence, Missouri, contain the ambassador's unpublished memoir on American-Iranian relations and a few letters on the question of Truman's claim that he sent an ultimatum to Moscow in 1946. Additional Allen material covering the entire postwar period has been collected in the *Allen-Augier Family* Papers at the Duke University Library. The *Clinton P. Anderson* Papers at the Truman Library contain one box on Germany but little else on foreign policy topics. On the other hand, the *Warren R. Austin* Papers in the University of Vermont Library are rich. As a senator until 1946 and ambassador to the United Nations, Austin participated in major postwar events. The collection includes material on Bretton Woods, Dumbarton Oaks, Latin America, the Korean War, and the United Nations Organization. A few memoranda of conversations with leaders like James F. Byrnes are noteworthy.

At the Princeton University Library, the *Bernard M. Baruch* Papers proved useful on a variety of topics, for the ubiquitous Baruch was never known for his abstention from public issues. *Thomas C. Blaisdell, Jr.,* has given his papers to the Truman Library. As chief of the Mission for Economic Affairs, 1945-1947, in London and an assistant secretary of commerce for international trade in 1948, Blaisdell was close to American economic diplomacy, particularly the issue of export controls and trade with Communist nations. The Clemson University Library holds the sizeable collection of *James F. Byrnes* Papers. Although uneven, these papers include a number of State Department memoranda, press conference transcripts (Dean Acheson and Byrnes), a log by Byrnes's assistant on the conferences at Potsdam, London, and Moscow, and miscellaneous correspondence. Of particular interest are letters between General Lucius Clay and Byrnes on Germany.

The papers of Under Secretary of State *William L. Clayton* in the Truman Library are spotty. Another group of Clayton Papers is housed at the Rice University Library and includes cables on the Paris Conference (Marshall Plan, 1947) and various Clayton speeches. I first examined the material in the *Clark Clifford* Papers when they were maintained in his Washington, D.C., law office. Now housed in the Truman Library, this valuable collection includes documents on the Truman Doctrine and Marshall Plan, as well as drafts of many of Truman's speeches. The Papers of *Oscar Cox* of the Foreign Economic Administration (1943-1945) are available to scholars in the Franklin D. Roosevelt Library, Hyde Park, New York. Useful are boxes on Russian reconstruction, UNRRA, Lend-Lease, Germany, and Cox's diary.

The *Joseph E. Davies* Papers at the Library of Congress include the former ambassador's memoranda on important conferences (particularly Potsdam) and on issues in Soviet-American relations. The Princeton University Library holds the significant collection of *John Foster Dulles* Papers, which address a wide range of topics. The papers of White House adviser *George M. Elsey* in the Truman Library are exceptionally rich for the preparation of major speeches. Working papers, handwritten notes made during discussions, and systematic drafts give the historian a sense of the process of decisionmaking. The family of Secretary of the Navy and Defense *James V. Forrestal* donated a large collection of papers to the Princeton University Library. Especially useful are memoranda of his telephone conversations, personal correspondence, and materials on his discovery of George F. Kennan's ideas. Many documents in the collection were not printed in Walter Millis' *The Forrestal Diaries* (1951).

In preparing a study of her father Will Clayton, Ellen Clayton Garwood conducted a number of interviews on the Marshall Plan with Dean Acheson, Lewis Douglas, and others. Transcripts are included in the *Ellen Clayton Garwood* Papers at the Truman Library. The Littauer Library of Harvard University houses the *Manuel Gottlieb* Papers. An official in the United States Office of Military Government in Germany, Gottlieb saved copies of minutes of Allied Council meetings on key issues like the level of industry. Ambassador *Henry F. Grady's* papers in the Truman Library are a disappointment because they contain so little on his tenure in Greece and because his unpublished memoir, "Adventures in Diplomacy," is shallow, yet the material on oil and Iran in the early 1950s is valuable. The *Joseph C. Grew* Papers at the Harvard University Library are helpful on the ending of Lend-Lease and the war with Japan.

W. Averell Harriman permitted me to examine documents on the Russian loan issue, East-West trade, and export controls in his private papers in Washington, D.C. Correspondence with large corporation officials and his own memoranda proved very useful. The complete collection will, I hope, be deposited in an accessible library. The Truman Library houses the papers of speechwriter and adviser *Joseph M. Jones.* They contain material, including drafts, which went into major addresses, especially Acheson's Delta Council address and the Truman Doctrine. In combination, the Clifford, Elsey, and Jones Papers make it possible for the historian to reconstruct the intense policymaking in the troubled months of early 1947. At the Princeton University Library, I had access to part of the *George F. Kennan* Papers. Because most of the material was closed to researchers, this collection proved to be diffuse. In the Library of Congress, the papers of *Julius A. Krug,* secretary of the interior from 1946-1949, contain material on raw materials, the Krug Committee, and the rehabilitation of western Germany.

For American relations with Poland, the papers of *Arthur Bliss Lane* in the Yale University Library are indispensable. Ambassador from 1944 to 1947, Lane was outspoken on most issues concerning Poland in Soviet-American relations. The *Isador Lubin* Papers in the Roosevelt Library are useful for the problem of German reparations. *Edwin Pauley,* who replaced Lubin as the United States Reparations Representative, supplied me with several speeches and memoranda on Germany from his private papers. *Paul R. Porter* has in his possession in Washington, D.C., a briefing book prepared for his successor as administrator of the Greek aid program in 1949 and 1950. The study is revealing for its demonstration of the depth and failure of American influence in Greece. Secretary of the Treasury *John W. Snyder's* papers in the Truman Library contain various items on important foreign policy issues. Very valuable are the papers of *Laurence A. Steinhardt,* Ambassador to Czechoslovakia. His letter books and general correspondence in the Library of Congress contain communications with State Department officials responsible for eastern Europe and with businessmen. The diary of *Henry L. Stimson* at the Yale University Library provides considerable background on the origins of the Cold War.

The official file of the *Harry S. Truman* Papers in the Truman Library is massive in size. Much of it consists of mail from citizens, although a few items help explain decisionmaking. This file can be researched by subject, because the efficient and exceedingly helpful Truman Library staff has catalogued the collection well. Truman's personal file contains, for the most part, polite and inconsequential correspondence. Scattered items of interest were also found in the files of the White House assistants. The file labeled "Correspondence . . . Not part of the White House Central Files" includes document 23, the memorandum of Charles Kindleberger, Jr., on the origins of the Marshall Plan, dated July 22, 1948. Also at the Truman Library are the papers of *James E. Webb*, director of the Bureau of the Budget and under secretary of state, on the European Recovery Program and Point Four. The *Harry Dexter White* Papers in the Princeton University Library contain memoranda on the Russian loan question and postwar Germany, written by both Secretary Henry Morgenthau, Jr., and White.

COMMITTEES, DEPARTMENTS, AND AGENCIES

At the Truman Library, the records of four groups appointed by the president contributed material for my study of postwar reconstruction. The *National Security Committee* and the *President's Air Policy Commission* linked the recovery problem and security. The *President's Committee on Foreign Aid,* or Harriman Committee, of 1947 studied the relationship of the United States to the European reconstruction crisis. The records of the *President's Materials Policy Commission* give the researcher considerable information on raw materials—sources, deposits, and shortages—and verbatim minutes of meetings.

In Washington, D.C., at the National Archives, the records of the *Department of Commerce* are a rich source. Well-documented in the general correspondence of the Office of the Secretary are the problems of trade with eastern Europe and Russia. Letters between businessmen and Commerce Department officials help explain the evolution of export controls. A few items in the *Department of Agriculture* records on food and trade were also helpful. The National Archives also houses the records of the *House of Representatives* and its committees. Useful for this study were the records of the Special Committee on Post-War Economic Policy and Planning, the Committee on Banking and Currency, and the Committee on Foreign Affairs of the 79th and 80th congresses. These collections contain letters to and from the committee chairmen, working papers, and special reports from government agencies. The records of the *United States Senate,* also in the National Archives, are an important group of documents. The records of the Committee on Foreign Relations, Committee on Banking and Currency, and the Special Committee to Investigate Petroleum Resources help explain a number of postwar issues.

The extensive collection of the *United Nations Relief and Rehabilitation Administration* in the United Nations Library, New York, is invaluable for UNRRA activities. The records contain considerable technical information on ordering and supplies, mission histories, and correspondence on UNRRA operations in particular countries. UNRRA programs in the Ukraine, Byelorussia, Czechoslovakia, and Poland are well documented. Several bibliographic aids help the scholar master this large archive.

SENATORS AND CONGRESSMEN

Many manuscript collections in this category are heavily weighted toward constituent mail and courtesy replies, but the patient researcher can dig out some useful material. The University of Kentucky Library supplied me with many of *Alben Barkley's* speeches from his papers housed there. The papers of Senator *Tom Connally* of Texas at the Library of Congress are quite disappointing, for they hold little information on his years in the Senate Foreign Relations Committee or on his participation in conferences. The papers of Senator *Ralph E. Flanders* of Vermont at Syracuse University Library are of particular interest for their transcripts of radio broadcasts on foreign policy topics. The papers of Senator *Robert C. Henrickson* of New Jersey and those of *Eugene J. Keogh* (member of the Herter Committee on Foreign Aid), both at Syracuse University, are sparse.

J. Howard McGrath (senator from Rhode Island and attorney general) deposited his papers in the Truman Library, and boxes on Europe and the Marshall Plan proved helpful. Senator *Claude Pepper* has placed his private papers in the Federal Records Center, Suitland, Maryland. A critic of the Truman administration and a tireless political commentator, Pepper studied most Cold War issues. Particularly interesting are records of his trips to Europe (including Russia) and the Middle East in 1945, speeches, and radio broadcasts to his constituents in Florida. Senator *H. Alexander Smith* of New Jersey also made a trip to Europe, in 1947, and his papers at the Princeton University Library include numerous memoranda and daily reports on visits to Greece and eastern European countries, among others. At the Dartmouth College Library the papers of Senator *Charles W. Tobey* of New Hampshire include a few letters and memoranda on his participation in the Bretton Woods Conference and on various Cold War issues.

PUBLIC LEADERS AND ORGANIZATIONS

The papers of *Winthrop W. Aldrich,* chairman of the Chase National Bank and a frequent government adviser, are housed in the Baker Library of Harvard University. The collection varies in quality for foreign relations issues, but boxes on Bretton Woods, the Business Advisory Council, the Citizens Committee for Reciprocal World Trade, the International Chamber of Commerce, and the Marshall Plan Committee, as well as his correspondence, show a multilateralist at work supporting the Truman administration. The *Chase-Manhattan Bank* of New York also supplied me with several Aldrich speeches from its archives. Another adviser and member of numerous committees was *Harry A. Bullis,* chairman of the board of General Mills. His company provided me with texts of a number of his speeches on foreign relations. The president of the American Bankers Association and an executive of the National City Bank of New York in the Truman years, *W. Randolph Burgess,* sent me copies of his speeches. He was particularly interested in the Bretton Woods institutions.

The Bancroft Library of the University of California, Berkeley, holds the papers of economics professor *John Bell Condliffe.* Active in the promotion of multilateral world trade through various committees and publications, Condliffe corresponded with government and business officials. His papers include numerous records of the Committee on International Economic Policy and the Committee for the International Trade Organization. The *Eugene Holman* Papers at the Syracuse University Library hold a box of speeches by the president of the Standard Oil Company of New Jersey. *Eric A. Johnston,* president of the United States Chamber of Commerce, frequently consulted with government officers and visited Stalin in Russia in 1944. Mrs. Johnston made his papers available to me in Spokane, Washington. Although the material for the 1940s is not extensive, there are richer sources for the 1950s and issues in the Middle East.

There are only a few items on UNRRA in the *Fiorello H. La Guardia* Papers in the Municipal Archives and Records Center of New York City. Some documentation on British-American relations and business contacts with Russia can be found in the papers of *Thomas W. Lamont* (chairman of J. P. Morgan and Company) at the Baker Library, Harvard University. Useful for UNRRA are the papers of *Herbert H. Lehman* at the Columbia University Library. *Frank McNaughton* was the Washington correspondent for *Time* magazine in the postwar years, and his papers in the Truman Library contain many informative reports on debates and policymaking, a good number of which were intended only for the eyes of *Time* editors and were not published. *John Francis Neylan,* longtime adviser and lawyer for William Randolph Hearst, was a vigorous critic of the Bretton Woods Agreements and an extreme anti-Communist. His files at the Bancroft Library, Berkeley, contain letters, speeches, and pamphlets on the World Bank and International Monetary Fund. In Buffalo, New York, I examined the spotty papers of *George E. Phillies,* a lawyer and leader of the Greek community in America. He organized the Justice for Greece Committee and corresponded with Senator Arthur Vandenberg, among others.

Some material on UNRRA can be found in the *Francis B. Sayre* Papers in the Library of Congress. Sayre was diplomatic adviser to UNRRA from 1944 to 1947. The *Richard B. Scandrett* Papers at the Cornell University Library are very useful for UNRRA and the Allied Reparations Commission. Scandrett served with Pauley in the delegation to Moscow and became a critic of the oil man's diplomacy. As the chief of the UNRRA mission for White Russia in 1946, Scandrett witnessed at first hand the destruction levied by the Germans on Russia and the impact of UNRRA aid. The publicist and friend of Acheson and other top officials *James Paul Warburg* was particularly concerned about postwar Germany. His papers at the John F. Kennedy Library, Waltham, Massachusetts, contain fascinating correspondence.

In San Francisco, I examined the *Bank of America* archives, which include correspondence between bank officials and government officers on questions like the Marshall Plan and foreign branch banking. The *Chamber of Commerce of the United States* Library in Washington, D.C., houses Chamber publications and minutes of meetings, including the texts of visiting speakers. The records of the *Committee for the Marshall Plan* are deposited in the Truman Library. This committee worked closely with the State Department in popularizing the Plan.

ORAL HISTORIES

Staff members of the Truman Library have conducted interviews with several European officials involved in the Marshall Plan for the *European Recovery Program Interview Project.* Also at the Truman Library are the oral histories taken by *Harry B. Price* in 1952-1953 for his book *The Marshall Plan and Its Meaning* (1955). Ellen Clayton Garwood recorded the *Marshall Plan Project* interviews, now found in her papers at the Truman Library. I also read a number of oral history transcripts at the Columbia University Library, the Princeton University Library, and the Kennedy Library.

OTHER SOURCES

My research took me to many other manuscript sources which did not prove fruitful for this book, and I have refrained from listing them here. For as thorough a list as possible of manuscripts and oral histories on the Truman period, consult Harry S. Truman Library, *Historical Materials in the Harry S. Truman Library* (Independence, Mo., 1971); Richard S. Kirkendall, ed., *The Truman Period as a Research Field* (Columbia, Mo., 1967); Philip M. Hamer, ed., *A Guide to Archives and Manuscripts in the United States* (New Haven, Conn., 1961); *National Union Catalog of Manuscript Collections* (Washington, D.C., various years); Oral History Research Office, Columbia University, *Oral History Collection of Columbia University* (New York, 1964, and supplements); and the bibliographies of the secondary works cited in the footnotes of this book. Various university and presidential libraries also publish guides to their collections, and the National Archives has printed indexes of its holdings.

INDEX

Abbink, John, 67
Acheson, Dean, 28, 76, 89, 194, 262; and
  Bretton Woods Conference, 150, 152,
  157; on Brown-Dirksen Amendment, 84;
  on economic aspects of peace, ix; and
  Germany, 255; and Greece, 185, 188,
  189, 195; and Iran, 180; and Marshall
  Plan, 208-13, 216, 218, 221, 223; and
  Paris Peace Conference, 123n; and
  Poland, 133n; and Soviet Union, 53,
  174; and Truman Doctrine, 197, 198n,
  200-203, 207; and Turkey, 192-93; on
  UNRRA, 78, 86-88, 95; and U.S. loan
  to Great Britain, 165-66, 171; and Van-
  denberg, 265
Adenauer, Konrad, 244
Africa, 41, 186
Akropolis, 187
Ala, Hossein, 180
Albania, 101, 184, 190, 202n, 204
Aldrich, Winthrop, 224
Allen, George V., 26, 180-82
Ambrose, Stephen, 263
American Exporter, 60
American Federation of Labor, 169n, 222
Americans for Democratic Action, 222,
  265
AMTORG, 60, 68, 71
Anaconda Copper, 101
Anderson, Clinton P., 92
Anderson, John, 161
Anglo-American: Combined Food Board,
  94; cooperation, 25, 171-73, 214, 256;
  intervention in Greece, 205; oil agree-
  ment, 177; presence in Iran, 178, 181;
  relationship to Soviet Union, 9, 204;
  technical mission, 185
Anglo-Iranian Oil Company, 21, 176, 182n
Arabian-American Oil Company, 175
Argentina, 22, 94
Arkansas Democrat, 168
Asia, 58n, 59
Atkinson, Brooks, 85

Atlantic Charter (1941), 2
Atlee, Clement, 160, 162, 186
Atomic bomb, 8-10, 12, 23, 26, 99, 159-
  60, 234
Atomic Energy Commission, 64, 200
Australia, 87, 94
Austria: aid to, 28, 88, 221; and Danube
  controversy, 109, 112, 114; elections in,
  116; occupied by U.S., 8; president's
  mission to, 244; river vessels seized in,
  25; supported U.N. Emergency Food
  Fund, 98; and UNRRA, 77, 95-97
Auty, Phyllis, 142

Balkan Federation, 139
Balkans, 15, 21, 79
Banque Nationale de Roumanie, 117n-18n
Baruch, Bernard, 39n, 67
Baruch Plan, 26
Battle Act (1951), 119n
Belgium, 79, 234, 249, 256
Beneš, Eduard, 108, 118, 131; and Czech
  nationalization, 121, 123-25, 130n
Berlin blockade, 73, 129, 226, 257-58,
  265
Bernstein, Bernard, 47
Bethlehem Steel, 58, 69
Bevin, Ernest, 186; and Marshall Plan, 213-
  18, 229
Bidault, Georges, 257-58; and Marshall
  Plan, 214-18, 229
Bierut, Boleslaw, 131-32
Bilateral agreements in eastern Europe, 14,
  104, 158
Bipartisanship in Congress, 265-66
Bizonia, 236, 245-47, 257-59
Black, Eugene, 154
Black Sea, 110, 111, 114, 191
Blaisdell, Thomas, 119
Bloom, Sol, 78, 87
Blum, John, 54
Bohlen, Charles, 28, 126, 199, 213, 226
Bolshevik, 70